MW01156435

ROBERT TAYLOR: A BIOGRAPHY

by CHARLES TRANBERG

Robert Taylor: A Biography

Published in the USA by:

BearManor Media
P.O. Box 71426
Albany, Georgia 31708
www.BearManorMedia.com

ISBN-10: 1-59393-615-X (alk. paper

)ISBN-13: 978-1-59393-615-0 (alk. paper)

Design and Layout: Valerie Thompson

Table of Contents

PREFACE

"Hollywood ain't what it used to be"!

I don't recall my father ever saying this, but if he were alive today reflecting upon the Golden Age of moviemaking during the '30s thru the '50s, I can assure you this is what he would be saying.

Chuck Tranberg meticulously and painstakingly researched, explored, and carefully chronicled this fascinating time in history. He offers us a glimpse into early Hollywood where the studio system incubated and dominated so many stars, Robert Taylor among them. He takes us through a time when feature-length films were made in weeks, and headline actors were making five-six films a year. What drove fans to the theatre during that era was a true admiration and fascination of the stars and the stories that they brought to life on the new silver screen.

What wasn't shown in a love scene was left up to the viewer's imagination. What wasn't depicted graphically in a war battle was left up to the history books. And what wasn't said through expletives was understood and appreciated as conversation the way it should be. Chuck explores the tension and interplay between producers, directors and actors, and the power struggles between the studio heads that drove the film business to where it is today. He includes story-lines and anecdotes about the movies, how they were made, who made them and why.

To the directors, producers, actors and film crews for and with whom he worked, my father was kind, generous, humble, modest, self-deprecating, hard-working, and the consummate professional. To his friends and fans, he was folksy, all-American, a Nebraskan through-and-through and reticent about fame. Because of the private man that he was, the press was an unavoidable annoyance that came with the job.

If asked to name the ten biggest stars of his time, his would not have made the list. I'm sure he felt that an autograph from him was a waste of time for the fan requesting it, but he never turned one down, no matter how intrusive on his private time. For every inch of stardom, he gave a mile of modesty. For every ounce of notoriety, he gave a pound of humility. His belief that he may have lacked acting ability or perhaps not fully recognized it was more than made up for in his belief and love of country, friends, family and the things most important to him. He was not outspoken or in-your-face about it publicly, but his love of country led him to courageously testify against his hatred of communism.

"Years ago they were twice the men and half the actor. Today they are twice the actor and half the men." This frequent quote from my brother-in-law and drama coach, Sal Dano, defined my father and his contemporaries.

Who he was, by many accounts, was indeed the best combination of gentleman and actor that ever graced the big screen.

TERRY TAYLOR

ACKNOWLEDGMENTS

The Golden Age of Hollywood has always been of great interest to and held enjoyment for me. I love the films that the studio system produced during their glory years. It's not that they were all great or even good, but they were made by people who loved movies, which is the big difference with the moguls of today. The stars of that era were more mysterious than today. In part this is because the press of the day, particularly the Hollywood columnists, worked hand in hand with the studios and protected them and published studio-fed publicity.

This book is a biography of one of the great stars to be produced by the studio system, Robert Taylor. I stress great star instead of great actor. Bob Taylor would be the first to insist that he wasn't a great actor. He was a modest man, sometimes too modest. While he wasn't a great actor, he certainly did develop into a fine one. In his early career he had to live down his own good looks. Many snide columnists labeled him "Beautiful Robert Taylor" as a putdown. He obviously hated it. His early films emphasized his romantic quality, but he wanted to move as quickly away from that image as possible and take on roles with a harder edge. He eventually succeeded. The great romantic figure of *Magnificent Obsession, Camille, Three Comrades* and *Waterloo Bridge* eventually played more complex characters, such as the would-be murderer in *Undercurrent*; the tortured war veteran who thinks he may have killed his wife in *The High Wall*; the Indian who seeks the same dignity as a white man in *Devil's Doorway*; the dedicated flyer given charge of the dropping of the Atomic Bomb and the effects it has on him and his family in *Above and Beyond*; the veteran cop who goes bad in *Rogue Cop*; and the sadistic Buffalo killer in *The Last Hunt.* He didn't really enjoy it, but he also made his mark in the epic and costume film realm in huge, popular pictures like *Quo Vadis, Ivanhoe* and *Knights of the Round Table.* Maybe not a great actor, but his body of work is as good as any produced by the studio system.

This book also intends to take a look at the studio system itself as it existed during the years that Robert Taylor was under contract to the greatest example of that system—Metro-Goldwyn-Mayer—from 1933 to 1958. Twenty-five years spent at one studio and he saw them come and go, outlasting such contemporaries as Clark Gable, Spencer Tracy, Robert Montgomery, William Powell, Katharine Hepburn, Greer Garson and Joan Crawford. The studio system could be compared to a factory churning out product, but in the case of MGM the product, even of its B pictures, was consistently glossy and well produced and overseen by the overpowering father figure known as Louis B. Mayer.

Bob Taylor the man was considered by most people who knew him as an open, considerate and friendly man who loved the outdoors, flying, barbecuing and, in his successful second marriage, his family. He also had a strong patriotism instilled in him from the days he was growing up on the prairies of Nebraska. In many ways the small-town boy he was never abandoned him. He never went Hollywood. He stayed in touch with friends from boyhood and beyond. His patriotism worked against him at times. In 1947 he was a so-called "friendly witness" before the House UnAmerican Activities Committee. He was strongly anti-Communist, as were most people, but by naming names he later paid for it with his reputation in Hollywood—mostly in the days after he was gone and couldn't respond.

He was married to two women. His first wife of twelve years was Barbara Stanwyck, a dedicated and talented actress who was four years older and sometimes treated him more like her child than her husband. He admired her tremendously and learned a lot about being a Hollywood professional from her, but came to believe he never really was in love with her. His second marriage was to actress Ursula Thiess, who was not a careerist in the way that Stanwyck was, and when she married Bob and had children she gladly abandoned her profession to be a wife and mother. It was a happy and loving union for both and lasted for fifteen years up to the day he died.

There are several people to thank for assistance in writing this book. First and foremost, I must thank his wonderful family. I am particularly indebted to his widow, Ursula Thiess Taylor, and his children, Terry and Tessa Taylor. I also want to thank his stepdaughter, Manuela, for putting me in touch with them. Along with his family I got valuable insights on Robert Taylor the man from his wonderful friends, Ivy Mooring and Art and Barbara Reeves. I am also thankful for the recollections of Beth Nadar, a boyhood friend from Beatrice, Nebraska, who has since passed. A special thank you, also, to Nancy Reagan for taking the time to answer some questions about her good friend (as well as President Reagan's good friend) Robert Taylor. Then there are the recollections of such co-workers as Arlene Dahl, Darryl Hickman, Arthur Hiller, Marsha Hunt, Robert Loggia, Ed Nelson, Fess Parker and Debra Paget.

There are many others to thank for their assistance. I am particularly thankful for the great and time-consuming work that Lisa Burks did for me in gathering articles from the Academy of Motion Picture Arts and Sciences Library in California. The information, which included letters from Taylor and unedited interviews with columnists like Hedda Hopper, was of great assistance to me. I'm looking forward to the day when Lisa's book on another great Hollywood figure, Franchot Tone, is published. Laura Wagner, as usual, was quite encouraging and provided me with many articles, book suggestions, quotes she had found from people who knew or worked with Taylor and contact information for several people. She herself is one of the foremost writers and historians on Classic Hollywood and her column is seen every month in *Classic Images.* E.A. Kral provided me with much information from his years of research on the early Nebraska years of Robert Taylor. I am indebted to him for his generosity of allowing me to use so much of it and for his encouragement of this project.

I am also indebted to the writers who came before me who wrote splendid biographies of Robert Taylor: Jane Ellen Wayne and more recently Linda Alexander. My thanks, too, to Scott O'Brien and Sandra Grabman for their encouragement and allowing me to use photos from their private collection in this book. They are both fine authors and colleagues at BearManor Media. My thanks, as well, to the staff of the Wisconsin State Historical Society Archives, which holds the papers of Dore Schary and Pandro Berman. My thanks to my friend Gary McFall who took the time to download the pictures I collected for this book and my special thanks to Valerie Thompson for the superb job she did on the design of this book. I would, finally, like to thank my publisher at BearManor Media, Ben Ohmart, for keeping classic Hollywood alive not only thru his publishing house, but his thru his own books.

It was a pleasure to write about Robert Taylor.

Charles Tranberg
Madison, Wisconsin
April 13, 2010

Chapter One
NEBRASKA UPBRINGING (1911-1929)

Ivy Pearson-Mooring arrived in Hollywood from Great Britain in the late 1940s to make a new beginning. To help make a living she became a valet to the stars and it was in this capacity that Mooring came to know Robert Taylor and his then-wife, Barbara Stanwyck. In time Taylor would make Mooring his secretary ("though he was a far better typist than I was"), and a friendship flourished. Eventually, after Taylor's divorce from Stanwyck, but before his marriage to his second wife, actress Ursula Thiess, Mooring would live in the same house as Taylor and another formidable presence, Taylor's mother, Ruth Stanhope Brugh. "To understand Robert Taylor," Ivy said nearly sixty years later, with a still-charming and soft British accent, "you must understand where he came from and that also means understanding who his mother was and her influence on him."[1]

Where he came from was Nebraska—in the heartland of America. It has been said that there is more corn in Nebraska than people. But there must be something in that corn, because the state has produced more than its share of creative people who went on to help mold the Golden Age of Hollywood: Harold Lloyd, Fred Astaire, Henry Fonda, Dorothy McGuire, producer Darryl F. Zanuck and Marlon Brando. It was on August 5, 1911, that Robert Taylor, or rather Spangler Arlington Brugh, was born in Filley, Nebraska. He would live for much of the next twenty years here and even when he became an established Hollywood star he would

1 Ivy Mooring to author

return many times. Barbara Stanwyck, Taylor's first wife, once said, "He never broke away from Nebraska and still has a sense of belonging there."[2] Taylor, only two years before his death, would write, "It happens that I like the people of Nebraska. They're the best, the most hospitable, the most honest, the most trustworthy people in the whole darned country."[3]

Filley is situated in Gage County in Southeastern Nebraska and in 1911 it had a population of only 194. Taylor's father, Spangler Andrew Brugh, was a twenty-two-year-old farmer when he married Ruth Adela Stanhope, a sixteen-year-old school girl. Farming, then as now, was risky and within a year, Brugh was working as manager of a grain elevator which was owned by Ruth's father. All of her life Ruth had been in fragile health due to a heart condition. She was cautious to exert herself and was often treated as an invalid by her family. The attention she received from a very early age would ultimately make her a very demanding person. In short, she expected to be pampered. Her husband was devoted to her and would keep house and cook meals, in addition to his work at the grain elevator. She would demand attention and even pity for the remainder of her long life. "Her attitude was, 'I'm on the verge of death,'" Ivy recalled. "She was very manipulative."[4] Years later, Ruth would say that her husband didn't want her to do chores—he preferred to come home and find her "dressed up pretty and sitting down with a book in the parlor."

When they married, Ruth's father told Brugh that due to her health he should not expect Ruth to live a long life and that her frail condition would be a detriment in bearing children. Brugh understood and was determined to make what years he and Ruth shared happy ones. He was also determined to help her get well. "All my life I had been in poor health," Ruth wrote in 1936, "with a weak heart. And as time went on, my health did not improve; it became steadily worse. Finally a doctor said that I would die within a very few years if I did not find a spot somewhere on earth beneficial to my ailing heart. He wanted me to travel. So did my

2 Axel Madsen, Stanwyck

3 E.A. Kral, Nebraska History Winter, 1994

4 Ivy Mooring to author

husband. We were not poor, but I knew that we did not have enough money to follow his advice—particularly after the heavy doctor bills over a period of years. And I refused to allow my husband to mortgage his life to save mine."[5] Ruth said it was at this point that Brugh decided to become a doctor in hopes of prolonging her life.

In 1909, he and Ruth moved to Kirksville, Missouri, where Brugh enrolled into the American School of Osteopathy. He wanted to become a doctor so he could better understand Ruth's condition and find some way to help her. For reasons unclear (perhaps financial?), Brugh left the American School just a year later and came back to Filley and his job managing the grain elevator. Despite Ruth's fragile condition, they were determined to have a child and just over a year after returning to Filley, August 5, 1911, young Spangler Arlington Brugh was born. Ruth later wrote, "When his father and I named him that, relatives asked us if we were 'trying to kill the child' . . . Spangler was a traditional name in the Brugh family, handed down from generation to generation. It was the first name of my husband . . . who was of Pennsylvania Dutch descent. It was also his father's name, and his grandfather's, and his great grandfathers."[6] The middle name, Arlington, was a favorite of Ruth's, and she always maintained that she recalled it from a novel she had read as a young girl. To differentiate the baby from the father, they began calling him by his middle name or "Arly" for short. The delivery did weaken Ruth and it took her several months to recover. "Most of the next winter after Bob's birth, I was in bed, too weak to move," Ruth later related. In the meantime, her husband engaged a local seventeen-year-old girl to help look after Arly. It would appear that Arly was not in robust health in that first month of his life. "The little son of Mr. and Mrs. S.A. Brugh has been seriously ill the last week," wrote a local newspaper, on September 5, 1911, before commenting that "[he] is much better at this writing."[7]

---

5 Ruth Brugh & James Reid, Movie Classics, 9/36

6 ibid

7 E.A. Kral, Robert Taylor: A Golden Era Hollywood Movie King from Nebraska, 10/8/93

Spangler Brugh had not given up on his determination to become a doctor and in early 1914 the family returned to Kirksville where Brugh resumed his medical studies. Occasionally, Brugh allowed Arly to accompany him to classes. Arly would later recall his father to journalist Adela Rogers St. Johns, "There are so many great men who are just country doctors, small-town doctors. They have so much understanding, so much strength. They give so much and help so many in trouble. My father was like that. I asked him one time what was the greatest study I could follow. And he just smiled at me and said, 'Human nature.'"[8] Ruth later asserted that when Arly attended classes with his father, he would try to pronounce the difficult medical terminology that his father was studying and through this he developed a stammer.

While living in Kirksville, the Brughs rented rooms from a farm couple who lived 1½ miles outside of town in hopes that by playing in the fresh air and away from the confinements of his father's classroom, Arly would lose the stammer. "We were panicky. We moved out into the country . . . and let him roam outdoors, where he would forget the big words," Ruth later recalled. "The farm couple we lived with had a little boy about Bob's age. The two of them were outdoors all day long; Bob even ate all of his meals on the porch. And in three weeks he was over his stammering. We lived there the rest of the time that my husband was in medical college—and Bob acquired a love of the outdoor life that he never has outgrown."[9] In January 1916, Brugh completed his three-year program and graduated with a doctorate in Osteopathic medicine. Dr. Brugh would embrace the theories of Andrew T. Still, a pioneer in Osteopathic medicine, whose motto was, "a sick person is ill all over and must be treated as a whole individual and not just for one ailment."

Shortly after graduating, the family moved from Kirksville to Fremont, Nebraska, where Dr. Brugh opened an office on Main Street. While in Fremont, Arly entered kindergarten. After only one semester he was promoted to the first grade. It is only speculation as to why he was promoted so soon, but certainly Ruth's early

8 Liberty, 10/24/36

9 Ruth Brugh & James Reid, Movie Classics, 9/36

encouragement of reading must have had something to do with it.

In September 1917, when Arly was six years old, the family moved to Beatrice, Nebraska (population 9,664, making it the fifth largest city in Nebraska at the time). Beatrice would become recognized as Taylor's true hometown, since he would now spend much of the rest of his childhood here. Dr. Brugh went into practice with another physician with an office on the second floor of a bank building in downtown Beatrice. Over the course of the next sixteen years the Brugh family would live in three houses in Beatrice: a single-story frame house from 1917–1921; a two-story frame house, in which the Brughs occupied the first floor and shared a bathroom with the tenants who lived upstairs, from 1921–1924; and finally their most expensive residence, a six-room brick house, which the family occupied from 1924–1933.[10]

Ruth occasionally worked as a receptionist for her husband, but, according to Nebraska historian E.A. Kral, "To many Beatrice people, her dominant characteristic was her infirmity, and the general public perception was that she enjoyed her illness."[11] As already noted, Ruth later admitted that Dr. Brugh didn't like her to overextend herself due to her precarious health, so he took on local women to help with the household chores and even, according to Kral, did much of the laundry himself. Ruth did cook, and while there is debate over how well her culinary skills were among some of her neighbors in Beatrice, Ivy, who lived with Ruth for several years during the 1950s, recalled that she did like to cook some of her son's favorite recipes from scratch.[12] Arly himself would recall more than two decades later the curious aromas which engulfed the home of a doctor. "I can remember still the warm, mixed odors of iodoform and hot corn bread and hot chocolate which were the mixed aromas of my dad's surgery and my mother's kitchen—the smell of home to me."

According to E.A. Kral, who has extensively chronicled Taylor's early Nebraska years, "I suspect he [Arly] was also aware that his

10 E.A. Kral, Beatrice Daily Sun, 10/8/93

11 ibid

12 Ivy Mooring to author

mother was regarded as 'different' by adults in the community, as did her husband who had to care for her illnesses, real or imagined. His mother did not live up to the expectations of others in the community, as she was described as 'dowdy' in dress when seen downtown."[13]

By the time he was eight years old Arly had a pony which he loved enormously, named Gypsy, or Gyp for short. He enjoyed riding Gyp and spent hours either riding him or being pulled while seated in a pony cart. The family couldn't keep Gyp in town, so the horse was lodged at a 160-acre farm, owned by Anthony and Rose Tyser Shimerda, which was bordered on the southern part of Beatrice. The Brugh and Shimerada families became very close, and Dr. Brugh even rented a cabin on the farm where the family would spend summers.

It was while visiting the farm that Arly began a life-long interest in hunting and fishing, often with his father and Mr. Shimerda. Doctor and Mrs. Brugh also tried to instill a sense of responsibility into the boy and among his chores were keeping the wood pile stocked and cleaning his own room. His father encouraged him in earning his own money by mowing his neighbors' lawns. His parents were disciplinarians. ". . . I don't ever remember being able to evade any punishments as result of a disagreement between them as to how many licks made a spanking. The notable thing about these spankings was not that there were many of them, but their reliability. As sure as they were due, I collected." Along with his parents, Arly attended services at the Centenary Methodist Church in Beatrice (where he sang in the church choir) and attended Sunday school classes from 1924–1928. However, as an adult, Robert Taylor wasn't a particularly religious man, according to his family and close friends like Ivy Mooring. He rarely attended church services. According to his son, Terry, he and his sister, Tessa, were encouraged to say bedtime prayers and attend Sunday school, but they rarely went to church services. "I have to assume that his religion did not play a significant role in his early life enough for him to pass that faith on to Tessa and me."[14]

13 E.A. Kral, Postscript on Robert Taylor, 1/16/04

14 Terry Taylor to author

Arly spent much of his time with his parents and older adults and had few friends his own age. Part of the reason for this may have been due to Ruth's continued over-protectionism. Several years later he would say, "I was almost always alone. I went to school. I was a good little boy, I am afraid. I liked school. I did well in my lessons and liked them. I never played hooky. I never was sent to 'see the principal.' I got on with the boys and girls in my classes. I was usually the room monitor and the president of the class or whatever that office is called in the grades . . ."[15] Despite this, he did receive ridicule from his classmates for the absurdly out-of-date outfits that Ruth would dress him in. He wore Little Lord Fauntleroy suits, to considerable teasing from his classmates, until the sixth grade. Another classmate would recall to E.A. Kral, "People in grade school would refer to Arlington as 'Little Lord Fauntleroy' in jest because of his immaculate dress." Ruth later commented, ". . . I used to dress him in Little Lord Fauntleroy suits. How he hated those suits, with their little silk blouses!," but that didn't stop her from doing it. Years later in an interview with the *Nebraska State Journal*, Taylor typically forgave his mother, ". . . for those Lord Fauntleroy suits I once had to wear."[16] Another former neighbor was quoted as saying that Arly was "considered a sissy" by the other children and that his teachers, "could have appointed him monitor of his class in grade school as a way of helping him."[17]

If Arly was seen in town it was usually being accompanied by his mother. Even when he was as old as twelve or thirteen years she required him to sit on the porch at home (probably reading a book) rather than play with kids his own age, which caused him to be teased by other children as a mama's boy. But there was something about Arly himself which made him a natural loner. He was a sensitive boy and enjoyed reading adventure stories. When he was allowed to go off, he often enjoyed solitary pursuits such as riding his pony or his bike. But sooner or later even Ruth came to the conclusion that the boy needed to interact with others his own age. "With the other kids in Beatrice," Taylor later wrote in

15 Gladys Hall, Robert Taylor's True Life Story, Dell, 1937

16 Nebraska State Journal, 3/1/37

17 E.A. Kral, Beatrice Daily Sun, 10/8/93

an autobiographical newspaper article, "I played sandlot baseball—as a scrub; went swimming at Riverside Park; played tennis, and had a lot of fun outdoors." At around the same time Ruth would portray Arly as being a "naturally . . . high strung child . . . he was very sensitive. If anyone spoke harshly to him about some little thing that he had done, he would not be able to eat or sleep. He still hates harsh criticism. He comes by that naturally; both his father and I were that way." Being a worrier was a characteristic which stayed with Arly for the rest of his life. He was an admittedly shy child. In 1937 he wrote, "I was not, I still am not, gregarious. I was then as I am now, uneasy when I am with more than one person. I preferred being alone on the prairie or in the woods, to playing football with the gang."[18]

Arly had a close relationship with his maternal grandmother, Eva Stanhope—who he called "Granny." One day Arly decided to ride his horse, Gyp, over to his grandmother's house. That was a distance of fourteen miles, quite a ride for a young boy and his pony. Before leaving on this journey Arly phoned his Granny to let her know he was coming and to please have something good to eat when he arrived. After a short while, Granny got another call from Arly. "I'm sorry, Granny, but I'm not even half way yet. Gyp keeps turning around and wanting to go home and we only go three yards ahead and then two back, and I don't think I'll ever get there. What'll I do?" Granny put it to him with the bark off, "You'd better make up your mind right now, young man, who's to be master—you or the horse." Arly arrived three hours later. Granny Stanhope was somebody that Arly never hesitated to come to if he had a problem or just needed somebody to talk with. She was a source of endless advice and support for him, and later, when he was "Robert Taylor," she took an active interest in his career by helping him answer his fan mail.[19]

The introverted Arly enjoyed music. He began practicing the piano when he was ten years of age. But it was the cello which eventually interested Arly the most. His mother later explained how this came about: "When he was about twelve, he wanted to

18 Gladys Hall, Robert Taylor's True Life Story, Dell, 1937

19 Hollywood, 11/38

take saxophone lessons. I did not want him to; a saxophone was so noisy and jazzy. So then he wanted to try the cello." Arly began traveling to Lincoln once a week to take lessons at the University School of Music (later part of the University of Nebraska). His instructor at the University School was a man named Herbert E. Gray. Gray had a "persuasive, dominant personality," recalled a former student in an interview with E.A. Kral. Ruth would later say that Gray was impressed with Arly from the start. "He told us that Robert did not handle the cello awkwardly, as most beginners do."[20] Professor Gray would be one of the most influential figures in Arly's early life and, as Arly later wrote, "it was largely because of Prof. Gray that I finally got to Hollywood."

At school, in Beatrice, Arly participated in the music program of public schools music supervisor B.P. Osborn. Throughout his junior high and high-school career Arly performed on the cello in school programs, including a solo performance titled "The Swan" in 1927.[21] But his musical talents were displayed throughout the state. In his junior year he and other members of his Beatrice High string quartet placed second in a state music contest. Outside of school he joined a community orchestra which played at church and community events and even in the pit orchestra at the Rivoli Theater in Beatrice. While being a musician was his prime extracurricular activity in school he also began appearing in acting roles in school plays and eventually the community theater of Beatrice.

As a senior he attended a state drama contest and was named state champion in the oratorical category. He did well, as he always did, but nearly everybody felt he was going to be a musician, not an actor. "No teacher in high school ever particularly encouraged him about his acting," Ruth later said. "We never thought much about his dramatic ability—neither did he. To us, it was only one of several talents he showed us."[22] Gray tried to dissuade Arly from a dramatics career—he wanted him to concentrate on his music. "He has a tremendous talent," he told Arly's parents. "But he must stop

20 Ruth Brugh & James Reid, Movie Classics, 9/36

21 E.A. Kral, Beatrice Daily Sun, 10/8/93

22 Ruth Brugh & James Reid, Movie Classics, 9/36

monkeying around with this acting business. Dramatics! Such a waste of time."[23]

Music and dramatics may have brought Arly out of his shell. By his senior year of high school he was a member of many prominent campus societies and clubs: the Boys Glee Club, the staff of his yearbook, Student Council, Forensic Club, Dramatic Club, National Honor Society and was even the senior social chairman! His easy, unassuming manner may have had a lot to do with it, but he also was developing into an extremely handsome young man who the girls certainly must have taken notice of. His classmates began to refer to him as "The Sheik," in reference to Rudolph Valentino, the movie heartthrob. It was not a nickname Arly cared for. Arly was not somebody who wanted to be sought out for his looks. He was conscious of the fact that some people considered him beautiful, a term which had a feminine quality to it. He would be self-conscious of his extreme good looks for many years, really until early middle age when his face lost much of the delicacy of his younger self and matured into rather rugged handsomeness. Meanwhile, he did very well academically in high school, very rarely getting anything under a B. When he graduated in 1929, he was among the ten members of the Beatrice High Chapter of the National Honor Society.[24]

Years later Arly summed up his upbringing by saying, "No one except my mother, father, and grandparents really 'influenced' my life or left any mark upon me."[25] Those influences continued, but now it would be from a distance. Arly was about to embark off on his own.

23 Jane Ellen Wayne, Robert Taylor, pg. 26

24 E.A. Kral, Beatrice Daily Sun, 10/8/93

25 Gladys Hall, Robert Taylor's True Life Story, Dell, 1937

Chapter Two
FROM NEBRASKA TO CALIFORNIA (1929-1933)

Following graduation, Arly spent the summer working in a bank in Beatrice, but as summer closed in on fall Arly enrolled at Doane College in Crete, about a 40-mile drive from Beatrice. Doane was a four-year coeducational liberal arts institution affiliated with the congregational church. Many of his classmates and friends could not afford to go to a larger and thus more expensive school so many enrolled at Doane. Given Dr. Brugh's income as a physician and his lecturing fees (as well as Arly's own academic accomplishments) Arly probably could have attended a larger college if he had wanted to. The thing which may have drawn Arly to Doane was the presence on the faculty of his music instructor, Professor Gray. Gray was still encouraging Arly to pursue a career as a concert cellist. Arly had mixed feelings about his future. There was a part of him which wanted to pursue a career in medicine like his father; others felt that with his oratorical skills he could pursue the law and Professor Gray believed his true future lay with music.

As a high-school graduation present his parents had given Arly a used car which was useful in making the 84-mile round trip drive from Doane to Beatrice on weekends to visit his parents. His father made Arly promise that he would not exceed 35 miles an hour, a promise Taylor later said he kept.[26] Arly took to Doane and enjoyed his first real taste of independence. ". . . Doane College days were great ones even though, actually, I was not plunged into any terrific adventures," Arly later wrote. "The

26 Omaha World Herald, 7/15/51

college was a small, church-endowed institution on the edge of a small town. I remember how we were away from the bustle and problems of big cities and how I liked that isolation. Our buildings were a comfortable red brick and classes were a pleasant divertissement. I never exerted myself too much in my studies. The countryside was too rolling; there were too many beautiful elms and maples, and there was that winding river that was a keen spot for canoeing." [27]

Arly participated, much to the consternation of Professor Gray, in pursuits which took him away from his music—oratory and dramatics. He won an oratorical contest in 1929 on the topic "Ten Years of Prohibition." Arly took an affirmative stand on the issue. He not only won a coonskin coat (highly valuable during the cold Nebraska winters) but a trip to Detroit, Michigan, to attend the national convention of the Anti-Saloon Leagued of America, and personally recite his winning oratorical essay. Years later Arly recalled this trip. "Oratory netted me my first trip to a metropolis. Contests were held in a number of colleges for the best speech on some topic I can't recall now." [28] (It's likely he could recall, but after the failed experiment of Prohibition decided not to admit he once spoke in favor of it!) He was not impressed by the big city. "The people in Detroit looked as though they had lived in apartments all their life and didn't go to the country often enough." [29]

But music was still a top consideration for Arly. While at Doane he played cello with the Doane Symphony Orchestra. More significantly, he and two friends formed a trio which they called "The Harmony Boys," performing at events all over Nebraska and even on the radio. Arly was the cellist as well as an occasional singer. A Beatrice friend named Gerhard Wiebe played violin and the third member, Russ Gibson, primarily played the piano but also could play trumpet and French horn when needed. The Harmony Boys got a job performing on radio station KMMJ on Sundays. In addition to the Doane Symphony Orchestra, Arly continued to be tutored by Professor Gray and together they would occasionally play with the Lincoln Symphony.

27 My Life by Robert Taylor as told to Ben Maddox, Screenland, 10/37

28 ibid

29 My Life by Robert Taylor as told to Ben Maddox, Screenland, 10/37

Dramatics also occupied Arly's time. "In my freshman year, I played the leading role in the campus performance of *Helena's Boys*," Arly later recalled, "greatly to the disgust of Professor Gray, who wanted to know why I 'fiddled about with such nonsense.' He said that I should concentrate on the cello, that I had the makings of a concert artist, what had I to do with playacting?' I couldn't tell him. I didn't know myself. I don't know now. I only knew that there was something in the musty smell of backstage I liked." [30]

It was as a member of the Doane Players that Arly first met a fellow thespian named Beth Naden. "Arlington was very nice and extremely good looking," Beth Naden Kellar would recall nearly 80 years later. "We were all aware of his good looks. It bothered Arlington because people would get so awestruck over his looks. He even hated looking at pictures of himself because his widow's peak was so prominent. The truth is that he was even better looking in-person than he was in pictures. But he had such a very nice personality and in spite of his good looks, and we always said 'in spite' of his good looks because everybody thinks that somebody who was as good looking as Arlington was would be stuck up, but he wasn't. He was very human." As a member of the Doane Players, Arly usually got cast as the romantic lead. "That bothered him too," recalled Naden. "He wanted to be challenged more. He would tell me how much he wanted to play the character roles, but with his looks he became typed as the juvenile or romantic lead." Naden also had the opportunity to meet Arly's parents. "My impression of his mother was that she was like the mother of an only child who was very handsome and in many ways treated him like he was fragile and could break. She was very possessive of him. The father was quieter, more like Arlington, while his mother was the more prominent and louder. Arlington definitely had her eyes. I later heard that she was supposed to be an invalid but she seemed very healthy on the few occasions I met her." [31]

The Doane Players later took a tour of Nebraska communities with *Helena's Boys.* (According to Miss Naden, when they toured back in those days it was usually by train, not by bus, because road

30 Gladys Hall, Robert Taylor's True Life Story, Dell, 1937

31 Comments by Beth Naden Kellar to author

conditions of the time were quite primitive and they could make better time by train.) Other plays Arly participated in during his two years at Doane were *The House Divided, Holiday* and *Alias, the Kid*. The drama coach was a woman named Mary Ellen Inglis, who also headed the Speech Department for many years. It probably can be said that Arly was almost as influenced by her as he was by Professor Gray. In fact, Inglis' daughter, Barbara Farries Hornady, later said, "There was a tug-of-war for Arlington's talents between the music and drama departments, and my mother chalked one up when her ex-student gave up plans to become a professional cellist and decided to become an actor instead." Of course, that wasn't immediately apparent. But it's also clear that Arly kept Mrs. Inglis in high regard even after he became an established film star. "As a youngster, now and then I would receive a gift from Hollywood: a blanket, a knit jacket and cap, a doll. Nothing extravagant. I believe they were thoughtful thank yous for my mother's single-mindedness in pushing Arlington's abilities. Although he was on location the two times my mother and I visited relatives in Southern California, as his guests we were allowed on the MGM soundstages, given private tours and allowed to eat in the commissary." (Mrs. Hornady later met Robert Taylor in 1946 when she was ten years old and she received her first kiss from the popular actor. "As we sat together on a bench or glider, I asked if I could give him a hug. 'Would you like a screen kiss?' he asked me. He put his right arm around my shoulder and leaned forward. Since I went to the movies every Saturday, I knew what to do: I bent my neck backwards and closed my eyes. Robert Taylor kissed my lips. Blood poured in my brain—all the good stuff I had read about love and passion became my own experience.")[32]

Arly began dating several girls while at Doane, none too seriously. He dated a dark-haired beauty named Kathryn Bender Boekel, a native of Crete. Many years later she told E.A. Kral, "He was a perfect gentleman, very attentive, very handsome, a 'ladies' man, and prompt, reliable, very honest, very intelligent, not a storyteller, did not gossip, was well groomed, meticulous, and had a bass voice." They dated for more than two years, and, as Miss Bender later said,

32 The Wilber Republican, 2/1/95

it was, "a matter of dating, not a serious love relationship or affair."[33] Arly also became infatuated with another young woman he met while playing at a concert in Clay Center. Her name was Blanche Gilsdorf. Blanche was not a student, but was working as a secretary. She was also dating another young man. "Arly was crazy about Blanche," recalled Beth Naden. "He would light up whenever he spoke of her or was around her, but she wasn't as crazy about him. She had another boyfriend and she couldn't decide between the two of them." Perhaps as a way of making up her mind, Blanche invited Arly and his parents to dinner and the opportunity to meet her parents. It didn't go well. Blanche came from a strictly devout Catholic family and the Brughs were Methodists. Clearly her parents were opposed to their daughter dating (and possibly marrying) outside of her religion. While they did go out a few more times (often with his parents acting as chaperones) the relationship, particularly from Blanche's perspective, was going nowhere.

Arly had an old-fashioned appreciation for women. He was courtly and very much a gentleman who had an idealized view of the type of woman he was attracted to. "Every woman I have admired has had the same qualities," Arly later wrote, "the identical characteristics. I couldn't care for a woman who didn't respect herself, who didn't have a passionate desire for making the most of life. It is easy for a girl to be ordinary; that demands no will at all. That makes, I feel, only for a shabby sort of a home. I think a girl should want a splendid home, but not in the material sense. As for surface traits, I've invariably been drawn to women who are tolerant, who are good sports. I'm not above relishing a dash of glamour, but to me glamour is not bleached hair and plucked eyebrows and gobs of make-up. It's that intangible understanding and sweetness that only the woman who has a first-rate heart has. Artificial girls bore me."[34]

In May 1931, Professor Gray made a professional decision which would have a big effect on Arly's future. A vacancy came up in the music department of Pomona College in Claremont, California. Arly still considered his calling to be music and now the person

33 E. A. Kral, The Beatrice Daily Sun, 10/8/93

34 Screenland, 10/37

who most influenced him and pushed him to study and succeed was leaving. Further compounding matters was when Professor Gray suggested that Arly follow him to California so that he could continue to tutor him. Ruth later wrote that Gray had spoken to her and Dr. Brugh "at great length" about Pomona College and its "high scholastic rating." Both parents seemed swayed by Gray's arguments in favor of Pomona, "The doctor and I believed that a larger college might be more beneficial," Ruth later recalled, "[and] we knew we could trust him [Arlington]" and, besides, Professor Gray had assured them that in addition to continuing to advise Arly he would keep an eye on him as well.[35]

Further complications arose when Arly, still just a college sophomore, was offered Gray's position at Doane College, certainly a validation of his musical talent. Arly was torn. He had the opportunity to be a music teacher or to follow his mentor to California and a new life. "I drove home to talk it over with my parents," Arly later wrote, "and we arrived at a decision that changed the course of my life . . . his [Gray's] enthusiasm for the California college and for my prospects of becoming a really good cellist led my parents to suggest that I should transfer to Pomona also. I agreed."[36] Over the years some have suggested that Arly went to California not so much because of music but because of his desire to become an actor in motion pictures. "He was a very good cellist," Beth Naden recalled, "and when he left Doane to go to California he followed his professor with ambitions to become a cello player . . . he liked acting, but it was my impression that his goal was to become a musician."[37] But clearly Arly was ready for a change. Moving to California would allow him true independence for the first time from Ruth, and, furthermore, he was restless. "In other words, I came to California, eventually to Hollywood, for the express purpose of taking cello lessons! It was just like that. And suddenly I was anxious to be on my way, even though I knew little of where I was going."[38]

35 Ruth Brugh & James Reid, Movie Classics, 9/36

36 Nebraska State Journal, 3/1/37

37 Beth Naden Kellar to author

38 Walter Ramsey, Movie Mirror

II

The adventure began almost immediately. He had assured his father that he would drive carefully at a restrained 35 miles per hour. Arly stopped in Laramie, Wyoming, where he met a married couple who told him they were hitchhiking to California. The man said he was a race car driver who was heading to California for a job. Arly invited the couple to ride along with him figuring that he could make it to California quicker with another driver. Furthermore, it would give him a chance to sit back and enjoy the scenery. The couple jumped at this opportunity. Before long they were on their way with the race driver taking the wheel with his wife next to him while Arly decided to get a bit of sack time in the backseat. Arly was a bit apprehensive when he saw the man drinking from a bottle of alcohol. But the drinking seemed to make no noticeable impact on his driving, so Arly relaxed and fell into a deep sleep. The next thing Arly knew he was waking up with a gash on his forehead and lying in a ditch with his car off to the side. There was an accident and apparently Arly had been tossed from the car, but there was no sign of the hitchhiking couple—they apparently were long on their way. "I wasn't killed because it just wasn't my time to go," Arly later said in recalling the incident.[39] But he did learn a valuable lesson—he never again picked up hitchhikers. Within a few days his car was repaired and he was on his way to California—without further incident.

As he drove into the state, Arly later recalled a sense of excitement which took force over him. "It's a funny thing, but I felt as though I were being drawn here, that something important to my life was in store for me. And the minute I saw those old purple hills and saw oranges actually growing on trees, I felt like a long-lost son coming home at last."[40] On his first day there he looked up an old friend in San Bernardino and paid him a visit. Arly and his friend and the friend's girlfriend took a drive to Lake Arrowhead where they all danced and laughed under a full moon.

He soon looked up Professor Gray and enrolled at Pomona

39 Walter Ramsey, Movie Mirror

40 ibid

College. His initial enthusiasm was depleted once he began classes because he was, for the first time in his life, completely alone. He had no friends on campus and felt a bit empty and homesick. "I never before had the experience of attending a school where I was a complete stranger," Arly later recalled. "It's a pretty lonely feeling . . . I was so utterly lonesome at first that the problem of starting to make friends had me baffled." He was insecure in unfamiliar surroundings and his natural shyness gave the impression to the other students that he was stuck up. "The other students seemed to think that I was lost in admiration of myself," Arly later wrote, "when all that kept me withdrawn was wishing for the sound of a Nebraska voice just saying, 'Hi'ya, Brugh.'" Slowly, but surely, he did begin to come out of his shell and the other students began to warm to him. What got him out of his shell was the usual—music, drama and speech—and tennis, though "not ambitiously enough to make the varsity." Arly also enrolled into a six-week lecture series on psychiatry which has led some to believe that he was interested in pursuing a career as a psychiatrist. Arly later downplayed this. "The time I gave to it has been considerably over-rated in various articles which have been written about me."[41]

One of the students that Arly became friendly with was Leonard Shelton, who was called Agee by his friends. He later recalled Arly as a "friendly and modest person with a great interest in music and drama." Arly recalled Pomona College as "a bigger college in a bigger small town [than Doane]. Only here it was balmy all the year around and the air was rich with orange blossoms." He was initiated into the Phi Delta fraternity. His friend Agee Shelton would recall Phi Delta as "a very sociable group. He was also a member of the Masquers, which was a club for students who were interested in drama at Pomona College." Indeed, it was drama which was now having a bigger impact on his life—much to the continued chagrin of Professor Gray, who continued to lecture Arly about concentrating on his music and to give up the distraction of dramatics.

Among the plays Arly appeared in at Pomona were *The Devil and the Cheese, Let Us Be Gay,* and he rounded up his first year at Pomona by appearing in the leading male role in *Camille*—never dreaming

41 Gladys Hall, Robert Taylor's True Life Story, Dell, 1937

that only a few years later he would be cast in the exact same role opposite the great Greta Garbo in the film. His good looks once again worked in his favor and he was often cast as the romantic lead. "I was crazy about doing those college plays," Arly later recalled, "but even when I had worked up to leads, I don't believe I ever seriously plotted an acting career for myself. Just because the school paper and the local critics happen to think you are pretty good behind the footlights doesn't necessarily mean you are launched on a career."[42]

All of this changed on December 2–3, 1932, when Arly played the pivotal role of Captain Stanhope in the Pomona College production of *Journey's End.* (Was it a further bit of serendipity that the part Arly played was Stanhope, his mother's maiden name?) *Journey's End* was set during the First World War and the role of Captain Stanhope is not merely a leading man type depended on good looks, but a role of a battle fatigued commanding officer often in conflict with his own feelings—certainly a part that Arly could relate to given the pulls in different directions he had regarding a vocation: Was he to be a doctor? A musician? Or an actor? A review in his college paper of his performance said, "Arlington Brugh gave an intense and finely drawn performance as Captain Stanhope, the harassed commanding officer whose nerves were near the breaking point."[43] Pomona was near Hollywood and occasionally talent scouts from the studios would come out looking for a new discovery. "Before the play opened," Arly later wrote, "we heard rumors that Metro-Goldwyn-Mayer was sending a scout to look for possible motion picture talent in the cast. Everybody was excited about it. It was then, for the first time, that I thought of films except as something to watch for an evening's entertainment." In truth, since coming to California (and probably festering before that), Arly wasn't sure if he wanted his vocation in life to be the cello. "At one time I wanted to study medicine, but I know how much you and Mother want me to master the cello," he wrote to his father. "Yet I cannot deny my love for the excitement of debate and acting."[44]

---

42 Robert Taylor's Always Been in Love, Movie Mirror

43 E.A. Kral, The Beatrice Sun, 10/8/93

44 Jane Ellen Wayne, Robert Taylor, pg. 26

Prior to the beginning of the second show, Arly and some of his fellow cast players looked out of a peep hole to see if the talent scout was in the seat that had been reserved for him. They saw nobody. Arly later related that they asked that the curtain be held ten minutes just in case the scout was running late. But they could hold it no longer and the curtain rose. After the show and with some surprise Arly was approached by a middle-aged man named Ben Piazza, who introduced himself as the MGM talent scout. He had seen the performance, but had sat in the back, not in the seat which had been reserved for him. He was impressed by Arly's performance and invited him to come to the studio to make a screen test. Little did Arly know that this particular talent scout was considered one of the best in the business, having "discovered" Jean Harlow and Rosalind Russell.

Arly did make a screen test which was directed by Harold S. Bucquet, who at that time was an assistant director at the studio, but would, within a few years, graduate to directing his own pictures, which included several *Dr. Kildare* films and more prestigious offerings such as *Dragon Seed* and *Without Love*, both of which starred Katharine Hepburn. His partner in the screen test was Evalyn Knapp, who was a leading lady of the '30s and into the '40s. Here is how Arly recalled his first experience before the cameras: "There was a reassurance in the efficiency and the matter-of-fact attitude of the people of the studio. I was plumped in front of a make-up man who had me ready in fifteen minutes. I was shown a dressing room to put on evening clothes and I was whisked over to a sound stage in a jiffy. The first word I spoke for the screen was 'hello.' It was intended to be a nonchalant 'hello' addressed to Miss Knapp as I entered the scene. In the brief sketch, which required expression of a variety of emotions, I had the role of a dramatic coach whose pleasant task it was to instruct a charming girl in the technique of a love scene. As the scene developed, the characters were to discover that they really were in love and not just acting. I tried to restrain myself from over emphasizing the emotional scene and to win for the character an amused chuckle and that sympathy which goes to a young man in the bewilderment of his first love. When I finished I was glad to settle for the mere survival of the ordeal. Those first tries result in a lot of nervous tension."[45]

Arly later related that the "whole ordeal" took about two hours from the time he entered the studio to the time he left the studio. He had received no feedback on how well he had done. Then two days later he received word that his test had been "quite satisfactory" and that they would keep him in mind if anything turned up at the studio for him. To Arly this was the old, "don't call us we'll call you." He later wrote, "I presumed that the officials were satisfied with the quality of the photography and the way the set was dressed, but that I had proven hopeless as an actor." He wrote home and explained the situation to his parents and received a letter in return from his father: "Be careful. Take your time. Finish your education before you decide."[46]

Within another week Arly heard back from MGM with an invitation to attend the studio's acting school. "But I'd never considered acting!" Arly later said. "I wouldn't quit college when I had only six months more to go to graduate. Yet I had no leaning towards any other field. The school plays had been fun, for a fact. I arranged to drive over three afternoons a week for instruction from their coach." It should be emphasized that while Arly was receiving these acting lessons at MGM, three days per week, he was not yet a contract player at the studio. Naturally, Professor Gray must have been terribly disappointed in his star pupil who seemed to have caught the acting bug rather than wanting to continue his training to be a concert cellist. But Arly continued his studies and continued his lessons with the cello—and he did see college through, graduating on June 9, 1933. "I graduated," he later wrote. "College was over with as sudden a bang as it had begun. Everyone now, though, was going somewhere to be something. There were promises to keep in touch. But what on earth was I going to make of myself? Mother and father had come out for the ceremonies and they were ready to drive home. Mother had beamed when she saw me playing the cello on the platform. My father said, 'Well, son—so you're not going on to medical school?' I don't know what seized me, but I answered, 'I want to stay out here for a month or so

45 Ladies Home Journal, October, 1936

46 Omaha World Herald, 7/15/51

longer. I had one nibble from the movies. I might get another.'"[47]

It wasn't quite as cut and dried as that. On the trip out, Ruth had had one of her occasional spells and still wasn't feeling well at the time of the ceremonies. This wasn't unusual to Arly. He had spent a lifetime with his mother recovering from various illnesses. What was different this time was the health of his father. After graduation, Ruth took Arly aside and told him, "Your dad isn't well." She proposed the idea that he come home for the summer and get a job and then from the familiar surroundings of Beatrice evaluate his future and, in the meantime, it would be a comfort to his father and her to have him around. Arly strongly considered her recommendation. Yes, he was taking acting lessons, but nothing yet had come from them. He really had nothing in California, all his roots and good friends were back in Nebraska. It was tempting to leave, but then his father, downplaying his health problems, told Arly how he had been talking to some of his classmates and heard that Arly might have a future as an actor and told him, in effect, to keep at it a little longer and see what happened. He gave him a check for $250 and he and Ruth started back for Nebraska.

Arly was studying at MGM under the guidance of its esteemed drama coach, Oliver Hinsdell. When he was an established star, he wrote of his experiences training under Hinsdell: "I remember our first session very well. He handed me a short side of lines and business which was excessively dramatic and which wound up with the line, 'He shot me. I'm dying.' I suppose the bit was as much a personality test as anything. I'm sure I couldn't have crowded a great deal of technique into the action, but I did read the concluding lines softly and with an awe-stricken manner. I think I should be too choked up with wonder and dismay at such dreadful luck to be noisy if I were wounded. At any rate, Hinsdell grunted 'Okay' when I had finished and he walked away. I didn't know but what he meant I was hopeless, but others in his charge later told me that he was expressing satisfaction. I can tell you I was pleased! But then I discovered that he started new pupils out on those lines because they tempt actors to build up a florid, 'hammy' piece of emotional over-acting, so I continued to practice restraint. In showing my

47 Screenland, 10/37

pleasure—much as Hinsdell restrained his enthusiasm over my first effort."

Within two months of his graduation from college, Arly heard from his mother again, this time by telegram informing him that his father's health had taken a turn for the worst and he was going to have an operation. She told him his condition was critical. "The bad news was a terrible shock," Arly later wrote. "On my way thru Pomona I stopped to tell my psychology professor, Dr. Robert Ross, and he offered to drive with me back to my father's bedside in Beatrice, Nebraska." When he got home he found his father "desperately ill" in hospital. After about two weeks, Dr. Brugh seemed to be recovering, and he told Arly, "I'm all right now, son. You go back to Hollywood and work hard." [48] Arly did return and within a month his father died. He was only 52.

In retrospect, Arly believed that he "let father convince me he was sure to recover and asked him to wish me luck to make good for him and mother. He did so as he sent me off. I don't know how he hid the pain he must have been suffering, for he couldn't really have thought himself out of danger when I returned to Hollywood. He wasn't." [49] This time Arly returned by plane for the funeral, which was held on October 18, 1933, at the Centenary United Methodist Church in Beatrice. At the funeral Arly silently paid tribute to his father thanking him, "for teaching me to handle situations. He had met life and death and all the exigencies of both with firm sympathy, with matter-of-fact common sense." Dr. Brugh's body was placed in a vault at Evergreen Home Cemetery in Beatrice. (In 1940, Arly—then Robert Taylor—had his father's body flown to California, where it was interred at Forest Lawn in Glendale, California.)

At this point Arly seriously considered staying in Beatrice and later said he went as far as getting a job at a gas station to help support his mother and himself. [50] The fact is that while Dr. Brugh provided a good living while he was alive, he also offered services on credit. Arly later recalled, "He had a good practice as long as he

48 Gladys Hall, Robert Taylor's True Life Story, Dell, 1937

49 ibid

50 ibid

lived. When he passed on, the income stopped. I went home to settle up the estate. He was like every other doctor. When he took the medical oath, he had to swear to do what he could to alleviate suffering. He would have done it, anyhow . . . When Dad died he had about $25,000 owing to him. I think, altogether, we've collected about $1,000 of it. He left us a lot of land on which we had to pay taxes. Maybe someday the land will be worth something. Then it was an added liability. It was during the Depression and we couldn't have sold it if we'd wanted to. He left some insurance. Not a lot but some. By the time we'd settled his bills, paid the expenses of his illness and funeral there wasn't much left. A few hundred dollars."[51]

Fortunately, Ruth determined that Arly should not give up the opportunities he had begun forging in California. The fact that he was still being tutored at MGM meant that they must have some interest in him. He also, prior to his father's death, had enrolled in a dramatics course at the Neely Dixon Dramatic School. He had determined before his father died to try acting for a year and if it didn't pan out this time, he would give it up and use his business degree. On November 25, 1933, Arly, Ruth and Grandmother Stanhope left for California. They only had a few hundred dollars to exist on.

51 ibid

Chapter Three
"MORE STARS THAN IN THE HEAVENS" (1933-1935)

In 1933 when people thought of Hollywood they probably thought of glitter and glamour in a world of make believe. But Hollywood was as much a factory town as Detroit and Pittsburgh. The Hollywood factories didn't churn out automobiles or steel, but they certainly did have quotas to fill for markets dependent upon their product. Hollywood factories went by names such as Metro-Goldwyn-Mayer, Warner Brothers, Universal, Paramount and Columbia. The produced product provided seventy minutes to an hour-and-a-half (on average) of escape for Depression-era audiences. The Hollywood factories produced these diversions, called motion pictures, out of their factories to fill their markets, theaters (many of which were owned by the major studios themselves), around the world. The biggest of them all in size and reputation was Metro-Goldwyn-Mayer. This was a studio that by 1933 had 4,000 employees and 23 soundstages and a backlot spread out over 117 acres. In 1933, MGM set its quota at producing one movie per week.[52]

MGM had withstood the effects of the Depression better than the other studios. For instance, in 1930, the first full year of the Depression, Warner Brothers reported an $8 million loss. RKO and Fox were also in the red. Of the major studios, MGM and Paramount managed to keep in the black. By the next year Paramount's $6 million in profits turned into a staggering $16 million loss, which led to that studio filing for bankruptcy. But MGM kept in the black with $8 million in profits. By 1933 weekly attendance in movie theaters was around 60 million. That's an impressive number, to be

52 John Douglas Eames, The MGM Story

sure, but, in fact, weekly attendance had declined by almost half since the beginning of the Depression. Despite the need for escape, it was still a struggle for many people during these years, when unemployment rose from just over 3% in 1929 to just under 25% in 1933, to even come up with an extra dime to see a movie every week. In short, the public became more selective of the films they saw.[53]

The chief executive officer at MGM was Louis B. Mayer. Mayer was one of the best-known business executives in the country and one of the wealthiest. Hard times for most Americans didn't affect Mayer and his family. They lived in an opulent beachfront mansion in Santa Monica which had thirteen marble bathrooms. His base wage was $3,000 per week at a time when many Americans made about $1,000 *per year*. But what really kept Mayer plush in cash (and helped motivate his decisions as an executive of a major motion picture studio) is that he had a deal that paid him, annually, a percentage of what MGM's parent company, Loew's Inc., netted. By 1939 Mayer's compensation was an undivided 6.77%.

Mayer was a hardnosed businessman who believed that to survive the Depression the company had to initiate salary cuts. He was no exception—the top executives of the studio in 1932 took a voluntary one-year wage cut of 35 percent for one year. He asked the employees at MGM to make a greater sacrifice: a wage reduction of 50 percent to avoid the lay-offs which other studios had initiated. Despite much grumbling—especially since MGM was in the black—his proposal was largely carried out. (The savings from these cuts, estimated to be around $800,000,went into the general fund of Metro's parent company, Loew's, and at the end of the year the top executives profited because they got a piece of the profits!) Mayer could be unscrupulous, but he didn't acquire his wealth through family connections. Mayer was that old-fashioned American success story—the self-made man—except that Mayer wasn't born in the United States.

Mayer was born Lazar Meir in Minsk in 1885. At the age of three he and his family moved to St. John, New Brunswick. His father went into the junk business and from young childhood Lazar worked

53 ibid

for his father. His mother sold chickens and made a mean chicken soup. (The recipe of which, years later, became one of the premium items on the Metro bill of fare.) At 18 Lazar set off for Boston and found work in a junkyard. There he met a nice, humble Jewish girl who was three years older than he and whose father was a butcher and cantor. Within a few months they were married and within fourteen months of the marriage their first child was born. By 1907 Lazar had two little girls he was supporting, but an economic downturn that same year put him out of business and Louis had to swallow his pride and move in with his wife's parents. But losing his junk business turned out to be a blessing in disguise for Lazar. Attempting to find work he met a man named Joe Mack who gave him a job selling tickets at his nickelodeon—Lazar's first exposure to the world of movies. The experience with Mack led to Lazar renting a dilapidated movie theater. With an investment of $650 Lazar fixed up the theater, doing much of the work himself. By the end of 1907 he had renamed his theater the Orpheum. What differentiated his movie theater from the others in Haverville was Lazar's determination to provide honest-to-goodness first-rate family entertainment rather than the more sordid adult fare that the other movie houses presented. This put Lazar in good stead with the church groups and leading citizens in town. In the next several years Lazar built on this success by acquiring more theaters and also ventured into the lucrative business of film distribution. What really put Lazar on the map was when, in 1915, he acquired the franchise to release D. W. Griffith's *The Birth of a Nation* in the New England region. Shortly after this Lazar became secretary in Metro Pictures Corporation and moved his family to California.

Metro was moderately successful and Lazar decided he wanted to produce his own films and formed Mayer Production Company. (By this time Lazar had Americanized his name; Lazar became Louis and Meir became Mayer.) He produced a series of pictures which featured the ex-wife of Charlie Chaplin as a way of exploiting the Chaplin name, much to Chaplin's chagrin. (When they met in a restaurant one night in 1920, Chaplin challenged Mayer to a fight. Louis obliged, and with one swing decked Chaplin.) Meanwhile, Metro Pictures Corporation was sold to Marcus Loew, who owned the Loew Theatre chain. Loew invited Louis to take over distribution of the newly merged company, so now Louis was working as chief operator for Loew's while still producing and distributing his own films. It was around this time that Louis decided he needed assistance with his work and hired a 22-year-old named Irving Thalberg, who had been in charge of operations at Universal, until Thalberg had the audacity to ask for a raise. When it was denied him, Thalberg made good on his threat to leave the studio. Louis knew of Thalberg's good reputation and hard work at Universal and hired him with a substantial increase in salary.

At the same time, another early movie company, Goldwyn Pictures, was on shaky ground. Goldwyn Pictures had a strong roster of stars and a splendid facility in Culver City, near Hollywood. But it had poor management, which had resulted in the man who formed the studio, Samuel Goldwyn, exiting it in 1922. Without Goldwyn, the studio floundered even more. It was another good opportunity for Loew to add to his impressive holdings and in 1924 Loew acquired Goldwyn Pictures. Mayer, with his strong management skills, was made the chief executive officer of the studio. Mayer's first decision in his new role was to make Thalberg his chief of production of the studio, now renamed Metro-Goldwyn-Mayer. The newly formed studio immediately took over production from Goldwyn of *Ben-Hur*, which was filming on location (with an out-of-control budget) in Rome. Within a year, *Ben-Hur* and the prestigious *The Big Parade* had put MGM on the map and were not only critical successes but hugely successful at the box office. In its first full year in operation MGM made a profit of over $4.7 million—in 1924 dollars.

Mayer ruled over his studio with an iron hand. He could make and break careers and frequently did. MGM was a producer's studio in a way that other studios in Hollywood at the time were not. Adolph Zukor at Paramount was more of a figurehead. He depended on his line producers and strong directors like Ernst Lubitsch and Cecil B. DeMille. At MGM Mayer made business decisions on properties to be filmed and talent to be acquired and, with Irving Thalberg, went back and forth about what directors would be right for what projects and which stars should be given what part—who should be rewarded with a plum role and who should be taken down a peg or two for the audacity of trying to show independence. Yes, MGM was a producer's studio, and while they did have under contract some very fine directors, like King Vidor, Victor Fleming and George Cukor, it seemed that the ones that Mayer especially valued were the speedy—yet efficient—directors like Woody Van Dyke, Richard Thorpe, Jack Conway and Sam Wood. They directed with factory efficiency—move the product along quickly—but made sure it had that special MGM gloss that made even their cheaper pictures look better than any other studios' standard B films. And these speed demons did produce some very fine pictures, indeed. Van Dyke was especially underestimated, but he did direct *The Thin Man* and one of MGM's biggest hits of the decade, *San Francisco*. If a production needed something extra and was considered one of the prestigious pictures of the year it might get a little more attention and somebody like Vidor or Cukor would be called in.

Yet, Mayer was also a sentimentalist who loved his adopted country for the opportunities it presented him. He espoused old-fashioned values, "his themes were God, country and mom's chicken soup."[54] He detested films which muddied any of those values. When asked at one time what film he was most proud of, he would point to the *Andy Hardy* series—the epitome of those values. It was on the question of what properties to be made into films that often caused friction between Mayer and his production head, Thalberg, who was much more cosmopolitan in his tastes.

MGM may have been a factory producing motion pictures to the masses, but Mayer saw his studio as more than that. He saw the studio as his home and the people who worked there as his family—and the family must take pride in what they do. Writer John Lee Mahin would later recall, "In the very early days, we used to play softball on Sundays, with Mayer pitching for one team and Thalberg for the other. A truck would come and take everybody to the back lot. And everybody would play—writers, executives, electricians."[55] Mayer was not the foreman but a father figure who would advise his children about what was best for them—*as he saw it*—and, like any

54 Ethan Mordden, The Hollywood Studios: House Style in the Golden Age of Hollywood

55 Aljean Harmetz, The Making of the Wizard of Oz

possessive, domineering parent, if his child disobeyed him he would not hide his sorrow, anger or disappointment. He would tell one and all, "If you have a problem, come to me." Producer Pandro Berman, who in the late '30s came to MGM from RKO, later summed up well the essence of Mayer and why he was successful in finding and cultivating talent: "I worked for two men in this business—Harry Cohen and Louis Mayer. Harry Cohen was a man who wooed you, and went to all kinds of lengths to get you to work for him, and admired you and respected you until the day you went to him. And on that day he lost interest in you because he said to himself, 'If this schmuck is stupid enough to come to work for me, he can't be the man I thought he was.' Louis Mayer was the exact opposite. He would woo you, win you, and the day you came to work for him, you were higher in his opinion than you'd ever been before, because if you were bright enough to come to work for Louis Mayer, you must be the man he wanted. And that's the truth about the two men. That's why Harry Cohen never kept anybody. They all left him. And that's why Mayer never lost anybody."[56]

Had Mayer decided to be an actor he might actually have succeeded. "Honest to God. Louis Mayer was the biggest ham I've ever met in America," recalled Berman. "He would start telling the story, and he'd get involved, and he'd start writing it, and he'd start acting it, and he'd start crying and he'd start praying . . . it was unbelievable!"[57]

Marsha Hunt, who was under contract to Metro for several years, recalls Mayer "did have a nose and ear for talent that was remarkable. He had his faults but he could sense talent. He gathered the very finest in all departments and brought them in together. But Mayer did make some bad enemies. Jules Dassin, for instance, has embittered memories of Mayer. Mine are very brief and pleasant and flattering."[58]

But the scales were not always in his favor—especially among his "children." Judy Garland always blamed Mayer and his studio for getting her hooked on uppers and downers and making her feel

56 Transcript of AFI interview with Pandro Berman, Berman Papers (WSHSA)

57 ibid

58 Marsha Hunt to author

insecure about her looks. Elizabeth Taylor, as a child actress, told Mayer to go to hell when she overheard Mayer yelling at her mother. Gene Kelly considered Mayer uncouth and much preferred his later head of production, Dore Schary, who he believed had better taste. On the other hand, Katharine Hepburn greatly respected "L.B." and was one Hollywood mogul she enjoyed negotiating with. As for Arly, he ultimately found Mayer, "kind, fatherly, understanding and protective."

Ivy Mooring, later Robert Taylor's secretary, later summed up the Mayer-Taylor relationship as "father and son," but, "He [Taylor] was a little afraid of Mayer. He never wanted to displease him and so he didn't turn things down that he thought were rubbish."[59]

II

Upon returning to California from Nebraska, Arly rented a three-room apartment for himself, Ruth and his grandmother to live in. There was only one bedroom which Ruth and her mother shared while Arly slept on the sofa in the living room. It was the best they could afford given their current circumstances. Arly also picked up where he left off when his father had died and returned to the Neely Dixon School and attending acting lessons with Oliver Tinsdell, the MGM coach. Shortly thereafter, he was offered the opportunity for a screen test at Samuel Goldwyn Studios for the Eddie Cantor film *Roman Scandals*. Decked out in a Roman Centurion outfit, complete with fig leaf in his hair and sandals on his feet (an early look at how he would appear fifteen years later in the film *Quo Vadis*), Arly was clearly ill at ease and it showed in his test. When the test was run for Goldwyn, the only response he had was that Bob was too thin. The test didn't lead to a film offer.

Meanwhile, back at MGM, Arly continued on with his training. One day in Tinsdell's class Arly was performing a scene from the play *When Ladies Meet*. It impressed an observer named Marcella Knapp, who worked in the studio's executive offices, and she arranged for yet another screen test. Arly thought the test was terrible: "When they see this, they'll throw me out of here for good." And,

59 Ivy Mooring to author

in fact, the test was not very good. For one thing the camera work was unfocused and Arly was ill at ease, but Metro executives found enough good footage of Arly to suggest that he had potential. On February 6, 1934, just over two months after returning from Nebraska, Arly signed a seven-year contract with MGM at a compensation of $35 per week, the lowest salary ever given a contract player at the studio up to that time. It was indicative that the studio might have thought that Arly had "something," but they really didn't know what. He certainly had good looks, but his acting was considered rough. Howard Strickling, one of Mayer's lieutenants, later said that Arly "had the looks, but not the training." If he could show improvement in the acting department he might make a good juvenile or secondary lead.

To be an MGM contract player, no matter how low the compensation, was pretty impressive and Arly was suitably awestruck by his surroundings. He enjoyed the collegiate atmosphere of the studio. "In my own case, I was part of the MGM stable. We called Metro the campus—and even the seasons became semesters. Camaraderie was shared at work and at play, up and down the line." The MGM that Arly came into in 1934 certainly had some of the top stars in the industry. Among the biggest names that Arly would occasionally see on the lot (but was still too green to get to know) were Greta Garbo, Clark Gable, Joan Crawford, Jean Harlow, Robert Montgomery, Wallace Beery, Norma Shearer (he knew off the bat that she was indeed somebody special since she was the wife of Irving Thalberg, and was usually assigned the most prestigious films at the studio, after Greta Garbo), William Powell and Myrna Loy. Among the Metro films which were in release at this time were *Bombshell, Queen Christina, Tugboat Annie, Manhattan Melodrama,* with *The Thin Man, Viva Villa!, The Barretts of Wimpole Street, Treasure Island, David Copperfield,* and *Tarzan and His Mate* were either in production or pre-production.

But at this time the most important person at the studio was, indeed, Louis B. Mayer. At first, like most of the lowly contract players, he observed L. B. from afar. "He was constantly on the move around the lot," Arly later recalled. "He knew every department—he knew the heads of every department—and he knew everyone's problems." It may have come as somewhat of a surprise that Mayer even understood Arly's problems—or perceived problems. One problem was his name. "Arlington Brugh" certainly had flair, but it wasn't really a star-making name. *New York Times* critic Bosley Crowther once pronounced the name, "intolerable."[60] It was at this crucial juncture that Arly got to know perhaps the second most important person at the studio—Mayer's personal secretary, Ida Koverman.

Koverman was an influential figure in her own right. She had befriended industrialist Herbert Hoover when working for the Consolidated Gold Fields in South Africa. Hoover was impressed by Koverman's organizational prowess and in 1924, when Hoover was U.S. Commerce Secretary, he named her executive secretary for President Calvin Coolidge's re-election campaign. Following that, she became executive secretary of the Republican Party of Southern California, a state that was Hoover's home base. In 1928, when Hoover was running his own campaign for the presidency, he asked Koverman to be the executive secretary of his campaign. It was in this capacity that Koverman was introduced to Mayer, who was one of many wealthy businessmen she was attempting to persuade to donate to the Hoover campaign. It didn't take much arm-twisting since Mayer was a fervent Republican and strong Hoover supporter.

One thing Mayer understood well was to have friends in powerful places, and there was no more powerful place than the White House. Following the election, Mayer offered Koverman the job of being his executive secretary, which she accepted. Mayer came to value her not only for her efficiency and organizational expertise, but because of her shrewd judge of talent. She was a patron of the arts and served as a director of the Hollywood Bowl. She was impressed by a young operatic singer named Nelson Eddy, and persuaded Mayer that Eddy should be signed by the studio, as a suitable leading man opposite the often-temperamental Jeanette MacDonald. The MacDonald-Eddy movies at MGM during the 1930s delivered heavy profits for the studio.

Koverman had taken a liking to Arly and early on when it was decided that the name Arlington Brugh had little marquee value it was Koverman who suggested to Mayer that "Taylor" would be a

60 Bosley Crowley, The Lion's Share, pg. 242

good last name for their new asset. "I wanted Stanhope," Bob recalled years later. "It was my mother's maiden name and I had been discovered playing Captain Stanhope." But Mayer always respected Koverman's opinions and overruled Arly, so his professional last name became Taylor. As for a first name, Mayer suggested "Robert." Again, Arly protested. "I told Miss Koverman there were already too many Roberts on the lot, Robert Young and Robert Montgomery, but Mayer had already left his office." So, along with a friend in the publicity department, Arly kicked around other possible first names and came up with "Ramsey"—Ramsey Taylor. But Robert Taylor it was and Robert Taylor it would remain. Years later, Arly, or as he was known by then, Robert Taylor, confessed that the subject of his name change was a "touchy" one, but, "I wasn't in much of a position to argue with anyone. Jobs were scarce and I considered myself pretty lucky to be offered one even at the rather meager salary of $35 per week. I held out for the name of Stanhope as long as I could, but it was largely a matter of being out-voted."[61]

With a new professional name Arly began using the name on the lot as well. Instead of introducing himself as "Arlington Brugh" he would say, "Hi, I'm Bob, Bob Taylor." It was part of the ordeal of getting used to a new name so that it became natural for him to say it and be referred to by it. For the next few weeks Bob collected his $35 per week and continued to take classes with Oliver Tinsdell. At this point Bob would later say he was referred to as "the Pomona mugger." Tinsdell immediately went to work toward correcting this. "I thought acting depended upon gestures and exaggerated facial expressions," Bob later said. "Mr. Tinsdell soon took away that amateurish idea."[62] Tinsdell "saw to it that I stopped overacting, mugging, and stepping on people's feet."[63]

But Bob was getting a bit discouraged as the weeks went on. On $35 per week it was difficult to support his mother and grandmother. He didn't see any rush by the studio to cast him in any pictures. He began to feel the whole experience might be a futile one. He thought perhaps he had nothing to lose if he asked for a raise. Bob went to

61 Jane Ellen Wayne, Robert Taylor pg. 33-34

62 Ladies' Home Journal, 9/36

63 Films of Robert Taylor, pg. 26

see Mayer, explaining his situation and asking for a raise. "Sit down, Bob," Mayer told him. "Bob," Mayer began, "God never saw fit to give me a son. He gave me daughters, two beautiful daughters, who have been a great joy to me." He then began to pour it on with the usual Mayer dose of pathos. "But if he had given me a son, Bob—if he had blessed me with such a great and wonderful joy—I can't think of anybody I would rather have wanted than that son to be exactly like you." Mayer went on for several minutes in this vein. Later, when he left Mayer's office, Bob was asked if he got the raise he sought. "No, but I got a father." [64]

Mayer did become a sort of father figure to Bob, and he took an active interest from this point forward in the young man's career. One day Mayer called Bob into his office. "How's your wardrobe, son?" he asked him. Bob explained to Mayer he had a couple of off the rack suits. "That's not good enough," Mayer told him and immediately sent him off to his personal tailor, "the best in Hollywood," Bob would recall. Mayer ordered four made-to-order suits and paid for them out of his own pocket. [65] For the next couple of years, or until Bob hit his major stardom, MGM continued to foot the bill for Bob's personal wardrobe.

MGM decided to introduce their young new contract player not in one of their own pictures but by loaning him out to Fox to appear in a Will Rogers film, *Handy Andy*. While this was not a Metro film, it was hardly a step down for Bob. Rogers, the cowboy-humorist, was one of the most popular and admired of American entertainers. He was also one of the top box-office stars of the day. Despite this being a Rogers film, Bob was disappointed that he was being "farmed out" for his first film. "My feeling was one of keen disappointment. Why couldn't I make my first picture in my own studio? Wasn't I good enough to work where I had been trained?" Bob later wrote. [66]

Handy Andy casts Rogers as a humble Midwestern pharmacist with a wife who has social aspirations. Mary Carlisle plays their daughter who the mother pressures to marry into the "right" family—meaning

64 Bosley Crowther, Hollywood Rajah, pg. 7-8

65 The Sunday Express, 8/12/62

66 Ladies' Home Journal, 9/36

one with social status. Carlisle, however, prefers the son of a local doctor, one of Rogers' longtime friends—and certainly not one of the young men that her mother has in mind for her. Bob was cast in this role (netting sixth billing). Bob would always recall how Rogers helped make him comfortable on the set of his first film. "Will Rogers' rare kindness to me made the experience doubly pleasant," Bob later wrote. "His consideration and encouragement made an immense difference."[67] Bob would recall, too, that the first day on the set for his first picture was "nerve-racking." He didn't get to perform in any scenes on that first day mainly because Will Rogers was having trouble with his lines. "It is true that Mr. Rogers held us up with his lines," Bob later said. "He could not memorize accurately, but he could ad-lib more quickly and humorously than any other actor I have ever seen."[68]

Bob came through the experience well. Fox began getting letters asking, "Who was Mary Carlisle's boyfriend in *Handy Andy*?" The film, as usual for a Rogers picture, did well at the box office. Bob also got his first major mention in the *New York Times* when the picture was released at the Roxy Theater in New York on August 3, 1934. "Robert Taylor makes the most of the part of the young man who is in love with Mary Carlisle," wrote the *Times* reviewer. When the film opened a few days later in Lincoln, Nebraska, the *Lincoln Sunday Journal & Star* made note in its headline: WILL ROGERS AND LOCAL LAD AT STUART. The review pointed out, "Doubly interesting is 'Handy Andy' to Lincoln people, first of course, because Will Rogers is the gum kneading comic and second, since it starts a Nebraska lad on what looks like a big first step into the land of the celluloid. This boy is on the screen as Robert Taylor, but to Beatrice, Crete and Lincoln people who knew him, he is Arlington Brugh."[69]

While Bob was appearing in films away from MGM he was still studying with Oliver Hinsdell and even appearing in productions put on by Hinsdell using MGM contract players. One such play was called "All Good Americans," which was presented in two

67 Lincoln State Journal, 3/2/37

68 Ladies Home Journal, 9/36

69 Lincoln Sunday Journal & Star, 8/12/36

performances at the Music Box Theater in late July of 1934. Proceeds from the performances would go to the Mt. Sinai Home for Chronic Invalids. The play would also be a chance for Metro executives to monitor the growth and audience reaction to their young contract players. In addition to Bob, the play included other such up-and-comers as Betty Furness and Mary Carlisle.[70]

Bob was then quickly loaned out to Universal where he received seventh billing in a Frank Morgan film titled *There's Always Tomorrow*. Morgan plays a husband whose wife and children take for granted and seem to have little consideration for. Bob plays Morgan's self-centered oldest son, Arthur. English actress Binnie Barnes plays a former employee of Morgan's who has always carried a flame for him which ignites again when they run into each other. Will Morgan give up his unfeeling family to find true love with her? Taylor's Arthur and the other children find out about Barnes and are convinced that Morgan is betraying their mother—even though he has not.

Bob made another good impression with his relatively small part in this film, but, naturally, when the picture was released it was Morgan who got the cream of the reviews (deservingly so) for his performance. Bob isn't even mentioned in the *New York Times* review of the film. Interestingly, more than twenty years later, Universal would remake this film with the same title but with Fred MacMurray in the Morgan role and Barbara Stanwyck, then Taylor's ex-wife, in the Barnes role. It was one of the two early Taylor films that Universal would remake in the mid-fifties directed by Douglas Sirk—the other being *Magnificent Obsession*. Of *There's Always Tomorrow*, Bob would only say that a "little more confidence became mine" by making the film.

Then, he finally appeared in a movie for his own studio, but it's more or less a bit part in a film called *Wicked Woman*. He plays a cad who's involved with leading lady Jean Parker and his big scene involves a fight he has with her brother (played by the much higher billed William Henry) and knocking him down a flight of stairs—causing a five-day coma.

Oddly, a starring role in a new short subject series of films under

70 LA Times, 7/23/34

the banner of *Crime Does Not Pay* proved to be one of Bob's big breaks at this point in his career. *Crime Does Not Pay* would become a hugely popular series which would run until 1947. The short was called "Buried Loot" and was filmed in late 1934. It was released in early 1935 and was a snug two-reeler, running approximately nineteen minutes. It cast Bob as a young bank clerk who is sent to prison for stealing $200,000 which was never found. He, of course, knows where the missing money is buried and just wants to wait out his time in prison and then when he is released retrieve the money. However, a fellow inmate convinces him to take part in an escape which is successful (Bob impersonates a priest to make his escape). They manage to escape to Canada where Taylor changes his name and causes an explosion which leads to plastic surgery which changes his features. But Taylor soon gets his comeuppance when he learns that all those that aided his escape were involved in an elaborate scheme by law enforcement to retrieve the missing money and proving, as the title of the series states, "Crime Does Not Pay."

Bob later recalled it as his first role of importance, but "I didn't realize it." MGM put him in this role, in part, to give him exposure but also to refine him—though Bob still thought he had the tendency to "mug a little."[71] The *Crime Does Not Pay* series became very popular with moviegoers and this initial offering probably gave Bob a wider audience than his previous films had. It was shown in theaters as a short-subject film supporting the major studio release, including ones starring the elite of the studio, such as Clark Gable and Joan Crawford—guaranteeing wide exposure. It seemed to work because afterward the studio began getting fan mail regarding the young man in the *Crime Does Not Pay* film. The studio now believed that Bob was ready to groom for stardom.

III

Bob had made enough of an impact on his loan-outs to Fox and his *Crime Does Not Pay* short that the studio was now ready to put him in one of its own features in a leading role. *Society Doctor* was shot over the course of about three weeks, between late November

71 Ladies Home Journal, Sept 1936

and mid-December of 1934. The working title alternated between *Ambulance Call* and *Only Eight Hours.* The film tells the story of two young doctors (Chester Morris and Bob) and the nurse they both romance (played by Virginia Bruce). Originally, Clark Gable was to play the Morris part, but since he had recently played in a similarly themed film, *Men in White,* Metro decided not to cast him in this picture. The Virginia Bruce part was first offered to Fay Wray, but she withdrew prior to filming.

The film was based on a novel and is quite melodramatic at times. While Bob is one of the leads, the primary male lead is played by Chester Morris. He plays a surgeon who has a run-in with a wealthy man with connections after disobeying his orders and performing emergency surgery on his son rather than waiting for the arrival of the family's more experienced doctor. Morris is fired, but a wealthy matron (Billie Burke) sets him up in private practice which alienates Bruce and moves her toward Taylor. At the end—shot by a gangster—Morris supervises his own operation to be performed by Taylor. Since Chester Morris was the nominal leading man he also, in the end, gets Virginia Bruce back.

There is a consensus that this was Taylor's most comfortable film performance to date and some of it may have to do with the fact that he was able to call upon his own experiences making rounds with his father. "There was a special spirit satisfaction for me in doing the doctor's role well," Bob later wrote. "I tried to get into the character some of the reverence I had for the memory of my father, who brought such compassion to the practice of medicine as one would expect of a doctor who learned his profession so he might save the life of his bride." [72] Bob later wrote that prior to just beginning production on this film he gave himself a pep talk. "What's the sense of all this tension? What's there to be afraid of?" he asked himself. He says that he began to feel himself relax and "was a lucky thing I achieved that sense of ease early in the picture, for I was playing my first substantial role and it was make or break." [73]

The critics took notice, too, with *New York Herald Tribune* critic Kate Cameron writing, "In a market where young leading men are

72 Lincoln State Journal, 3/3/37

73 Lincoln State Journal, 3/4/37

so scarce a commodity that the same players are used over and over again until one is likely to grow weary of the same faces, the appearance of an actor with the potentialities of young Mr. Taylor is to be hailed with cheers. Clark Gable, Robert Montgomery, Franchot Tone, Gene Raymond, Gary Cooper, Joel McCrea and Chester Morris, push over and make room for Robert Taylor!" The *New York Times* praised the film as "spotless white and with an appropriate sense of glamour and nobility." The review called Bob a "promising newcomer."

Bob realized that he must have made a good impression in the film when he was called into the office of Howard Strickling, MGM's publicity director who was often referred to as "the fixer" because of his knack for getting stars out of fixes which might harm their careers. Bob later recalled that Strickling spoke with him about two subjects. "One, I was to be careful about getting into scrapes or situations which might injure my reputation. If I did get into trouble, such as being arrested for speeding, I was to report immediately to him, so the department would know the truth before a highly colored picture could be printed in the papers . . . Two, I was to tell my life story to one of his writers. I was to tell the truth. And I was to continue to tell the men of his department anything of interest which might happen to me from day to day."[74] It was clear that this chat with the head of publicity for the whole MGM studios was an indication that Metro had finally realized that Bob had arrived and they were about to throw the entire studio publicity machine behind him.

The push was now on and in the next seven months Taylor would grind out four more films. The chemistry with Virginia Bruce was so good that Metro immediately cast them in another film to follow up *Society Doctor. Times Square Lady* tells the story of Bruce, a nightclub singer, whose father dies and she inherits his dog track, hockey team and a nightclub run by Taylor. The father's attorney/executor employs Taylor to help him swindle Bruce, but he falls in love instead. The chemistry was strong between Taylor and Bruce off screen as well. Miss Bruce was slightly less than a year older than Bob but had been in films since 1929 and by the time of *Times Square Lady* she had made more than twenty films. In

74 Ladies' Home Journal, November 1936

1932 she had married the faded silent screen star John Gilbert, who had struggled to make the transition to talking pictures. They had a child in 1934, but his alcoholism was taking a toll on their marriage and by 1935 they had divorced. Taylor and Bruce began quietly dating, but MGM didn't approve of the match. They really didn't want their up-and-coming young actor to be tied to a divorcee with a young child. Whatever the story, the romance didn't last long after the completion of *Times Square Lady*.

West Point of the Air, released less than a month after *Times Square Lady* but completed beforehand, is mainly a Wallace Beery film about a veteran army sergeant who wants to make a man out of the son who has continually disappointed him. If you thought that the son would be played by Taylor, wrong; the second lead is another Robert—Robert Young. In fact, Bob has very little to do in this picture. He plays a fellow air cadet and only has two or three lines. Bob would get his chance to co-star with Beery on an equal basis in four years time when they both appeared in *Stand Up and Fight*.

Bob's next substantive film is *Murder in the Fleet*, an uneasy mixture of adventure, suspense and comedy. Bob plays a lieutenant on a battle cruiser experiencing a series of murders committed by a saboteur intent on blowing up the ship. Bob cuts a fine figure in his naval uniform, but naturally he needs a love interest. Jean Parker plays a girl who he had once proposed marriage to and now wants him to leave the Navy to take a civilian job with her father. But the love story does take a backseat to the suspense and comedy relief (provided by Nat Pendleton, Una Merkel and Ted Healy minus his Stooges). The *New York Times* in its review didn't care for the comedy relief. "The film isn't a bad bit of moviemaking, but its incessant and ghastly comedy becomes a great nuisance." The review did applaud Bob and the truly thrilling finale of the picture. "*Murder in the Fleet* can be complimented on the most chilling episode the screen has worked up in months. When Robert Taylor is locked in combat with a maniac in the powder magazine, which is being flooded to prevent the madman from blowing up the ship, the chances are you will have enough excitement to last you until the next Frankenstein picture." *Murder in the Fleet* proved a nice bit of diversion for audiences and allowed MGM to feature Bob as an action hero to the delight of his fast-rising fan base.

Bob was next cast in a big hit for the studio, *Broadway Melody of 1936*, the second of four *Broadway Melody* pictures the studio would produce—and the best. Jack Benny is top billed as a Walter Winchell-type Broadway columnist who continually prints gossipy items in the newspaper about a Broadway producer (Bob) and the show that he is producing. Eleanor Powell gives the standout performance in a dual role playing a phony French Chanteuse as well as the former small-town girlfriend that Taylor now has little time for.

The picture features several top-notch songs by the team of Nacio Herb Brown and Arthur Freed (before Freed became the studio's leading producer of musical pictures). The songs include "Broadway Rhythm," "On a Sunday Afternoon," "Sing Before Breakfast," and, in a beautiful sequence featuring Powell, "You Are My Lucky Star." Taylor gets a chance to sing "I Got a Feelin' You're Foolin'" with June Knight.

Eleanor Powell was hired off the Broadway stage to make her film debut here. At first she was to be offered a specialty tap dance number but, after watching her do a wide range of dances, Louis B. Mayer decided to test her for the leading lady part—which, to her horror (she felt she wasn't ready for a leading role in her first picture), she won. She later recalled her initial introduction to Robert Taylor. "I'd never heard of Robert Taylor, and I don't think many people had," she recalled. "He was under contract; he was getting $35-a-week jobs. They figured they'd take this young boy with the widow's peak out of stock, get all the girls excited. Bob Taylor was petrified of me—I'd been in the New York Theater and he imagined me like Tallulah Bankhead. But he knew more about the camera than I did!"[75] Of course he did since this was now Bob's ninth picture compared to Powell's first. Powell felt the film turned out well. "The reason it turned out so well, I believe, is that it was a very good story per se. It was a solid, dramatic story, and they embellished it with the songs and dances the way they should do every musical comedy. Set a good foundation and then fill in the other things instead of starting off with a song."[76] As a result of this picture, Powell was given a seven-year MGM contract.

---

75 John Kobal, People Will Talk

76 ibid

Jack Benny and Bob became friends as a result of their appearing in this movie together. Over the years Bob would appear on Benny's highly popular radio series many times. He even filled in for Benny one week in 1948 when Benny took the week off. The program (which included Bob's interaction with Benny's supporting cast) was very popular and the following week when Benny returned to the show the biggest laugh was provided by a phone call from his sponsor suggesting that Benny take another week off! When Taylor married Barbara Stanwyck, the Taylors often were seen out on the town with Jack Benny and his wife Mary Livingstone. Livingstone gushingly called Taylor "Shangri-La with a widow's peak" on one Benny show he was a guest on.

Two years later, Bob and Miss Powell appeared in *Broadway Melody of 1938*; however, they didn't play the same roles, though once again Bob plays a Broadway producer putting on a show. The highlight of this film is the presence of fifteen-year-old Judy Garland, who made a huge impression singing "Dear Mr. Gable" to a picture of Clark Gable. Buddy Ebsen also makes a good account of himself with his distinctive eccentric dance style. Bob, now the major star, he wasn't yet when he did the last *Broadway Melody* film, is largely wasted—as pointed out by *Variety* in its review: "With little to do he is beautiful as ever. He is asked to contribute nothing but his beauty to the production."

IV

Magnificent Obsession is based on a 1929 novel by Lloyd C. Douglas. Douglas was the son of a minister and, eventually, ordained into the Lutheran ministry himself. In mid-life Douglas began writing novels of which *Magnificent Obsession* was his first. His writings—obviously influenced by his religious upbringing and life experiences—are highly moralistic and most have religious themes. Three of Douglas' novels would be adapted into motion pictures, *Magnificent Obsession* (twice), *The Robe* (which when released as a novel sold an extraordinary 2 million copies), and *The Big Fisherman. Magnificent Obsession* is allegedly based on a real-life physician friend of Douglas', a neurosurgeon that always went the extra mile for his patients and the community in which he lived.

Magnificent Obsession is the story of a reckless playboy named Bob Merrick who nearly dies due to his own stupidity. He is resuscitated using a hospital's only resuscitating machine. Meanwhile, at the time that the machine is being used on Merrick, beloved Dr. Hudson suffers a fatal heart attack and cannot be revived due to the machine being used on Merrick. Meanwhile, Hudson's much younger wife, Helen, returns from a trip and finds out the truth and is bitter toward Merrick. In fact, most people at the hospital are of the opinion that the wrong man was saved. Instead of the saintly doctor, who spent his life saving people and making anonymous donations to help others, a drunken, selfish, spoiled playboy who hasn't contributed anything to mankind is kept alive. Merrick eventually wants to make amends to Helen, who rejects his superficial attempts. Dejected, Bob gets drunk again and ends up at the house of a sculptor named Randolph, who was a friend of Dr. Hudson's. He may be the only one who understands Bob's situation and even sympathizes with him. He tries to explain why Dr. Hudson was so beloved. Randolph tells Bob to, "Make contact with a source of infinite power"—quite obviously a supreme Godly power. He tells Bob to live a life of giving toward others and do it in an anonymous way, like Dr. Hudson. It is the "magnificent obsession" that Dr. Hudson had.

Bob misunderstands the advice. He still thinks giving away money is the solution to his problems. He asks Helen, who he meets by chance, to allow him to drive her home, and she reluctantly agrees. In the course of running out of gas he gets a little frisky and Helen makes a dash for the exit of the car—just in time to be hit by a passing car. Helen recovers but is blinded. Bob has done it again. This time he takes what Randolph told him seriously and begins to re-evaluate his life. He begins to anonymously look out for Helen. He also seeks to immolate Dr. Hudson by working his way toward becoming a doctor. Eventually, Bob wants to restore Helen's eyesight.

The film differs from the novel in that while Merrick is indirectly responsible for Dr. Hudson's death he isn't the indirect cause of Helen's accident and blindness. In the book Helen moves to Europe where she is involved in a train accident which blinds her, and Merrick—seeking redemption—eventually restores her sight.

Universal bought the film rights to the book for $12,500. This was to be one of their two high-quality A pictures of 1935–1936 (the other one being *Show Boat*) and the studio, then known mostly for its horror franchise of *Dracula, Frankenstein* and *The Invisible Man*, was willing to spend the money to make this film look as good on screen as possible. The studio had sought out Frank Borzage, the talented director of *A Farewell to Arms*, to direct, but Warner Brothers refused to loan him out. So Universal went to John Stahl, its own very talented director of such previous hits as *Back Street, Only Yesterday*, and *Imitation of Life*. This film was seen as the ultimate "woman's picture" and putting Stahl in charge of it with his previous track record made perfect sense. He also was a sure hand with female stars, including Irene Dunne, Margaret Sullavan and Claudette Colbert. While the studio had toyed with the idea of casting Jane Wyatt in the leading role, Stahl was adamant about wanting a star name for Helen and suggested Irene Dunne, who was promptly hired at a fee of $75,000 for eleven weeks' of work, plus $7,500 for each additional week; ultimately, Dunne would earn over $100,000 for her services.[77]

For the Merrick role, Douglas Fairbanks, Jr. was interested, but neither the studio nor Stahl really wanted him. Bob had already made *There's Always Tomorrow* on loan-out to Universal and in the time since he was emerging as a new romantic star. Stahl arranged to see some of Bob's MGM films and thought that Bob might work as Merrick, but wasn't entirely convinced. Irene Dunne had the right to approve her leading man, so he asked her to a screening for her opinion. Dunne would later recall, "I remember sitting with John Stahl, who was to be our director, looking at some film of Robert Taylor. Neither of us knew much about him. I did know John, however, and he was the kind of director, who if he were in heaven, would tell God where to sit, and then complain about the lighting. But I like to remember that I told John I thought Taylor would be entirely right for the part of Robert Merrick."[78] But, ultimately, Stahl shot a screen test of Bob on July 5, which impressed the studio enough that they did agree to borrow Bob from MGM. Bob

77 Thomas Schatz, The Genius of the System

78 Jane Ellen Wayne, Robert Taylor, pg. 37

certainly didn't cost as much as Dunne had, but MGM made sure they made a profit. Bob was now making $400 per week, but MGM charged Universal $2,400 for the loan out. Bob got his $400 per week while Metro pocketed the other two grand. Bob, for his part, would always credit L.B. Mayer with "shrewd showmanship" in his willingness to allow him to be loaned out to Universal for this film. L.B. obviously saw that this film, based on a bestselling novel, would be quite popular and would give Bob additional box-office luster when he returned to MGM.

The film began shooting on July 12, 1935, and Stahl, a perfectionist, kept the film in production for over three months, a long time for those days. Part of it was due to working with Bob—a still relative newcomer whose first major film this really was. Years later Bob told Hedda Hopper that Stahl was, "a pretty tough man to work for, but I thought all the scoldings and goings on were part of the business. Forty takes was a little new to me, but I thought that was what I was getting paid for. If I'd known what I know now, I'd have said, 'stuff this.'"[79] Darryl Hickman, who later would work for Stahl in the memorable *Leave Her to Heaven*, would recall Stahl as a "pain in the ass and not a very pleasant man."[80] The pain was worth it, however, as Bob would give his most accomplished performance yet.

The studio and Stahl almost came to blows just before filming began on the film. While the studio paid $12,500 for the rights to the book, they spent over five times that much on writers adapting the book into a doable screenplay. Ultimately, $65,000 was shelled out to a dozen writers in constructing the screenplay. Universal, which was going through tough times economically, wanted to lay off all the writers once the filming began, but Stahl blew a fuse when he heard that idea. He liked to have writers available if changes were needed during filming. He angrily informed the studio, by memo, "If any writers are taken off . . . you are doing it at your own risk, and I absolutely forbid it . . . this is absolutely final."[81] He got his way. He felt his use of doing several takes was more a form of sadistic punishment than the act of a man who was trying to get the right

79 Hedda Hopper Papers, Margaret Herrick Library, (AMPAS)

80 Darryl Hickman to author

81 Thomas Schatz, The Genius of the System

take. It was an exacting shoot, but Bob would always credit Dunne with helping him get through it. "I was a mighty green newcomer getting a very important break," he later said, "and she was an established star. I learned right then how gracious a 'big timer' could be. She helped over a lot of rough spots and gave me a feeling of confidence right when I needed it the most." [82] After sixty-seven days of shooting, the picture closed production in late September. But it was clear there would need to be extensive retakes. *Magnificent Obsession* began twenty-five days of retakes in early September. When the film finally closed production, Stahl had about eighty hours of film to cut down to less than two hours. The cost of the picture came in at around $950,000—a very expensive film for 1935.[83]

Bob's performance is good in this film. He makes the transition well from reckless youth to determined doctor. His drunken scene, however, is a little over the top and he seems heavily made up in the early 1930s' fashion, but it certainly doesn't hide his extreme good looks. He does a credible job. Bob may also have been inspired by the character he was playing. He had always looked up to his father, Dr. Brugh, and he admired the way his father worked to become a doctor to help his mother in much the way that Robert Merrick is determined to become a brain surgeon so he can cure Helen Hudson's blindness.

When one reporter asked Bob what the motivation behind his work in the film was, Bob, who enjoyed his psychology class in college, gave a convoluted explanation. "A screen metamorphosis is more psychology than histrionics. The thing is to analyze the character you are playing and then the various stages of self-development become a logical outgrowth of that individual finding himself." Wow! When the words hit print, L. B. Mayer called Bob into his office and told him, "You sounded like your jockstrap was on too tight!"[84] In other words, this wasn't the image that MGM wanted for their new, young star.

82 Hollywood Citizen News, 4/22/46

83 Bob and Irene Dunne would recreate their roles on radio's "The Lux Radio Theatre" on 4/26/37

84 Linda Alexander, Reluctant Witness: Robert Taylor, Hollywood & Communism, pg. 90

Portrait Gallery #1

Young Arlington, age 12, in a Boy Scout uniform riding his pony, Gyp

Arlington with his parents, Dr. and Mrs Spangler Andrew Brugh, 1929

Early MGM publicity photo of Robert Taylor, 1934

Bob flanked by a bevy of showgirls, *Broadway Melody of 1936*

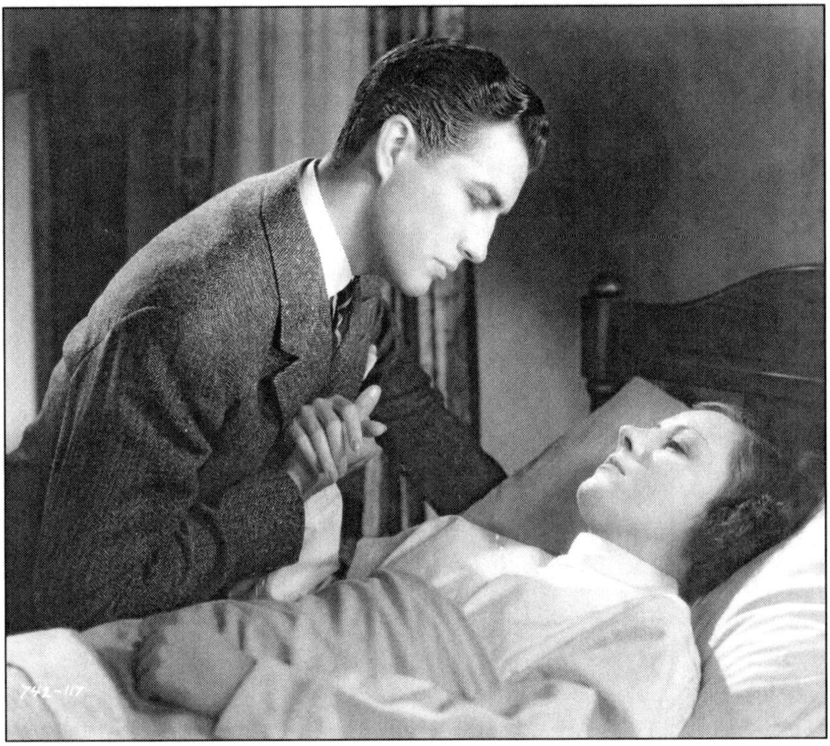

Bob in his break-out role opposite Irene Dunne in *Magnificent Obsession* (1935)

Bob and Charles Butterworth, *Magnificent Obsession*

Reckless playboy, Bob Merrick, trying to charm his nurse (Sara Haden), *Magnificent Obsession*

Chapter Four
1936: His Great Year

When released, *Magnificent Obsession* made Robert Taylor the talk of Hollywood. A new screen idol had been discovered—the successor to Valentino, Gilbert, and—perhaps—Gable. Columnist Adela Rogers St. Johns profiled Bob around this time and summed it up this way: "Our girls and women have declared for Robert Taylor, and that is as important an indication of our return to old-fashioned femininity as was the return of the trailing skirt, the soft girls and the picture hat."

Magnificent Obsession was an immediate smash hit when it was released on December 30, 1935, at Radio City Music Hall. (It would be the first of several Taylor films which would, over the years, make their debut at New York's premiere movie house.) Several contemporary articles of the time point out swooning women in the audience when Bob is on screen. Just as moviegoers would do sixty years later with the tremendous world-wide success of *Titanic*, many (particularly women) would come back to see the film a second or even a third time—the major reason being Bob Taylor. The ad campaign that Universal used to promote the film was a bit over the top, calling Dunne's and Taylor's performances "the finest in motion picture history."

The *New York Times*, however, was negative, calling *Magnificent Obsession* a "mystical film" and "its movements are never remarkable for their conviction or plausibility." Of the leads, the review says, "Miss Dunne rises to what probably should be respectfully referred to as dramatic heights as the blind girl." Bob got the worst end of the stick. "Mr. Taylor plays the reformed wastrel with such aggressive charm that the only word for his performance is cute." The *Variety* review was much better. "If its 110 minutes' running time makes it appear a bit sluggish, the sensitive and intelligent development ultimately makes the . . . progression appear justified." The review calls Taylor and Dunne a "stellar pair." *Commonweal*, perhaps unsurprisingly, liked the film a great deal and called the work of Dunne and Taylor, "sheer artistry." The *Chicago Tribune* called *Magnificent Obsession* a "splendid" film and said that Bob was "perfectly grand" as Merrick. One of the best reviews Bob received was in the student newspaper of the University of Illinois Urbana-Champaign, which wrote of their fellow young American, "Mr. Taylor is revealed as a dramatic actor of exceptional ability and fully justifies the Hollywood announcement that he is one of the most important screen discoveries of the year."

No matter what any critic thought, the film proved a great success at the box office, primarily with female viewers. Many theaters held the film over beyond the norm. And, just as L.B. hoped, Taylor returned to MGM a bigger star due to this film—and he was now ready to give him bigger assignments opposite some of Metro's prestige female stars to cash in. 1936 would be the year of Robert Taylor.

II

Bob was next cast as a carefree playboy once again when he was assigned by Metro to appear opposite Janet Gaynor in *Small Town Girl*. This would be the first of a series of films that Bob would star in over the next few years opposite some of the most glamorous and popular female stars of the era.

Gaynor is the small-town girl of the title who craves more excitement than her pedestrian life has thus far permitted. Enter Bob as a rich playboy who swings into town on his way to the big Yale-Harvard football game. He wants to celebrate early and asks for directions to a roadhouse. Gaynor is taken by his looks, his sense of fun and his shiny new automobile. He isn't quite like anybody in town—particularly her hayseed beau Elmer (played by James Stewart). When invited to accompany him, she readily accepts and by the end of the night Taylor is thoroughly drunk and he insists that they get married. Realizing that this is the way to permanently end her humdrum existence a less-inebriated Gaynor allows a Justice of the Peace to marry them. Naturally, the next morning . . .

The film went into production just two months after Bob had completed *Magnificent Obsession* and just days before *Obsession* opened at Radio City Music Hall in New York. It was clear to Mayer that Bob was on the threshold of becoming the studio's newest heartthrob. Initially, Metro was going to cast Jean Harlow as the small-town girl, but her persona wasn't exactly that of a naïve who craves excitement. You can bet that wherever Harlow is she will find excitement. Instead, the studio borrowed Janet Gaynor from Twentieth Century-Fox. Fox was open to this because in recent years Gaynor's once hot popularity was cooling and she was now playing second fiddle to the studio's biggest star, seven-year-old Shirley Temple. At first, Gaynor was less than thrilled to accept the loan-out. She didn't want to do a film where she was considered second choice. She also didn't want to take second billing to Robert Montgomery, who had been announced in the press as the playboy. Taylor's newfound popularity was enough of an incentive to take Montgomery off the picture and put Taylor in, and because Bob was still a relative newcomer to pictures he was given second billing behind Gaynor.

Initially, the film was to be directed by Jack Conway, but ultimately the directorial reins were given to William Wellman. Making this film was not easy for the director known as "Wild Bill" since he and Gaynor didn't get along. It was so bad that at one point Wellman requested to be taken off the film, a request Metro denied. By this time it is conceivable that Gaynor sensed that her career was running out of momentum and she was only two years away from retirement, and this may have made her difficult on the set and with her director. While Wellman and Gaynor didn't get along (though they would team up for *A Star is Born* the next year) he found Bob unusually cooperative and professional and a friendship was born. The two would go on to make *Westward the Women* fourteen years later and Wellman would recall Bob as only one of two actors he truly liked (the other being Joel McCrea).

Bob and Gaynor had no problems either. She took him under her wing and tried to teach him better fashion sense. Up to this time he was known for wearing colorful sweaters. Gaynor thought that with his perfect profile and glamorous looks he should dress more conservatively. "Your looks make it unnecessary for you to dress conspicuously," She told him.[85] When *Small Town Girl* was released only three months after *Magnificent Obsession*, it proved a big hit—confirming Bob's growing popularity. The *New York Times* critic wrote, "Mr. Taylor and Miss Gaynor are a pleasant co-starring combination and, if Metro heard the cooing from the feminine contingent in yesterday's audience, they probably will be teamed again in the future." On the other hand, the *Pittsburgh Press-Gazette* found the film entertaining only "in early reels" and was one of the first reviewers to point out something that would become more discussed as Bob's stardom cemented itself: "Taylor is much, much too handsome."

Bob was next loaned out to Twentieth Century-Fox to star opposite Loretta Young in *Private Number*. Young is cast as a servant girl in a mansion where Bob is the son of the house. (Yep, another wealthy young playboy role for Taylor, who was seemingly getting typed in these parts, not that female audience members seemed to care.) They fall in love while at the family summer cottage in Maine and secretly marry before Taylor returns to college. Unbeknownst to the rest of the family, all seems perfectly fine with Young returning as personal maid to Taylor's mother (Marjorie Gateson). But she soon discovers the truth when Young becomes pregnant and the slimy family butler (a menacing Basil Rathbone) finds out and goes to the mistress with the truth. Young is ordered out of the house and Rathbone and Taylor's parents do their best to keep them apart in hopes that Taylor will get an annulment. This is soap with a capital S.

The film was based on a far racier play titled *Common Clay*, which had starred Jane Cowl on the stage. Two previous film versions were also produced—one during the silent era and then another in pre-Code Hollywood starring Constance Bennett. This film was also Miss Young's return to films after a year's absence. It is generally accepted today that during that year in seclusion Miss Young gave birth to the love child of Clark Gable, conceived while on location

85 Robert Taylor, J.E. Wayne, pg. 44

shooting *Call of the Wild.* Miss Young later said she adopted the little girl. In a press release dated 2/29/36, Fox publicity wrote, "For Miss Young this picture will mean her return to her home studio as a star after a year's absence caused by prolonged sieges of illness." Young enjoyed working with Bob calling him, "a surprisingly normal person, neither fussy nor conceited. He was simply doing his work and letting matters take their own course." [86]

During the making of the film Bob was asked about all his romantic escapades that he was purported to be having when he was really just a nose-to-the-grindstone working actor. Of course, most of the stories in the papers were studio-manufactured publicity and it's a good bet that this response by Bob was the same thing. "At a time when I was working every day without a let-up, grabbing meals on the fly and tumbling exhausted into bed at 9 p.m. every night, I was rumored as being out every night with a different girl," Bob is quoted as saying. "What's more, not only was it just an idle rumor, but I was also accused of trying to play the social game too heavily. The rumors, as I can see them, were based on the fact that a few times I would go out to dinner every night as soon as I was through work, and generally take the actress with whom I was working at the time. After dinner, we would go our separate ways to get a good night's sleep in order to be fresh for the next day's work. Being a bachelor, I eat all my meals out, so that leaves me wide open for rumor." He concluded, "Hollywood is a small town with a knitting circle complex—which doesn't bother me personally. What I can't stand is having my family and other people hurt and embarrassed by idle gossip." Needless to say, Bob was seen around town with his co-star, Janet Gaynor, but no real romance developed.

Private Number was briskly directed by Roy Del Ruth and has a fast-paced 75-minute running time. It was premiered at Radio City Music Hall in New York City on June 11, 1936, and became another huge hit for Bob. The *New York Times* critic was astonished by the caliber of acting. "Believe it or not, the picture is well acted throughout," he wrote. "Mr. Rathbone is as hateful as Miss Young is charming, and Mr. Taylor is manly to a fault." It is worth noting

86 Barbara Stanwyck, Al Diorio, pg. 100

that the critic hit upon something which was beginning to bother Bob, that he was adored as a heartthrob to scores of women, but that he really didn't register with male filmgoers who saw him as less of a man for the types of roles he played. Before long Bob would begin to demand a toughening of his screen image.

III

Zeppo Marx was the "other" Marx Brothers when the brothers were appearing in Paramount films. He was, for lack of a better description, the straight man of the team. After the Four Marx Brothers were fired by Paramount after completing *Duck Soup* in 1933, they wondered if their film career was over. Soon enough, however, Irving Thalberg signed them to an MGM contract. But coming over to Culver City would not be the Four Marx Brothers but the pivotal Three (Groucho, Harpo & Chico). Zeppo believed himself to be easily disposable and besides he wanted to make real money as an agent rather than a performer. He opened an agency with an office on Sunset Boulevard and soon enough Zeppo was one of the top agents in town. One of his clients was Barbara Stanwyck, one of the most successful stars of the era. She also became a close friend of Zeppo and his wife Marion.

At this time Stanwyck was going through an extremely difficult period in her life. She was in the midst of a divorce from an extremely unpleasant man named Frank Fay. Fay was a red-headed, handsome, hard-drinking Irishman who had an ego without restraint. He had been a successful vaudevillian when he came to Hollywood in the late twenties. He had nowhere near the success in films that he had on the stage. Barbara had faithfully followed him to Hollywood and found herself cast into films—emerging as a far bigger star than he. Fay already had a reputation for being an egomaniac and bastard to boot and almost everybody detested him. The noted radio wit and comedian Fred Allen once said, "The last time I saw Frank Fay he was slowly strolling down Lovers' Lane holding his own hand." [87] Compounding this was an alcohol problem kicked into gear by the fact that his wife was a bigger star than he was. He was physically

87 The Jack Benny Show, Milt Josefsberg, pg 314

and mentally abusive to Barbara. Once, after their divorce, Barbara was filming a scene for a movie where her leading man loses control and is supposed to violently slap her. The actor didn't want to hurt her and held back causing the director to do several takes. As they were preparing for a fifth take, Barbara went up to the director and said, "Why don't you get Frank Fay as technical advisor for this scene." [88] It was the classic "Star is Born" story of one star on the way up and one star on the way down, but, unlike Norman Maine, Frank Fay was no sympathetic protagonist. (Fay was by no means untalented. As mentioned, he had huge success on stage and later returned to Broadway to star in the Mary Chase play *Harvey* to much acclaim.)

Marion Marx and Barbara became close friends. In many ways they were cut from the same cloth. Both women could be quiet and introverted, yet when they had something to say they didn't hesitate to give their opinion with the bark off. Barbara used Marion as a sounding board of her troubles. It was therapeutic for her. At one point during this difficult period Barbara, her adopted son, Dion, and a nurse appeared on the Marx's doorstep and ended up staying several weeks until Barbara was able to lease a house—right next door to the Marx's on Bedford Drive in Beverly Hills. Gradually Barbara came out of her funk as her divorce from Fay became final at the end of 1935. Barbara began to be seen in public. One of her frequent companions at this time was George Brent, another was her brother Byron.

Bob was emerging as the new star of the year at about the time that Barbara signed with MGM to make *His Brother's Wife.* Her co-star was Robert Taylor. Among the things that many people in Hollywood admired about Stanwyck was how she took control of her career. She was one of the few actresses of her time not to be tied to a binding contract with any one studio (such as Bob and MGM). Stanwyck knew little about Taylor, except that she did know he was a strong up-and-comer. Marion convinced Zeppo that they should introduce Stanwyck to Taylor away from the studio and make a night of it.

Marion told Stanwyck that they were going to try a new nightclub

88 The Jack Benny Show, Milt Josefsberg, pg. 315

on the Sunset Strip called the Trocadero, and they had somebody they wanted her to meet. When Barbara asked who, Marion decided to play coy and only said "RT." Marion had a thick New York accent and Barbara thought she had said "Artig" who she thought was somebody who worked at Zeppo's agency. Reluctantly, Barbara decided to go. That night, waiting at the table to greet them was Robert Taylor. Marion and Zeppo introduced them and then made their way to the dance floor leaving Barbara and Bob to get to know one another.

When Bob asked Barbara if she would like to dance, she declined. "I'm sorry, but I'm waiting for a Mr. Artig," she told him. Bob was doubly puzzled since Zeppo and Marion had invited him to the Trocadero for the express purpose of being Miss Stanwyck's dinner date so that they could get to know one another prior to making their movie. Bob asked her what the gentleman's name was again. And Barbara replied "Artig" but said she may be pronouncing it incorrectly. Bob mulled it over for a bit and then it came to him—Artig—R.T., and told Barbara, "R.T—that's me!"[89] They ended up having a good laugh over it which helped break the ice.

The evening turned out to be an extremely pleasant one. Bob and Barbara talked and danced and found themselves enjoying each other's company. The following morning, Barbara received a box of roses with a card from Bob thanking her for "a thoroughly delightful evening."[90] He definitely wanted to see more of her. They were mutually intrigued with one another. Taylor summed up his feelings of the time when he was quoted as saying, "Barbara is not the sort of woman I'd have met in Nebraska." Stanwyck famously said of Taylor, "The boy's got a lot to learn and I've got a lot to teach." Unfortunately, that quote would sum up the tone of their entire relationship.

They couldn't have been more different in backgrounds. Barbara Stanwyck was born on the so-called "other side of the tracks." Like Bob, she came into the world with a different name than the one she would go out on. She was born Ruby Stevens in 1907, making her four years older than Bob. But those four years were significant

89 Axel Madsen, Stanwyck, pg. 109

90 Barbara Stanwyck, Al DiOrio, pg. 99

when it came to life situations faced by the two of them. Her early life had matured and in many ways hardened Barbara. Ruby was the last of five children born in the New York borough of Brooklyn. At the age of two her mother died from a fall off a streetcar. Within weeks of her mother's funeral her father had left, presumably to work on the Panama Canal, but he was never seen, nor heard from again. From that point forward Ruby and her brother Byron made the rounds of foster homes. Stanwyck later said, "Growing up in one foster home after another didn't give me any edge on the other kids or any excuse for whining, protesting, demanding. Besides, why whine?" That would be her philosophy through-out her life. She took what came her way, no matter the knocks, and rode with it.

By the time Ruby was thirteen she had had enough of school. She needed to make a living. She became a showgirl. She later would have opportunity to put this persona on display in some of her movies. Certainly there is some of Ruby Stevens in Sugarpuss O'Shea in *Ball of Fire* and Dixie Daisy in *Lady of Burlesque*. Within a couple of years Ruby would be a Ziegfeld Girl. By the time she was nineteen she was in a Broadway play called *The Noose*. It was at that time that Ruby Stevens got the stage name of Barbara Stanwyck. The last name came from a real-life actress named Jane Stanwyck, who appeared in a play titled *Barbara Frietchie*. Soon afterward, pianist and wit Oscar Levant introduced Barbara to Frank Fay and it was, by both accounts, hate at first sight. But they warmed to each other after meeting at the funeral of a mutual friend. They married in 1928 and soon both were in Hollywood where his career failed to prosper while hers built on one success after another. She was the kind of actress who could play any type of role required of her in all types of genres.

Her big break came when Frank Capra, an up-and-coming director at Columbia, cast her as the lead in *Ladies of Leisure* (1930). She became his favorite of all of the actresses he worked with (as she did with other directors such as William Wellman and Mitchell Leisen). Part of the reason directors wanted her was because of her complete professionalism. She was always on time. She always knew her lines. She was cooperative and helpful. She became a favorite of the working men on the sets, grippes and lighting technicians, because while she took her job seriously she never took herself seriously. Capra used her again in such films as *The Miracle Woman* and *The Bitter Tea of General Yen*. But her best films were such pre-Code goodies as *Night Nurse, Baby Face*, and *Illicit*. She could be bad but with a sympathetic edge—you admired her moxie and ability to put men in their places. Certainly she didn't always play the bad girl. One of her earliest successes was the screen adaptation of Edna Ferber's *So Big* playing a sympathetic school teacher in a farm community who yearns for a better life for her son.

By 1932 the Fay marriage was in deep trouble. They thought that a child might bring them closer together, so they adopted a month-old baby that they named Dion. Neither Fay nor Barbara seemed suited to parenting. The real problem was Barbara's success and Fay's ego couldn't tolerate it, so the drinking and abuse became more frequent. By the end of 1935 they were divorced with Barbara getting sole custody of Dion. Barbara was a realist who dealt with the curve balls as they came her way. "I've always been a little sorry for pampered people—and of course, they are very sorry for me," she once said.

Metro decided to use the Stanwyck-Taylor budding romance to its advantage in publicity for *His Brother's Wife*. While Bob and Barbara weren't publically acknowledging their romance, the press was making much ado about their being seen out on the town together and rumors were escalating about their relationship. Metro believed (rightly) that pairing Bob with his rumored love interest would spark box-office receipts.

The plot is something else again. Bob is a scientist who is working on finding a cure for spotted fever. Barbara plays a model he meets in a gambling joint and, of course, they find themselves attracted to each other. Since Bob doesn't have to leave for ten days they decide to spend it together in New York City. During the course of those ten days they fall in love. Before leaving there is one little problem—Bob owes a gambler (Joseph Calleia) five grand and doesn't have the money, so he approaches his brother (John Eldredge) for the money. That comes with a catch: he'll bail Taylor out only if he forgets about Stanwyck and leaves immediately for South America. Naturally, Barbara doesn't take this very well and to get revenge she marries the brother, a totally loveless marriage. The love scenes between Bob and Barbara are very convincing and speak volumes for the passion each felt for the other in the early days of their relationship. Initially, this was to be a Jean Harlow-Clark Gable picture, but as often happened that casting didn't pan out.

To direct the picture MGM put one of its best directors in charge, W. S. (Woody) Van Dyke. He had a reputation for being a speed demon. In fact, many of his pictures are quickly and efficiently done, but quality is not sacrificed for this is the director of such classics as *The Thin Man* and his recently completed *San Francisco. The Hollywood Reporter* put out a news item that the 137-page script was shot in 14 days, but the truth is that the shooting schedule was a more traditional 40 days from the middle of June to the end of July of 1936. Van Dyke did like to shoot as few takes as possible because he felt that the fewer takes the more spontaneous the performances—and he was delighted to work with both Bob and Barbara who were always professional and could get the job done on the first two or three takes. Bob later explained Van Dyke's approach. "Woody cut as he shot," he said. "He used his camera as though it were a six-shooter and he was the fastest gun in Hollywood. Actors rarely got more than one take on any scene, and then the camera was moved rapidly to another set-up. It was, of course, going from the sublime to the ridiculous, but it seemed normal. It was the age." [91] He later told Hedda Hopper that once he was filming a scene and saying his line when Van Dyke called out, "That's it." "He'd cut you right off in the middle of a word . . . I didn't know what town I was in." [92]

When the film premiered at the Capitol Theatre in New York in August of 1936, Frank Nugent of the *New York Times* conceded that the picture was "incredibly romantic, glossily produced, expertly directed and peopled by the sort of players most often encountered on the covers of the fan magazines," but couldn't help but chiding casting Bob as a scientist. "Mr. Taylor, crown prince of charm and heir apparent to the throne of Clark Gable, seems to have gained such a hold on the feminine movie-going contingent . . . we must admit to certain reservations about Mr. Taylor's personification of a

91 Film Fan Monthly, June, 1969

92 Hedda Hopper Papers, Margaret Herrick Collection, AMPAS

laboratory scientist seeking the cause and cure of spotted fever." Oh well, it was another hit for Bob.

Shortly after completing *His Brother's Wife* Bob saw his name up in lights for the first time in star billing while driving with Barbara down Hollywood Boulevard. They approached Grauman's Chinese Theatre where the picture was playing. He recalled the incident to Hedda Hopper nearly twenty years later when she asked him what the best piece of advice anybody ever gave him was. "You can't print it, but I'll tell you. It must have come from Stanwyck, of course. We're driving down Hollywood Boulevard years ago, and they used to have a business in front of Grauman's Chinese of putting the stars name up on a pennant giszmo. I looked up and it said Robert Taylor and Loretta Young in—so and so. I said, "How do you like that—my name is above Young's.' 'Buster,' said Barbara, 'You're starting to get that shitheel feeling.' She's a very positive person." In other words, he was getting a big head. Hedda tried to egg Taylor on by saying, "She must have torn down your ego," to which Bob replied, "No, not at all. She treats herself rougher than anybody in the world."[93] For the rest of the year Bob and Stanwyck would date, but they would continually in the press downplay their relationship—which, in fact, was deepening. By the end of the year, when newspapers were speculating as to when Bob and Barbara would marry, Stanwyck publicly said, "I will not marry Robert Taylor." True enough—of course, she wasn't inclined to marry anybody at this time—and neither was Bob.

Bob's run of 1936 films continued with his being cast for the first time opposite Joan Crawford in *The Gorgeous Hussy*. The film was based on a historical fact about a Washington innkeeper's daughter (Crawford) who becomes the hostess and confidant of the widowed President Andrew Jackson (flamboyantly played by Lionel Barrymore), a friendship which causes Washington society to gossip and shun her.

Bob is cast as Bow Timberlake, a naval lieutenant, who marries Crawford's character early on in the proceedings and then dies in battle—never to be seen again. Bob looks handsome and isn't required to do more than be romantic, which was good enough for this part and good enough for his fans. Producer Joseph L. Mankiewicz

93 ibid

surrounded Crawford with several choice actors to work off of in this picture: Melvyn Douglas, James Stewart, Louis Calhern and Franchot Tone, who, off screen, had just recently married Miss Crawford. MGM stalwart Clarence Brown was selected to direct the historical drama, the only one Crawford ever made. In fact, David O. Selznick, who just recently had left MGM to found his own studio, advised Crawford not to do a historical picture because her persona was "too modern" and would confuse her fans.

But Mankiewicz convinced her otherwise, and this was the first of several pictures that he would produce for Crawford during his years at MGM before leaving in the mid-1940s for Twentieth Century-Fox and a stunning career as the writer-director of his own films, which included back-to-back Academy Awards for *A Letter to Three Wives* and *All About Eve*. Mankiewicz would recall Crawford as "the prototype movie star—there will never be another like her." [94] In truth, Crawford wanted to get away from the shop-girl-who-makes-good formula roles that she had been playing to great success earlier in her career and jumped at the chance to do a costume picture. In part, she wanted to prove that she was as versatile at doing those types of films as her studio rival, Norma Shearer, who was filming *Romeo and Juliet* and would soon star in *Marie Antoinette.*

The chief assets of *The Gorgeous Hussy* are a strong cast, some excellent performances (especially by Barrymore, Beulah Bondi, and Douglas), and topnotch production values. The lavish production cost 1.1 million (a formidable price tag in those days) and didn't hold back on sets and costumes. Despite all of this, the film tends to drag and Crawford *does* seem out of place in a historical costume picture. But she wasn't alone. A young James Stewart, sporting side-burns which make him look rather silly, also seems out of place as one of Crawford's many suitors. Like Bob, Stewart was being built up by MGM and allegedly Mayer asked Crawford to "look after" Stewart on the set. Crawford reportedly replied, "What about Robert Taylor? Do I change his diapers, too?" [95] Crawford and Bob did, however, get along. Crawford would recall Bob as a "gentleman"

94 Joseph Mankiewicz, Pictures Will Talk, pg. 81

95 Jane Ellen Wayne, Crawford's Men, pg. 145

who had "beautiful manners."[96] Bob would remember Crawford years later as "A very talented actress whose real ability wasn't recognized until *Mildred Pierce* won her the Academy Award. Joan has a lighter side, however, that not everyone knows about. I remember when she had us all drinking milk on the set for health and energy. Next, she suggested I stop smoking. When I didn't, she decided to ration my cigarettes. Whenever I'd leave a package about, she'd pick it up and cut each cigarette in half—the little vixen!"[97]

While the film made a modest profit, letters to the studio and Crawford herself confirmed what Selznick had told her: They didn't want Joan Crawford in a historical costume picture; she listened, and never again appeared in one (although she would have consented, like most other actresses in Hollywood, had David Selznick offered her Scarlett in *Gone with the Wind*). Most of the reviews for the film ignored Bob's meager contribution and concentrated on Miss Crawford. The *New York Times* thought that her Peggy was a "maligned Anne of Seven Gables, a persecuted Pollyanna, a dismayed Dolly Dimple." *Variety* was more supportive saying that Crawford "fills the role and the billing." *Commonweal*, on the other hand, was complimentary and called the picture "well rounded entertainment." Though his role was brief, Taylor made an impact with the MGM hierarchy. His romantic look in a period film helped persuade the studio that Taylor would make a suitable Armand in Greta Garbo's next film, *Camille*.

IV

In the fall of 1924 Louis B. Mayer was in Rome supervising the filming of what would ultimately become one of his fledging new studio's first important pictures and one of the great successes of the silent era, *Ben-Hur*. But at that time things were not going well and expenses were mounting. Mayer was working night and day and his health was becoming an issue. Despite the pressures on him, Mayer still had an eye out for new talent and while in Rome he made a side trip to Berlin to check out various European films. One of the

96 ibid, pg. 235

97 Hollywood Citizen News, 4/22/46

films was Mauritz Stiller's *The Atonement of Gosta Berling*. Mayer was correctly told that Stiller was an important European director and he should consider signing him for American pictures.

Mayer watched the film very intently and made comments throughout, not so much about the plot or the brilliance of Stiller's direction, but about the film's leading lady. "Look at that girl!" Mayer cried out. "There's no physical resemblance, but she reminds me of Norma Talmadge—her eyes. The thing that made Talmadge a star is the look in her eyes." When the screening ended, Mayer was ecstatic. "Stiller's fine, but the girl, look at the girl!" To get the girl Mayer signed Stiller, who, nevertheless, insisted that the girl be part of the deal anyway. But the important thing to Mayer was the girl and he signed the nineteen-year-old Greta Garbo to a contract paying her $400 per week. That face and especially those seductive eyes were made for the silent era.

Garbo came late to the silent era, but she had a huge impact on it. She became a new kind of woman, and, in the words of film historian David Thomson, Garbo was "passionate but restless and insecure." She made ten silent films with titles which summed up her passionate, yet elusive persona: *Flesh and the Devil, Love, The Devine Woman, A Woman of Affairs* and *The Kiss.* Often teamed opposite her real-life lover, John Gilbert, audiences, especially women, flocked to see her films. One journalist wrote of her, "Greta Garbo will fascinate people, but I wager she will always remain more or less a mystery."[98] That mystery became part of her screen persona. She said it only in one film, but "I want to be alone" became not only part of her screen personality, but ultimately became associated with the later elusive Garbo who walked away from her career. Her films were important to the studio in European markets where they often outperformed her North American grosses. Garbo was so universally known that the studio and public dropped the Greta and referred to her simply as "Garbo."

When *The Jazz Singer* changed Hollywood forever and made silent pictures obsolete, many of the reigning stars of the silent era went with it. New actors were brought out from the New York stage; correct diction was considered a virtue in the new sound medium.

98 Norman Zierold, Garbo, pg. 40

Some of the silent actors had great faces, but less-than-distinguished voices. (Legend has it that Gilbert's career was ruined because his voice didn't match his romantic image.) The question at MGM, with regards to Garbo, was "How would she adapt to the talkies?" with that thick Swedish accent?

Garbo's first talking picture was eagerly awaited by audiences who wanted to know if her voice was everything they imagined it to be. MGM made sure they promoted it as an event: "GARBO TALKS!" cried the advertisements. When she makes her first appearance in *Anna Christie*, she takes a few moments and then utters the immortal, "Bring me a Vhiskey . . . and don't be stingy about it, baby." The husky voice fit the actress and the characters she played. Sound only enhanced Garbo's popularity and deepened her mystery. Through the mid-thirties she was at her peak as she appeared in such popular and enduring films as *Mata Hari, Grand Hotel, Queen Christina,* and *Anna Karenina* (perhaps her greatest performance).

Garbo's name on the marquee was enough to bring in audiences, particularly women who related to her screen suffering. MGM began using her films as a way of build up their roster of leading men and give their careers a boost because of being associated with Garbo. Thus, Clark Gable was cast opposite her in *Susan Lenox: Her Fall and Rise*; Robert Montgomery in *Inspiration*; and Melvyn Douglas in *As You Desire Me*. MGM had intended to cast the relatively new Laurence Olivier in *Queen Christina*, but Garbo had insisted on John Gilbert, who, since losing his MGM contract, had descended into alcoholism. In 1936 Garbo's next film would be *Camille*, and the studio decided that Robert Taylor had shown enough promise to be cast opposite the great Garbo in a film which would be his most challenging to date and would go a long way in establishing him as the studio's leading romantic idol.

Camille, based on the well-known novel by Alexandre Dumas (which apparently Dumas based on an actual woman he came to know in Paris), is the story of Marguerite, a fashionable Parisian courtesan who ultimately sacrifices the love of the younger Armand Duval. Armand's father tells Marguerite that Armand's love for her would ruin his aspirations for him and begs her to give him up. Marguerite complies with this request and tells Armand that she prefers the high life of Paris to being with him and literally laughs in his face. The dejected Armand leaves. Eventually, Marguerite develops tuberculosis, and with this disease her social life in Paris dries up and she becomes impoverished. Armand later finds her and reassures her that his love for her hasn't diminished and that he will be there for her forever. At the end, in one of the screen's best remembered "death" scenes, she dies in his arms.

Camille was one of the last films to be personally supervised by Irving Thalberg. He kept Garbo happy by giving her one of the studio's top directors, George Cukor, a director Garbo admired a great deal, especially for his handling of the film *David Copperfield*, which had been one of MGM's most prestigious releases of the previous year. But what kept Garbo happiest of all was that Cukor had agreed with her demand for her usual cameraman, William Daniels, to photograph her. Garbo felt at her most secure around people she trusted, and her trust for Daniels, who was cinematographer for 14 of her 26 films, was explicit. As for the cast surrounding Garbo, MGM gave her the best of its stellar supporting players, including Lionel Barrymore (playing Armand's father), Jessie Ralph, Henry Daniell and Laura Hope Crews. As for her leading man Garbo generally took who the studio gave her and understood that they were considered one of the many accessories which surrounded her.

For Armand, Thalberg only considered Bob. He had shown so much promise over the past year and, once again, the clincher for Thalberg may have been Bob's performance opposite Irene Dunne in the previous year's *Magnificent Obsession*, a film more contemporary than *Camille* but containing some of the same soap opera elements that appealed to women. *Obsession* highlighted Bob's incredible appeal with female audiences as well as his romantic quality, which would be an important element for *Camille.* Thalberg believed that Bob "needed only to be immensely attractive, which he was, and to portray great love for Garbo, which he could." [99]

Despite this, some of the MGM hierarchy thought that Bob was too inexperienced to be cast opposite Garbo in one of MGM's premier films of the year. Thalberg dismissed this and believed that the lack of experience might actually work in Bob's favor; there was a boyish quality that Thalberg believed that Bob could best bring

99 Bob Thomas, Thalberg, pg. 308

out as opposed to a more experienced leading man. In the end, Thalberg probably saw Bob's attractiveness and freshness as being paramount and in contrast to Garbo's mystery and aloofness. George Cukor also championed Bob. "Historically it's a bad part [Armand], because it's usually played by old actors, and you don't forgive an old man for being so foolish," Cukor believed. "Robert Taylor was a wonderful looking young man, and he was touching and passionate. It turned out to be a very good idea, casting him as Armand."[100] Cukor also believed that Bob was able to do something that many other actors could not do—successfully work with a strong actress-personality. "A lot of actors . . . cannot play scenes with women, and Taylor really did it. You believed that he loved her, and he was young enough to make them chemically a very nice couple."[101] In short, Cukor felt that with Bob cast as Armand the part "came alive."[102] Bob enjoyed working with Cukor as well. He would make one more film with him (*Her Cardboard Lover*) and stayed friendly with him for the rest of his life. At one point he sent some rare books to Cukor along with a note which said, "They certainly are not as elaborate as my personal feelings of gratitude to you, but if you enjoy them only partially as much as I have enjoyed working for you then I shall have been fortune in my choice."[103]

Garbo believed that most of her leading men were in love with her, and perhaps she was right, but she dismissed most of them to author Antoni Gronowicz. Of Gable she said, "He knew his shortcomings, which I had spotted right away, including a stiffness that was close to the quality of wood." Robert Montgomery "showed more enthusiasm than talent." Garbo, on the other hand, seemed to have a soft spot for Bob. "He was a very well brought up young man, a bit shy perhaps," Garbo recalled. "I was often actually rather ill during filming. He used to have a gramophone with him that he would play because he knew I liked music. It helped distract me."[104]

---

100 American Film 3, February, 1978

101 ibid

102 Gavin Lambert, On Cukor, pg. 114

103 Robert Taylor to George Cukor, undated, Margaret Herrick Library, AMPAS

104 Antoni Gronowicz, Garbo: Her Story

But early on in the filming, which began in late July of 1936, Garbo kept her distance from her leading man. Cukor introduced them for the first time on Stage 23 at MGM where much of the film was shot. "She [Garbo] was polite but distant," Cukor recalled. "She had to sell herself on this picture of an ideal young man. She knew if she became friendly, she'd find out he was just another nice guy." Garbo herself conceded that her emotional commitment to Marguerite "was so complete that I was unable to maintain emotional contact with people whom I met during work on this film." Bob didn't know exactly what to make of this distance. He had always enjoyed good relationships with his leading ladies and was fascinated by Garbo, as most of her leading men were. Again, Garbo may have misinterpreted his friendliness for love. "Robert Taylor was most attentive, trying without success to make me respond to his love," recalled Garbo years later. "I noticed his ardor, and I became especially patient with him in explaining how he must act, since he was young and inexperienced. But I never spent any time with him in the evening after work." Bob later conceded that "I was scared to death at the thought of appearing opposite Garbo in *Camille.*"[105] The shooting of *Camille* coincided with the early days of Bob's relationship with Barbara Stanwyck. He would tell Stanwyck of his intimidation in working with a star of Garbo's stature and that he didn't seem to be forging any kind of personal relationship with her. Barbara, who was also fascinated by Garbo, advised Bob to, "just be natural. Treat her as you would anybody else."

Garbo was in many ways a Method actress. "She doesn't act; she lives her roles," supporting actor Rex O'Malley later recalled. "She was 'Camille' during the entire filming of the picture . . . Beautiful beyond words of description." But slowly yet surely Bob made inroads and was able to crack through and forge a relationship with the elusive Garbo. She was "an uncanny craftsman with a playful sense of humor," Bob would later recall. His solicitousness deeply impressed her; not only playing his gramophone to calm her tattered nerves, but his innate kindness. Between scenes Bob began telling her of his upbringing in Nebraska, ". . . he told me that his best friend during his youth in Nebraska had been a Swede," Garbo

105 Norman Zierold, Garbo, pg. 85

recalled years later. "I have never liked sitting in the sun. I have a delicate skin and have to be careful not to get sun burnt. But Robert Taylor was the exact opposite. He worshipped the sun. And then he was forced to abstain from the outdoor life for the weeks we were filming since we both had to be equally pale . . . [He] was actually a kind and well-bred man." [106]

Camille was filming at an agonizingly slow pace and the tension was getting to Garbo. "I have never worked under conditions like these before," she wrote a friend. "I sometimes start crying from tiredness . . . I've been feeling out of sorts the whole of last month and still had to work." Sadly, for the *Camille* Company a break came when the producer of the film, Irving Thalberg, died after a short illness. Over the Labor Day weekend, Thalberg and his wife, actress Norma Shearer, had gone vacationing near the ocean with friends. Thalberg loved playing bridge and played for hours on a veranda overlooking the Pacific Ocean. The sea air was cool and Thalberg, who had a heart condition, caught a cold which ultimately developed into pneumonia. He died two weeks later and production of four of his films which were currently filming was postponed: *Camille, The Good Earth, A Day at the Races* and *Maytime*. The studio as a whole was shut down on September 17, the day of his funeral at Wilshire Boulevard Temple. Every MGM contract player was expected to pay their respects to Thalberg, who was universally acclaimed as a "boy genius"; he was only 37 when he died. Bob came, bringing with him Barbara Stanwyck, but they were all there: Jeanette MacDonald, Clark Gable, Joan Crawford, Spencer Tracy, Myrna Loy, William Powell—all, that is, except Garbo, who, as always, did as she pleased and welcomed a day off as a way to rest and recuperate from the burden of filming.

One of the last influences that Thalberg had on *Camille* was the filming of Marguerite's death scene. Thalberg thought that the first version was too talky for a woman on the verge of death. He also wanted the scene moved from the bed to a chaise lounge, so it was filmed again with these changes which made it even more effective. [107] It wasn't difficult for Garbo to play the dying scene since she was ill

106 Sven Broman, Conversations with Greta Garbo, pg. 148

107 Bob Thomas, Thalberg, pg. 262

during much of the shooting and in her weakened and pale condition helped make the scene one of the most memorable ever filmed. Another memorable scene from *Camille* involves Marguerite's passionate kissing of Armand's entire face. This was yet another Garbo innovation and Bob had only expected the usual screen kiss on his lips. "She was supposed to kiss me once, and do you know what she did," Bob asked Clark Gable, who was fast becoming one of his best friends on the Metro lot. "She kissed ya twice?" Gable responded. "She kissed me all over my face!" Gable asked Bob what he did about that. "Nothing, she's the aggressor in love scenes."[108]

Principal photography on *Camille* ended on October 27, 1936; three months after filming began, an unusually long time for a picture in those days of factory-like efficiency. But the cast and crew were not finished yet, as extensive retakes followed a less-than-enthusiastic sneak preview in Santa Barbara in November and went into December. On the final day of shooting retakes Garbo gave Bob a gift, a ceramic Buddha, as a good luck charm. The picture was finally completed and ready for its release by New Year's Day. The film went on to be a huge success worldwide for the studio with, as expected, Garbo receiving the lion's share of the accolades. The *New York Times* film critic, Frank Nugent, called Marguerite Garbo's "best performance," but also praised Bob. "Robert Taylor is surprisingly good as Armand, a bit on the juvenile side at times, perhaps, but certainly not guilty of the traditional sin of the many Armand's of the past—callowness." The *New York Times* put the picture on its Top Ten list for the year of 1937. *Commonweal* was enthusiastic: "Miss Garbo's and Mr. Taylor's work is as fine as any in their bright careers . . . Their association should be continued." *Time* magazine's reviewer said that Bob gave an "assured and competent performance." Bob came out of the experience enhanced by working opposite one of the greatest stars of the era and in one of the most acclaimed pictures of the year. His Armand stood his ground and his interpretation of the role, under Cukor's skillful direction, was a very solid piece of acting and enhanced his already high appeal with female fans. "Taylor was a talented actor who became quite expert," recalled Cukor, "but for a while he was frightened off

108 Jane Ellen Wayne, Gable, pg. 148

by being called 'beautiful Bob Taylor.'"[109] Cukor later added to this statement when he told writer and film historian Richard Schickel, "He liked, he wanted to play sort of rougher parts, which he did perfectly well. But when people have this gift of picturesqueness and beauty, I think it should be exploited."[110]

For Bob, working on *Camille* had been the most exciting event of his career up to that time. In his usual modest and self-deprecating way, he came to think of it as an education and Garbo as one of his great teachers. "I don't think Garbo was a Method actress," Bob recalled. "But she certainly knew what it was all about. One of the great secrets of acting, of course, is to think. I've never learned it but Garbo knew. She thought with her eyes, photographically. The muscles in her face would not move, and yet her eyes would express exactly what was needed. Working with her was perhaps my greatest acting lesson, though I probably didn't learn enough from it."[111] When the film premiered in Stockholm, it was Bob who was there, not Garbo. Garbo was later very touched to learn that while in Stockholm Bob sent her mother "twelve gorgeous orchids."

While Bob was able to crack through the fabled Garbo reserve while making the picture, they went their own ways afterward and Bob only saw the great Garbo once more, years later, when she returned to MGM long after she had retired. She was sitting in the commissary when Bob and a friend walked in. "My companion suggested I go over and say hello," Bob recalled. "I would no more go over to Garbo than I would drop dead in the commissary. I respect her feeling for privacy too much."[112] Though she and Bob never spoke to each other again after filming *Camille*, a residual of regard remained with Garbo for this nice young man with the good manners who cared enough about her to try and comfort her during the difficult days of filming. When she heard, more than thirty years later, that Bob had died, at only fifty-seven, Garbo broke down and cried.[113]

---

109 Gavin Lambert, On Cukor, pg. 115

110 The Men Who Made the Movies, pg. 182

111 Norman Zierold, Garbo, pg. 86

112 ibid

113 Sven Broman, Conversations with Greta Garbo

V

While *Camille* was filming, Bob made it well known that unless he got a dramatic raise in salary he would go on strike following the completion of the picture. Here he was the hottest young actor in motion pictures and making $750 per week. Certainly with the money his films were bringing in he deserved more. What is surprising is Bob going so public. Surely his representatives believed that they couldn't get what they thought Bob was worth behind the scenes so pressure was put on the studio by using the Hollywood press. Much mention was made of the 7-9,000 pieces of fan mail that Bob was receiving *every* week. "Bob gets more fan mail than any star on the lot," one studio representative told columnist May Mann. Another told her, "Everyone likes Bob Taylor. He's just the same now as before he became famous. Neither affected nor conceited." [114] MGM, however, felt that they deserved credit for building Bob up from $35-per-week contract player to $750-per-week star in little more than two years and the money and time they invested into Bob should be taken into consideration. The studio pointed out that for a long time they had provided Bob with his wardrobe for everyday wear—not only for business purposes and that they foot the bill to send replies and pictures for all that fan mail that Bob received (at a tune of some $2,000 per month). However, there would never be any doubt that Bob would get a raise; the studio had big plans for Robert Taylor and didn't need him on strike but on a soundstage making movie love to one of their roster of leading ladies to the delight of millions of female fans. In the end, he got a huge raise which brought his salary up to $3,500 per week and would earn him a cool million over the next seven years. [115] By this time Bob had put his mother up in a rented house in Beverly Hills. In addition to that he had hired a servant for Ruth and provided her with a car. He was living in another rented house in Beverly Hills along with a valet and an Irish setter he was extremely fond of named Jack. The house that Bob rented was small (six rooms) but comfortable. He was more interested in cars. By now he had

114 Deseret News 11/12/36

115 Hartford Courant, 11/27/36

two cars and according to one nationally syndicated article was negotiating on a third. In addition to this he had bought land in Coldwater Canyon, an area above Beverly Hills.[116]

For Bob the sense of excitement of the picture business was beginning to fade. "I'm tired of trying to figure it out, so I'm going to take it for granted. The shine is beginning to wear off, anyway. Making pictures is routine now—just a job of hard work." He was also modest. "I guess I am sincere, all right. I have to be. I'm no actor—I mean not a technical actor." He expanded on this. "There are parts I couldn't play if I rehearsed for years. I couldn't be a hand-kissing, continental type of guy. The parts I have, I must feel. And maybe people like me because they know I'm a pretty normal kind of pretty ordinary American."[117]

His travels got headlines across the country. When he went to Dallas for the Cotton Bowl and crown its Queen, she promptly fainted at his feet. In New York he was met by thousands of fans who got dangerously close and began tearing at his clothes. It took fifteen New York policemen to lift him up and get him out of harm's way. Naturally, he found this annoying and embarrassing. The visit was supposed to be a vacation, but it turned out to be anything but—and he came to terms with how his life had changed in just a short time. "I flew to New York for my first visit there," he later said. "I had less than a week in the city. A year or two ago, I might have made the trip and wandered aimlessly among the crowds unnoticed. Now, they have seen me on the screen and it was pretty difficult to get around without recognition." He also had to come to terms on adjusting his life and personality to fit this new lifestyle. "Hollywood changes you inside and out," he said. "I realize the difference between the person I am and the one I was two years ago. I have had to break off old habits and cultivate new ones as I readjusted myself, or as nature did it for me, to meet the metamorphosis of Hollywood. According to the philosophers I studied at school, the process is quite enough to change a personality."[118]

In the fall of 1936 Bob made a trip back to Beatrice, which got

116 Kentucky New Era, 9/10/36

117 Kentucky New Era, 9/9/36

118 Eugene Register-Guard, 10/18/36

plenty of newspaper headlines coast to coast. Certainly, MGM arranged and paid for the trip, but Bob enjoyed returning home and visiting with old friends in familiar stomping grounds a great deal. It had all the hallmarks of the classic small-town boy makes good. Hundreds of fans met him as his plane arrived at the Lincoln Airport, but that was nothing compared to what he would meet when he arrived home.

As Bob entered Beatrice he was welcomed by a huge banner which read BEATRICE WELCOMES YOU, ROBERT TAYLOR. There was a huge crowd estimated at 20,000—far higher than the population of Beatrice. People came as far as Kansas, Iowa and Missouri to welcome Arlington Brugh home. Bob, sitting on the top of the backseat, was driven in a yellow topless car. The car was driven an old school mate of Bob's, now a private in the State National Guard. There was a police motorcycle escort, color guards from the American Legion and marching bands to welcome him, including those from Beatrice High School and Doane College. According to newspaper accounts of the day, "A mob of school children followed, on bicycles or afoot, each grasping a piece of paper and screaming for an autograph." When he arrived at his lodgings, the Hotel Paddock, Bob was met by his Grandmother Stanhope who jokingly asked him, "Do you remember me?" [119] Bob was thrilled by the reception, though maybe a bit humbled by it, too. "New York was nothing like this," he said. "I never spent a more enjoyable day in my life." [120]

In a press conference with reporters at the hotel, Bob did allow that he had received a raise in salary from MGM. Of course, this made perfect sense because Taylor was now one of the biggest stars in the country. The popularity he had attained with *Magnificent Obsession* was immense. And the pictures he was turning out since had cemented his popularity. He was asked about what leading ladies he would like to work with in the future and he replied that there were only three he hadn't worked with as yet: Myrna Loy, Jean Harlow and Luise Rainer. (In the near future he would get to work with two of these three.) When asked what his favorite film was, he

119 Lincoln Evening Journal, 10/28/36

120 Reading Eagle, 10/30/36

didn't mention his star-making *Magnificent Obsession* or the popular *Small Town Girl* or even the recently completed *Camille*. No, he said his favorite picture was *His Brother's Wife* with Barbara Stanwyck. (Though he did admit that *Magnificent Obsession* was the "hardest work" he ever had done.) When asked what films he would like to make, he said he wouldn't mind remaking the Valentino classic *The Four Horsemen of the Apocalypse*, though he was quick to point out that he doubted he would be as effective in the part as Valentino. He admitted to no rivalry with Clark Gable. He called Gable a good friend and, "We often read each other's fan mail, and get a big kick out of it." He pointed out that *Camille* was virtually completed; all that remained were some retakes.

He attended an assembly at the high-school auditorium where "students gave Taylor a full minute ovation which threatened to shatter the windows." [121] He was introduced by the manager of the local Rivoli Theater. Bob recalled that he had lived in Beatrice at the time that the school and the theater had been built and was there on the opening night of the theater. While on stage he pointed to the orchestra pit and said, "I used to play cello down there. I sang on this very stage, too." He recalled how as a freshman he introduced a speaker to dedicate the new high-school auditorium. "I rehearsed a long time," he said, "but when the time came my knees shook and I didn't know what to say. That's the way I feel now." [122] In the afternoon, Bob made a car tour of Beatrice with two old boyhood friends to see how things had changed or, more likely, how things had pretty much stayed the same. Among the places visited was his old house at 901 6th Street, now under new occupation. After that he went to another reception at the Rivioli Theater and was introduced by the Governor of Nebraska himself. In remarks to the crowd, Bob reminisced about his days as an usher in the theater. But his day wasn't over yet. It was nearly eleven o'clock at night when he returned to the Paddock Hotel for another reception. When he arrived in the ballroom, the orchestra began playing "There's No Place like Nebraska," and as if on cue Bob began dancing with the girl nearest him. The locals were quoted as saying how he was

121 Lincoln Evening Journal, 10/29/36

122 Reading Eagle, 10/30/36

just the same good guy they knew as Arlington Brugh.

The next day the press was full of the news that Bob had made a "date" with a local Beatrice girl, Vera Bascom, described in the Lincoln paper as a "comely blonde." Bob and Vera had known one another when Bob had worked at the radio station KMMJ. When Bob arrived at her house to pick her up, he seemed surprised to find the press there and asked them to let him have a free night without all of their questions and flashbulbs and that if they did he would reward them with all the pictures they wanted the next day at the big football game in Lincoln. He told them he "didn't want to play Garbo," but couldn't they give him a break? They apparently relented and off Bob drove with his date.

The next day Bob (accompanied by his mother, bodyguard and an assortment of high-school and college friends) motored to Lincoln for a luncheon, football game and dinner. It was a whirlwind three days and afterward he said goodbye and returned to Hollywood. (Through the years he would return to Nebraska and Beatrice frequently, though not with the fanfare of this first trip back at the height of his initial fame.) But that didn't mean that his days of causing public commotion were over. Just days after returning to Hollywood, Bob appeared to vote in the 1936 Presidential election between Franklin Roosevelt and Kansas Governor Alf Landon. He caused commotion at his prescient and ended up spending some thirty minutes signing autographs. [123] No word on whom he voted for, but as a Midwestern Republican it is assumed he voted for fellow Midwestern Republican Landon.

In a national survey of girls aged sixteen to twenty to find out who their favorite movie actor was, Bob came out in front by a mile. He received four times more votes than the man who came in second, Clark Gable. [124] Theater owners also noted his allure when they listed him number four on the annual listing of the top ten box-office stars in the country. In 1935 he had rated 83rd in the same survey. Now the only stars who rated above him were Shirley Temple, Clark Gable and (paired together) Fred Astaire and Ginger Rogers. *Time* wrote that Bob shared a distinction with Rudolph

123 Lincoln Evening Journal, 11/4/36

124 Lincoln Evening Journal, 11/4/36

Valentino, "for whom the use of freight elevators and fire escapes is more of a necessity than an affectation. Crowds often try to pull buttons off his clothes, clip his curls for souvenirs." [125] But perhaps the most impressive assertion of Taylor's popularity in his great year of 1936 came not in the United States but in the London Observer (confirming Taylor's popularity with worldwide audiences), which noted, "1936 will go down as the year of Edward VIII, the Spanish war and Robert Taylor."

125 TIME, 1/18/37

Chapter Five

"NOW YOU ARE A MAN, BOB" (1937-1939)

MGM felt that Bob needed a change of pace when it cast him in a comedy, *Personal Property*, opposite one of the studio's top female stars, Jean Harlow. Bob never felt comfortable in comedy and during his long career he appeared in relatively few films in this genre, but when he did do a comedy he had a nice flair. While the studio felt he needed a change of pace in genres, he still played his stock character of this period—the irresponsible playboy.

As was the case with many films at this time, *Personal Property* was a remake of a previous MGM film, *The Man in Possession*, from 1931, which starred Robert Montgomery and Irene Purcell. Set in England, Jean Harlow is an American widow who has hit hard times. Bob's playboy is disowned by his family because they see him as spoiled and irresponsible. As usual, Harlow uses her considerable charms to marry into Taylor's family—not with Taylor, but with his more responsible and staid brother (Reginald Owen). Turns out that the family she thinks is well-heeled financially is also experiencing hard times. In fact, the family thinks that Harlow is well-off and is encouraging Owens' marriage as a way to get back on its feet financially. Taylor sees through both sides and decides to have a bit of fun himself. Naturally, through all of this Taylor and Harlow find themselves falling in love. Bob enjoyed working with Jean who he described as "full of laughs, yet her fun never seemed to interfere with her work." [126]

Assigned to direct once again was speed demon Woody Van Dyke. This time he really did do a rush job in getting the picture completed

126 Hollywood Citizen News, 4/22/46

in approximately two weeks. One of the reasons for completing the film as quickly as possible was because Harlow was already exhibiting signs of the fatigue that would sap her strength as the year 1937 wore on leading to her untimely and tragic passing at age 26 in June. This was, ironically enough, a happy period in Harlow's life. Over Christmas, William Powell, who she was dating, gave her an 85-caret star sapphire ring which she took as an engagement ring, even if Powell didn't. Sadly, it seemed that Harlow was more in love with Powell than Powell was with her. After two failed marriages (one to Carole Lombard), Powell was gun-shy about walking down the matrimonial path again. *Personal Property* would be the last film that Harlow would complete. (She died while making *Saratoga*, completing about two-thirds of her scenes.)

Prior to beginning production on this film in January of 1937, Bob and Harlow worked together on a *Lux Radio Theatre* production of "Madame Sans-Gene" (a comedy which takes place in post-revolution France).[127] Like most of her co-stars, Bob liked and was protective of Harlow, who was known to most people on the MGM lot by her nickname "Baby." Taylor later recalled Harlow as "warm, outgoing, [and] deeply kind."[128]

Following completion of *Personal Property* Bob and Harlow left almost immediately by train with other stars to attend President Roosevelt's annual Birthday Ball on behalf of the March of Dimes held in Washington, D.C. Neither Bob nor Jean Harlow were well during this time as they both had the flu bug, but that didn't stop them from making over 20 appearances during the course of the trip. One of the highlights was a luncheon with Eleanor Roosevelt. At the time Mrs. Roosevelt was quoted as saying that the president didn't mind playing second fiddle to Robert Taylor. "In fact," she said, "he admitted romantic appeal is more persuasive than statesmanship. He likes his movies and is a big fan. He told me they do the world just as much good as any politician in the long run."[129] On the same day as the ball Bob and Harlow were asked to attend another event

127 This was Bob's second appearance on Lux Radio Theatre. On October 28, 1936 he appeared in "Saturday's Children" opposite Olivia de Havilland.

128 Films of Robert Taylor, pg. 11

129 Robert Taylor, J.E. Wayne, pg. 70

in nearby Baltimore. "So off we went," Bob recalled years later, "riding with J. Edgar Hoover in a bullet-proof limousine, and escorted by screaming motorcycles expertly ridden by State Troopers." He later admitted the experience was "exciting." [130] Having completed *Personal Property*, and embarked on this fast-paced trip, both Harlow and Bob returned exhausted and ill. According to Bob's grandmother, writing to a friend in Nebraska, Bob was, "pretty well tired out. He does not enjoy these trips to the larger cities. They wear him out." [131] The fatigue Harlow had for so long never faded as she went into her final decline. Years after she died, a book came out on Harlow which portrayed her as an alcoholic slut. Bob was one of several Hollywood stars who knew the real Jean Harlow to come forward and denounce the book as "trash." Bob further said that she was "not at all the monster some writers have made of her." [132]

II

It seems like those who are built up eventually need to be brought down and Bob was no exception. As 1936 turned to 1937 the star of the year began to get increasingly negative press while his films continued to be popular.

In February of 1937 began a host of headlines datelined Beatrice, Nebraska, regarding Bob's 82-year-old grandfather, Jacob A. Brugh. What the articles found outrageous was that Bob's grandfather was on relief receiving only $16 per month. In contrast his movie-star grandson was making $3,500 *per week*. According to Ruth, it was not the responsibility of Bob to look after his grandfather. "He has two sons and two daughters and I also have contributed to his support ever since the death of Bob's father, and shall continue to do so." It was also pointed out that when Bob had been in Nebraska the previous fall he had given his grandfather $20, paid for some groceries and paid a $15 coal bill. However, the state of Nebraska believed that Bob should be helping to support his elderly grandfather. The state, according to Irl D. Tolen, State Assistance

130 Film Fan Monthly, June, 1969

131 Reluctant Witness, Linda Alexander, pg. 109

132 Films of Robert Taylor, pg. 11

Director, sent a registered letter to Taylor regarding the financial condition of Brugh, and it had been returned "unclaimed" from Hollywood. According to Tolen, he wrote, "In view of the fact you are amply able to contribute to the support of your grandfather, we are directing this communication to you, requesting that you reinstate your support to Mr. Brugh so that he may not continue to be on a public charge." Tolen acknowledged that Bob was not "legally responsible" to take care of his grandfather, but said he had a "very heavy moral responsibility."

Then Bob's grandfather got in the act blaming Ruth for the lack of support. "She thought I would hold him back," he told reporters. "She never liked me." He then praised Bob as "the greatest actor they got out there in Hollywood." He was also confident that he would hear from his grandson. In fact, Bob did get in touch with the County Assistance Director and let them know he would take care of the situation. "He appeared to me to be more worried about his grandfather than about unfavorable publicity," the Assistance Director told the press.

One of the nations' most widely-read columnists, Westbrook Pedler, even wrote a column on the situation. "One of our beautiful male movie actors suffered a little embarrassment recently," Pedler's column began. (He doesn't name Bob in the article, but it's obvious that he is referring to him and the well-publicized story.) He pointed out that while the beautiful actor was collecting that $3,500 every week, the old man was reduced to a diet of coffee, oatmeal and bread while living in a shack on $4 per week. Much of the rest of the article goes into the plight of the destitute in the nation and how little many have to live on. [133]

By February 25 the newspapers announced that the grandfather had been taken off of the pension rolls and he had moved in with his son, Jacob Brugh, who owned a farm. No additional information was given as to how Bob was going to help him monetarily. However, just a week later, Grandfather Brugh was in the news again when it was announced that he had died of influenza at age 83. Bob announced in the press that he couldn't attend the funeral services because he was shooting a film, but that Ruth would attend.

133 LA Evening News, 2/24/37

The film that Bob was working on that prevented him from attending his grandfather's funeral was *This is My Affair*, which re-teamed him with Barbara Stanwyck and loaned Bob out to Twentieth Century-Fox. This would be Bob's final loan-out from MGM for nearly twenty years as MGM greedily kept him steadily working in their own films from this point forward. Despite its romantic title, the film is basically a crime drama which casts Bob as a Navy lieutenant who goes undercover on a mission under the direction of none other than President William McKinley. McKinley's directions are that he must resign his commission and assume a new identity as he infiltrates a mob situated in the Midwest pulling off a series of bank robberies which are causing a wave of hysteria. There he meets and falls for a nightclub singer (Stanwyck) who has connections to the mob he is trying to bust up. Along the way President McKinley is assassinated—the only man who knew the truth of the mission other than Bob. The film had the working title of *The McKinley Case*, but that was hardly the kind of title that would attract female movie-goers, even if it's more appropriate than *This is My Affair*. During a story conference Zanuck told his writers, "For the time being, the new title . . . is to be kept confidential. However, we want to work this title into the dialogue somewhere."

During the making of the picture Taylor admitted that he had a "Lon Chaney complex," meaning that he wanted very much to play the kind of character parts that Chaney had done in the silent and early talkie days. There is a scene in the picture where Taylor's character is condemned and rotting away in prison and apparently Bob wanted to play the scene using make-up, including applying heavy circles under his eyes to make himself look more haggard. But director William A. Seiter insisted that Taylor play it without all the make-up flourishes, and just show his fatigue thru acting.

In her role as a nightclub singer Barbara got the chance to sing the song "I Hum a Waltz." It was common practice that songs are recorded earlier and played back when the scenes are shot, with the actor mouthing the words. Bob attended the recording session and sat himself in the orchestra, near the cello player. As Stanwyck was recording the song, Bob cupped his hands under his chin and gazed romantically into her eyes. Apparently, this proved too distracting for Barbara, who stopped singing and allegedly called out, "Bob

Taylor, if you don't stop looking at me like a mooing cow, I'm going to walk right out of here. You come out of that orchestra so I won't see you while I'm trying to sing." As usual, she won—with Bob laughingly taking another seat, this time behind Stanwyck's gaze.[134]

The film was shot over a 40-day period and includes a stellar supporting cast, including Victor McLaglen, Brian Donlevy, John Carradine and Sig Rumann. Frank Conroy, cast as William McKinley, is very effective and truly evokes the image of the man he portrays. The film is well directed by Seiter and its period look and costumes add immeasurably to the atmosphere. It was yet another Taylor picture to have its opening at Radio City Music Hall. The *New York Post* critic wrote, "The big news for the fans is that Mr. Taylor and Barbara Stanwyck are paired as hero and heroine. The former does a fairly creditable job with the role of secret service ace and he makes love to Miss Stanwyck persuasively. Neither she nor Mr. Taylor know much about counterfeiting an emotion—at least neither of them steals the show from the other."

Following the completion of *This is My Affair*, Bob took a vacation to Hawaii while Barbara plunged into what would be one of her signature film roles: playing the self-sacrificing mother from the wrong side of the tracks in Samuel Goldwyn's production of *Stella Dallas*. The film brought her more praise than any other she had done up to that time. The *New York Times* said her performance was as "courageous as it is fine." In late July Bob escorted Barbara to the premiere of the picture in Hollywood. Goldwyn hired extra security knowing that a star-studded group of guests would be attending, including Claudette Colbert, Ginger Rogers, Gary Cooper and Harpo Marx. The crowd was large (some 2,000 people gathered) and noisy, but it wasn't the crowd that got the attention but a security officer who didn't recognize Barbara and tried to eject her from the premiere and how Bob came to her rescue.

The officer somehow had mistaken Barbara for an autograph seeker trying to sneak into the premiere! According to newspaper reports, she was grabbed by the officer so hard that would develop black-and-blue bruises to her arms as she vainly tried to explain who she was. Apparently, she and Taylor had become separated in

134 Barbara Stanwyck, Al DiOrio, pg. 106

the lobby of the theater and as she was making her way back to Bob the officer grabbed her thinking that she was approaching Bob for an autograph. The officer allegedly said, "No, you don't," as he grabbed her.

Bob pushed his way thru the crowd toward the now-weeping Barbara and approached the officer while the crowd, understanding what was happening, cheered him on by yelling, "Sock the cop." Taylor was angry and actually challenged the cop by saying, "I'll punch you in the jaw." However, other officers soon arrived and explained the situation to the officer who had manhandled Barbara. The officer apologized saying, "Gosh, I didn't know who she was."

Bob wasn't mollified and wanted to have the officer arrested, but Barbara came to the officer's defense. "Nothing doing, Bob," she told him. Goldwyn had been appraised of the situation and rushed over also tried to cool Bob down. "The man did what he was hired for," Goldwyn said. Bob soon calmed himself down and the couple continued on their way into the screening.[135]

III

A Yank at Oxford is the film which answered the question "Does Robert Taylor have hair on his chest?" It was a film that Bob very much wanted to make because he felt that his screen persona needed some toughening up. He had gotten tired of cracks about being a "pretty boy" and comparing his "beauty" to that of his leading ladies. Up to now he had basically played playboys who looked good in a tux with one of MGM's top female stars on his arm. He was the dream lover of thousands upon thousands of women who sought escape at the movies. That was part of the problem. While he was the romantic idol to countless women, he offered little to men. Men could identify with somebody like Clark Gable. He was a "he-man" that men could understand women being attracted to. They wanted to be Clark Gable. Not many men could identify with Robert Taylor at this point. They sneered at his image; in effect many considered him a "pretty boy." But the reality was that Bob himself wasn't satisfied with his screen roles and wanted to diversify. What many

135 Fresno Bee, 7/23/37

men didn't realize was that Bob was an outdoors man who loved to hunt, fish and ride motorcycles. It's not that he wanted to give up being a romantic leading man, he would continue to play such roles for the remainder of his career, but he wanted to develop other sides of his screen persona—more true to himself. "I've always been a nice guy in pictures and I'm glad to be a louse at last!" he said regarding the character he plays in *A Yank at Oxford.*[136]

Bob plays Lee Sheridan, an arrogant young athlete with a swelled head. He is the star athlete of his small Midwestern College where he has won medal after medal in track and field. He has known the adulation (no doubt since childhood) of his friends, classmates and of his newspaper publisher father (played by Lionel Barrymore). It has made him more than self-assured and confident but incredibly cocky and egotistical. The dean of his college gets Lee admitted to Oxford and, upon leaving, the town rolls out the red carpet at the train depot. Practically the entire town comes out to cheer him on. There is a brass band and speeches. It is nothing less than what Lee would expect—and he promises to show the English kids how it's done. Needless to say, his attitude wins him no friends when he arrives at Oxford and for the first time in his life he experiences being an outcast. But, despite this, a pretty English girl (Maureen O'Sullivan) is smitten by him, although she is the sister of one of his rivals. Eventually, Lee learns lessons in sportsmanship and how to be a member of a team rather than just thinking about himself. The film gives Bob the opportunity to demonstrate his athletic prowess in track and field as well as rowing. But the most talked about scenes in the picture were the ones which showed off his solid legs, muscular arms, and yes—his hairy chest! Putting those doubts to rest.

A Yank at Oxford would be the first film shot at Metro's new British studio. The reason for opening a studio in Great Britain was, as usual, economics. In the mid-1930s the British government decided to impose a quota on the number of foreign films that were shown in England. It was hoped that this would help their domestic film studios. To get around this MGM decided that they would begin film production in England with a series of pictures that would get

136 Robert Taylor, J.E. Wayne, pg. 80

wide release not only in England (a major market) but all around Europe and still be accepted in the United States. Enter *A Yank at Oxford* and Robert Taylor for box-office assurance. In fact, while publicizing the new venture in London, Louis B. Mayer said of Taylor, "If ever there was an American young man who could logically by culture and breeding be called a Britisher, it's Robert Taylor." [137]

Initially, the screenplay was given to Frank Wead, best known as a Navy aviator. In between World Wars, Wead turned to writing and eventually screenwriting and wrote the story or screenplays for such films as *Ceiling Zero, Test Pilot* and *The Citadel.* His life was later filmed by director John Ford in the motion picture *The Wings of Eagles* with John Wayne playing Wead. Wead wrote over 100 pages of a screenplay before it was given to novelist F. Scott Fitzgerald to revise. Fitzgerald, the author of such literary classics as *Tender Is the Night* and *The Great Gatsby*, felt something was "missing" from Wead's story. Fitzgerald believed that there was little difference between the characters that the Yank encountered at Oxford and those he encounters in the USA. He felt that the girl, as written by Wead, could have been "found next door in Lakedale, USA," so "Fitzgerald . . . set out to stress the Yank's Yankness and Molly's [O'Sullivan] Britishness." [138] Fitzgerald thus revised the script, but ultimately even Fitzgerald's script would be rewritten. Fitzgerald would later write that, "Very few lines of mine are left in 'A Yank at Oxford,' . . . but the sequence in which Taylor and Maureen O'Sullivan go out in the punt in the morning, while the choir boys are singing on Magdalene Tower, is mine, and one line very typically so—where Taylor says, 'Don't rub the sleep out of your eyes. It's beautiful sleep.' I thought that line had my trademark on it." [139] In two years in Hollywood, Fitzgerald would only get screenwriting credit on one film—ironically another one with Bob, *Three Comrades.* Still, it seems that when we watch the film that the cultural changes that he suggested to differentiate Taylor from O'Sullivan and his Oxford classmates were adopted. Ultimately, the screenplay credit would be given to Malcolm Stuart Boylan, Walter Ferris and George Oppenheimer.

---

137 The New Republic, 3/23/38

138 Crazy Sunday's pg. 112

139 Correspondence of F. Scott Fitzgerald, pg. 498

For Bob the journey to England to shoot the picture turned out to be a trial for him. Luce publications like *Time* and *Life* seemed to take particular delight in going after him. It was *Life* which coined the phrase "beautiful Bob Taylor" when writing about him. It was not done in a complimentary way either, and other publications picked up on it. Newspapers across the country were printing stories about Taylor being asked such inane questions as "Would you rather be brainy or beautiful?" It was publicity such as this that more than convinced MGM that they had to toughen Bob's persona or else he would dissolve into a laughing stock. Columnist O.O. McIntyre of the *Los Angeles Examiner* wrote a column on the subject. "If I had a hand in piloting the career of Robert Taylor," he wrote, "I would soft pedal the Pretty Boy stuff in a hurry. It is heading toward turning a no doubt deserved favorite into a National Laugh." He pointed out that a trailer announcing the newest Taylor picture was booed "without a single hand clap" at a local theater. He likened Bob to the child actor Freddie Bartholomew who he said was being perceived by the public as a "namby-pamby" due to his role in *Little Lord Fauntleroy.* (MGM would attempt to toughen up Bartholomew in 1937, too, by casting him in Captains Courageous.) McIntyre suggested that if MGM wanted to bury the "pretty boy" angle soon they should allow him to be cast as Rhett Butler in *Gone with the Wind.*[140]

Bob's arrival in New York on August 19, 1937, in preparation for his leaving for Europe, was met by screaming fans and a sneering press corp. Against his better judgment he met with members of the press and, as usual, they asked demeaning questions such as, "Do you think you are beautiful? He finally snapped. "I'm a red-blooded man," he told the reporters, "and I resent people calling me beautiful. I've got hair on my chest." They tried again with, "Would you rather be brainy or beautiful?" in which he replied, "I haven't much choice in the matter." One reporter asked him if he would ask Spencer Tracy to teach him to act. Bob just grinned at that one and replied, "I couldn't think of anyone better. I may do it." He then did something he would do throughout his career: downplay his own talent. "You know I'm really lucky to be where I am. All I play is straight

140 LA Examiner, 9/26/37

stuff—I'm not much of an actor, you know." And (as usual) he was asked about Barbara. "She calls me Bob—and I call her Boobs. That's all I can say about it now."[141]

Bob sailed for England in late August of 1937, taking the Cunard steamer *Berengaria*. The *Berengaria's* construction began in 1910 and was put to sea in May, 1912, only a month after the *Titanic* disaster. It was one of the most luxurious ships still baring the Cunard brand. The Port of New York was one of chaos as more than 2,000 fans waited eagerly for Bob. The contemporary newspapers reported that dozens of women fainted. One woman got through the guards that were accompanying Bob and was able to touch him. She shouted, "Folks, I'll never wash this hand as long as I live." When Bob finally got on board and was situated in his suite, he began to speak with reporters. In the midst of the press conference sounds came from beneath his bed—and two young women were dragged out by police. (Bob, years later, acknowledged that this had been a studio publicity stunt.) Finally a half-hour late, the *Berengaria* pulled out to sea.[142] Seven days later, the arrival at Southampton was another scene of chaos with more than 5,000 people dockside to welcome him.

Initially, Bob was put up at the Claridge Hotel, but eventually he would be housed in a quaint little village called High Wycombe. The filming of *A Yank at Oxford* was the beginning of a love affair for Bob and England. He loved the traditions, such as afternoon tea, and the countryside with its small villages. "Bob never tired of coming to England," related Ivy Mooring, born and bred in England and later Bob's secretary. "He hated doing the 'costume pictures' he later made in England, but he loved the country and the people."[143]

Vivien Leigh was cast in the picture by British producer Michael Balcon over L.B. Mayer's objections. But by the time Mayer had made his objections known it was too late to recast the part, and, needless to say, she is highly effective playing a vixen. Bob got along well with her and observed that between scenes she was often

141 LA Daily News, 8/20/37

142 LA Times, 8/22/37

143 Ivy Mooring to author

caught reading the worldwide bestseller, *Gone with the Wind*, and trying out a Southern accent, long before she would be cast as Scarlett O'Hara.

The picture was shot over the course of some three months with several interruptions due to weather. By the time he returned to the United States in mid-December he was ready to come home. He and other cast members departed on the *Queen Mary*. When the ship arrived in New York, he met the press wearing candy-striped pajamas and a stubble. The press was at it again. Reporters asked if he would expose his chest so that they could confirm he had hair on it. He declined this offer. (They only had to wait a few months and the film would confirm that he did, indeed, have hair on his chest.) He was asked (again), "Would you rather be brainy or beautiful?" This time he replied, "That was four months ago and I don't know what I said. But if I were faced with that question again I know what I'd do. I wouldn't say a damned thing." One reporter got a little tough. "Come on, Taylor, Let's get this thing settled. Did you or did you not say you were beautiful?" Bob handled that with aplomb. "I'll ask you one. Would a man say that about himself? Would you?" Lionel Barrymore, also on board, came to Bob's defense. "Bob is a fine lad. He has no vanity at all." When asked if he thought Taylor was too handsome, Barrymore replied, "Huh? He can't help that." [144]

Three days later, Bob returned to Los Angeles by airplane. He was again met by reporters, this time somewhat less hostile. He expanded on his treatment along the way. "Just what does a fellow have to do to be a regular guy anyway?" he said. "Of course I'm glad that I'm a popular actor, but I certainly don't get a kick out of a lot of girls who ought to know better pawing me and mauling me. And I resent those interviews which made me out a fop . . . Well, I've learned a lot. If you belong to the public you've got to take plenty of wear and tear. But don't get me wrong I'm not sore." He summed it up this way: "You might say that I'll be a sadder and wiser guy." Naturally, he was asked about Barbara and rumors of their getting married. "We're still good friends. Very good friends. But we have made no plans for marriage. Before anything more is said on that

144 LA Herald, 12/13/37

score, we'll have to have some good, long talks."[145] He then picked up Barbara and went to his mother's house for dinner. When he went to the studio, he was summoned to see Mayer who told him the rushes he had seen of the film were outstanding and then said, "Now you are a man, Bob."[146]

When the film opened in February 1938, *A Yank at Oxford* proved to be a big hit at the box office. The reviews, on the whole, were good. Frank Nugent of the *New York Times* was still suspicious of Bob, "for we still regard that widow's peak with cynicism," he wrote, but added, "In fact, we find ourselves rooting for Mr. Taylor." He added that in all the film is "quite a pleasant spoof." The *New York Daily News* was enthusiastic. "Looks very much like a Robert Taylor year. *A Yank at Oxford* is his best picture and Robert should thank his lucky stars because when he left for England several months ago, the pendulum could very easily have swung the other way." It could be said that *A Yank at Oxford* succeeded. From this point forward he would alternate between romantic films and more masculine portrayals. In fact, one upcoming film in particular would redefine him even more—playing a prizefighter in *The Crowd Roars.* Years later he would say of this film, "I really socked it to 'em in that, and I only wish I had made it a year or so before I did . . . there'd have been less nonsense in the press."[147] From this point forward "Beautiful" Robert Taylor receded into the past.

Shortly after returning home Barbara told Bob that Frank Fay was instituting a custody battle over their adopted son Dion, and that he may drag Bob's name into the case. The custody battle began in December of 1937 and would run over the course of several weeks. Fay accused Barbara of not allowing him the right to see Dion so that the boy could become more "accustomed" to Bob.

In January Barbara, on the stand, admitted that Bob was a frequent visitor to her home and that he did play with Dion and, on "numerous occasions," gave the boy gifts. One gift which the attorney for Fay tried to enter into evidence was a $50 check made out to Dion from Bob. The judge, Goodwin Knight, a future Governor

145 LA Examiner, 12/17/37

146 Robert Taylor, J.E. Wayne, pg. 86

147 Films of Robert Taylor, pg. 69

of California, sustained an objection over this from Barbara's attorney telling Fay's attorney, "I don't care how many times Mr. Taylor came to her house. This is her personal life and has nothing to do with this proceeding." Clearly, Fay was trying to show that Barbara was using Bob to alienate Dion's affections for Fay—through bribery if nothing else.

Barbara fought back by claiming that Fay was a violent drunk. She wanted him to undergo psychiatric testing. She told the court, "He is an unfit guardian for the child. He drinks too much. Why, he even fell into Dion's crib once and fell asleep, keeping the boy awake with his snoring." But Fay's attorney's punched back claiming that Barbara was an inattentive mother. She was asked if it was true she had spent most of Christmas Day at the races "instead of at home with your child." Barbara admitted she had. In the end Fay did win a victory. The court ruled that he was to be allowed to have Dion every other Saturday and then be allowed to visit the boy at Stanwyck's home every Tuesday and Thursday afternoon, but Judge Knight stipulated that he lose these rights if he ever appeared drunk while either visiting the boy or when the Dion visited him. This was only a temporary victory, however, since Fay became bored with the boy and eventually stopped requesting to see him. Barbara wasn't much better—soon enough she was sending him off to military school. (She told the press, "I don't want him to one of those so-called movie children. The spoiled and pampered variety. That's why I'm sending Dion to military school soon." [148])

Left unsaid in court was that Stanwyck and Taylor were not only "good friends" but also neighbors. In the fall of 1936, Barbara built a house on 170 acres of land in Northridge, in the San Fernando Valley. Barbara tapped Paul Williams, the first African-American to be admitted to the American Institute of Architects, to design the house. The house was built as a French-English stone manor atop a hill and included four fireplaces, a swimming pool and a tennis court. The rest of the property was used as a ranch for breeding and housing thoroughbreds, due to Barbara's passion for horse racing. The ranch was named Marwyck, combining Marx (Zeppo and Marion were partners with Barbara) and Stanwyck. As the relationship

148 Al DiOrio, Barbara Stanwyck, pg. 118

between Barbara and Bob deepened, Bob purchased twelve acres just down the road from Barbara. He built a home which he called his "hideout," and also purchased several horses. Some of the horses were thoroughbreds which he would store at Barbara's stables. Other horses he purchased and kept in his own stables for his own riding pleasure. When possible, Bob, often with Barbara, would go riding in the 5,000 acres that were being preserved in the hills behind the ranch.[149]

IV

Taylor's next film was *Three Comrades*, based on a bestselling novel by Erich Maria Remarque, the author of the anti-war novel, *All Quiet on the Western Front*, which Universal filmed in 1930 to great acclaim. Taylor plays Erich, one three lifelong friends who are veterans of the German army who set up an auto shop in postwar Berlin. They meet Patricia, an attractive woman who came from an aristocratic family but has fallen on hard times. She has a radiance about her that enthralls everyone who meets her. From the moment they meet Erich and Pat are attracted to each other. Erich's friends believe he should marry her and press him to do so. But there is a secret that Patricia has been keeping from Taylor and his friends: she has Tuberculosis. The disease is stable right now but could return at any time and would be an almost certain death sentence for her. She and Erich marry. There are tragic consequences for the Comrades and Patricia before the film goes into its fadeout. The Germany of the early 1920s was ravaged from the war and economic and political chaos is among the themes that the film explores.

The cast is distinguished. Playing Patricia is Margaret Sullavan; a radiant screen actress who made far too few films and yet made a strong impact in those that she did appear in such as *The Moon's Our Home, The Shop Around the Corner* and *The Mortal Storm*. In *Three Comrades* we can understand why these three men are captivated by her vivacious beauty—inside and out. Bob enjoyed working with Sullavan, describing her as "enchanting. Her talent warranted a much bigger career than Hollywood ever allowed her." Appearing

149 Screenland 11/38

with Bob, as his fellow Comrades, are Franchot Tone, a superb actor who never became the huge star in pictures he should have, and Robert Young, who had been toiling in films since 1930, and despite some good performances over the years would find his greatest success on television as the patriarch of *Father Knows Best* and the kindly doctor *Marcus Welby, M.D.* Young recalled Taylor in a 1986 interview with Leonard Maltin. ". . . Taylor, who was perfectly capable as an actor, but he was so damn handsome, that he, like Tyrone Power, looked almost feminine. He was what you might call a beautiful man. Not a handsome man, but a beautiful man. He was a wonderful. Wonderful person. And a good actor, too." [150] In addition to these talented actors, the supporting cast is equally impressive: Guy Kibbee, Lionel Atwill, Henry Hull, Charley Grapewin, Monty Woolley and George Zucco.

F. Scott Fitzgerald received his only screen credit for writing this film. He felt that the Remarque novel was "just short of first-rate," but "tells a lovely, tragic story." However, the producer of the film, Joseph Mankiewicz, was frustrated by Fitzgerald's over-analytical and talky script and ended up hiring an MGM contract writer named Edward Paramoure to collaborate with him on a rewrite. Despite having written some superb films, like *The Bitter Tea of General Yen, Trouble for Two* and the 1936 version of *Three Godfathers*, Mankiewicz thought of Paramore as "a Hollywood hack," but someone he felt might be able to rein Fitzgerald in. (For the record, Fitzgerald also didn't think much of Paramour, having worked with him once years before.) In the end, however, Mankiewicz himself ended up rewriting major portions himself (though he receives no screen credit for this). In many circles thereafter Mankiewicz became known as "the man who rewrote Fitzgerald." This was not out of character for him. MGM executive Edwin Knopf would later say, "It is both Joe's strength and his weakness that he thought that he could rewrite anyone." Mankiewicz concedes that "when I rewrote Scott's dialogue people thought I was spitting on the flag." [151] The bottom line for Mankiewicz is that he believed that Fitzgerald, like most novelists, had an ear for how dialog is written

150 Robert Young to Leonard Maltin, Movie Crazy, pg. 14

151 Pictures Will Talk, Kenneth Geist

in novel form but not cinematic. He did feel that Fitzgerald could capture the time period represented, as well as understand the girl, Peg, who had parallels with his wife, Zelda, and who suffered from mental illness and spent years in a sanatorium. But, according to Mankiewicz, the thing that really caused him to rewrite Fitzgerald's dialog was when Margaret Sullavan said she simply couldn't "play this"—meaning the lines that Fitzgerald had written, which looked good on the printed page but were awkward when reciting them.[152]

Sullavan told Frank Borzage that the "dialogue is beautiful, but there is too much of it."[153] She felt that the "camera, rather than the dialogue," should tell the story. Mankiewicz agreed. According to author Lawrence Quirk, Franchot Tone also objected to the wordiness, but he came to rue it. "I could have kicked myself because I had cut off my nose to spite my face—half my footage was cut, and I had only myself to blame."[154]

The most significant change from the screenplay written by Fitzgerald is that the time period of the film was changed from the 1930s, during the uprising of Adolf Hitler, to the early 1920s. Fitzgerald also wanted to use the film as a platform to expose the Nazi brutality against the Jews, but this was either excised or toned down considerably in the released picture. Many of the changes were at the request of the Hays Office. In fact, the writer of the novel, Erich Remarque, charged that the Production Code and the German government were in cahoots to tone down the film's indictment of Nazi Germany and that MGM backed down.[155]

Perhaps the scene which broke the camel's back as far as rewriting Fitzgerald involves Erich calling Pat for the first time. As a way of illustrating the divinity of their love, Fitzgerald cuts to Saint Peter sitting at a telephone switchboard in heaven and personally rings Pat. That was enough for the front office. "What the hell does he think he's writing about?" Eddie Mannix allegedly screamed when he saw the script. But one extremely effective scene that Fitzgerald wrote that Mankiewicz kept involved Erich escorting Pat to a fancy

---

152 ibid

153 Lawrence Quirk, Margaret Sullavan, pg. 87

154 Ibid, pg. 89

155 New Masses, 2/15/38

nightclub and wearing rag-tag clothing that is basically pinned together because he can't afford anything better. Pat still has an elegant dress to wear and they are dining with some snobbish acquaintances of hers. Despite repeated efforts by Pat to get him to dance, Erich refuses to do so, knowing that if he moved too much his suit would come undone. However, he finally consents to dance with Pat and the suit does come undone much to the laughter and ridicule of Pat's "friends." He is deeply embarrassed. This was an example of Fitzgerald adapting the novel to the cinema because in the novel all of Erich's discomfort verbalized thru his thoughts, here Fitzgerald was able to let the audience see it.[156]

Despite the toning down there are a number of scenes with a political bent to them, though Nazism has been eliminated. Fitzgerald, naturally, wasn't happy with the result of the rewritten script, "My producer could not resist the fascination of a pencil and managed to obviate most signs of my personality." Later, when seeing the completed film, Fitzgerald called Mankiewicz an "ignorant and vulgar gent." He did acknowledge that about 1/3 of the picture was his script, but with "all shadows and rhythm removed."[157] However, when Fitzgerald's wife, Zelda, later saw the picture she was more enthusiastic. She reported to Fitzgerald that "most of the scenes are gratifyingly strong and full." She also appreciated the comedic moments in the picture, "sophisticated, realistic, and of a bitter delight." She did believe that there wasn't enough "dramatic continuity," which she thought deprived the film of suspense. She also lauded the love scene on the beach between Taylor and Sullavan, calling it "superb."

The director is Frank Borzage, who had helmed such distinguished pictures as *A Farewell to Arms* and *Man's Castle.* Borzage was also one of the most honored directors of the time having already won two Academy Awards for his directing of *Seventh Heaven* (1927) (the first director so honored) and *Bad Girl* (1931). He had worked with Margaret Sullavan only a few years earlier on the excellent *Little Man, What Now?* for Universal which, ironically, was also set during the 1920s in Germany and was bolder politically than *Three Comrades.* The resulting film was right up Borzage's ally as he had a reputation

156 Crazy Sunday's, pg. 139

157 ibid, pg. 148

for being a director who could bring out the romantic quality in almost all of his films. Robert Young, who worked with Borzage more than once, would recall him as a "sentimental slob but . . . a lovely, lovely man."[158]

Bob wasn't enthusiastic about making this film, even though he had been associated with it throughout its development. MGM bought the novel in 1936 and in 1937 it announced in the trades that Taylor, Joan Crawford and James Stewart were going to make the movie. Then later it was announced that the cast of the three friends would be Spencer Tracy, Taylor and Robert Young along with Luise Rainer as Peg. Eventually, Tracy and Rainer left the project and Stewart was again announced as one of the friends before the final cast of Sullavan, Taylor, Franchot Tone and Young were finally cast.

Bob didn't want to make the picture because he didn't want to play a German, especially a sympathetic one at a time in history when Germany was once again arousing the ire of the world with its belligerence and treatment of the Jews. He told Mayer he would rather not do the film. Now many writers have tried to say that Bob rarely objected to the films he was offered by Metro. In fact, he did object to several, but the difference is that he wasn't the type of actor, like Bette Davis and James Cagney, who would rather go on suspension than make the film (and also MGM was not the type of studio that would allow that). Bob later said, "I never did see the sense in endless quarreling with studio bosses and energy-draining displays of temperament. My way was right for me. My metabolism doesn't lend itself to the Davis-Cagney brand of high-pressure careering."[159] So when Mayer told Bob that this film was going to be a big prestigious studio project and that he wanted Bob to be part of it, Bob gave in despite his lack of enthusiasm.

Bob and Sullavan got along well enough, but she wasn't particularly keen on him as her leading man. She later called his performance, "nice but gut-less."[160] She later said she had, "found myself in danger of playing down to him rather than getting him to play up

---

158 Movie Crazy, pg. 30

159 Films of Robert Taylor, pg. 11

160 Lawrence Quirk, Margaret Sullavan, pg. 90

to me." Off camera, she advised him to be more firm in standing up to Mayer and demanding better parts to which Bob allegedly replied, "Fighting the boss is not in my metabolism."[161]

When *Three Comrades* was released in June of 1938, it received generally good reviews. The *New York Tribune* proclaimed it a "memorable motion picture" and said that the acting was "uniformly excellent." Frank Nugent, writing in the *New York Times*, ecstatically called it a "beautiful and memorable film." Nugent liked the cast, particularly Sullavan, whose performance he called "shimmering." Bob, however, didn't fare nearly as well. Nugent thought he was "good occasionally, but most often is merely acceptable." That is unfair to Bob since his Erich is one of his most effective early performances. His scenes with Sullavan are universally good. Among the highlights being a series of phone conversations that the two have on split-screen which explore their longing and love for one another. Another strong Taylor scene shows Erich tenderly removing falling snow from the face of one of his deceased comrades who had been shot in the back while standing up for his political beliefs. It is a film beautifully played by each of its four lead actors, despite the drawback of not being more relevant to the events then occurring in Nazi Germany. *Commonweal* was mixed. It felt the film was "too sentimental," but tossed a bouquet to Sullavan and Tone by calling their performances "entirely convincing."

One of the few purely negative reviews the picture got at the time, strangely enough, was from the industry bible, *Variety*, whose critic said, "There must have been some reason for making this picture, but it certainly isn't in the cause of entertainment. It provides a dull interlude, despite the draught of the star names." *Variety* also pointed out the obvious—the dated nature of the story. "There is developed in the film no relation between the historical events of that period and the Reich of today. The story is dated and lacks showmanship values of current European movements." Much to Metro's chagrin the picture didn't perform well at the box office. Despite this it did turn up on several critic's best ten lists.

161 ibid

V

1939 began with an embarrassing article in *Photoplay* magazine titled "Hollywood's Unmarried Husbands and Wives," The article dealt with the supposedly platonic "friendships" between several unmarried Hollywood star couples, including Bob and Barbara, Clark Gable and Carole Lombard, George Raft and Virginia Pine, Charlie Chaplin and Paulette Goddard and Gilbert Roland and Constance Bennett. "Just friends to the world at large," the article reads, "yet nowhere has domesticity taken on so unique a character as in this unconventional fold." The meaning was pretty clear to anybody who read between the lines. These "friends" were more than friends but actually living together, unmarried. "Nowhere has domesticity, outside the marital state, reached such a full flower as in Hollywood," the article continued. "Nowhere are there so many famous unmarried husbands and wives." Today, it's hard to understand how this could be considered a scandal. But in 1939 Hollywood studios did their best to protect their stars from embarrassing or unwanted publicity and certainly didn't want anybody to think that their stars were "living in sin" with one another. In most cases, the columnists and the studios worked hand in hand. The studios would give columnists (such as Hedda Hopper and Louella Parsons) information in exchange for favorable treatment in their columns. But this didn't mean that columnists didn't, on occasion, stray off the reservation. Hedda, for instance, had a vendetta against Charlie Chaplin while Louella would go after Orson Welles, especially after *Citizen Kane* and Welles' alleged attack on Parsons' employer, William Randolph Hearst. But on the whole the "I'll wash your hand, if you wash mine" deal between the reporters and the studios worked fine.

Of Bob and Barbara the article stated, "Barbara Stanwyck is not Mrs. Robert Taylor. But she and Bob have built ranch homes next to each other. Regularly, once a week, Barbara freezes homemade ice cream for Bob from a recipe his mother gave her." Carole Lombard and Clark Gable got the same treatment. (Gable, incidentally, was still married to another woman, though separated.) "Carole Lombard is not Clark Gable's wife, either. Still she has remodeled her whole Hollywood life for him. She calls him 'Pappy,' goes hunting with him, copies his hobbies, and makes his interests dominate hers."

With two of Metro's top male stars subjects of this article, Mayer knew he had to do something quick since letters were pouring into the studio and the Hays' Office regarding the article. Metro, in particular, under Mayer's firm hand, was the studio which embodied home, mother and apple pie. Was it coincidence that in February Bob and Barbara formally announced their engagement? One day Gable took Bob aside and said, "Baby, betcha Carole and I beat you to the preacher!" [162]

VI

1939 is considered one of the all-time great years in Hollywood history. Many critics consider it the greatest ever with regards to outstanding films being released in one golden year. Among the films that MGM released that august year were: *The Women, Ninotchka, Goodbye, Mr. Chips, The Wizard of Oz, Gone With the Wind,* and *The Shop Around the Corner.* The other studios had strong entries as well: *Dark Victory, Stagecoach, Destry Rides Again, Mr. Smith Goes to Washington, Love Affair, Young Mr. Lincoln, Only Angels Have Wings* and *Wuthering Heights.* Unfortunately for Bob, while Hollywood was having one of its best years he was entering into a professional slump.

Bob's first project of the year was a film that few thought could have missed: a comedy opposite one of the screen's most popular actresses, Myrna Loy. Loy had reached great popularity as Nora Charles in the Thin Man films and scored in other hits such as *Libeled Lady, Test Pilot* and *Too Hot to Handle.* In 1937 she was proclaimed "The Queen of the Movies" with Clark Gable voted as her King. Unfortunately, the film that Metro selected to pair Loy and Bob is not in the league of their better films. *Lucky Night* is plagued by a weak script, heavy-handed direction by Norman Taurog and a curious lack of chemistry between its stars. It had ingredients of screwball comedy at a time when the screwball rage was running out. Loy plays an heiress whose love life has thus far been unexciting.

162 Robert Taylor, J.E. Wayne, pg. 95

She longs to find a man who will knock her off her feet. Her father tells her to give up the high life and seek employment—and maybe find the man she is looking for. She takes his advice and meets a fellow job seeker, played by Bob. They hit it off and gamble a nickel into a night of excitement and one too many. They wake up married to one another. They decide to make the best of it and eventually come to the realization that they really do love each other, only after they separate.

Loy is one of the rare Taylor co-stars who didn't particularly like him. "The studio thought it would be a good idea to team me with Robert Taylor, Metro's reigning heartthrob," she later wrote in her autobiography. "Our first day on the set I played records, which we did sometimes to fill those endless waits between shots . . . I was listening to some wonderful Cuban music when Robert Taylor approached, 'Do you have to play that sexy stuff all the time? It's the dirtiest music I ever heard.' That was my first day with him. I thought, 'Oh, brother!' He was a bit stuffy, but we got along all right—during the picture, that is: later on I didn't get along with him." In fact, Loy's overall opinion of Bob is clouded by the role he played in the House UnAmerican Activities Committee (HUAC) hearings of the late 1940s. Loy was a lifelong liberal who publicly opposed the hearings and the blacklist that resulted and took a dim view of those who supported the committee, the so-called "friendly witnesses." She called Bob one of the "tattletales." Loy also alleges that during the filming of *Lucky Night* Bob tried to cook up a "triangle" with hopes of making Barbara Stanwyck jealous. "He wanted her [Stanwyck] to think I was after him," Loy wrote nearly forty years later. "Barbara's maid mentioned this to Theresa [Loy's maid], who assured her that nothing could have been further from the truth. I'm not sure Barbara believed her, because on the last day of shooting she came by in a limousine and whisked him off to be married." (Not quite true, Bob and Stanwyck "whisked" off to be married during the making of his next film, *Lady of the Tropics*, with Hedy Lamarr.)[163]

When the picture was released in early May, the reviews were lukewarm at best. Frank Nugent in the *New York Times* found the

163 Myrna Loy, Being and Becoming, pg. 156

fault with the script, calling it "embarrassingly bad." The *New York Post* was slightly warmer, but not much. "Mr. Taylor is aggressively dashing but he scarcely fits the role of an introspective rebel against conventions." *Commonweal* called it a "mess."

Next, Bob was assigned to the aforementioned *Lady of the Tropics,* which teamed him with the sultry Hedy Lamarr. Lamarr had been signed by MGM in 1937 (she had actually been "discovered" by Mayer in England while he was there to launch the filming of *A Yank at Oxford*), but had been loaned out since then by the studio to appear opposite Charles Boyer in the romantic hit *Algiers* for independent producer Walter Wanger. *I Take This Woman* was to be Lamarr's first Metro film, but it was delayed (ultimately she would make it in 1940 with Spencer Tracy), so Metro assigned her *Lady of the Tropics* and Robert Taylor.

Lady of the Tropics casts Bob as an American playboy who meets, falls in love and then marries a Eurasian woman (Lamarr) in Saigon. What then follows is the uphill struggle to allow his wife to leave the country with him. The film, written by Ben Hecht, also explores the racism and double standards she experiences in French Indochina. The chemistry between Bob and Lamarr is fairly non-existent, but they certainly do look good together, but ultimately it is, once again, the script that does them in. The best part of the film is the presence of the lovely Gloria Franklin, playing Lamarr's sister. Her rendition of the song "Each Time You Say Goodbye I Die a Little" is the highlight of the film. For Taylor the highlight of making this film was his marriage to Stanwyck and return to the set all within about forty-eight hours. For Lamarr, the film and Taylor held no real attraction; they are barely mentioned in her autobiography. In *Time* magazine the producer, Sam Zimbalist, said, "Hedy is just a nice girl, not at all vain, and a hard worker. She has a natural allure . . . If anything, we've attempted to tone down the sex appeal she exudes." [164] He succeeded.

The film is significant in one respect; it was while in the middle of making this picture that Bob and Barbara finally, after three years of being together, tied the knot. It was a Saturday and both Bob and Barbara worked on their pictures when it was common practice to

164 Time, 8/28/39

work at least half-a-day on Saturdays with the expectation that Sunday would be their day off. At 7:30, that evening of May 13, they drove to San Diego to the home of Thomas Whelan, a San Diego attorney. The party included Marion Marx, Barbara's matron of honor, and Uncle Buck, who acted as Bob's best man (he also gave the bride away). Others in attendance were Zeppo Marx and Ida Koverman. The wedding party arrived in San Diego at around Midnight on the 14th. Whelan, a deputy county clerk, and his wife prepared a buffet supper just prior to the ceremony.

One other tiny thing they had to do before the wedding was give an exclusive scoop to Louella Parsons. Parsons later recalled that she received the call while she was sitting down to dinner at Constance Bennett's house. According to Parsons, when Bob was told she was sitting down to dinner he asked, "Where did we come in—between the soup and salad, or the fish and chips?" [165]

Bob wore a plain brown business suit while Barbara had on a navy-blue crepe silk dress. After supper the wedding party moved to the living room which overlooked San Diego Bay. The room had the fragrance of freshly cut roses which came from the Whelan's garden. Judge Phillip Smith, Justice of the Peace for San Diego Township, then conducted the brief ceremony. According to newspaper accounts, the Judge seemed a bit flustered as he had to clear his throat several times during the ceremony. Bob was said to be nervous while Barbara was the picture of serenity. The wedding ring that Bob gave Barbara was Gold with rubies around it and matched a bracelet that he had given to her the previous Christmas. As a wedding gift Bob gave Barbara a Gold St. Christopher Medal that was inscribed GOD PROTECT HER BECAUSE I LOVE HER. [166] Shortly thereafter, the wedding party returned to Los Angeles and the newlyweds to Barbara's ranch to spend the rest of the night before going to a midday press reception at the Beverly Hills Café.

At the reception Bob drew laughs when he told the assembled reporters, "Here I am married today and tomorrow I've got to be back at work making love to another woman." Bob revealed that they had actually decided more than two weeks before that they

165 St. Petersburg Times, 6/6/43

166 Barbara Stanwyck, Al DiOrio, pg. 120

would get married at the first available moment. In fact, they had taken a trip to San Diego on the 6th of May for a license from Whelen, who was a mutual friend. When asked where they would live, Barbara explained that, "we'll live on my ranch for the time being. I don't know where we'll live ultimately. Perhaps we'll sell either my home or Bob's or perhaps sell both of them and build a new house." Bob added, "And whichever one sells first, we'll move into the other."

At the press gathering the two held hands and smiled sweetly at one another, but didn't do what the reporters requested—kiss. "We'll just smile and look silly, I guess," Bob said. When asked if they would have children, Bob replied, "Well, we'll raise horses definitely."[167] From the reception Barbara returned to the ranch while Bob went to console Ruth, who hadn't been told of the wedding until they had returned from San Diego. She had never really warmed to Barbara, who she felt had already eclipsed her own hold on Bob.

So the question remains why did they decide to get married at a time when both were deep into production on films and couldn't enjoy a decent honeymoon. For the longest time MGM had opposed Bob getting married. They believed that it would damage his romantic quality. Bob couldn't care less; he didn't care for the screaming fans tearing at his clothes. In some ways he felt that if he did get married it might bring an end to the mob scenes he encountered anytime he stepped outside. Barbara, for her part, wasn't sure she wanted to get married so soon after her marriage to Frank Fay, and thus she never pressured Bob in the three years that they were together to marry her. The *Photoplay* story from January had undoubtedly changed some minds. Barbara and Bob were named as one of the unmarried couples and you didn't have to read between the lines to understand that the article was alleging what everybody in Hollywood knew: they were basically living together for much of the time, even though they had separate residences. Mayer, fearing a backlash, now came to the conclusion that Bob and Barbara marrying wouldn't necessarily be a bad thing. Further, they had been

167 press clips on wedding and reception from LA Times, Examiner, Citizen News, NY Herald Tribune 5/15/39

together for so long as a couple that people were beginning to wonder why they didn't tie the knot. The fact that Ida Koverman was a guest at the wedding is indication enough that MGM sanctioned the union; otherwise it is certain that the secretary of Louis B. Mayer would not be among the wedding guests.

To this day many have said it was an arranged wedding. Certainly, it was sanctioned by the studio and given its blessing but that doesn't necessarily mean it was a loveless marriage. There is every evidence to believe that Barbara was in love with Bob and even after they were divorced she would always regret the end of this marriage. Bob may have been less certain, but at the time he had been with Barbara for three years and he deeply respected her and certainly felt a kind of love for her. He had grown up around a strong, dominating woman and here was another one. In many ways it seemed normal for him to be with a woman who in some ways reminded him of his mother: a strong, determined woman who looked out for him. Ivy Mooring, later Bob's secretary and his confidante, when asked if she thought that the Taylor-Stanwyck marriage had been arranged replied, "No, and neither did Bob. He was from Nebraska, you know, and had these Midwestern values. He and Barbara had been together for a long time and to him marrying her was the next logical next step." [168] The nicknames that they used for each other also tended to show who really seemed to wear the pants in the house. Bob referred to Barbara as "Queen" while she, maternally and one assumes with affection, called him "Junior."

168 Ivy Mooring to author

Portrait Gallery #2

Bob and Barbara Stanwyck in a row boat from *His Brother's Wife* (1936)

From left to right, Victor McLaglen, Brian Donlevy, Bob and Barbara Stanwyck, *His Brother's Wife*

Publicity photo with Janet Gaynor, *Small Town Girl* (1936)

Another publicity shot, 1936

Camille with Greta Garbo contained one of Bob's signiture romantic performances.

Bob and Garbo, *Camille*, 1936

Bob carrying the dying Greta Garbo, *Camille*

Film poster of *Personal Property* (1937), the last film Jean Harlow completed.

Bob at Oxford, *A Yank at Oxford*, 1938

Bob on the set of *A Yank at Oxford*

An enchanting photo of Bob with Margaret Sullavan, *Three Comrades* (1938)

Bob, Margaret Sullavan and Franchot Tone in the snow, *Three Comrades*

Bob and Maureen O'Sullivan, *The Crowd Roars*, 1938

Bob wasn't only paired with leading ladies, here he is with Wallace Beery, *Stand Up and Fight*, 1939

Greer Garson, Lew Ayres and Bob from *Remember?* (1939)

At Lionel Barrymore's birthday party: First row (LEFT TO RIGHT), **Norma Shearer, Barrymore, Rosalind Russell. Back row** (LEFT TO RIGHT)**: Mickey Rooney, Robert Montgomery, Clark Gable, Louis B. Mayer, William Powell and Bob** (PHOTO COURTESY OF TERRY TAYLOR).

Bob loved horses, another publicity photo, circa 1939.

Chapter Six

Hitting His Stride (1940-1943)

Elizabeth Naden Kellar, Bob's old friend from college days at Doane, had made her way out to Hollywood to attend a convention. By chance Bob and Barbara were at the same event when they ran into each other. "Elizabeth Naden! What are you doing here?" he exclaimed as he warmly greeted her with a hug and then introduced her to Barbara. They all went outside to hide behind a fleet of cars so to avoid fans and catch-up. "Arlington had a problem with so much publicity all at once, " Kellar recalled of the chance meeting almost seventy years later. "He was a quiet type and it bothered him. Barbara was older, friendly, and very protective of him." Kellar also recalled that Barbara and Bob had a chauffeur who she called "Unc" who drove them that day.[169]

The chauffeur, who Barbara referred to as "Unc" is no doubt "Uncle Buck." When Bob married Barbara, he accepted into his household "Uncle Buck." Uncle Buck was James Buck McCarthy, a song-and-dance man in vaudeville when Barbara met him. He was her sister Millie's boyfriend and he took an interest in the younger Ruby Stevens. The young Ruby came to call him "Uncle Buck" and he helped her get one of her first jobs in show business. She never forgot his kindness toward her, and even though he never married Barbara's sister, Uncle Buck would be family to Stanwyck. From the mid-thirties on he would live in her various homes and run the household.

Bob ended 1939 by teaming with the fast-rising Greer Garson (fresh off *Goodbye, Mr. Chips*) in the comedy *Remember?* The film

---

169 Beth Naden Kellar to author

was pretty well drubbed by most critics. Its reputation continues to this day. with Leonard Maltin calling it a "blah comedy" in his *Movie and Video Guide*. But the film is actually quite amusing at times and better than its reputation. Neither Taylor nor Garson has a strong reputation for performing comedy, and yet when on the few occasions they were allowed, such as *Many Rivers to Cross* (for Taylor) and *Julia Misbehaves* (for Garson), they perform admirably enough. They also have good chemistry in this film, which Taylor lacked in his earlier comedy that year with Myrna Loy. The story itself is about an unhappily married couple who are heading for divorce court until they both take a potion which causes amnesia. This blocks out the memories of their marriage and the troubles they experienced and allows them to basically fall in love again. Luckily for the film, it has a first-rate comedy director in Norman Z. McLeod (the director of the Marx Brothers comedies *Monkey Business* and *Horse Feathers*), who makes this a brisk 82-minute film. Also aiding the picture immeasurably is a superb supporting cast, including standout performances by Lew Ayres, Billie Burke, Reginald Owen and Henry Travers.

When released, the *New York Times* spoke for the majority of reviewers when it wrote in a rather unoriginal way, "The story of 'Remember?' is one which you are going to find easy to forget." Taylor also wanted to forget *Remember?*, calling it a "regrettable dud," but with the compensation of working with Greer Garson who he called a "lovely and accomplished" lady[170] as well as "the acme of charming refinement."[171]

Bob's confidence by the end of 1939 was at a low. After three consecutive years in the top ten among box-office stars, Bob didn't make the cut in 1939. His films didn't generate the kind of buzz his earlier ones did and he was showing definite signs of a slowdown in his popularity with audiences. Perplexed, Bob arranged a screening at Universal of *Magnificent Obsession* to try and discover what it was that he had lost in the last three years. "What baffled me was that it was an instinctive piece of acting when I didn't know any better," he recalled. "I'd sit there in the darkness, getting myself all pepped

170 Films of Robert Taylor, pg. 79

171 Hollywood Citizen News, 4/22/46

up and then the picture would end—and boom!—down I'd go again." [172]

What he needed was a good script and when he got it he didn't really realize it. When he received the script of *Waterloo Bridge*, he very nearly turned it down. "The plot sounded uninspiring and the character struck me as ingenuous, wholly uncomplicated, just another of those juveniles from which I'd been trying to get away," he later recalled. [173] Luckily, the producer, Sidney Franklin, persuaded Bob he was perfect for the part of Roy Cronin. Reluctantly, Bob took on the role which would become his personal favorite of all of his films.

Waterloo Bridge was a play by Robert E. Sherwood, and was adapted by Universal as a film in 1931, which starred Mae Clark and Douglass Montgomery. The MGM version is told in flashback and opens with Bob standing on a bridge at the outset of another war, WWII, reflecting on the past Great War more than twenty years before and the love he found and lost. Roy Cronin is a soldier who falls in love with Myra, a ballerina. They plan to marry before he is shipped to the front, but are prevented from doing so due to army regulations. Her love is so great for him that when he is shipped away she sees him off from Waterloo Station, missing a performance which leads to her being fired from the ballet company she works with. She vainly attempts to find work, but nothing turns up as she sinks into poverty. She then learns that Roy may have been killed in action. Not caring about anything anymore she allows herself to sink into prostitution to earn a meager living. Months later she again encounters Roy at Waterloo Station. She is joyful that he is alive and attempts to hide the fact that she has been working as a prostitute. They decide to pick up where they left off and he takes her to his country home to meet his domineering mother, but her guilt about her recent past haunts her and she comes to believe that she isn't worthy of him and runs away to meet her doom.

MGM had negotiated the rights to the Sherwood play just months before from Universal. In close contention for the rights

172 Robert Taylor, J.E. Wayne, pg. 99-100

173 Saturday Evening Post, 7/27/46

was Selznick-International, which had just produced the biggest film of all-time, *Gone With the Wind*. MGM had just put up money, distribution and Clark Gable for *GWTW*. It was not surprising that somebody would think of Vivien Leigh for Myra since they needed an English girl—not to mention she had just dominated the screen in the most popular movie ever produced up to that time. Metro lost no time negotiating with David Selznick (who owned Leigh's contract) for Leigh's services for *Waterloo Bridge*, a film he had intended to star her in had he succeeded in buying the film rights. Getting Leigh meant one problem for MGM: her requests that her lover, Laurence Olivier, be cast opposite her as Roy. Not yet married, Leigh and Olivier were at the height of their passion. Now she was asking MGM if they didn't think that "Larry's" accent was just a "shade more natural" than Bob Taylor's. [174] But MGM had other plans for Olivier—casting him opposite Greer Garson in *Pride and Prejudice*. Leigh wasn't happy, but had no choice in the matter. She would write her estranged husband, with whom she managed to remain friendly all the while openly living with Olivier, "Robert Taylor is the man in the picture, and as it was written for Larry, it's a typical piece of miscasting. I am afraid it will be a dreary job." [175]

Despite this, Leigh would not act the prima-donna on the set. Why should she when she had David Selznick. Selznick demanded that Leigh be given top billing over the more established Taylor (a demand which Bob easily agreed to, and understandable in its way due to *GWTW*). Furthermore, in one of his infamous memos, Selznick spelled out his demands for the camera work on the film. He explained that they had to test several cameramen on *Gone With the Wind* before finding one who "caught her very strange beauty." He insisted he be consulted on and be given approval of the cameraman. He further asked that MGM protect her from bad close-ups "or anything of the kind will be re-taken, just as though she were your star, under contract, instead of ours." [176] Selznick need

174 Love Scene: The Story of Laurence Olivier and Vivien Leigh by Jesse L. Lasky, Jr. with Pat Silver pg. 105

175 Vivien by Alexander Walker, Weidenfeld & Nicolson, 1987 pg. 139

176 ibid

not be worried, the cinematographer selected, Joseph Ruttenberg, had won an Academy Award for his work on the 1938 film *The Great Waltz* and had also photographed such films as *Three Comrades, The Shopworn Angel, The Women* and had just finished shooting *The Philadelphia Story*. The close-ups in *Waterloo Bridge* are among the most lush and beautiful ever filmed and Ruttenberg won another Academy Award nomination for his work.

MGM surrounded Leigh and Taylor with its usual excellent supporting players, including Lucile Watson (as Roy's aristocratic mother) and C. Aubrey Smith, the very personification of the British Empire in his nearly one hundred films. Mervyn LeRoy, who had been a top director at Warner Brothers before coming to MGM a few years earlier to function primarily as a producer (he had produced *The Wizard of Oz* the prior year), returned to directing with this film.

The film began production in late January of 1940 and would be in production until the middle of March. It was a relatively smooth shoot. Leigh eased into the production and her apprehensions disappeared. She later told LeRoy that she enjoyed making *Waterloo Bridge* more than she had the ordeal of *Gone With the Wind*.[177] While she may have preferred Olivier, she got on well with Bob. Bob later recalled that while Leigh was being hailed as one of the greatest stars ever discovered, "this hadn't gone to her level little head. She proved a grand coworker, an intelligent, talented actress." He also said, "One of the most pleasant experiences Hollywood has brought me has been working again with Miss Leigh. When I first met her in London three years ago . . . she was just beginning to win recognition. She had an intense enthusiasm. And she still has. I was interested in talking to her about Scarlett O'Hara and got a typical reaction. She would like to have done over more than half her scenes in *Gone with the Wind*. They didn't satisfy her." [178] He would later add that Leigh was a "completely effortless actress. She works strenuously in her roles; yet few persons realize it. She can clown about the set one moment and the very next do a perfect dramatic scene before the camera."[179]

177 Mervyn LeRoy, Take One

178 St. Petersburg Times, 4/6/40

179 Hollywood Citizen News, 4/22/46

One of the technical problems making the film dealt with the fog. Much of the outdoor scenes set at Waterloo Station involved fog. LeRoy would recall that the soundstage was "always full of the acrid smell of what the studio manufactured for the effect." The studio was also saving money by the extensive use of fog as LeRoy also pointed out. "We could suggest a locale, and the fog would be so thick we didn't have to be too specific with our sets. There was one scene of Vivien walking on a bridge. All we did was build part of the sidewalk and string some lights across it, then fill the set with fog, and we had our bridge."[180]

One of the most memorable sequences in *Waterloo Bridge* involved Bob and Vivien in a nightclub on New Year's Eve. The sequence is memorable in part due to Vivien and Bob dancing as the orchestra played "Auld Lang Syne." The rendition of this song (used as a love theme) and the close-up of Taylor and Leigh, looking passionately at one another, followed by cuts to the orchestra (where each member has a candle on his music stand and one by one, they snuff them out) is incredibly romantic. As LeRoy later wrote in his autobiography, "Before all the candles were extinguished, the message was clear—they had fallen deeply, completely, in love. Not a word had been uttered."[181] The *New York Post* and other reviewers specifically pointed to this scene as one of the best in the picture. The *Post* wrote, "A dance by two lovers in a candle lit cabaret the night before his departure for the front will live in tender memory."

This would be the first picture that Bob Taylor would sport the pencil-thin mustache he would wear in several films over the course of his career. It had been pointed out that the majority of British officers wore a mustache during the First World War and so the decision for Taylor to wear one was considered one based on research. It struck a chord with his fans and made him look a bit more mature and so it stuck. It also struck a chord with Barbara, who made a special trip to MGM to view tests of Taylor in costume, wearing the newly grown mustache and giving her assent.[182]

---

180 Take One, pg. 147

181 ibid

182 Pittsburg Press, 2/27/40

Waterloo Bridge with its dynamic love story and combination of Leigh and Taylor was a big winner at the box office and restored Bob's confidence. The critics were, on the whole, generous as well. The *New York Times* Bosley Crowther was surprised that Bob gave such a "flexible and mature performance." *Variety* thought that the picture was "played with great sincerity, forcefully directed, compellingly translated into film and produced with distinction." In her widely syndicated column Louella Parsons wrote, "If you ever had doubts about Bob as an actor, his performance in *Waterloo Bridge* will dispel them. He is superb." One of the few poor reviews was by *Commonweal*, which wrote that the film was "slow-moving, sentimental and unconvincing." But most of the critical plaudits went to the picture and Miss Leigh, who, as she did in *Gone With the Wind*, dominates the screen time. Still, for Bob, it was a tremendous success as he was not playing one of his young, immature lovers, such as his Armand in *Camille* or Merrick in *Magnificent Obsession*, but he was performing with ease and conviction a mature characterization in a love story which touched the hearts of the many that saw it.

Bob would come to consider *Waterloo Bridge* his favorite film. He later said that the characters were "real, three-dimensional people—something which by no means always happens on the screen. It was one of those subtle situations in which everything clicks." [183] He would also say that he "felt surer of myself in scenes with Vivien Leigh in *Waterloo Bridge* than I have in any dramatic role that I have played." He went on to say, "I am not at all egotistical about some of the egotistical things that were said about me in *Waterloo Bridge*. Instead of being satisfied with myself, I feel that I have just made a beginning in the right direction, with a lot yet to learn." [184] Mervyn LeRoy would recall, "Bob Taylor, in his later years, when he knew he was dying, grew sentimental. Most actors keep and cherish prints of their pictures, but Taylor never had any. He told friends then that he would like a print of one picture he had made—*Waterloo Bridge* . . . he showed it often in his last months." [185]

---

183 Saturday Evening Post, 7/27/46

184 The Montreal Gazette, 11/30/40)

185 Take One, Mervyn LeRoy

II

Bob was attracted to the script of *Flight Command* because it again gave him the opportunity to get away from the romantic leading man roles he was coming to detest. Once more Bob is cast as a cocky young man whose arrogance earns him his comeuppance. When a member of the Navy "Hell Cat" squadron dies in a flying accident, a new recruit, a recent graduate of Pensacola, Alan Drake (played by Taylor), is assigned to take the dead cadet's place. Drake is certain that he was selected by the squadron and their much-admired commanding officer Bill Gray (Walter Pidgeon) because of his scholastic achievements, but these men, the best of the best, don't want a relatively inexperienced cadet, and they take a dislike to Drake whose arrogance turns them off. In the course of the story Gray's wife (Ruth Hussey) finds herself becoming close to Drake, especially after her brother, another flyer, is killed while trying out an experimental instrument. Meanwhile, the men of the squadron hear of marital problems between their commanding officer and his wife and assume Drake is at fault, making him more of an outcast. However, Drake redeems himself when he saves Gray, whose plane is in danger of crashing when it runs out of fuel. Hussey, realizing she still loves him, returns to her husband and by the final fadeout Drake is an accepted member of the Hell Cats.

Selected to direct the film is Frank Borzage. Borzage seemed an odd choice given that many of his films were romantic in nature and often featured a strong female lead that the camera could gaze upon in loving close-up. The female lead of this film, Ruth Hussey, does a superb job, but her story is secondary to the action between Taylor and his fellow cadets. Borzage himself was a pilot and had a strong admiration for the Air Force and does a fine job of helming this film which one might think would be right up the ally of directors like Victor Fleming, Howard Hawks, and William Wellman.

The flying sequences are compelling and superbly filmed and for that recognition must be given to Paul Mantz, commonly known as "Hollywood's Pilot" for his stunt work and directing of aerial sequences for such films as *Air Mail* (where he became the first pilot to fly a plane thru a hangar on film), *Ceiling Zero, Only Angels Have*

Wings, God is My Co-Pilot, and *Twelve O'Clock High.* Mantz also became friendly with many Hollywood stars with an interest in aviation, such as Bob, Clark Gable and Jimmy Stewart, and owned an air service business that was extensively used by his connections in Hollywood and nicknamed the "Honeymoon Express" due to the stars who used him to get to Nevada for quickie marriages. Sadly, Mantz died in 1965 while filming a stunt for the film *The Flight of the Phoenix.*

The reviews were mixed. The *New York Times* acerbic new critic, Bosley Crowther, called the picture "moldy" and full of "obvious clichés." But he, like most of the other critics, applauded the flying sequences calling them "beautiful." On the other coast the *Los Angeles Times* praised the picture and the topical nature of the film (released while Europe was at war and less than a year before Pearl Harbor), "It is probably the first feature of its type . . . and has exceptional news value in the light of events today." The film went on to be a solid winner at the box office.[186]

Another consequence of making this film was to become Taylor's passion for aviation, which would last the remainder of his life. Shortly after completing the picture he began taking flying lessons, much to Barbara's chagrin. She hated flying and whenever possible would opt for the train rather than fly. Bob's love of flying never interested Stanwyck and in the end was just another of the issues that drove them apart. Bob could easily get away for a weekend with his buddies by flying to some hunting location or rather than travel with his wife on the train would fly on ahead of her and meet her when she arrived. Barbara did get a good quip, however, out of Bob's obsession with flying: "Bob can do anything a bird can do, except balance himself on a barbed wire fence."[187]

Bob's next picture allowed him to take on the Nazis head-on, in the filming of Ethel Vance's bestselling novel *Escape* (bought by Metro in 1939 for $50,000). Bob plays the American-born son of a former

---

186 Bob performed a radio adaptation of "Flight Command" on Lux Radio Theatre on 3/24/41. He made two more appearance in the next year on "Lux"—in "Penny Serenade opposite Barbara on 4/27/42 and then was joined by Rita Hayworth and Robert Preston for "Test Pilot" on 5/25/42.

187 Tay Garnett, Light Your Torches & Pull Up Your Tights

famed German actress who is awaiting a death sentence at the hands of the Nazis at a concentration camp in the Bavarian Alps. After hearing from a friend that she had been arrested, the son arrives in Germany to search for his mother. He receives aid from a countess, the American-born widow of a German nobleman and currently the mistress of a Nazi general. The countess is played by Norma Shearer, the former Queen Bee of the Metro lot, and still a force to be reckoned with because of her share of Metro stock.

The script is tight and suspenseful, which would have been perfect for the talents of the newly-arrived British director Alfred Hitchcock. Taylor's character in this film has much in common with Hitchcock's usual hero, the ordinary man up against extraordinary circumstances. In fact, Metro originally offered him the project and Hitchcock was intrigued, according to Shearer biographer Gavin Lambert.[188] However, Hitchcock knew that MGM was a producer's studio, which kept most of their directors under strong supervision, and turned the project down. He had just been under the close eye of David Selznick while filming *Rebecca*, an experience that was less than optimal for Hitchcock. Instead, he went on loan-out for Walter Wanger to make *Foreign Correspondent* and was basically left to call his own shots. With Hitchcock out, *Escape* ended up going to Mervyn LeRoy.

The filming went quickly, four weeks with a few days of retakes later on (these retakes were directed by George Cukor). The only problem was that the actor that LeRoy cast as Shearer's Nazi husband, Paul Lukas, needed to be replaced because, in LeRoy's words, he was "misinterpreting" the role.[189] Luckily for LeRoy, the man that he originally wanted to play the part, Conrad Veidt, was now available and stepped in and did a suitably menacing job. Bob got along well with Shearer, but the relationship had little warmth. Later on when asked to describe Shearer he gave a two-word answer, "A perfectionist."[190] They would work together again two years later in the escapist comedy *Her Cardboard Lover*, a film which fizzled at the box office, and led Shearer to retire from the screen.

---

188 Gavin Lambert, Norma Shearer

189 Mervyn LeRoy, Take One

190 Films of Robert Taylor, pg. 11

Escape premiered at Radio City Music Hall on October 31, 1940, to strong reviews. *TIME* magazine said the picture was "a powerful true bill against Nazism's ruthlessness." The *New York Times* applauded LeRoy for following the novel's construction with "fidelity," and called the picture, "the most dramatic and hair-raising picture yet made on the sinister subject of persecution in a totalitarian land." The *Times* lauded the supporting actors, but was more reserved about the two leads. Bob seemed to come out slightly better than Shearer. "Robert Taylor, as the young American, plays with becoming self-possession but a hint of obtuseness which is bad. Norma Shearer as the countess, is much too affected for the role." Still, the final verdict of the *Times* is that the "picture crackles with vitality." *Commonweal* praised the "powerful visualization of terrifying scenes of suspense," and called *Escape* a "stirring" film. *Modern Screen*, however, found the two leads "excellent." The film, produced for $1.2 million, was a moderate hit at the box office, bringing in nearly $1.4 million domestically and just over a $1 million in the shrinking foreign markets for a net profit of $345,000. One market which it didn't have access to was Germany where Adolf Hitler banned the film because of its anti-Nazi message.

III

In 1940, Barbara sold the Northridge ranch house to actor Jack Oakie. By the late summer Bob, Barbara and Dion (who still spent much of his time away at military school) moved into a new home, a large 16-room mansion near North Arden Road in Beverly Hills. *Screen Guide* magazine wrote a story on the house: "[It] hasn't a gaudy room in it, lacks all the modernistic gadgets which they had in their ranch house (now for sale). Upstairs, Bob's room and Barbara's are separated by a small study. She sleeps in her own quarters when one or the other or both are working in a picture, have to get up at 6 in the morning, retire at 10. Bob's room is decorated in mannish style, with a huge bed filling most of the room. Beyond that is a tiny gymnasium where Bob works out, gets a massage after a tough day at the studio. Downstairs, leading off the formal living rooms, is a room that looks like Madison Square Garden—Don's stamping-grounds, cluttered with games, ships, croquet mallets. Strangely, the house has no back door. The only way to get into the back yard is through the bar, a hole-in-the-wall spot stocked with choice liquors, touched only by guests on party evenings." [191]

When Barbara first spoke about this house to reporters, she was combating rumors that the Taylors were about to split up. They spent so much time apart due to their mutually busy careers, and the Hollywood community had noticed. In fact, at the time that she spoke with the press, Bob was relaxing at their Palm Springs home while Barbara was in Hollywood. But she was adamant. "Bob and I are building a house in Beverly Hills," she said. "Does that sound as if we were getting a divorce?" [192]

Bob also got into the act of replying to these divorce rumors. He wrote an open letter to the editor of *Motion Picture* magazine. "The rumor, though unfortunate, did not come as a surprise to either Barbara or myself," he wrote. "Actually we have been expecting it. It seems most inevitable that when picture people have been married over a year, rumors of this sort arise . . . May I assure you and hope that you will assure your readers, in turn, that all such rumors are entirely unfounded and untrue." [193]

At home Barbara wasn't exactly the domestic type. If she wasn't working on a picture, she was invariably reading one book after another. It wasn't uncommon for her to begin and finish a book in one day. Except for the one day per week the cook had off she stayed out of the kitchen. She did, however, enjoy redecorating rooms and moving furniture. "I have a passion for moving furniture from one place to another," she related. "Bob says he'd never sit down in any room in the dark because he'd be sure to land on the floor. I love to change colors in furniture, too. If I could afford it, I'd redecorate my house every month. When Bob sees me eyeing the davenport, he knows it will be changed from gray to lipstick red next week!" [194]

While Ruth is often portrayed as being at odds with Bob's marriage to Barbara, at least outwardly she tried to put a pleasant

191 Screen Guide 8/40

192 Robert Taylor, J.E. Wayne, pg. 104

193 Motion Picture Magazine 4/41

194 Barbara Stanwyck, pg. 128-129

spin on it to friends. "Arlington is so grand to me," she wrote a friend around Christmas, 1940, "and now I have a daughter, she is so dear too. They act like they could not give me enough . . ."[195]

By the early forties Bob and Barbara were one of Hollywood's golden couples. While Bob was making his comeback with films like *Waterloo Bridge* and *Escape*, Barbara was keeping up the pace. She was enjoying huge popularity in such films as *Remember the Night* (opposite Fred MacMurray), *Meet John Doe* (with Gary Cooper) and showing a strong comedic edge in *The Lady Eve* (with Henry Fonda) and *Ball of Fire* (Cooper again). In fact, this last named film earned her a second Academy Award nomination for her performance as a showgirl who teaches a timid professor slang (as well as how to come out of his shell). In fact, the early to mid-forties would constitute the strongest period of Barbara's film career.

Jack Benny and his wife Mary Livingstone were among the best friends that the Taylors had. The Bennys and Taylors would often be seen at the races together and Jack and Bob occasionally went to the fight and ball games together. Benny's daughter Joan recalled the Taylors as "my parents' closest friends after the [George] Burnses." She admired Barbara a great deal "for her talent and loved her looks" and her ability not to speak down to her as a child. They were regulars at the sparkling parties that Jack and Mary threw at their Beverly Hills home on Roxbury Drive. Joan would recall the "glittering parties . . . how beautiful the women were in their evening gowns and jewels and how handsome the men in their dinner jackets." Joan recalled Barbara looking "slim and elegant" with Bob and other guests such as the Van Johnsons, George and Gracie Burns, the Ray Millands, Robert Montgomerys, Gary Coopers, and Danny Kayes.[196]

Bob also enjoyed working with Benny on his highly-rated Sunday evening radio series. Two episodes in particular standout. On February 13, 1938, a Valentine's Day-themed episode, showed Bob's attempts to teach Benny how to play a love scene. A highlight of this episode is a cello-violin duet between Jack and Bob. The other interesting episode came years later, in 1948, when Bob subbed

195 Linda Alexander, Reluctant Witness, pg. 147

196 Sunday Nights at Seven, pg. 61-62

for Jack when Benny was ill. The show, which included Bob interacting with Benny's roster of supporting players, went over very well. In fact, the following week Jack acknowledged this when he did a gag where Benny's sponsor calls him mid-monologue to suggest that Jack take more time off!

Bob and Barbara, like many of their friends, had a home in Palm Springs. Joan Benny would recall that her first boyfriend was Dion, who she knew as "Skip." "He was adorable with his freckles and sandy blonde hair," she later recalled. "He sent me my first love letter—in almost indecipherable capital letters scrawled all over the page it said with classic simplicity, I LOVE YOU. I was four and he was five. Together we picked wild flowers in an enormous field behind the El Mirador, rode our bikes and explored the neighborhood. And possible each other as well."[197] For the most part, Dion was gone attending military school, and was home mainly at holidays and only a short time during the summer, when he was boarded off to camp. But even when he was around, Barbara and Bob rarely had time for the boy. They were too busy working at a furious pace. The boy grew closest to "Uncle Buck." This doesn't mean that Bob never took interest in him. When he was around, he did try to interest Dion in some of the things he was interested in, hunting, fishing, horses, but these turned out to be things that didn't seem to interest Dion. In short, they never really bonded. Dion called him "Gentleman Bob" and liked him, but thought he had no real say in his upbringing.[198]

When they did have friends over (such as the Reagans, Bennys and the Marxs), it was more likely than not to be a laidback affair such as a patio barbecue with Bob in front of a grill watching over the steaks while Barbara made a salad. Barbara, for all of her bravado on film, was very much an introvert privately—in contrast to Bob who greatly enjoyed getting together with friends. "I don't believe I'll ever get over the fear of going into a group of stranger," she once said. "If I'm to visit Ty Power and Annabella and know that the Millands or the Bennys are to be there, I'm all right. But if I think I won't know anyone, I suffer horrors."[199]

197 ibid

198 Stanwyck, Madsen, pg. 180

199 Barbara Stanwyck, pg. 129

Another couple that Bob and Barbara knew socially was Ronald Reagan and his wife Jane Wyman. Both Reagan and Wyman were under contract to Warner Brothers. When Reagan first came to Hollywood in 1937, he was invited to the same talent agency which represented Bob among other major stars. Reagan made a good impression with his tall, dark good looks. The agent immediately picked up the phone and called a casting director at Warner Brothers and told him, "I've got another Robert Taylor sitting in my office." Reagan later said that he heard the response over the phone, "God only made one Robert Taylor." [200]

In October of 1940 the first peacetime draft was enacted in response to the war in Europe. Bob was given his draft number. "Robert Taylor may be a heart throb to millions of American girls," wrote United Press, "but to the draft board he is simply No. 363." The article added, "However, the board has to take into consideration the fact that he's a married man." Among the other actors given their conscription numbers were: Henry Fonda (#132), Tony Martin (#374), Cesar Romero (#1811), Ray Milland (#2658) and John Payne (#3511). [201]

IV

Bob's next film, *Billy the Kid*, was one he greatly enjoyed making because it offered him his first chance to play in a genre that he would become increasingly identified with in his postwar career—the Western film. *Billy the Kid* also became Bob's first film shot in Technicolor. The film was to be a color remake of an earlier film also produced by Metro, directed by King Vidor and starring cowboy actor Johnny Mack Brown. At the time that this new version of the Billy the Kid story was being discussed and filmed Howard Hughes was getting a great deal of publicity out of his version of the story (titled *The Outlaw*) originally directed by Howard Hawks (though ultimately Hughes himself would take over the direction), and starring Jack Buetel (as the Kid) and Jane Russell's bosoms. Due to censorship problems, among other things, this film was not released (and then only a limited release) until 1943 and finally got a full

200 Ronnie & Nancy, pg. 68-69

201 Pittsburg Press, 10/27/44

theatrical release in 1946 when it cleaned up at the box office. Bob's version was produced between December of 1940 and April of 1941 and released at the end of May.

Chosen to direct was Frank Borzage and it was he who, on December 16, 1940, took a team of some 150 technicians and actors to the beautiful Monument Valley to begin location filming. The Monument Valley had been used as a backdrop for previous films, most notably in 1939 for John Ford's *Stagecoach*. This, however, would be the first time that the majesty and beauty of the valley would be seen in color. Borzage filmed for some four weeks but because of mental exhaustion (and, according to his biographer, too much booze[202]) due to his divorce Metro relieved him of his duties. Borzage had managed to complete much of the location shooting and when the cast and crew returned to Culver City Metro assigned a short-feature director, David Miller, to complete the picture. It is Miller who gets directorial credit. Miller would go on to direct such films as *Flying Tigers* (with John Wayne), *Top o' the Morning* (Bing Crosby), *Midnight Lace* (Doris Day) and *Captain Newman, M.D.* (Gregory Peck). It appears that with Borzage out and Miller in that there was a script rewrite which de-emphasized the role of the daughter and led to Maureen O'Sullivan leaving the picture and Mary Howard being brought in.

Dressed all in black and essaying his first screen villain (with shades of gray) Taylor turns in a good performance. He isn't yet as comfortable with the Western genre as he would get in later years, but he looks as solid in a Western film as the young John Wayne did in his first big Western role, *The Big Trail* (1930). (From 1949–1967, Taylor would appear in eleven Western films as well as host and occasionally act in the Western anthology series *Death Valley Days*. Taylor became so identified with the genre that he posthumously won the Golden Spur Award, which is given out annually for outstanding contributions to the Western genre.) Taylor later said that he "loved that picture." Initially, he said that when he filmed his death scene he wanted to have a "hard glint" in his eyes. But because of his blue eyes he didn't think he could put it over in Technicolor, so he went to an eye doctor who gave him drops to

202 Dumont & Kaplansky, Frank Borzage

make his pupils contract. "He fixed me up all right," Taylor recalled. "Then, soon as the lights trained on me for my death scene I went blind and production had to be called off. Next time I did it straight—with my own blue eyes."[203]

Bob told reporters that he had wanted to make a Western ever since he began working in films. "In fact, if I had my choice I'd never have done anything else. Bill Hart and Tom Mix were my earliest film idols. When I was a kid I would see their films over and over again. One day I took my lunch to the movie theatre and stayed through nine showings of a Mix picture." He also was so taken with Arizona that he said he is considering buying a ranch there. "I want a practical cattle ranch and the more acreage the better."[204]

For the most part Bob got good reviews for *Billy the Kid.* The *New York Post* thought that Bob gave a "distinguished performance" and looked well on a horse and handling a gun. The *Chicago Tribune* thought that the film was "engrossing and colorful" and that "many of us are busy thinking how handsome Mr. Taylor is, that we forget the chap really can act." But, as was often the case with Bob, the *New York Times* dissented, calling the film "just another routine horse opera" and that Bob's Kid is "stuffed with too much straw. Vaguely, he gives the impression of a kid in a new cowboy suit." *Commonweal* snickered at how the studio cleansed the Kid: "My! What a nice boy has been made out of Billy the Kid." Audiences seemed to like the results as the film became one of Bob's biggest box-office hits.

Bob's next picture was a welcome change of pace—a screen comedy—his first since *Remember?* in 1939. Taylor proves in this film that he could be a quite enjoyable light leading man. Certainly he was no Cary Grant at screen comedy, but he allows himself to loosen up considerably and appears to be having a good time on screen in this drawing-room comedy.

When Ladies Meet is based on a play which had been made into a motion picture for MGM back in 1933 with Ann Harding, Robert Montgomery and Myrna Loy. Taylor plays a playboy newspaperman

203 NY Times, 2/2/47

204 Montreal Gazette, 6/24/41

who is trying to win back a former flame, a novelist (Joan Crawford), who has been having a dalliance with a married publisher (Herbert Marshall). He plans to bring Crawford together with the married publisher's wife (Greer Garson) at a country house, owned by the amusing Spring Byington, in hopes that the two will discover each other's identity and that Crawford will come to her senses and leave Marshall for him.

At the time this film was made Crawford was in a career slump, having been named "box-office poison" a couple of years earlier. Her more recent pictures had not been terribly successful at the box office. At the same time Greer Garson was on her way up. She had appeared in such prestigious and popular films as *Goodbye, Mr. Chips, Pride and Prejudice*, and *Blossoms in the Dust.* There were also rumors that Metro was trying to get rid of Crawford, one of their top actresses since 1925, by giving her inferior projects while building up Garson. In the midst of filming Garson was nominated for an Academy Award for her performance in *Blossoms in the Dust* while Crawford was overlooked for her excellent work in *A Woman's Face.* Garson, who was enjoying the opportunity to work in a modern screen comedy, didn't want to engage Crawford in a feud. "Joan was just completely nonplussed when I refused to feud with her," she told her biographer. "She tried very hard to feud with me because she felt it was natural to feud with every other actress on the lot."[205] In fact, within two years, Crawford would be gone from MGM and Garson would be the new Queen of the lot thanks to her Oscar-winning performance in *Mrs. Miniver* (a film, incidentally, that Norma Shearer turned down in order to work with Bob in the comedy *Her Cardboard Lover*). Despite whatever tension there may have been on the set between the two leading ladies (for the record Crawford gets top billing) the film is smoothly directed by Robert Z. Leonard and it is fun seeing these three essentially dramatic actors let their hair down and perform engagingly in a comedy.

When the picture opened, the reviews were mixed. The *New York Times* thought that the film was dated and somewhat talky. Bob came out best as far as performances. "Robert Taylor does all right—in fact, he does surprisingly well—as the bouncing newspaper writer

---

205 A Rose for Mrs. Miniver

whose job and whose ardor are conveniently vague." The *New York Post* was even more positive about Taylor's performance. "Taylor has most of the real action and a great deal of the comedy to interpret and he is rarely at a loss." *Commonweal* also praised Bob's comedic performance: "Robert Taylor is sprightly as the man about town."

V

Mervyn LeRoy directed Bob for the third time in two years with *Johnny Eager*. In it, LeRoy, who also produced, teamed Bob with one of his sexiest leading ladies, Lana Turner. MGM expected box-office dynamite and, in fact, its ad campaign screamed TNT indicating the dynamic star teaming of Taylor and Turner. Bob specifically asked to do this film. "If the studio had any misgivings about it [his playing a criminal], it was only because I personally like the script so much," he said at the time. "Mr. Mayer ribs me about that because I've pleaded to do pictures that turned out sort of badly, and I've battled to keep out of pictures that went ahead to become hits." (He may have been specifically thinking of *Waterloo Bridge*.) [206]

For Bob it was another tough guy role. In it he plays the title role, a ruthless racketeer who is paroled and seemingly going straight working as a taxi driver. But behind the scenes he is still deeply involved in the rackets, including the operations of a lucrative dog track. Enter Miss Turner playing the do-good daughter of the crusading district attorney (played by Edward Arnold) who had put Johnny behind bars in the first place. They meet in his cab and when he finds out who she is he decides to use her as a pawn, going as far to "gaslight" her into thinking she has committed murder. Eventually, however, Johnny falls in love with Turner and in the typical production code fade-out he must redeem himself and pay for his sins.

No doubt about it: Taylor's Johnny Eager is a no-account ruthless bastard—and Bob plays him with gusto. It is one of his finest pre-war screen performances. Turner, too, excels in a part which allowed her to prove she was an actress as well as a sex goddess. She never had a better opportunity prior to this film and wouldn't have

---

206 Kentucky New Era, 9/18/41

as good a chance again until she made *The Postman Always Rings Twice*. Along with Taylor and Turner is Van Heflin, in the showy role of an alcoholic confidante of Eager's. Heflin gives a fine performance and won the Academy Award as Best Supporting Actor for his work, but this is Taylor's picture all the way—and, unfortunately, the Academy decided to overlook him when they made their nominations for Best Actor. Along with Taylor, Turner, Heflin and Arnold, the cast impressively includes Robert Sterling, Barry Nelson, Paul Stewart and Glenda Farrell.

Off screen there was TNT too between Taylor and Turner. Three years into his marriage to Barbara it became increasingly apparent to Bob that while he respected Barbara enormously and felt a kind of love for her, it wasn't a deep-seated, passionate kind of love. He was also feeling increasingly smothered by her. On screen he and MGM had been taking pains to develop a more masculine screen image while in his private life he often felt overwhelmed by his wife. Needless to say, Bob found Turner's fresh sexiness quite alluring. He later admitted that during the filming of *Johnny Eager* he "couldn't take my eyes off her . . . there were times I thought I'd explode." He found her coquettish. "Lana Turner wasn't very career-minded, and preferred men and jewelry over anything else." Just the sound of her voice saying "good morning" made Taylor "melt." He admitted that he never really went after blondes, but, "Lana was the exception." He summed up his feelings for Lana crudely, but with perfect honesty: "She was the type of woman for whom a guy would risk five years in jail for rape." [207]

Turner, in her autobiography, would admit that Bob had the kind of looks "I could fall for," and that they engaged in a romantic flirtation (at least on her part) which included passionate kisses, but nothing more. The one stumbling block to pursuing a more romantic (or sexual) relationship with Taylor, according to Turner, was Barbara. Lana didn't want to be cast as the "other woman" who stole Taylor from Stanwyck. Bob told Lana that he was unhappy at home with Barbara and had fallen in love with her. Furthermore, he was going to tell Barbara about his love for her and wanted a divorce so he could presumably marry Lana. Turner writes that she

207 Forties Film Talk, pg. 357, Doug McClelland, McFarland, 1992

asked Bob not to do this. "Don't make me the solution for your marital problems," she told him.[208] But he did it anyhow and the result was that Barbara, feeling betrayed and hurt, left him for several days, staying at the house of her maid, Harriet Coray.

The filming of *Johnny Eager* also coincided with a trip to the hospital by Barbara on October 7, 1941, suffering from gashes to her arms and wrists. Bob later explained to reporters that the injuries occurred when Barbara tried to open a sealed window at their Beverly Hills home and accidentally broke her hand and arm thru the glass. According to one Stanwyck biographer, there was talk around Hollywood that this was a suicide attempt by Barbara, who was distraught over Bob's confession to her about Turner and his wanting a divorce. From that point forward Turner contends she cooled it with Bob, until he finally understood that they would not have a future together. There are those who dispute that Taylor and Turner never were lovers and believe that while Taylor was sexually attracted to Turner he wasn't going to leave Barbara for her. Whatever the story, according to Turner, Barbara was not the forgive-and-forget type.

Johnny Eager did turn out to be TNT at the box office, but even more satisfying for Bob was that he got mostly good reviews for his work. *Variety* said that Bob handled his characterization "effectively." The *New York Times* said that under LeRoy's direction "Taylor seems nearly as cold-blooded as he sounds" and that Taylor and Turner "strike sparks." The *New York Daily News* opined that Bob's Eager is "really tough—he pulls no punches." But not all the reviews were positive. *TIME* magazine labeled *Johnny Eager* as yet "another attempt to hirsute handsome Robert Taylor . . . It's no use. Mr. Taylor won't toughen up. He's too nice to be a melodramatic mobster, and he shows it."

Just six weeks after *Johnny Eager* had been completed, Hollywood, like the nation as a whole, was taken by surprise by the Japanese attack on Pearl Harbor. The United States was now at war not only with Japan but with Germany and its allies. Hollywood had already begun to take on the Nazis in some films (including *Escape*), but now the studios would be on a wartime footing and they were only

---

208 Lana—The Lady, The Legend

too willing to use their resources to aid the war cause not only by producing patriotic wartime pictures and sell war bonds but to sacrifice to the military some of their stars. For instance, David Niven had already returned to his native England to join the Royal Air Force. James Stewart had enlisted into the Army. MGM hoped that their two biggest male stars, Clark Gable and Robert Taylor, would be exempt due to the fact that they were married and overage, Gable in particular, at 40 years of age.

The Hollywood stars began traveling to sell war bonds. One of the most enthusiastic from the get-go was Carole Lombard. Less than a month after the war started she began a war bond drive which took her into the Middle West. Traveling with her mother she had completed the tour and was in a hurry to return to Hollywood and her husband, Clark Gable, who was shooting a movie with Lana Turner. The plane she was traveling in made it to Las Vegas for refueling and then in the midst of a storm took off again. Minutes later the plane crashed into the side of a mountain; all on board were killed instantly. Gable was inconsolable. The Hollywood community only slightly less so. When Bob received word of Carole's death, he was quoted as saying, "There is nothing one can say. It is too terrible."[209] Barbara and Bob attended her funeral. Gable reluctantly completed his picture and announced that he would honor Carole's memory by enlisting into the Air Force. MGM couldn't talk him out of it. The King was going to leave, but they wanted to hold on as long as possible to Bob, who was also eager to enlist, and cast him in two wartime pictures. Bob did make a contribution to the war effort in February by donating his monoplane, which had been grounded since the outbreak of the war (on the Pacific coast amateur aircraft was grounded for the duration of the war). The donated plane was given to the Los Angeles Sheriffs Air Squadron.[210]

The first of the wartime pictures was *Stand by for Action*. The film cast Bob as a cocky Harvard-educated Lieutenant and aide to a Rear Admiral ("Iron Pants" Thomas), played with crusty authority by Charles Laughton. Brian Donlevy is cast as Taylor's adversary, a

209 LA Times, 1/18/42

210 Hartford Courant, 2/25/42

Lieutenant Commander who came up by his bootstraps and thinks that the Taylor character is trying to delay his ship's return to action. The Rear Admiral assigns Donlevy to a long-out-of-action destroyer and then makes Taylor his executive officer; they now will have to find a way to work together to aid the war effort. Along with the three leads is Walter Brennan, cast as an aging seaman who Taylor champions when Donlevy wants to put him out to pasture. Marilyn Maxwell, Henry O'Neill, Chill Wills, Douglass Dumbrille and a young pre-directorial Richard Quine fill out the cast. Robert Z. Leonard directs and co-produces the film, and one of the three writers is Herman Mankiewicz, who also co-wrote *Citizen Kane* with Orson Welles.

Initially, this film was meant to star Robert Donat, who had won an Academy Award for his performance in *Goodbye, Mr. Chips* in 1939, with Edmund Gwenn cast as the Rear Admiral, and was to be set in England and focus on the war in Europe. Instead, due to the intensity of the actual war in England at the time filming was to begin, the decision was made to bring the film back to Hollywood *sans* Donat, with a rewrite script (but not basic story) changing the location from England to the United States and dealing with the US Navy and the war in the Pacific rather than in the Atlantic. This is a typical Robert Taylor film characterization from the thirties about a willful young man, who has all the advantages, who is taken down a peg or two and ends up being a better person because of it.

One of the most stirring scenes in the film occurs when Charles Laughton recites the Declaration of Independence. He did it in one take and by memory. Leonard suggested cue cards, but the British actor knew the Declaration by heart and refused Leonard's gesture. When the scene was completed, the cast and crew gave Laughton a spontaneous round of applause.

While *Stand by for Action* certainly had its patriotic heart in the right place, it didn't fare too well with critics. Bosley Crowther of the *New York Times* compared it unfavorably with the Noel Coward British war film *In Which We Serve*, which he called a "superior picture." Bob didn't fare much better. "Mr. Taylor—how shall we say?—is not impressive in a very fatuous role." But, then, none of the other actors were applauded by Crowther, who felt Donlevy was merely "adequate" and that Laughton played his part like "a character out of H.M.S. Pinafore." Despite the less-than-stellar critical reaction, the film went on to be a solid winner at the box office.

Faring much better with critics was Bob's second 1943 wartime drama, the excellent *Bataan*. *Bataan*, while not a fact-based film is pulled out of the headlines of the actual war, much like the 1942 Paramount film *Wake Island*. (In fact, its story is partly based on the 1934 John Ford film *The Lost Patrol*, where members of a brigade are killed one by one until there is only one man left to heroically die fighting to the end.) *Bataan* tells the story of the battle of the Philippines during the end of 1941 and into 1942 as the Japanese invaded and gradually overran the combined American and Filipino troops. The Americans made a last ditch effort in the Bataan Peninsula, where they heroically held for several months, but eventually the Japanese won the battle and this led to the infamous Bataan Death March. Our film tells the story of one such brigade, which held out until the very end, with Bob leading a rear guard suicide mission, trying to protect the American retreat along the peninsula. In many ways it is a character study of men under fire and the courage of war. Bob plays a grim, hardened, and unshaven sergeant in a cast which includes George Murphy as a Air Force lieutenant; Lloyd Nolan as the wisecracker in the outfit, but still someone all can depend on; Thomas Mitchell as a career soldier; and Robert Walker, in his film debut, gives a strong performances as a young, homesick sailor. Also included in the film in good performances (mostly) devoid of the usual Hollywood stereotypes are Desi Arnaz as a Spanish soldier, Kenneth Spencer as a black soldier and Roque Espiritu as a Filipino soldier.

Bataan was well directed by Tay Garnett, who had been around Hollywood since 1922 both as a film writer and director. Among the films that Garnett directed prior to *Bataan* include *One Way Passage, China Seas,* and *Seven Sinners*. Garnett was a journeyman director who often did better than efficient work. His biggest film would come just after the war when he directed Lana Turner and John Garfield in the *film noir* classic *The Postman Always Rings Twice*. Garnett was justly proud of *Bataan*. He later wrote that he was determined to make the film and offered a pay cut to MGM just to get the directorial reins, "that turned the trick."[211]

The film did not utilize outdoor sets, but was shot entirely on Soundstage 16 at MGM, and at times looks it, but that doesn't take away from the intensity of the action in the least. Garnett would later recall that he decided to utilize the ground fog that is prevalent in a humid jungle climate. To create this the special effects department devised a plan to dump dry ice into tubs of water. Then, using fans, it blew the vapors onto the set effectively creating this tropical atmosphere. There was one problem: the fumes were lethal. When submerged in the manufactured fog, the extras, who were supposed to be advancing upon Taylor at the end as he is alone and manning his machine gun, were required to hold their breath and keep their eyes closed, and only breathe when they lifted their heads above the ground fog. It was dangerous, but effective on film. At the end, after Taylor is killed and falls back into the grave he himself dug, the picture was supposed to dissolve with the camera peeled on the motionless machine gun Taylor had been manning, but this was considered too downbeat of an ending for Louis B. Mayer, who instructed Garnett to dissolve to a shot of the American flag and the voice of Gen. Douglas MacArthur proclaiming "I shall Return."[212] Garnett understood what Mayer was aiming for—to allow the audience to leave the theater with hope, but he still didn't like it. "I still deplore what I regarded as a betrayal of artistic integrity."[213]

Garnett was happy with his cast. "Bob Taylor was one of the world's great gentlemen," he later recalled of his star. "He was serious minded, hard working, and keen. In spite of his astounding good looks, he was determined to be a fine actor, and not merely a star."[214] Garnett wasn't the only one on the *Bataan* set to be impressed by Bob; his co-star Lloyd Nolan felt that Bob was underrated by many people because of his good looks and that Taylor himself was inclined to downplay his own talent. "I think Bob Taylor had to fight two things—his great beauty as a man," Nolan told Jane Ellen

---

211 Tay Garnett, Light up Your Torches, pg. 257

212 Tay Garnett, Light up Your Torches, pg. 257

213 ibid, pg. 257

214 ibid, pg. 254

Wayne, "and his lack of confidence in his talent as an actor."[215] Bob was pleased to do this film, which allowed him to be dirty, grimy and tough. It is one of his finest pre-war films and the ending where he is the last man standing holding off an advancing Japanese Army is particularly memorable. Also memorable is the scene where a dying Desi Arnaz recites the *mea culpa* in Latin. Arnaz hadn't liked the scene as written and asked Garnett if he could recite it "not in Spanish or English, but in Latin, as we did it when I was a kid in Jesuit school."[216] Garnett checked with Bob who, according to Arnaz, loved the idea. This sequence and the ending scene with Bob are the two most remembered from this film.

The reviews for *Bataan* were better than those for *Stand by for Action.* Even Bosley Crowther, who had disdained the earlier film, was enthusiastic. He called *Bataan* "harrowing" and applauded MGM for not presenting "prettified" facts. However, it seems that Crowther couldn't quite bring himself to totally applaud Bob's performance. "Mr. Taylor is believable as the sergeant, even though he does rush about a bit too much with a dark scowl." The *Time* magazine critic wrote, "*Bataan*'s scenery is realistic down to the last carload of tropical foliage—and its drama is constantly loud and overemphatic. But there are a few stretches when the military situation calls for silence, the noisy sound track quiets down and, for a moment, incredibly enough, Hollywood's war takes on the tense, classic values of understatement." Bob was no less enthusiastic about *Bataan.* He told Louella Parsons that he considered the film one of his four personal favorite pictures of those he made. The other three were *Magnificent Obsession, Waterloo Bridge* and *Johnny Eager.*[217]

In October MGM asked Bob to join several other leading stars at the studio in making a guest appearance as himself in the frothy comedy *The Youngest Profession.* Child actress Marcia Mae Jones recalls the day Bob filmed his scene. "I played another mean girl. The day Mr. Taylor was to arrive they said we should rehearse the scene beforehand. I was supposed to believe that he was not going to arrive so when we rehearsed I opened the door and there he

215 Robert Taylor, Jane Ellen Wayne, pg. 110

216 Desi Arnaz, A Book

217 St. Petersburg Times, 6/6/43

stood. I couldn't remember my lines as he was the most handsome man I had ever seen. Everybody broke out laughing, even Mr. Taylor."[218]

In December Bob and Barbara announced that they were petitioning the Superior Court to change their names. Spangler Brugh wanted to be known as Robert Taylor and Ruby Stevens wanted to be known as Barbara Stanwyck not only professionally but in all personal and business matters as well. Both gave the same reason; they were both known under their stage names as a result of their careers and had acquired property and other legal obligations under those names. In short, it would simplify matters. (The court would grant their request early the following year.)

By the end of 1942 Bob had completed his slate of films and was ready to join such Hollywood stars as Clark Gable, James Stewart, Tyrone Power, Ronald Reagan and Henry Fonda by putting on the uniform of his country and serving in the armed services in a time of war. Metro had other ideas.

218 Growing Up on the Set, pg. 175

Chapter Seven

MR. BRUGH JOINS THE NAVY (1943-1945)

The Navy swore in one Spangler Arlington Brugh on February 9, 1943, and commissioned him as a navy lieutenant, junior grade. The examining officer, Lt. John Canady, told newsmen gathered to witness the event, "Taylor passed his mental general classification and his mechanical aptitude tests with the highest grades reported here in many months—all A's and B's." He added, "And as far as his physical is concerned, he passed his flyers physical with a . . . 13—and 14 is as good as you can get."[219] He was given orders to report to Corpus Christi, Texas, within thirty days to begin training and where he would be assigned one of three duties: ferry commander pilot, transport pilot or flight instructor. Bob told reporters he hoped it would be transport or ferry pilot. At the Corpus Christi Navy Training Center he would begin four months of intensive training. In the meanwhile, he would remain on inactive duty. Bob said he was "tickled to death" becoming a navy flier. "I've been anxious to get into this. I want to do whatever I can do well to help the war effort—and I think I can do a good job of this for the navy."[220]

Just three weeks before he was sworn into the Navy, Bob was the subject of an erroneous report in the nation's newspapers. The Nazis had announced that Bob had been captured and interned in Spanish Morocco. The German News Agency spread the report that Bob had been a crew member of an American bomber that had been forced down and that he had tried to escape, but he and his fellow airmen had been "taken prisoner." MGM knocked down the

219 LA Daily News, 2/11/43

220 Schenectady-Gazette 2/9/43

report almost immediately. Bob was working on a film and had not been out of California for weeks, much less abroad. Why the Nazis decided to spread such an easily repudiated report is not clear, but it may have been meant for propaganda purposes within their own carefully controlled media.

What happened next infuriated Bob. MGM wanted him to star in a big-budget propaganda picture—*Song of Russia*—and went so far as to arrange a deferment of his active duty status until after he made the film. At one point it was reported that director Gregory Ratoff called on the Soviet Ambassador complaining that he wanted Taylor for the film, but he was going to be starting his military service within a month. According to Washington columnist Drew Pearson, the Soviet Ambassador lambasted this. "I don't understand this country," said the Ambassador. "You take the men who can do most for morale and send them off to shoot a rifle. In my country we exempt leading actors from military service." According to Pearson, the Ambassador then called the War Information Chief, Elmer Davis, who arranged with the Secretary of War, Frank Knox, to release Taylor so he could do the Russia film.[221]

It is hard to believe today that *Song of Russia* would become one of the most controversial films of Bob's career and one he was adamantly against making. Of course, it was after the war that this film became an issue because of the Cold War between the United States and the Soviet Union, but when this film was made Russia was an ally of the United States in the war against Nazi Germany.

Bob was always an anti-Communist and his reluctance to act in the film was due to purely political reasons. MGM, like all the other studios, was making patriotic pictures for wartime audiences. MGM had already made and released such films as *Mrs. Miniver*, an unabashedly sentimental salute to our wartime ally, Great Britain, and the English people. Other MGM releases from early in the war years included *Pilot #5*, *Journey for Margaret*, *A Guy Named Joe* and the two wartime films starring Bob, *Stand by for Action* and *Bataan*. Bob had enlisted into the Navy and was awaiting his orders, but Louis B. Mayer had another patriotic picture that he wanted Bob to make before leaving and the result was *Song of Russia*. *Song of*

221 Washington Merry-go-Round/Drew Pearson, 3/10/43

Russia, in Bob's view, was more or less a valentine to the Communist system (complete with happy, music-loving villagers content with the Russian Communist system—a system he deplored). Mayer was also under government pressure to make a film which was friendly toward the Russians since they were our allies in the European war and were giving signals that they were willing to help us in the Pacific against the Japanese once the Nazis were defeated.

The story itself is pretty innocuous. Bob is cast as an American symphony conductor on tour in Russia. He meets and falls in love with a Russian peasant girl (Susan Peters) who also loves and has a talent for performing classical music, and the music of Tchaikovsky in particular. They marry but because of the war they are torn apart. They are reunited toward the end but when a young boy (Darryl Hickman), who Taylor has taken under his wing, is killed by German bombs, Taylor pledges to stay in Russia and join in the fight against the Nazis. However, Taylor and Peters are eventually persuaded to return to the United States, largely for propaganda purposes, to spread the word of Russia's plight against the Nazis.

However, in Bob's view the Russians presented in *Song of Russia* were not honestly portrayed. Basically, Bob felt that the film didn't treat the Communist system with proper contempt. It showed the Russian people working contently in their co-ops by day and then singing and dancing happily by night. Bob felt that the movie could be a salute to the bravery of the Russian people without glorifying its Communist political system. Ayn Rand, who testified in 1947 before the House UnAmerican Activities Committee (HUAC), took *Song of Russia* and other films she considered pro-Communist to task by stating, "Communist propaganda is anything which gives a good impression of communism as a way of life. Anything that sells people the idea that life in Russia is good and that people are free and happy would be Communist propaganda. Am I not correct?"

Song of Russia was certainly not the only movie to be held up as Communist propaganda during the Cold War. *Mission to Moscow* (1943), based on the memoirs of Joseph E. Davies, the U.S. Ambassador to the Soviet Union from 1936–1938, was, perhaps, even more criticized than *Song of Russia*. The film was produced by Warner Brothers, and Jack Warner later testified that the picture had been made "when our country was fighting for its existence, with Russia as one of our allies. It was made to fulfill the same wartime purpose for which we made such other pictures as *Air Force, This Is The Army, Objective, Burma!, Destination Tokyo, Action in the North Atlantic*, and a great many more . . . If making *Mission to Moscow* in 1942 was subversive activity, then the American Liberty ships which carried food and guns to Russian allies and the American naval vessels which convoyed them were likewise engaged in subversive activities. The picture was made only to help a desperate war effort and not for posterity."

Later, Louis B. Mayer also testified before HUAC and gave his explanation as to how MGM came to make *Song of Russia*. "It was in April of 1942 that the story for *Song of Russia* came to our attention," Mayer explained. "It seemed a good medium of entertainment and at the same time offered an opportunity for a pat on the back for our then ally, Russia. It also offered an opportunity to use the music of Tchaikovsky. We mentioned this to the Government coordinators and they agreed with us it would be a good idea to make the picture."

Eventually, Bob did, of course, make the movie—in large part to be done with this commitment so he could get on with his stint in the Navy. Though he was never at ease with it. The film was shot between mid-March and late May of 1943. Darryl Hickman was cast as the young boy that Bob's character takes under his wing. Hickman "well remembers" this film and his enjoyment of making it with Bob. "Taylor was a real nice man and he wasn't condescending to kids like some actors were," Hickman recalls. "He treated me as an equal." He was also a lot of fun to be around. "I would bring a ball and a mitt to work and between scenes when I was out of school, we would play catch together." But what got even more attention from Hickman was that Bob would ride a motorcycle to the studio and offered to take Hickman for rides. "My mother wasn't crazy about it, but Bob would come up to her and say, 'Darryl would like to go for a ride on my motorcycle,' and she would okay it. It was only around the studio grounds and he never sped." [222]

In the midst of making the picture Bob spoke to reporters and

222 Darryl Hickman to author

told them he was "anxious" to complete the film and get on with his military service. "I don't care where they send me," he told them. "Any front where I'm stationed is all right with me, but I want action."[223]

Gregory Ratoff was chosen to direct this film primarily because of his Russian background. He was born in St. Petersburg, Russia, in 1897, and served in the Czar's army and later joined the Moscow Art Theater. In the United States Ratoff acted (his most famous role being as the producer who takes Marilyn Monroe under his wing in *All About Eve*), wrote, produced and directed. Among the films he had directed prior to *Song of Russia* were *Intermezzo, A Love Story, The Corsican Brothers* and *Adam Had Four Sons.* Hickman recalls Ratoff as "having a big-time understanding of music, which was wonderful for this film because it had so much music in it." He also calls Ratoff a "wonderful director because he knew the acting process and so he was able to more easily convey what he wanted to actors because he was one himself."[224]

Bob's leading lady, Susan Peters, had just made a big hit in *Random Harvest* in which she had been Oscar-nominated. Her star was on a rise when she made this film, but it was not long afterward that she suffered a terrible accident when she was accidentally shot and paralyzed from the waist down. She made a valiant effort to work again, and did so, but her career really never recovered. Hickman recalls Peters as a "quiet lady and I had the sense that she was not a very happy lady. She was never very forthcoming."[225]

When the film was released, Bosley Crowther in the *New York Times* liked the film for the most part. "This is frankly a musical picture, scored to Tchaikovsky's immortal works. The spirit and sweep of the music which the great nineteenth-century composer wrote is the touchtone for most of the action in this vivid romantic film, and a fine blend of music and image is achieved in the best cinematic style." Crowther also liked the acting, including Taylor, who he says "makes a very good impression as a young American caught in Russia by love and war." He calls Susan Peters "extraordinarily winning."

223 St. Petersburg Times, 7/4/43

224 Darryl Hickman to author

225 Darryl Hickman to author

Three years later in his HUAC testimony, Louis B. Mayer would also sum up *Song of Russia* as little more than a innocuous musical, "little more than a pleasant musical romance—the story of a boy and girl that, except for the music of Tchaikovsky, might just as well have taken place in Switzerland or England or any other country on the earth."

With *Song of Russia* finally completed, Bob was able to begin his Navy commitment.[226] He checked into the Navy Air Training Base in Dallas, Texas, to begin his basic training just days after his thirty-second birthday. Following his basic training, he was transferred to the Naval Air Station in New Orleans, where he received three months of instructor training. Bob's hopes to be either a ferry pilot or fighter pilot were turned down. It was felt that he would serve the Navy best as an instructor. Following his training, Bob earned his wings, and graduated fifth in his class on January 11, 1944. In fact, Commander R.E. Gillespie made a point of saying that Bob "finished his training with one of the best records among the graduates." It was noted that Barbara didn't attend the graduation ceremonies; she was recovering from the flu, but she had cabled her congratulations.[227] In fact, the day after graduation, Bob was allowed a short leave so he could visit Barbara before arriving at the Naval Air Station in Livermore, California.

Part of Bob's duties as a flight instructor would be to supervise the making of training films. In all, he would make some seventeen training films with an average length of about twenty to thirty minutes. The pictures were not to be for general release, but rather to be shown to the young pilots as part of their training. According to the commander in charge of the division, the films constituted a "new approach to flight training" and believed that they would improve performance by the young cadets by as much as twenty-five percent. Taylor would serve as the instructor in the film as well as the narrator. "In twenty-minutes," according to Commander Frederick Reeder, "we will be able to give cadets the benefit of hundreds of thousands of hours of work done before them in a

226 Just before leaving Bob, Barbara & Robert Young acted in a radio adaptation of "The Philadelphia Story" for Lux Radio Theatre.

227 St. Petersburg Times, 1/9/44

particular phase of training by the best men the navy has."[228]

One of the films that Bob participated in making during the war was shown to the public. It was considered to be one of the finest documentaries produced during the war. The documentary was *The Fighting Lady*. It was produced for Twentieth Century-Fox by Louis De Rochment, a producer for the *March of Time* newsreels. *The Fighting Lady* followed life aboard an unnamed aircraft carrier over the course of some fourteen months. It showed the actual crew and pilots and their adventures in such war fronts as Guam, Saipan, Tinian and a major battle against the Japanese fleet task force in the Philippine Sea. De Rochment called the film a "new drama or an adventure in pictorial journalism."[229]

The Fighting Lady was released in late 1944 and ran ninety-two minutes. It garnered good reviews at the theaters it appeared in. "Not even thrill maker Alfred Hitchcock could match the excitement of this racy biography of an anonymous aircraft carrier," wrote one reviewer. "It is a human story of the gallant ship and her men, highlighted by some of the most dramatic scenes on celluloid." The film tells the story of the glamour boys (pilots), 90-day wonders (reservists), so-called "trade school boys" (Annapolis men), and the zoom pigeons (air crewmen). The film was made in color and showed such harrowing scenes as a plane landing with its un-dropped bombs pouring molten thermite on the flight deck. It also showed scenes of Japanese torpedo planes flying directly at the carrier and the efforts to shoot them down before they are hit. The film didn't try and hide the brutal truth of war—young men are killed or grievously wounded.[230] Bob's contribution as narrator of the documentary was uniformly praised. The *New York Times* said his running commentary was "excellent," while the *New York World-Telegram* wrote, "Taylor's is a stern, self-effacing voice with no trace of the movie star."[231] *The Fighting Lady* would go on to win the Academy Award as the best documentary of 1944.

Bob was praised as an excellent instructor who was just one of

228 Milwaukee Journal, 7/31/44

229 Contemporary 20th-Century-Fox Press Release

230 Milwaukee Journal, 12/22/44

231 Films of Robert Taylor pg. 195

the guys and made no pretense at being a celebrity. "I figured I had two strikes against me before I came to bat," he later said. "I was an actor and an officer." [232] With his close-cropped military haircut he wasn't easily recognized and even among those who did recognize him he never acted the big shot—and never spoke of acting or movies. He was commended by all for being down to earth and made several friendships while in the Navy. One of the most significant, and one which would last for the rest of his life, was with a fellow naval instructor named Tom Purvis.

Bob met Purvis when he was transferred back to New Orleans, once the training pictures had been completed. He was to resume his duties as a flight instructor, but Bob pointed out that he really hadn't done much flying over the past year and asked for a refresher course. His commanding officer agreed, and assigned Purvis, who was roughly Bob's age, to bring him up to par. 6'3" and 240 pounds, Purvis was an imposing figure. He, like Bob, was born in the Middle West—in Purvis' case, Illinois. They would bond like brothers and Bob felt comfortable speaking about almost anything with Purvis. At first Bob was concerned about how Purvis would perceive him. He continued to be apprehensive about how new people would accept him; as one of the guys or some Hollywood actor who got his wings. He soon was relieved to see that Purvis accepted him as a fellow pilot, and so he allowed himself to lower his guard.

On one of their refresher courses Bob and Purvis left for a flight which took them from the deep south into the Middle West and it was somewhere over the Mississippi River that Purvis tested Bob by asking him to take the plane into a right slow roll. They were some 5,000 feet up and in an open plane and Bob did the roll perfectly. Purvis complimented Bob on the perfect roll, but found that the color had drained from Taylor's face. Was he experiencing air sickness? Nope. He explained to Purvis that he had lost his cigarette lighter out of the pocket of his shirt. "It's down there in the Mississippi River," he said.

Purvis, confused, asked him what the big deal was about losing a cigarette lighter. Bob explained to Purvis that it was no mere cigarette lighter, but rather a gift from Barbara—solid gold with a replica of

232 Robert Taylor, J.E. Wayne, pg. 113

his Naval Station Emblem—costing about $300.

Purvis told him to just tell Barbara the truth and that she will probably have a good laugh about it. Wrong. "You don't know Barbara," was Bob's reply to Purvis. (When she did find out the truth, Barbara merely bought him a new one as a replacement.)[233]

Except for a few rare leaves by Bob and one visit to New Orleans by Barbara, the Taylors were, like most military spouses, separated during the slightly more than two years that Bob was in the Navy. Barbara was proud of her husband. When she visited him in New Orleans, Stanwyck told the reporters who showed up to meet her, "Don't ask me about the movies. Ask me about the navy. We're navy. And while I'm here I plan to be just a navy wife."[234] Barbara, who detested flying, feared for Bob spending so much time in the air and sent him several St. Christopher medals. "She doesn't trust me for nothing in a plane," Bob said. "But anything she says is good for me, I'll wear." One comment that Barbara made came dangerously close to the truth. Seeing that Bob lost 14 pounds and sported a navy crew cut, Barbara said, "He's still the handsomest man I've ever laid eyes on, but he looks about eighteen—people will think that I'm his mother!" Barbara had a wonderful figure and smooth skin, but she had prematurely graying hair, which she didn't hide when she wasn't working.[235]

Professionally, the war years were good ones for Barbara. It was during this time that she made one of her best films—containing one of her finest performances—that of the manipulative, icy-veined blonde, Phyllis Dietrichson, who drives a supposedly self-assured insurance salesman to kill her husband—in the classic *film noir Double Indemnity*. It would earn her a third Academy Award nomination (at the same ceremony that Bob's documentary, *Fighting Lady*, was also nominated). Furthermore, she was the highest paid woman in Hollywood, according to published reports; she earned slightly more than $323,000 in 1943.

In January of 1945 Bob was sent to New York by the Navy to help publicize *The Fighting Lady*. Barbara joined him while he was

233 Robert Taylor, J.E. Wayne, 114-115

234 Fresno Bee, 2/12/45

235 Al Diorio, Barbara Stanwyck, pg. 134

there, and he also sat down for an interview in his hotel suite with columnist Earl Wilson. Wilson described him, in his article, as "wondrously handsome" with his crew cut and mustache.

Bob told Wilson that he doubted he would return to acting if the war lasted "as long as I think it will." He added, "Nobody will remember Robert Taylor." He was as self-deprecating as usual. "I'm not a great actor and never will be. I got in pictures because I was a good-looking guy." He thought that one day he might actually end up a director. He was happy about the way he could go undetected by the young flyers he trained. "They never show that they know you from a load of coal cars." [236]

Even though it appeared that the war against Nazi Germany in Europe might be coming toward an end, the secondary war, but one no less intense, against the Japanese in the Pacific, might last well into 1946 and end up costing hundreds of thousands of more lives. Nobody knew that scientists were developing a powerful bomb that was hoped, if used, would end the war in a matter of months. Bob was in New Orleans when he learned of the Nazi surrender in May of 1945. Just three months later, after the United States used the Atomic Bomb—twice on Japan—the Japanese surrendered. It was now August of 1945, and the war was over, but Bob wasn't immediately discharged. He would remain a Navy flight instructor until his active discharge in November of 1945. "It's good to be home," Bob said at the time, "but it's rather tough to leave the gang you've been with so long. You get that lumpy feeling about where you tie your tie." [237] He was home and ready to resume his career, but wasn't sure how the studio or the fickle public would react.

If Barbara believed that absence makes the heart grow fonder, she was in for a rude surprise. After the war, Bob more than ever craved activities which he knew Barbara didn't enjoy and thus would make no attempt to join him. These included flying, hunting, and fishing trips. He was still fond of Barbara and respected her fine qualities, but it seems as if the war years had made him question whether he really wanted to be married to her—if he was truly in love with her.

236 Miami News, 1/15/45

237 The Evening Independent, 11/6/45

"The war matured Bob," his friend and future secretary Ivy Mooring would recall. "He began to question whether he wanted to remain tied to Barbara. He was tiring of mother figures."[238]

238 Ivy Mooring to author

Chapter Eight
POST-WAR SLUMP (1946-1949)

Ivy and Len Pearson came to the United States shortly after the war ended. Len had grown up in the same village as David Niven's wife, Primmie. To escape from the harsh economic conditions of post-war Europe, the Nivens agreed to sponsor Len and Ivy and bring them to the United States. They guaranteed jobs for them. Len would be David's valet and Ivy would be a combination maid/cook. Tragically, within a few weeks of settling in the United States, Primmie died from a fall down stone stairs while attending a house party at Tyrone Power's home. Niven was inconsolable and poured himself into work. One movie would take him back to England and Niven decided to rent out his house and the guest house that Ivy and Len lived in on the property. Ivy and Len had fallen in love with California and the warm climate—and, too, Ivy was pregnant and they wanted their baby to be an American citizen. They decided to stay.

Len started a business as a valet to the stars. In this capacity he would organize their wardrobe, shine their shoes and press their suits. He soon had a clientele that included Keenan Wynn, Mervyn LeRoy, Dick Powell—and Robert Taylor. The word of mouth of this service recruited other clients and soon Ivy was helping with the business and in this capacity got to know Bob and Barbara Stanwyck. The relationship that Ivy forged with Bob would last for the rest of his life and strengthen. Eventually, Ivy would lose Len to a brain tumor and Bob would bring her on as his private secretary, "even though he typed better than I did!" And she would also become godmother to Bob's first child, his son Terry. Ivy offers an insight into the deteriorating Taylor-Stanwyck marriage.

She would often come over to the Taylor home and do the ironing. Ivy recalls Stanwyck as, "very nice to me, but it was clear that there were problems in their marriage." She says that Barbara became very jealous of Bob, especially of his weekends away with the guys flying and hunting. She was jealous of friends Bob met and kept in touch with in the Navy, Ralph Crouse (who he would arrange a job for at MGM as his pilot) and Tom Purvis. It got so bad that when either one would call the house, Barbara, if she answered first, would tell Bob, "Your wife is on the phone."

One day Ivy was discussing Len's deteriorating condition with Stanwyck. "Len is very confused these days," she told her. "So am I," Barbara replied. "I can't understand Bob's behavior—he's gone off the rails."

Barbara began to drink quite a bit during this period of time. "It was a very tense relationship," Ivy recalls. "Barbara would drink a great deal of champagne and would become a different person." It was at times like this that Barbara would even lash out at Ivy. "She would insinuate that something was going on between me and Bob. Of course it wasn't. She was just looking for any excuse she could because Bob had lost any desire he may have had at one time for her."[239]

Barbara began to assault Bob's masculinity. Perhaps it was a defense mechanism to help deal with the fact that Bob apparently didn't find her attractive sexually any longer. Arlene Dahl recalls that the first time she met Bob was at a party shortly before she was to begin filming a movie with him, the Western *Ambush*. "Barbara would embarrass him and attack his masculinity in front of all of these people," Miss Dahl recalls. "She would loudly say to him that he was 'too pretty' and that his 'leading ladies couldn't stand it.' Bob would just stand quietly by; he never stood up to her. She told him he should grow a beard for the film, so that he looked like a real man—like Joel McCrea." Miss Dahl was not surprised when he arrived on the set of Ambush sporting a full beard, "we hardly recognized him." Dahl was actually happy when she heard that Bob and Barbara had broken up. "I was hoping they would. He was too good of a man to waste on a woman like her."[240]

239 Ivy Mooring to author

240 Arlene Dahl to author

Tom Purvis, who lived in Illinois, came out to California for a visit. Bob wanted to put him up at the house, which had lots of room, but Barbara didn't believe in being either a house guest or having guests in her house. At least that is what she told him. More probable is that she didn't want to have one of Bob's hunting chums hanging around the house. Bob already spent so much time away from her that she didn't want to share him at home, too, with one of his buddies. Instead, Bob put him up at the Beverly Wilshire Hotel, giving him a suite to boot, and paid the bill. When his friends did visit Bob at home, it was not usually a hospitable scene they were invited in to see. "When I did go there I had to listen to Barbara yelling at Bob and watch him taking it," one friend told Taylor biographer Jane Ellen Wayne. "He never fought back."[241]

One of the problems that existed in the marriage is that Bob apparently lost his sexual attraction to Barbara. "She was no longer sexually attractive to him," Ivy recalls. "He wasn't attracted to her in that way any longer. Bob didn't have a big libido anyway, which caused a great deal of tension with Barbara. She would say, in front of me, 'It's too hot that will be his excuse this time,' for not having sexual relations with her. I think he came to the conclusion that you don't have sex with your mother—which is how he saw Barbara."[242]

More and more Bob would seek escape with his friends in activities that Barbara loathed, such as hunting trips. Bob knew Barbara would not want to come. Once, Barbara did join a hunt. It was when she and Bob, along with Ernest Hemmingway, Gary Cooper and various guides, went deer hunting in Sun Valley, Idaho. Stanwyck later recalled that Bob stood on one hill, Cooper on another and Hemmingway on a third hill while the guides created a commotion so that the deer would enter the valley below them creating a clear shot for the hunters. "It wasn't hunting," Barbara recalled. "It was the damndest ambush I'd ever seen."[243] It disgusted her. Yet it was Stanwyck, not Taylor, that man's-man Hemmingway gained an appreciation for. He felt that Bob was a "miniature man" who played he-men on screen but "the actual model that the lens enlarges is neither very

241 Robert Taylor, J.E. Wayne, pg. 125

242 Ivy Mooring to author

243 Axel Madsen, Stanwyck, pg. 181

gay nor very impressive." On the other hand, Stanwyck, he found, "very nice with a good tough Mick intelligence."[244]

If Bob was depressed about his marriage he was equally distressed over his career prospects since coming home from the war. It was as if MGM didn't know what to do with him. Bob made thirty-six motion pictures in the nine years from 1934–1943, when he joined the Navy. In the three years after he came back he appeared in only five films, averaging about one per year. If Barbara was attacking his masculinity at home she was also showing him up in the profession, too. During the same period of time Barbara made ten films and was in great demand. In 1948 she would be nominated for a fourth time for an Academy Award for her breathless performance as an invalid suspecting that her husband has arranged for her to be murdered in *Sorry, Wrong Number.*

The films that Bob made from 1946–1949 were not inconsequential films. MGM didn't put him in conventional films to cash in on his previous romantic leading man quality. Most of these films have a dark, *noir* quality that was in vogue during these years.

MGM finally settled on Bob's first postwar picture, *Undercurrent*; it would team him with a strong leading lady, Katharine Hepburn, cast against type as the fragile and socially awkward daughter of a small-town college professor (played by Edmund Gwenn). She marries an industrialist who completely dominates and bullies her into becoming the stylish social matron he wants her to be. Once married, he comes and goes at his own pleasure and won't tell his wife what he is up to and, in effect, to mind her own business. He has a brother (Robert Mitchum) she has never met. The brother isn't spoken about, and she is given the impression that he is a black sheep of the family—but is he? The wife decides to look into her husband's background and discovers a man who may be pathologically unstable, who once beat a horse so severely it had to be put down. She gradually discovers that he may also be a murderer. It was a complex part in a suspenseful film, but Bob didn't exactly jump for joy when the studio sent him the script. He thought it would be a typical woman's picture. "Then they told me that Hepburn was doing

244 Hemmingway: A Life without Consequences, James Mellow, pg. 525

the feminine lead, I was sure of it. But I did it anyway. I needed a picture badly."[245]

The director of the film was Vincente Minnelli who had proven himself an effective director of some very innovative musicals up to this time, including *Cabin in the Sky* and *Meet Me in St. Louis*, the film in which he met the woman who would soon become his wife and one of MGM's biggest stars, Judy Garland. But could he handle a suspenseful melodrama such as *Undercurrent*, with a strong-willed leading lady like Hepburn?

Producer Pandro Berman, who had produced several of Hepburn films of the thirties at RKO (*Morning Glory, Alice Adams* and *Stage Door*), was confident that Minnelli could handle the job, and went to Hepburn for final directorial approval, which she reluctantly granted. Hepburn, at this stage, was in need of a hit as her last couple of films, especially *Dragon Seed*, in which she played a Chinese peasant, were box-office disappointments. Minnelli met Hepburn at the studio and she told him, "I'm sure we'll get along." Minnelli later was a bit uneasy about how she phrased it. "It sounded like both an order and a threat. I never met anyone with such self-assurance. She made me nervous. And here was I, theoretically the captain of the ship, being made to tiptoe through my assignment."[246] Berman warned Minnelli that Hepburn would be a "hand full" and Minnelli recalls that she would come to him daily with suggestions, "and some were very bad." She wasn't pleased with her leading men either. Hepburn thought that Bob was too much of a "lightweight" to handle such a strong role, but reluctantly accepted him because the studio, especially Mayer, whom she admired very much, wanted Bob in the part and he was, after all, a huge star.

Hepburn didn't take well to Mitchum, who she thought was very common. Mitchum didn't exactly take to the high and mighty ways of Miss Hepburn either and began to act up on the set doing practical jokes and indulging himself with impersonations, including Katharine Hepburn. Spencer Tracy, Hepburn's frequent screen partner and off-screen companion, often lampooned the Great Kate's Bryn Mayr voice and sometimes haughty manner, but that was okay since

245 NY Times, 2/2/47

246 I Remember It Well, pg. 171

Tracy was somebody Hepburn genuinely admired as a person and as an actor. But, by God, she wasn't about to take it from Mitchum! She read him the riot act in front of the company. "You know you can't act. If you hadn't been good looking, you would never have gotten a picture. I'm tired of playing with people who have nothing to offer."[247]

Eventually, Hepburn warmed up to Minnelli's direction. In his autobiography Minnelli writes that the turning point came when Hepburn was filming a scene where she has to break down completely as she confronts Bob, playing her husband. "Kate ended the scene with honest tears." So moved by the scene was Minnelli that he ran up to Hepburn and threw his arms around her and kissed her. "That was absolutely beautiful." Minnelli said that "from that moment on, she became ultra feminine." But Minnelli soon discovered that while things with Hepburn were improving that his relationship with Bob, which was "cordial" up to this point, was in danger of deteriorating. "He'd taken my chronic vagueness as disinterest, I suppose, and though he never voiced any complaints, I was aware of his dissatisfaction. Bob's wariness, that I was throwing scenes to Kate."[248]

Minnelli believed that Bob was effective in the part of the psychotic husband because the audience wouldn't believe that Bob Taylor (at least at that time in his career) was capable of playing such a terrible man. "Though Bob had gotten over his pretty boy reputation," recalled Minnelli, "you still couldn't disguise his charm. The audience simply wouldn't take him for a murderer . . . until that climactic scene with his brother." To get the deranged look that Minnelli wanted from Bob in this scene he told Bob to do the scene without blinking. "I figured his eyes would get wider and have a teary, frantic look. Bob did it beautifully."[249] In fact, Bob followed his director's direction so completely that he was sent to the studio's doctor to be given some medication for his deeply reddening eyes! In the end, Minnelli was impressed by Bob's performance. "He [Taylor] out acted her," Minnelli told writer James Baldwin years

247 George Eells, Robert Mitchum, pg. 77

248 I Remember It Well, pg. 174

249 ibid

later, "and stole the picture as the demanding and sadistic husband. It was Kate who was miscast." Hepburn herself later changed her tune about Bob being too "lightweight" in his role. "I never got to know him very well," she later said, "but I considered Bob one of the most underrated actors in the business."[250] As for Bob, he recalled Hepburn fondly. "I've never met anyone like her. She has the keenest sense of humor of anyone I've met. She's also a good business woman. She only makes one picture a year—and she makes sure it's a good one."[251] Years later, Hedda Hopper asked Bob if he had talked politics with Hepburn. "No. She's too fast for me."[252] For Minnelli, the film was also memorable due to the birth of his and Garland daughter, Liza, during its production.

Undercurrent was shot between January and May of 1946 and held its New York premiere on November 28. The *New York Times* felt that the screenplay had problems, but was complimentary toward the actors. Hepburn gives a "crisp and taut performance." Taylor, "back from his war service accelerates a brooding meanness as her spouse." Mitchum, "fairly appealing in a crumpled, modest way." Minnelli's direction "used atmosphere and mood well." The *New York Herald Tribune* enthusiastically welcomed Bob back to the screen, "Taylor's performance has new presence and dignity . . . a strong performance." Variety thought that picture had "heavy drama with femme appeal." Bob's first post-war picture was also a much-needed box-office success. The film cost $1.6 million to produce and grossed $4.2 million and showed a profit of slightly more than a million dollars on the Metro log.[253]

It would be more than a year before Bob would go before the cameras again. "The studios weren't prepared for us," he told the *New York Times* in 1947, "so many of us, all coming back at once [from the war] just not enough scripts to go around." Bob said that much of his idleness was his decision. "I've turned down twelve scripts" since *Undercurrent*. He said he wanted to make sure he

250 Robert Taylor, J.E. Wayne, pg. 123

251 Hollywood Citizen News, 4/22/46

252 Hedda Hopper Papers, Margaret Herrick Library, AMPAS

253 Hepburn and Bob would recreate their roles in a radio version of "Undercurrent" on Lux Radio Theatre, 10/6/47

selected the right parts. "Barbara has four pictures on the shelf and she has just finished another. Well—someone in the family has to work." He conceded that he no longer got the wild adulation that he had received in the thirties and what more recently established male stars, like Frank Sinatra and Van Johnson, received. "I guess I've graduated—matured . . . it's been a long time—now I have to act for a living."[254]

While the studio was looking for the right properties for their returning stars, Bob did do occasional radio work to keep his name before the public. The first radio show he did after coming back from the Navy was a condensed adaptation of *Magnificent Obsession*, which was broadcast over the CBS radio network on December 4, 1945. Over the next year he did five more radio adaptations. He recreated his roles in "Johnny Eager" (opposite Susan Peters in the Lana Turner role) on *The Lux Radio Theatre*. He did an adaptation of "Men in White" for *Armed Forces Radio Theatre*. Barbara joined him playing the Vivien Leigh role in a radio adaptation of "Waterloo Bridge" for *The Lady Esther Screen Guild Theatre*. But his finest radio work may have been in two episodes of *Suspense*. The first was titled "The Argyle Album," about blackmail and murder, but the best was aired on December 5, 1946, and was titled "The House in Cypress Canyon." It's an eerie story involving werewolves, blood oozing under doors, screams in the night, and quite unlike anything Bob ever did before or would do again.[255]

In early 1947 Bob and Barbara went on vacation to Europe. They arrived by ship in Paris on February 20, where they hoped to spend a couple of weeks sightseeing on the continent. Within days of arriving, however, on February 24, it was announced that Barbara had been staying at the American Hospital in Neuilly virtually since their arrival while Bob had been situated in their suite at the Hotel George V. The strange explanation given was that Barbara had found the suite in one of Paris' best hotels too cold, and chose instead to be put up at the hospital—while her husband, with whom she was supposed to be vacationing with, stayed at the hotel. The Taylors

254 NY Times, 2/2/47

255 Bob made one more radio appearance on Suspense in "Four Hours to Kill" on 1/12/50

denied that Barbara was ill, except for a minor cold, and that the couple had met several times for dinner. In retrospect, given their increasing estrangement, it seems likely that something unpleasant happened between the couple on the voyage over which cast such a pall over the entire trip. Such a pall that they decided it would be best if they spent more time separated than together.[256]

However, they were together in March when they journeyed across the channel to London for the opening of Barbara's film *The Other Love*. Seven police officers had to hoist Bob and Barbara on their shoulders and carry them into the Empire Theatre through a throng of 5,000 fans. "It was so overwhelming I was terrified for a few minutes," Barbara recalled.[257] Barbara came through the encounter with only her clothes disheveled. Bob wasn't as lucky; he received a bruised right eye.[258] They returned to New York in early April by ship. They took the train to Chicago where Bob would board his twin-engine Beach craft and fly back to Los Angeles. Barbara, hating flying, would continue on the train. "This character Taylor," she said, "will fly with no ceiling and no visibility. I will fly when I can see the roof of my house in Hollywood from Chicago."[259]

Once, Barbara did allow herself to fly with Bob. He recalled one of these times as "the proudest moment of his flying experience." One day in the late forties, Barbara said to Bob "quite unexpectedly" at breakfast that it "looks like good flying weather today. The mountains are so clear against the sky." She then asked him if he would fly her to Palm Springs that day: "I tried not to let her see my amazement. She had avoided flying, made no bones about saying she did not like it, and I never made a point of it. So, much as I wanted to take her up in 'Missy,' as I call my plane, I bided my time, hoping for such a thing to happen—and here she was asking to take off with me. Away we went. Out of the corner of my eye I noticed she clutched the arm of her seat so tightly her knuckles were white. Believe me; I kept that plane on a steady keel! No smart-alec show-off tricks that day. We came down so gently I surprised myself.

256 Axel Madsen, Stanwyck, pg. 147

257 LA Daily News, 3/28/47

258 LA Times, 3/28/47

259 LA Daily News, 4/7/47

And the only comment she made was 'You're a helluva pilot.' That was the proudest moment of my life. It was a thrill greater than anything my movie career ever offered." [260]

Within a month of returning home to California Bob reported to MGM for his second post-war film, his first in over a year. The film was *The High Wall,* and in some ways it's one of Bob's most interesting films. It is a true post-war *film noir. The High Wall* tells the story of a man returning from the war having a hard time fitting in with the general population. He suffered severe head injuries as an Air Force pilot and the condition, later diagnosed as hematoma, makes him act in a paranoid and anxious fashion. He discovers that his beautiful wife has been having an affair with a hypocritical publisher of religious materials. He intends to confront his wife and in the course of doing so a knock to his head renders him unconscious and when he wakes up he finds his wife has been strangled to death. Even he isn't sure he didn't commit the murder. He is found guilty of her murder (in fact, he confesses to the crime, believing he actually did commit the crime) and is sentenced to an asylum where a sympathetic psychiatrist (played by Audrey Totter) eventually helps him uncover the identity of the true murderer.

MGM decided to forgo one of its regular house directors and brought in a freelancer, Curtis Bernhardt, who had made his reputation by directing a string of hits for Warner Brothers starring their strong roster of female stars: Olivia de Havilland and Ida Lupino in *Devotion*; Bette Davis in *A Stolen Life*; and most memorably Joan Crawford in *Possessed.* Bernhardt was born in Germany and became an actor and producer on stage in Berlin. He turned to direction in 1927 and turned out several German films, including one with Marlene Dietrich. When the Nazis came to power in 1933, Bernhardt immigrated to France where he directed several French films up to 1939 before arriving in Hollywood in 1940. Barbara Stanwyck, who made one of her favorite films, *My Reputation*, under Bernhardt, told Bob that Bernhardt was "a highly talented director, but a son of a bitch." [261]

---

260 Hollywood Album, late forties

261 Curtis Bernhardt: Directors Guild of America Interview, Mary Kiersch, Scarecrow Press, 1986, pg. 127

As in *Possessed* there is a strong psychological element in *The High Wall*, and it may have been because of that that MGM wanted Bernhardt to direct the picture. Bernhardt would later recall that psychoanalysis was in vogue in Hollywood in post-war Hollywood. "On the slightest provocation people went to a psychiatrist. Everybody: writers, directors, stars, producers," recalled Bernhardt.[262] But to Bernhardt the idea of *The High Wall* was more than an examination of psychoanalysis; it was "a chance to bring directly to the American people the experience of war. In the American picture this experience is treated as a kind of ballyhoo concept."[263] Bernhardt strove to show how the Taylor character's injuries in the war contributed to what ultimately happened to him on the home front. Bernhardt enjoyed working with Bob but wasn't blown over by his skill as an actor. "Robert Taylor and I had a great relationship. But Taylor was less an actor than he was a nice man. And Taylor always played himself."[264] Of course, many of the great screen actors (such as Cary Grant and Gary Cooper) are accused of "playing themselves," but given the complex roles that Bob played, and played extremely well, in the postwar years, such as in *Undercurrent, The High Wall, Above and Beyond*, and *The Last Hunt*, to name a few, Bernhardt's opinion of Bob's abilities as an actor are off base.

The script was co-written by Sidney Boehm and Lester Cole. Lester Cole was a name that would be long associated with Bob Taylor. Cole was one of the names that Taylor supplied in his testimony before the House UnAmerican Activities Committee (in the fall of 1947) when asked by the committee for names of possible Communists. But at the time, according to Cole in his autobiography, Taylor was very high on the screenplay for *The High Wall* and enthusiastically wanted to work with him again—going too far as to wanting to help Cole get a raise.

In the role of the psychiatrist, Audrey Totter equals Bob in giving a superb performance. Totter was a fine actress who excelled at playing bad girls, and had a voice had made her one of the most requested

262 ibid

263 Curtis Bernhardt: Directors Guild of America Interview, Mary Kiersch, Scarecrow Press, 1986, pg. 127

264 ibid, pg. 93

actresses in radio. Movies cashed in on that voice, too. In *Bewitched* (1945) she provides the evil voice which taunts Phyllis Thaxter; and then in *Ziegfeld Follies* (1946) she is the voice of the unseen telephone operator in a sketch starring Keenan Wynn. Her big break on-screen came in 1946 in one of the studio's top *noir* films, *The Postman Always Rings Twice*, playing the blonde tramp that John Garfield picks up. This led to leading lady status in the Robert Montgomery Philip Marlowe film, *Lady in the Lake* (1946), which used a subjective camera. Totter and Bob work very well together in *The High Wall*, as her sympathetic psychiatrist slowly comes to believe that Taylor really didn't commit murder.

One day filming of *The High Wall* went well into the night, and Bob and Totter were famished and went looking for food at the studio commissary, but found it had already closed for the night. They then went looking for a restaurant but found them so crowded that it would take a great deal of time to both get seated and eat their food. Finally, Bob told Totter, "Let me take you to the best restaurant in town." He took her home where Barbara made them bacon and eggs, "and it was great,"[265] recalled Totter.

The High Wall premiered in New York on Christmas Day, 1947, which prompted Bosley Crowther of the *New York Times* to joke in the opening paragraph of his review, "It simply wouldn't have been Christmas on the local movie scene without at least one good psychoneurotic spreading comfort and joy . . . . All of these cheerful ingredients are in this happy little film, plus a couple of juicy murders and any number of cackling lunatics." Crowther also pointed out that "the chief maniac" is "our old friend Robert Taylor, who can look fiercer than any nut we know." *The High Wall* returned a profit, but a meager one.

II

Bob had always been a conservative politically and it is one of the few areas that he and Barbara still had in common, though Bob was far more outspoken and public about his politics than Barbara was. They belonged to the Motion Picture Alliance for the Preservation

265 Films of the Golden Age, Summer 1999

of American Ideals. The Alliance had been founded by the director Sam Wood in 1944 and along with the Taylors it boasted such members as Clark Gable, Walt Disney, Adolphe Menjou, Victor Fleming, Cecil B. DeMille, Ginger Rogers, Irene Dunne and Gary Cooper. Its charter made clear that it was fighting the infiltration of Communism into Hollywood films. Rabid anti-Communist author Ayn Rand wrote a pamphlet for the organization which summed up its ideas:

> The purpose of the Communists in Hollywood is *not* the production of political movies openly advocating Communism. Their purpose is *to corrupt our moral premises by corrupting non-political movies*—by introducing small, casual bits of propaganda into innocent stories—thus making people absorb the basic principles of Collectivism *by indirection and implication.*

One of the things which the Alliance wanted was for studio personnel to sign loyalty oaths. Some members, such as Sam Wood, were vehement about this—even extending to their private lives. When Wood died in 1949, his will specified that his heirs would have to sign a loyalty oath before they could claim any inheritance.[266]

Shortly after beginning production on *The High Wall*, Bob was among a group of Hollywood officials who appeared voluntarily before the House UnAmerican Activities subcommittee on May 14, 1947, to support the committee in its probe of alleged Communism in Hollywood. The group included actor Richard Arlen, Leila Rogers, mother of Ginger Rogers and rabid anti-Communist, and Henry Ginsberg, the vice president in charge of production at Paramount Pictures. The testimony was taken in special session at the Biltmore Hotel in Los Angeles. By far the biggest bombshell was made by Bob who testified before the subcommittee that he was "forced" into appearing in *Song of Russia*, a film that he felt favored Russian ideologies over American. According to Bob, the pressure was applied by Lowell Mellet, a former White House aide to President Roosevelt and an official in the Office of War Information. The pressure,

266 Hollywood Directors, pg. 467

according to Representative J. Parnell Thomas, the committee chairman, included keeping Taylor from joining the Navy until the picture was completed. Bob testified that he felt that *Song of Russia* was Communist propaganda. The film, "favored Russian ideologies, institutions and ways of life over the same things in our country," Bob testified. When informed of Bob's accusations, Mellett replied that it was "too silly to deny. I certainly didn't compel Robert Taylor or anyone else to do anything."

In his testimony Bob said, "If there is anyone against Communism, it is me. I'm agin 'em. I am very strongly against Communism and I think its influence is serious enough that more actors should become aware of it. I always try to make my position in the matter emphatically clear and I always welcome any opportunity that I have to do anything I can against Communism." Bob was asked if he thought that Communist influence in Hollywood would try to punish him for his testimony. "If there is going to be any pressure from the Communist party, they are welcome to start right now," Bob replied with a huge smile on his face. At one point Bob was asked if Barbara had been invited to testify. No, she hadn't, Bob replied, "but if she had, she would be tickled to death to come down and she would come running."

Within days of his testimony a Soviet film director, Sergei Gerasimov, published an open letter in the official Russian government newspaper, *Investee.* According to Gerasimov, Bob lacked political "morality" if he really did act in *Song of Russia* against his own beliefs. "Conscience, honor and even the very elementary representation of decency are tied up conveniently with the dollar, for which Taylor, according to his own statements, sold his 'American convictions,'" Gerasimov wrote. "There was a time when it was stylish to become enthusiastic in one's sympathies toward the Soviet Union. Hollywood made quite a bit of money out of it and so did Robert Taylor." In the conclusion of his letter, which was excerpted in newspapers throughout the United States, Gerasimov wrote that *Song of Russia,* "despite considerable naiveté, made a generally good impression on him because it was permeated with a sympathetic attitude towards the U.S.S.R," [267] which during the war was an ally of the United

267 LA Times, 5/26/47

States in the war against Fascism.

This was just the beginning for within five months of this testimony Bob was invited to appear in Washington before the committee as a so-called friendly witness. Bob wasn't the only one. Among the other "friendly" witnesses were Gary Cooper, Louis B. Mayer, Leila Rogers (who actually said, "I know Dalton Trumbo is a Communist because in a picture he wrote my daughter [Ginger] was forced to say, 'Share and share alike, that's democracy'"), Adolphe Menjou, Robert Montgomery, Ronald Reagan, George Murphy and Ayn Rand. But once again on the first day of the hearings, October 22, 1947, it is Bob who took the headlines.

Bob's testimony in October is remembered primarily today because he "named names" of people who he suspected might be Communists. What is forgotten about his testimony is that it differed somewhat from his testimony in Los Angeles the previous May in one important respect. He softened the assertion that he had been pressured to make *Song of Russia*. He still testified that he had objected "strenuously" to playing in the film because he felt it was Communist propaganda, but, "If I ever gave the impression in anything that appeared previously that I was forced into making *Song of Russia*, I would like to say in my own defense, lest I look a little silly saying I was ever forced to do the picture, I was not forced because nobody can force you to make any picture. I objected to it, but in deference to the situation as it then existed I did the picture." He now testified that Lowell Mellett, the head of the movie division in the Office of War Information, did come out to Hollywood to discuss production of the picture, but that nobody in the government proposed its filming.

Despite this, Bob was still outspoken in his disdain for Communism and alleged Communism in Hollywood. When asked if he would refuse to act in a picture that included somebody he considered to be a Communist, Bob replied, "I certainly would. If I were even suspicious of him being a Communist I would have to insist either it was him or me. Life is too short to be around people who bother me as much as they do." Asked in follow-up if he considered them a "rotten apple in the barrel," Bob replied, "Yes sir, most certainly." The audience, which included a good share of women (who showed up largely due to Bob's presence on this first day), applauded him when he testified, "If I had my way, they [Communists] would all be sent back to Russia or some other unpleasant place."

But the high point of Bob's testimony (or low point, based on your opinion) is when he was asked if he could give the names of individuals he believed might be Communists. He was asked if he had ever noticed any elements within the Screen Actors Guild that he would consider to be following the Communist Party line. "Well, yes, sir; I must confess that I have," he began. But he softened it as he continued. ". . . there is always a certain group of actors and actresses whose every action would indicate to me that if they are not Communists that they are working awfully hard to be Communists. I don't know. Their tactics and their philosophies seem to me to be pretty much party line stuff."

At this point the hearings took a brief recess and when they returned Bob was asked the key questions. "Do you recall the names of any of the actors in the Guild who participated in such activity?" What he said next must be made clear, "*Well, yes, sir; I can name a few who seem to sort of disrupt things once in awhile. Whether or not they are Communist I don't know.*" Clearly, Bob was stating that these people might be disruptors at Guild meetings, but that they were not necessarily Communists. He was then asked to "name them for the committee."

Then it happened, the thing that would haunt Robert Taylor for the rest of his life and his reputation well after his death. "One chap we have currently, I think, is Mr. Howard Da Silva. He always seems to have something to say at the wrong time." Da Silva was a well-known actor in the Broadway theater having originated the role of Jud in the landmark musical *Oklahoma!* He also appeared in Broadway productions of *Golden Boy* and *Abe Lincoln in Illinois.* In Hollywood he had appeared in such films as *Abe Lincoln in Illinois, Keeper of the Flame, The Great Gatsby* and as the bartender in *The Lost Weekend.* But was Bob saying that Da Silva was a Communist? No, he clearly states that he is somebody who "always seems to have something to say at the wrong time."

After naming Da Silva as somebody who usually had something to say at the wrong time, Bob went on to add another name, "Miss Karen Morley also usually appears at the Guild meetings." Like Bob, Morley had come to Hollywood from the Midwest—in her case Iowa—and began her career at the Pasadena Playhouse before breaking into movies in 1930. She was signed by MGM and appeared in such films as *Inspiration* and *Mata Hari* (both with Greta Garbo), *Arsene Lupin* (opposite John Barrymore); *Scarface* (with Paul Muni); and *Dinner at Eight*, one of Metro's biggest hits of 1933. After she left MGM, she did appear in such films with a liberal political bent as *Our Daily Bread, Black Fury*, and *The Last Train to Madrid*. She returned to MGM in 1940 to appear in *Pride and Prejudice*, which starred Greer Garson and Laurence Olivier. But did Bob call her a Communist in his October, 1947 testimony? No. He said, "Miss Karen Morley also usually appears at Guild meetings."

So, did Bob clearly call anybody a Communist during his testimony? The closest he came was when he named writer Lester Cole as a "reputed Communist." Bob was asked, "Are you personally acquainted with any of the writers whom you consider to be Communists or who follow the Communist Party line?" Bob replied, "I know several writers—I know of several writers in the motion picture business who are reputedly fellow travelers or possibly Communist. *I don't know about that.*" He is saying that several may be Communists, but he didn't have any personal knowledge if that is in fact the case. Then it came. "You have no personal knowledge of it yourself?" Bob could have easily said, "Yes, that is correct," but instead he said, "I know one gentleman employed at the studio at which I am employed. Mr. Lester Cole, who is reputedly a Communist. *I would not know personally.*"

Cole, who had written the film *The High Wall*, would later write in his autobiography that just months before Bob made this testimony he had read his script of the film and "went to L.B. [Mayer] and demanded that henceforth I write all his films. He wanted me put under contract for the length of his contract." [268] In a deposition to his lawyer on September 10, 1948, nearly a year after these hearings, Cole said, "Robert Taylor, who was prominently photographed and written about throughout the nation, identified me, if I can recollect his words, by saying he had been told that a gentleman named Lester Cole was a communist and identified me that way, and said that at the time—this was given quite some publicity—that he would

268 Lester Cole, Hollywood Red, pg. 256

never knowingly work with a person that he thought or was told was a Red. Of course, this was a bald faced lie, because . . . Taylor and I had been in continual conference on the script of *High Wall*, at which time he told me—thanked me for the script, told me that it was the finest job he had in five or six years, that he hoped I would do more films for him." Of course, in Bob's defense, *The High Wall* was filmed and completed months before his testimony before the committee on October 22. It is possible, though not likely, that Bob wasn't aware of rumors that Cole was allegedly a Communist at that time. But what mattered to MGM at the time was the bottom line. Just prior to *The High Wall* Cole had written a highly profitable film called *The Romance of Rosy Ridge*, and at the time was high on MGM's list of screenwriters.

The bottom line is that Bob did publicly name three people: Howard Da Silva, Karen Morley and Lester Cole. But he didn't explicitly call them Communists. He clearly says each time that he had no knowledge, but clearly the committee expected names and he provided them—and did so without really knowing for sure if they were or were not Communists. In essence, Bob was just confirming rumors and the Committee clearly wanted him to do so. This is why many people in Hollywood still hold Robert Taylor in contempt for what he did on October 22, 1947.

So why is it that Robert Taylor's testimony is held against him when the following day, October 23, a bigger star, Gary Cooper, also testified before the committee as a "friendly" witness? And Cooper's testimony is rarely held against him, even among those on the left? In some ways Cooper was putting on a performance. He was "Mr. Cooper Goes to Washington." Where Bob had been formal, and business like, Cooper was shy and diffident. He diminished the Red threat in Hollywood. Yes, there were Communists in Hollywood, just like anywhere else, but like anywhere else they are a small minority, and that by and large the Hollywood film community, like the country as a whole, was full of patriotic Americans. Furthermore, when pushed to name names, Cooper, would give his "aw-shucks" performance and basically scratch his head and say he couldn't "off-hand think of any." At the end of his testimony he got a standing ovation. When Cooper next saw Bob, he said, with a grin, "I got a much bigger hand than you did."[269]

Bob truly did believe what he told the committee. He did feel he was a patriotic American and that the industry did have a problem with those who wanted to spread Communist or leftist propaganda. But it's highly doubtful that he truly wanted to testify. He understood that if he didn't it might be detrimental to his own career, but he also believed it was his patriotic duty to appear before the committee. Bob's son, Terry, says, "It is very likely that pressure was put on him too [to testify]. That said, while he clearly was outspoken against Communism and the dangers he felt that it posed on our freedoms and liberties, he would have regarded the Washington hearings as his moral and civic duty regardless of the controversial attention that it ended up attracting."[270]

In later years Bob would never discuss his appearance before HUAC. "It was a closed book," says his friend Ivy Peason-Mooring. It pained him too much to discuss it. But he did see Communism as a real threat. He did feel that certain writers put propaganda in their scripts. He did feel that "Sen. McCarthy was a brute, but that it had to be done and McCarthy was the one who was doing it."[271]

Marsha Hunt had been one of several actors blacklisted (or graylisted) during the Communist witch hunts of the late forties thru mid-fifties. In 1960 she was invited to appear on *The Detectives*, Bob's television show. Miss Hunt recalls Bob as being especially gracious and welcoming toward her and she suspects that in a small and very human way he was trying to make amends for what happened on October 22, 1947.[272]

III

The Bribe is the first of three films to team Bob with Ava Gardner, a dark-haired, voluptuous beauty with a husky southern draw, who by this time had already been the spouse of Mickey Rooney and Artie Shaw. Though she had been in films (in mostly

269 The Last Hero: A Biography of Gary Cooper, Larry Swindell, pg. 276

270 Terry Taylor to author

271 Ivy Mooring to author

272 Marsha Hunt to author

minor roles) since 1941, her career was on the rise by the time she teamed with Bob in The Bribe thanks to persuasive performances in *The Killers, The Hucksters* and (ideally cast) as Venus, the Goddess of Love, in *One Touch of Venus*. By the late forties she was emerging past Rita Hayworth as the screen's top love goddess. MGM felt it would be good to cast Bob with the fast-rising Gardner in his third postwar picture in four years.

In her autobiography Gardner gives a pretty good synopsis of the film: "Set on some fictitious island off the coast of Central America, which looked suspiciously like Mexico on MGM's all-purpose back lot, *The Bribe* had me tangentially connected to a nasty plot to smuggle surplus American aircraft engines into South America. I was excused from my usual slinky black dress and put into Mexican huaraches and fetching native blouses to match the climate. And though I seemed to be happy singing and dancing in the local cantina, my main job was to take one quick look at Mr. Taylor, a federal agent dead set on catching those smugglers, and fall into his arms." To this summary we can add that John Hodiak is cast as Gardner's husband, a U.S. flier who aids the smuggling ring led by Vincent Price and Charles Laughton. Producer Pandro S. Berman assigned MGM stalwart Robert Z. Leonard to direct. This would be Leonard's third film with Bob. Their previous films being *When Ladies Meet* and Bob's final postwar film, *Stand by for Action*.

For Bob this was his third interesting part since emerging from the service. MGM seemed to be trying to find suitable scripts for him and that may explain why he would go more than a year between film assignments compared to the multi-pictures he would make every year prior to his war service. Bob wasn't alone. While he had only three releases between 1946 and 1949, the king of the lot, Clark Gable, just appeared in five films between 1945 and 1949. Robert Montgomery, another returning veteran to the MGM stable, was also used infrequently by the studio and, unlike Bob and Gable, was often loaned out. A fourth returning veteran, Mickey Rooney, was so discouraged by how MGM was using him in the years since he returned from the war, that he asked and received a termination of his studio contract. Yet, especially compared to his friend Gable, Bob was being used rather interestingly by MGM in terms of film assignments: the psychotic murderer of *Undercurrent*; the brain

]eral agent, tempted to look the other way, of The Bribe. Bob was miles away from the gorgeous young lover roles which had defined his earlier career.

Bob thought that *The Bribe* was nothing special, just a potboiler and he isn't far from the truth. He told Gardner that he thought that the film was one of the worst films he ever made. Bob and Gardner got along very well during the filming and, as often happened on movie sets, the two indulged in a love affair. According to Gardner, the affair spanned at most about four months, but was very passionate while it lasted. Gardner would refer to it as a "magical little interlude." Gardner, of course, knew that Bob was married to Barbara Stanwyck, "but the marriage had been on the rocks for a long time." [273]

Prior to her affair with Bob, Gardner had been seeing movie tough guy Howard Duff, but that had ended just prior to filming on *The Bribe.* "I was available," she later recalled. Gardner recalled Bob as a "warm, generous, intelligent human being. " Bob and Ava couldn't hold a clandestine affair behind closed dressing room doors at the studio alone, so they had to find somewhere to meet that would be out of the way and where nobody would recognize them—a tall order. Taylor ultimately came up with Ruth's house. Ruth allowed this because she never really took to Barbara, but she still wasn't happy about it. One night Ava would recall Bob having words with Ruth. "Mother, would you rather I go to a cheap hotel?" [274]

The affair ran its course, but Gardner had happy memories of it and Bob. "Bob, despite all his efforts, couldn't break the mold of the beautiful lover. The film world remembers him that way, and I have to say that I do, too." [275] While they would make two more films over the next four years they never resumed their affair, but did remain fond friends. Ironically, just months after completing *The Bribe,* Ava went into another film, *East Side, West Side,* which paired her with Barbara Stanwyck. Ava suspected that Barbara had found out about her affair with Bob because she was cool toward her throughout the filming even going as far as to avoid a formal introduction.

---

273 Ava: My Story, pg. 134

274 Ava Gardner: Love is Nothing, Lee Server, pg. 158

275 Ava: My Story, pg. 135

When *The Bribe* opened in New York, *The New York Times* dismissed the film as "lurid" and "absurd." Bob's secret-service agent "grimly goes through the paces" and Gardner, "performs the sultry siren with her hips draped in nobility." *The Bribe* didn't take the country by storm. It grossed only about $1.6 million in North America and ended up in the red by over $300,000.

IV

Ambush returned Bob to the Western genre for the first time since *Billy the Kid* in 1941. It was a genre he came to enjoy a great deal and would appear increasingly in for the remainder of his film career. He certainly would be more comfortable in the Western genre than the other genre he would appear in with some regularity over the next several years—the costume picture.

The producer of *Ambush* was Bob's friend Armand Deutsch, whose first picture for Metro as a line producer this would be. Deutsch was happy with the assignment. "*Ambush* seemed just fine to me," Deutsch recalled years later. "It was certainly not the kind of project assigned to the front-rank producers, but had the makings of a respectable program film to be produced with second-tier stars and a competent director."[276] The screenplay was assigned to one of Metro's top writers, Marguerite Roberts. Roberts had already written or contributed to the screenplays of such Taylor films as *Escape*, *Undercurrent* and *The Bribe*. At this point in the picture Deutsch had no illusions that his picture would be nothing more than a solid programmer.

One day while Deutsch and Roberts were still hammering out a screenplay, Bob Taylor dropped by unannounced at his office on the Metro lot. It seemed odd to Deutsch that Taylor would drop by. "We were friends by now, but . . . in MGM's stratified hierarchy major stars had no need to cruise around the offices of fledging producers."[277]

Bob told Deutsch that he had a problem. Dore Schary wanted him to star in one of his personal productions, a war picture called

276 Bogie and Me, Armand Deutsch

277 ibid

Battleground. Battleground was going to be made with an all-star cast and a strong director in William Wellman. Schary was very big on the picture. Bob, however, wasn't. It's not that he didn't think it was a good project, but he felt at this time in his career he needed a personal star vehicle, rather than appearing with an all-star cast. He wanted out of *Battleground* and had a plan which involved Deutsch. He wanted Deutsch to go to Schary and help plead his case. At some point during this meeting Bob's eyes settled on the draft of the script for *Ambush* which sat on Deutsch's desk. Bob asked to read it. Deutsch wasn't keen on the idea since it was an early draft. Deutsch continued to balk at the idea, but Bob grabbed the script off his desk and responded, "Bullshit, Don't make such a big deal out of it. I'll just read it and get back to you in the morning." [278]

The next morning an enthusiastic Bob called Deutsch to tell him that he loved the script and he intended to get out of *Battleground* to make Deutsch's little programmer! Deutsch knowing that the film wasn't intended to be made with a star of Bob's caliber was insistent; he would pick up the script from Bob's house and they would not even consider such a thing. He would have to find another project to use to get out of *Battleground.*

A few weeks passed and Deutsch was summoned to Schary's office to discuss the screenplay and budget for the picture. To his surprise, when he walked in, he found Schary with Bob Taylor. Schary informed Deutsch that Bob had read Ambush and was insistent upon making the picture. Schary told his producer, "You're a lucky guy." [279] Suddenly, *Ambush* took on a different light at the studio. It was no longer a programmer to star one of the studio's second-tier leading men, but a star vehicle for Robert Taylor. After a few days Schary called Deutsch back to his office to inform him that veteran MGM director Sam Wood liked the script and wanted to direct it. Wood had directed such films as *A Night at the Opera, Goodbye, Mr. Chips, Kings Row, Command Decision* and *The Stratton Story*. He had also directed (uncredited) some scenes of *Gone With the Wind.* Now Deutsch not only had a name star but also a prestigious director. The budget of his film also increased. His programmer was

278 ibid

279 Bogie and Me, Armand Deutsch

now an A picture. Schary informed Deutsch that his good luck might be a blessing in disguise. That with an important star and important director assigned to his picture that he Deutsch) may be taken off the film and a more experienced line director assigned. Deutsch felt his heart fall.

Deutsch decided to plead his case with Wood, if he could get the director's blessing to continue as producer of the film it would be a major source of support. When Deutsch got to Wood's office, he came in to find Bob also present. For twenty-minutes Deutsch plead his case to Wood. Finally, at the end of that time, Deutsch put his hand up and told Deutsch, "You'll do. Most producers are stupid as hell anyway. You couldn't be any worse than they are." [280] Though Bob never admitted it to Deutsch, he was sure that it was Bob who had put in a good word for his friend and made sure he was kept on the picture.

Ambush cast Bob as a civilian scout working for the U.S. Army. Naturally, there is a love story among the Indian attacks and this one involved Bob romancing beautiful young Arlene Dahl away from an Army captain (played by John Hodiak). Miss Dahl, only twenty-one at the time, was a veteran of only six previous films before being cast in *Ambush*, her most popular being as Red Skelton's leading lady in *A Southern Yankee.*

The casting of Arlene Dahl as the film's leading lady was the only flare-up during the production between director Wood and producer Deutsch. Wood favored casting a more well-known leading lady opposite a star of Bob's caliber. Once again Deutsch turned to his friend Bob Taylor for advice. Taylor told Deutsch to hold firm, "Don't fight the front office about this. You'll lose. The part isn't strong enough for a big star and Sam knows it. He's just been too nice to you and wants you to suffer a little. He's the one to stand up to, not the front office. Deutsch stood his ground with Wood, who responded, "You're getting to be a real producer real quick. Unable and unwilling to do a goddamn thing." [281] Arlene Dahl was in the picture. The picture would be shot over a two-month period from early June to early August of 1949, mostly on location in

280 ibid

281 Bogie and Me, Armand Deutsch

outside Gallup, New Mexico.

Arlene Dahl had wonderful memories of Bob Taylor. "Fred Astaire and Bob Taylor were the two gentlemen of Hollywood." She recalls that because it was so early in her career that Bob took her under his wing. "We forged a great friendship on that film. He knew I was a newcomer and this was only my sixth picture and I wasn't as sophisticated about such things as camera angles and lighting and he was very helpful. Bob made me feel at home. He was my confidant. Just a sweet, wonderful man." [282]

Dahl recalls that *Ambush* was also the final film that Sam Wood would direct. "I think the location shoot did him in." Shooting the picture during the height of the summer in the southwest was not an easy task for any director, especially one who turned 66 during the shooting of the picture. (Wood would die within six weeks of completing *Ambush.*) She said she did not realize that Wood didn't want her for the picture, but she is sure that Bob probably did go to the bat for her. She recalls Wood as a "very contained man—not a woman's director at all! He was decidedly a man's director and he liked doing those kinds of thing. The romance in pictures didn't mean a thing to him." [283]

The day before the picture ended Dahl confessed to Bob, "because we felt comfortable with each other," that just a couple of years before when she was still a high-school student she had written MGM for an 8x10 glossy of him. Bob asked her if she had gotten it. She said she had and "I told him it was signed." The next day, when she arrived at the studio to begin the final day of shooting the picture, she found in her dressing room, "the most beautiful sterling silver frame with a picture of Bob, signed by him, of course, and then a card next to a wrapped box. The card said that years before, when he was doing *Camille*, Garbo had given him this to wish him luck. He signed the card 'Love, Bob.'" Dahl unwrapped the box and inside of it was the ivory-carved Buddha that Garbo had given the young, relatively inexperienced Bob Taylor. "I still have it," Dahl says today. [284]

---

282 Arlene Dahl to author

283 ibid

284 ibid

V

In early November of 1948 Bob began production on one of the worst films of his career. *Conspirator* was the second film shot at Metro's newly built Elstree studio, and casts Bob as, of all things, a Communist agent. Of course, it was a propaganda film of the worst kind. Bob plays an English serviceman who meets a visiting American at a ball who finds a mutual attraction. They are soon married and the wife comes to the realization that her husband is a Russian spy. Of course, she wants him to quit. He tells her that he is a 'loyal supporter of the greatest social experiment in the world." Whatever, says his bride, "All I know is its wrong and I hate it!" The Communists don't like that he married behind their back since it's a "serious breach of discipline." They tell him that he must eliminate his new bride—or they will do it for him.

Even though Bob would be away from home over the holidays filming *Conspirator*, he was excited to be back in England. "I came more than ten years ago to make *A Yank at Oxford*," he recalled, "but I had almost forgotten what a stimulating experience it can be to work amid surroundings that are entirely different from those one is accustomed." He noted the postwar austerity in England and commented, "I know I shall return to Hollywood with a deeper appreciation of the problems faced by the British government and the people themselves under the current austerity program. All of this helps to broaden anyone's viewpoint . . . I'll be glad to get back home, of course, but I feel that I'm returning as a better-informed American citizen, and yes, a better actor too."[285]

The only thing novel about the film is the choice of Bob's leading lady, sixteen-year-old Elizabeth Taylor, in her first adult role. "I was sixteen but looked about twenty-four," Miss Taylor later said.[286] Bob was thirty-eight at the time and looked every year of his age. Elizabeth's California tutor accompanied her to England and in between romantic scenes with Bob she had to buck down and study algebra, composition and history before being called to shoot another scene. "It kind of made your eyes crossed," she later

285 MGM News, 1/10/47

286 Elizabeth, Dick Sheppard, pg. 60

explained.[287] One Taylor biographer would suggest that when the young actress balked at having to return to her studies, her older co-star would tell her that his wife, Barbara Stanwyck, was a true professional who would always do what the studio asked of her. "Elizabeth, in the interest of being polite to her costar, who was old enough to be her father, would bite her tongue."[288] Still, Miss Taylor took a liking to Bob, telling the press, "He is just as wonderful as everyone in Hollywood told me he was. I have to admit I did get nervous when he took me in his arms and made love to me, but the director said I shouldn't be upset."[289] Bob seemed to enjoy those romantic scenes. "They told her to kiss," he said, "and she kissed!"[290] Elizabeth was an "amazing youngster," he recalled, "she will be talking on the set just like a regular teenager. Then suddenly she will go into a dramatic scene with me and change into a grown young woman. She is an excellent actress with great talent."[291]

The film, directed by Victor Seville, who the previous year had made the interesting *Green Dolphin Street* and would do a fine job adapting Rudyard Kipling's *Kim* a year later, sat on the shelf for over a year before being released in March of 1950. The *New York Times* called the picture a "lugubrious affair" and a "disappointment." As for the leads, "Miss Taylor and Mr. Taylor are capable of doing better. " The *New York Post* did acknowledge that Taylor and Taylor "are the two most beautiful people on the screen." The reviews didn't help and the film was a box-office failure, Bob's second in a row after *The Bribe*.

Bob's next film was much more interesting and cast him in one of the best roles of his career, playing an Indian. Bob Taylor playing an Indian? Well . . . yes, he was cast as a Shoshone Indian who wins the Congressional Medal of Honor by fighting with Union forces at Gettysburg in *The Devil's Doorway.* The film is a sympathetic look at the struggles of Native Americans, as Bob's character, Lance Poole, back from the war a hero, returns to his native Wyoming and

287 ibid

288 Elizabeth, J. Randy Taraborrelli, pg. 60

289 Robert Taylor, J.E. Wayne, pg. 142

290 Elizabeth, Dick Sheppard, pg. 62

291 LA Examiner, 5/1/49

has to grapple with white sheep herders who want to take over his land. Anthony Mann, directing his first Western, would become identified with the genre in a series of films during the 1950s with James Stewart (including *Winchester '73* and *The Man from Laramie*) as well as top examples of the genre as *The Tin Star* (with Henry Fonda) and *Man of the West* (with Gary Cooper). It's a shame that Bob, who enjoyed the Western genre so much, wasn't able to work with Mann in any of his subsequent Western films.

Mann was offered a Western by MGM and jumped at the chance after reading the scenario. "In fact, that . . . scenario was the best script I've ever read," Mann later recalled.[292] When asked what MGM leading man he wanted to play the lead, Mann selected Bob Taylor without hesitation. To play an Indian the Metro make-up artists darkened Bob's skin and most critics agreed that he did look the part. Production on the film began on location in Grand Junction, Colorado, in mid-August of 1949 with principal photography to run approximately two months.

The film was not only enlightened in its treatment of Indians, but also in its treatment of women. When white settlers try to take over his land, Poole goes to the only attorney in town, one O. Masters, who turns out to be a woman (played by Paula Raymond). Raymond had mixed memories of the film, but she did enjoy working with Bob. "I've heard it was one of Bob Taylor's favorite pictures because for once he was able to play a different type of character. He was the charming leading man in most of his pictures. He was a nice guy. Easy to work with . . . professional."[293] But Miss Raymond also believed that Bob "felt inferior to his wife, Barbara Stanwyck." She recalled that once Anthony Mann showed her a note that Bob had sent him. "He signed it Mr. Barbara Stanwyck."[294]

While Raymond got along fine with Bob, she tried to keep her distance from their director. "When I was off screen, I would hide," she recalled. "The director was Anthony Mann. I had not-too-impressive credits from Columbia, yet I was co-starring with a big

292 Anthony Mann, Jeanine Basinger, pg. 83

293 Films of the Golden Age #17, Summer 1999

294 Interview with Paula Raymond, Western Clippings Magazine by Mike Fitzgerald

star. Anthony Mann didn't want me because I was not a star, not an equal to Taylor." But later she contends when they were on location, Mann tried to get her into bed, but she avoided his advances. A year later she worked with Mann again opposite Dick Powell in *The Tall Target*, "This time . . . Mann left me alone." [295]

There are a number of good scenes in the picture. One scene in particular early on in the picture is visually strong. It involves Taylor riding into town to deposit the money he earned by selling cattle into the bank. Yet, as he rides into town, the streets become filled with herds of sheep blocking his path while in the sky large dark clouds fill the sky. The storm clouds in the sky are an omen for the hell that will break loose against Taylor and his fellow Indians by the sheep herders who dominate the county. The use of black-and-white photography by Mann and director of photography John Alton is superb, as is the use of sound effects. For instance, there is a fight in a saloon, a dark and forbidding place where no Indians are to be served. A fight takes place, with punches being punctuated by the sounds of the thunder and crackling of the lightning from the storm brewing outside. It makes for a compellingly hard and realistic cinematic experience. The ending is well done as well, particularly the final scene in the picture when Taylor, after having done everything he could to legally protect his land, ultimately loses to the white sheep herders. In his Civil War uniform and wearing his Congressional Medal of Honor he salutes the soldiers who have now driven him off his land and then falls dead.

While *The Devil's Doorway* was completed in October of 1949 it was not released until nearly a year later. The studio was unsure how the film—sympathetic to the Native American—would play. They also knew that 20th Century-Fox was working on their own pro-Indian film, *Broken Arrow*, and wanted to see how that film would go over. While *Devil's Doorway* was completed before *Broken Arrow* it was held back. When *Broken Arrow* was released, the Delmer Daves film starring James Stewart became a big critical and box-office hit, which offered hope to MGM for *Devil's Doorway*.

Unfortunately, the film was completely overshadowed both critically and at the box office by the Fox film. Many critics, not

295 ibid

realizing the MGM film was actually shot before the Fox film, thought that *Devil's Doorway* was a quickly made imitation to cash in on the popularity of *Broken Arrow.* But in many respects *Devil's Doorway* is a much more complex and visually superior film than *Broken Arrow*. Bob did, however, get some good reviews for his performance. "Robert Taylor may strike you as a rather peculiar choice to play a full-blooded Indian, but give the man credit for a forceful performance," wrote the critic for the *New York Post*. Director Anthony Mann, however, was nevertheless pleased by his picture and compared it to the more popular *Broken Arrow*. "I think the result was more powerful than *Broken Arrow*, more dramatic, too." [296]

296 Jeanine Basinger, Anthony Mann, pg. 89

PORTRAIT GALLERY #3

Bob and Vivien Leigh in his own favorite movie, *Waterloo Bridge*, 1940

Vivien Leigh, Bob and C. Aubrey Smith, *Waterloo Bridge*

Bob as Roy Cronin in his best film, *Waterloo Bridge*

Spring Byington, Bob and Joan Crawford, *When Ladies Meet* (1941)

Bob in his first western, *Billy the Kid* (1941)

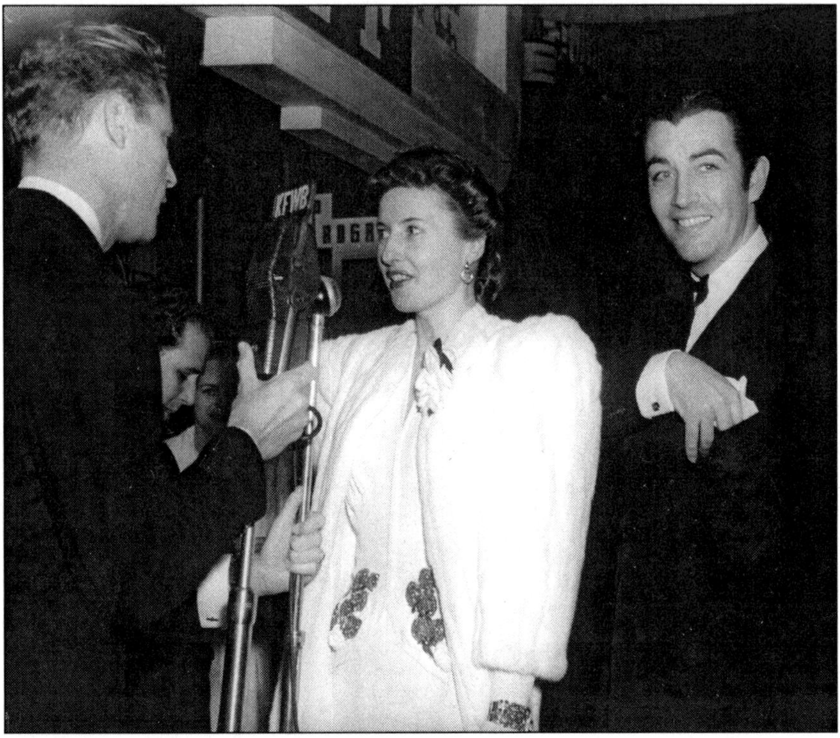

Barbara and Bob at the premiere of *Meet John Doe*

There was TNT behind the scenes of *Johnny Eager*, too, with Lana Turner

Bob fighting for his life, *Johnny Eager*, one of his favorite pictures.

Bob offering a drink to Lloyd Nolen, *Bataan* (1943), PHOTO COURTESY OF SANDRA GRABMAN

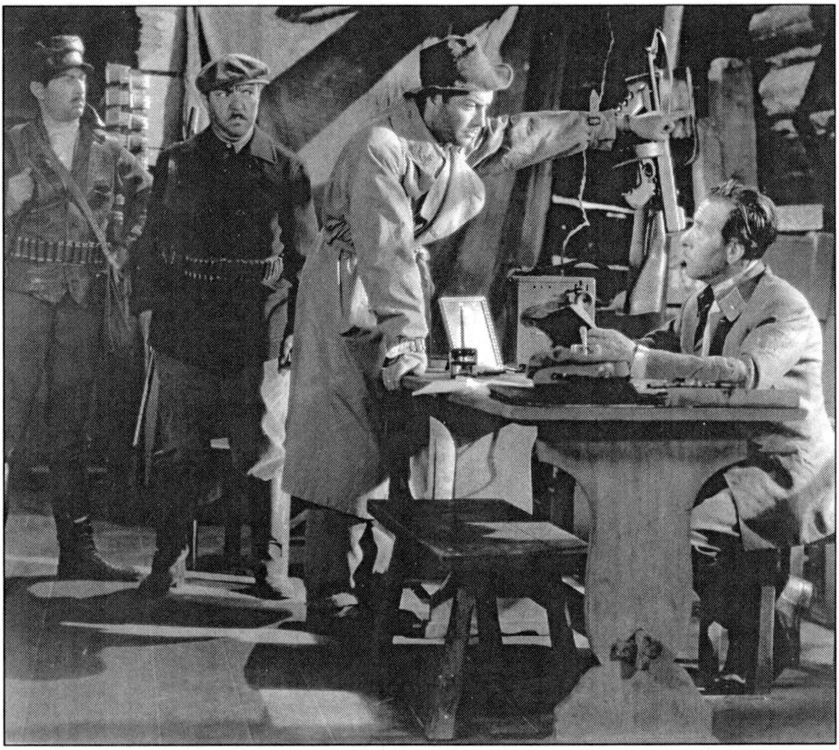

Bob didn't want to do *Song of Russia* (1944), but did, so he could get on with his stint in the Navy.

Bob in Naval uniform (1944)

Bob's first post-war film, *Undercurrent* (1946), teamed him with Katharine Hepburn

Bob with Robert Mitchum in *Undercurrent*.

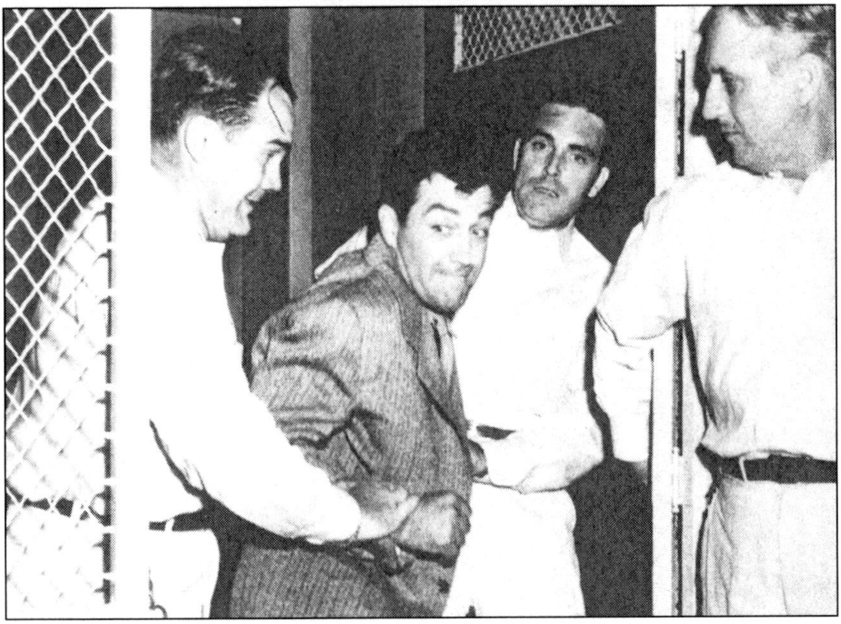

One of his most interesting pictures, *The High Wall*, 1947

Bob engaged in a brief, but passionate affair with Ava Gardner while making *The Bribe* (1949)

Bob with his Beechcraft plane (1946). He had a passion for flying—something Barbara loathed (PHOTO COURTESY OF TERRY TAYLOR)

Leon Ames and Bob in *Ambush* (1950)

Elizabeth Taylor had her first grown up role opposite Bob in *The Conspirator* (1950)

Another studio portrait of Bob, late forties.

Cast against type as an Indian seeking dignity in *Devil's Doorway* (1950)

Chapter Nine

"WELL, SON YOU ARE GOING TO STAR IN THE BIGGEST OF THEM" (1950-1953)

MGM had been negotiating for the rights to Henryk Sienkiewicz's 1895 novel *Quo Vadis* almost since its inception as a motion picture studio. Metro had had a huge hit with *Ben-Hur*, and saw *Quo Vadis* as a sure-fire box-office hit on the same grand scale. The novel, when published, became an international bestseller and was translated into many different languages. The title is from the Gospel of St. John and is translated as "Whither goest Thou, Lord?" And the answer is "I am the way, the truth, the life."

Eventually, MGM did acquire the rights to *Quo Vadis* and over the years several announcements were made about producing the picture. One of the earliest came in 1935 with the announcement that Wallace Beery would star as Nero with Marlene Dietrich as his wife, Poppaea. In 1939 Louella Parsons wrote in her column that Hunt Stromberg, one of Metro's leading producers at the time, would be producing a version of the novel with Robert Taylor in the lead. Nothing ever came of this. Then in 1942 the studio made another premature announcement that the picture would be made with Orson Welles as Nero from an S.N. Behrman script. The publicity continued on into the next year with various announcements that Walter Pidgeon, Lana Turner and Thomas Mitchell were being cast and that Ernst Lubitsch was under consideration as director. Again, the production languished, but finally was revived in 1949, with the *Hollywood Citizen-News* announcing that MGM would begin production in the summer. This time the stars would be Gregory Peck and Elizabeth Taylor with John Huston directing. However, an eye infection caused Peck to drop out of the film. Already in pre-production with some $2 million spent and sets built, the film would only be delayed, not cancelled, until a new leading man was found. But, then, John Huston, who was feuding with the original producer. Arthur Hornblow, dropped out of the film.

Mayer quickly assigned a new producer, Sam Zimbalist, and director, Mervyn LeRoy. Needless to say, LeRoy was less than overwhelmed. He read the novel and cabled one of the writers, Sam Bierman: I HAVE FINALLY FOUND A BOOK I COULD PUT DOWN.[297] However, LeRoy did understand that the needed ingredients to make an epic blockbuster were in the book and the script fashioned by Bierman and John Lee Mahin. LeRoy then contacted the movies king of the biblical epics, Cecil B. DeMille, and questioned him as to why the Bible has proven to be profitable. "I'll tell you, Mervyn," DeMille informed him. "The Bible has been a best-seller for centuries. Why should I let two thousand years of publicity go to waste?"[298] LeRoy couldn't refute that. He would proceed to film a story with all the elements: big stars, colorful characters, madness, orgies, man-eating lions, spectacular battle scenes, thousands of extras, man-eating, the burning of Rome, and early Christianity.

As an added insurance, LeRoy had a private audience with Pope Pius XII and asked The Holy Father to bless his shooting script of *Quo Vadis*. The Pope did as requested. He laid his hands on the script and, first in Latin and then in English, said, "May your film be a successful one."[299] Later, the Pope confessed to LeRoy that he was a fan of the cinema and especially enjoyed *Going My Way*, particularly the scene where the elderly priest takes a little drink of whisky.

When recasting the key role of Marcus Vinicius, the studio approached the King of the lot, Clark Gable, who turned the role down flat—there was no way he would appear in toga and sandals. Gable told Schary, "I'm not going to be seen in a Roman toga with my bloody knees sticking out. It's not my thing and I won't do it."[300] Stewart Granger was then considered for the part, but after

297 Mervyn LeRoy, Take Two, pg. 169

298 Ibid, pg. 170

299 Take One, Mervyn LeRoy, pg. 171

300 Clark Gable, J.E. Wayne

he declined a long-term contract the studio decided not to cast him in such an important role in a film they correctly believed would be a blockbuster.

Enter reliable Bob Taylor. Bob wasn't keen on accepting the role either. "When the part of Marcus Vinicius in *Quo Vadis* first was offered to me, I was quite dubious about it," Taylor later recalled. "You see I almost broke into the movies wearing a toga and the result almost sent me back to Nebraska." [301] Mayer poured it on as well, "Yes, son, you are going to star in the biggest of them all." [302] However reluctant Bob felt about playing a Roman centurion, he decided to do the picture. In part because he needed a big box-office hit; his postwar box-office record was mediocre at best. It also would provide Bob the opportunity to spend several months away from Barbara, as the friction at home was becoming more unbearable. Surprisingly, Barbara urged Bob to accept the part. The professional in Stanwyck understood that *Quo Vadis* could provide her husband's career with a needed jolt. The other actors had already been cast when Bob was brought aboard. Joining him were Peter Ustinov in the colorful role of Nero; Leo Genn as Petronius; Patricia Laffan as Poppaea and Finley Currie as Peter. However, after the film was delayed, Elizabeth Taylor was assigned to another film. To play the part of Lygia, the Christian girl who believes in Jesus, LeRoy tested hundreds of girls over a three-month period of time. LeRoy felt he needed an unknown and thought he found her in Audrey Hepburn, but the studio vetoed her, wanting a more established actress in the part. Deborah Kerr was soon signed. [303]

Quo Vadis tells the story of General Marcus Vinicius returning to Rome after three years in the field. He meets and falls in love with Lygia, a Christian, who doesn't want to have anything to do with him since the Romans persecute believers in Christ. Vinicius is a hero to the Roman people and he convinces Emperor Nero to give her to him for the services he has rendered for Rome. Despite her being used in this way, and resenting it, she does fall in love with Vinicius. The other part of the story concerns the increasing madness

---

301 LA Daily News, 5/7/53

302 Stanwyck, Axel Madsen, pg 274

303 Take One, pg.171

of Nero and his atrocities which culminate in the burning of Rome. Nero puts the blame for what he did on the Christians and orders the Christians to be rounded up and killed. Vinicius, who over time has grown sympathetic to the plight of the Christians, must save Lydia and her family.

Production of the film was to begin in May of 1950 at the Cinnecitta Studios in Rome. Prior to leaving Bob had one more urgent matter to take care of:

> Dear Sirs:
> This will undoubtedly strike you as a presumptuous request and I hasten to beg your pardon for intruding on your time in this matter. However, I have no way of obtaining the information I desire. In the very near future I shall be leaving for Italy, where I shall be engaged in the making of a motion picture for a period of at least eight months. From the inquiries I have made thus far it seems extremely unlikely that I will find it convenient to obtain your Glenlivet Scotch Whiskey in Rome . . . Over a period of time I've come to consider all other brands of Scotch Whiskey to be second rate and strenuously dislike the prospect of six months in Italy without your Glenlivet . . . the assurance that I will have ample stocks of Glenlivet during my stay there is one of the most urgent elements of my present departure efforts . . .
> Very Truly Yours,
> Robert Taylor[304]

He also worked with Barbara on *Screen Guild Theatre* in a radio adaptation of one of Barbara's most famous films, "Double Indemnity." Barbara recreated her role as the manipulative Phyllis Dietrichson while Bob took on Fred MacMurray's role as the insurance agent, Walter Neff, driven to murder. It would be their final radio program together, but not the last time they would act together.

304 A Double Scotch by Paul Pacult, pg. 202

II

When Bob arrived in Rome, the studio spared no expense in keeping their star happy and comfortable. He was given the entire top floor of an apartment house, five servants including butler and valet. For his convenience he was given two cars, one sporty so he could enjoy tooling around in and the other a more formal limousine with chauffeur. His meals were prepared by a chef who once served the King of Italy. In the midst of filming, Bob's friend Tom Purvis paid a visit. "My God, I didn't know what the hell I was eating when that chef prepared dinner for us at the apartment," Purvis later said. "When I got back home my wife asked me what kinda food I had and she coulda kicked me when I answered, 'don't know.'"[305]

While Bob was set up comfortably in his apartment, he was also putting in long hours at the studio. He was up by five and often not in bed until ten at night. He worked six days per week, with Sundays off. Working conditions were not always the best. There was a heat wave in Rome that summer. It was often unbearable and caused some morale problems as the weeks went by. Eddie Mannix, sent by Dore Schary to keep an eye on the production, sent sometimes daily reports to Schary. On July 4, he wrote, ". . . the usual complaints about the weather, we have had two weeks of very hot days and nights. As a rule the nights cool off, it should break in a day or so, if not afraid we will be forced to work at nights, which I do not like to, but it may be the only way out." He also informed Schary that the weather was causing delays, "We continue to lose time and unless we do more with a second unit the show will be in production until early December. I hope not."[306] (A few days earlier Mannix had written Schary that the temperature on the sets had been 105 degrees.)

Mannix was also pleased with how well Zimbalist and LeRoy were cooperating together on the picture. "They both are working together like partners—asking one another for help on all matters—so pleased with their attitude to one another."[307] It was probably a

305 Robert Taylor, J.E. Wayne, pg. 146-147

306 Eddie Mannix to Dore Schary, Schary Papers (WSHSA)

307 ibid

complete turnaround from when Arthur Hornblower and John Huston had been working on the film as producer and director several months before.

For his part Schary had cabled Mannix that on the whole the footage he was receiving from them was very good particularly, "all material with Ustinov (as Nero) very exciting and interesting." He found the "big spectacle stuff also very impressive indicating scope and vitality." On the down side, Schary felt that the "camera in intimate scenes could be used a little more effectively, I have feeling that the cutting will appear to make picture static unless we employ camera at times more ingeniously." But, overall, "Actors doing fine job and picture developing good style." Among the actors, the only real problem, as far as Schary was concerned, was with Leo Genn, cast as Petronius. He felt that Genn was "playing a little too soft and should be a bit more masculine." Mannix, in his follow-up, agreed. "Having trouble with Leo Genn to make him a little more stern and manly—to me is completely overpowered by Nero." A couple of days later, Schary responded to Mannix's concerns about how long it might take to complete the picture, with his prediction that filming may drag out until December. "My feeling about the picture is that we cannot help anything by developing a state of panic, and as a matter of fact a few items that have appeared in papers were harmful and were caused by panic that never should have been permitted to start." But all in all, Schary was bucking him and the entire company up: "I am positive, along with you, that we are going to have a helluva wonderful picture."[308]

Deborah Kerr was another in a long list of fetching leading ladies that Bob worked with. "When one thinks of his extraordinary good looks, he had every right to be a bit spoiled, but not Bob," recalled Kerr. "He was unassuming, good natured and had a wonderful sense of humor . . . I felt he was a much better actor than he was given credit for."[309]

Meanwhile, Barbara was hearing word back in the States that Bob was being seen around Rome with a minor actress who was playing a slave girl in the picture. Her name was Lia De Leo, a red-headed

308 Dore Schary to Eddie Mannix, Schary Papers (WSHSA)

309 Robert Taylor, J.E. Wayne, pg. 147-148

twenty-five-year-old divorcee. De Leo later said that Bob was "tired of her [Stanwyck] and told me so. It was evident that after meeting me, a divorce was the only possible solution." She also said that if it were up to Bob, he would marry her, but "I don't think it will happen because I am reluctant to marry again."[310] Years later, Miss De Leo, when asked if Bob ever discussed his marriage with her, she had partially changed her story, saying she really didn't understand the language and, "I'm a person who never asks questions." She said that when they did talk she would nod her head as if she understood what he was saying, and sensed that he wanted to divorce Barbara.[311] As a lover she recalls Bob as "a very great, good lover. Maybe I inspired him."[312] Apparently, Miss De Leo was reluctant to admit that she was probably no more than a movie location dalliance. Yes, his marriage with Stanwyck was all but over, but certainly Bob had no intentions of divorcing Barbara so he could marry De Leo.

Stanwyck allegedly checked with Howard Strickling, Metro's publicity chief, to make sure that this wasn't studio publicity. Strickland assured her it wasn't. According to Stanwyck biographer, Axel Madsen, the Queen Bees of the Hollywood gossip machine, Hedda Hopper and Louella Parsons, were on the phone to Stanwyck asking for comment. Hopper came right out and asked her if Bob wanted a divorce. Telling Hopper that she would find out, she called her back a few minutes later and said, "He says not today, Hedda. Sorry. Goodbye."[313]

Stanwyck had committed to go to London to make the movie *Another Man's Poison*. She and her close friend and publicist, Helen Ferguson, flew over. This was unusual because she hated flying and when traveling abroad she usually sailed. This caused some warning signals among the Hollywood gossips as well. As it turned out, the script of *Another Man's Poison* was being overhauled, and this gave Stanwyck the perfect opportunity to fly into Rome and check out the rumors for herself. She arrived at Bob's lavish apartment and

310 LA Times, 2/23/51

311 Linda Alexander, Reluctant Witness

312 ibid

313 Stanwyck, pg. 276

asked him pointblank if the stories about his womanizing were correct. He didn't deny them. She then, either out of anger or to frighten him, said that a divorce was in order. Bob said "fine." So, that was that. The breaking point had come. It is said that Stanwyck never stopped loving Bob, and that she had asked for a divorce in the heat of the moment, and came to regret it, but as a proud woman she wouldn't be the one to back down. If anybody were to back down it would have to be Bob, as he had done so many times in the past. But this time Bob was firmly in control. His months of independence from Barbara had made him see that the marriage wasn't worth saving.

Needless to say, neither Bob, nor Barbara, had ever discussed the other disrespectfully in the press and they weren't about to begin now. No mention of a divorce was made in the press. Bob was still to be in Rome for several more months. The announcement would be delayed until they both were back home. Barbara wasn't about to make it appear that a little starlet had ended her marriage. (Of course she didn't; the breach had been brewing for years.) But the columnists would certainly make it seem as if she was the motivator. Instead, the Strickling unit went overboard with exaggerated claims of gifts from each spouse to the other and expressions of their undying love. They then put on a act of Bob showing Barbara the sights in Rome, which made it appear in Hollywood that the rumors had been false and the couple were just fine, exactly what Stanwyck and Bob wanted. But the most telling sign of what actually happened was when Stanwyck informed the producer of *Another Man's Poison* that she had to withdraw from the picture because her life "was in shreds" and she was unable to perform.[314] This was certainly not expected of a pro of Stanwyck's reputation.

There was still a film to complete. The arena sequence in *Quo Vadis* took about three weeks to shoot, in often excruciatingly hot weather. Thousands of extras were used. LeRoy estimated the number as high as 60,000! Stars passing through Rome asked to be part of the crowd of extras and among those who did so included Elizabeth Taylor, who asked LeRoy if she could be an extra specifically to get away from her then-husband Nicky Hilton. Her wish was

314 ibid

granted. A star-to-be was also among the extras: a young Sophia Loren. The production was still problem-plagued. Robert Surtees, the cinematographer on the film, would recall, "We were able to secure only three or four setups per day. Camera motors broke down; sound equipment blew; the Italian electricians, new to their jobs, allowed lamps to go out during takes." [315]

Of the arena scenes involving the lions versus the Christians, LeRoy would recall, "I had a gun which I shot off three times. I shot the first bullet; everyone was ready. I shot the second; the cameras turned over and they all yelled 'Ready!' I shot the third; the screen opened and the lions all rushed out. They looked up at the sun and went right back in." LeRoy asked the lion tamers, who were also among those playing the persecuted Christians in the picture, what they should do. They told him to starve the lions for about two weeks. "So I jumped to other scenes and for two weeks all night long you'd hear these lions growling for something to eat. After two weeks we were ready to shoot. The lions rushed out into the sun, looked up and went back in again. I could never get the shot the way I wanted it. I had to break it up into different shots." But the pace did quicken once the heat broke and the picture finished production by mid-November of 1950, and Bob was free to fly back to the United States.

Back in the States Bob and Barbara didn't immediately announce their separation and allowed the charade to last a bit longer. For one thing, within a week of returning Bob went under the knife undergoing a two-hour abdominal operation at the Stanford Hospital in San Francisco. He had been suffering from a double hernia. Barbara was at his side. Stanwyck told the press that the operation was a success in part "due to Bob's splendid physical condition he came through in very fine shape." Yet he was expected to remain in the hospital for two weeks. [316]

On December 15, 1950, the bombshell hit the press when Bob and Barbara issued a joint statement announcing that they were separating and that a divorce would soon follow. The press release said that they had come to this decision, "reluctantly and unhappily,"

---

315 Voices from Film Experience, Jay Leyda pg. 449

316 LA Examiner, 11/23/50

and that the reason was due to the long separations they have endured "professionally" during their eleven-year marriage. "Our sincere and continual efforts to maintain our marriage have failed. We are deeply disappointed that we could not solve our problems." The statement went on to say, "We unhappily and reluctantly admit that we have denied the rift to even our closest friends, because we wanted to work this out together in as much privacy as possible. Neither of us has any other romantic interest whatever."[317] One unnamed confidant of the couple was quoted as saying, "They never could get together. They were always separated by an ocean or a mountain or the gate of some movie studio."[318]

Certainly, professional separation may have played a role, but the simple fact is that the couple was mismatched. Bob had interests such as flying and hunting that took him increasingly away from home—and Barbara. She was, on the whole, a homebody who had no real hobbies and spent most of her days when not on a soundstage reading. When they met, Bob was a younger (wet behind the ears) actor and Barbara was an experienced professional who was happy to take the younger actor under her wing. Bob always admired her for her professionalism and learned a lot about the industry from her, but that is not enough to build a foundation for a successful marriage. She continued to try and dominate him throughout their marriage. If he did anything that displeased her she would go for the jugular by attacking his manhood. She would refer to his friend and frequent hunting/fishing partner Tom Purvis as "your wife." Years later when working on the film *Ride, Vaquero!* Anthony Quinn asked Bob, over drinks, why he and Stanwyck had divorced. "Ah, Tony," he said. "That woman, she always wants to run the fuck."[319] In short, Bob had grown up and no longer required a mother figure looking out for him.

After the separation Bob moved in with his mother. He took the small maid's room as his own. Ivy Shelton recalls that Bob, who Ruth liked to call "Buddy," provided well for his mother. "He gave her a house, car and even paid for a companion to come and take

317 LA Times, 12/16/50

318 San Mateo Times, 12/18/50

319 Anthony Quinn, One Man Tango

her out once a week," Ivy recalled. "The companion would take Mrs. Brugh out on Bob's money." The companion, named Ralph, would usually visit Ruth on Wednesdays for lunch, which, according to Ivy, were always taken in her bedroom. Ruth became dependent on Bob because she had been so dependent on Bob's father during her own years of marriage. Furthermore, Ivy believes that Ruth was "afraid of losing Bob," which was one reason why she never thought that any woman was good enough for him.[320]

Yet he had his Midwestern guilt to contend with. "He felt guilty," Ivy Pearson recalls. "Yet the divorce relieved him. He was a very lonely man. He would just sit in his apartment by himself, he rarely would go out. I would tell him, 'Any lady in America would go out with you—why are you sitting alone?' he would just shrug."[321]

The production of *Quo Vadis* proved a watershed in Bob's life and career. The months of separation from Stanwyck allowed him the freedom to reflect and understand that his marriage was something he didn't want any longer as well as giving him the resolve to stand up to Barbara. Professionally, it put him back on the map again as the picture became MGM's biggest success at the box-office since *Gone With the Wind.* The picture was the most expensive film produced up to that time, costing $6-$7 million. Its first week take at New York's Capitol Theatre set a box-office record, reportedly twice what *Gone With the Wind* had grossed in its first week at the same theatre. It grossed in its initial release an estimated $12.5 million in domestic rentals. LeRoy later said that, with foreign markets figured in the gross, it was closer to $50 million. Critically, the film was praised for its lavish spectacle, but some critics felt that the spectacle overwhelmed the performances. Bosley Crowther, in his *New York Times* review, said that the film is "combined a perfection of spectacle and hippodrome display of a luxuriance of made-to-order romance in a measure not previously seen. Here is a staggering combination of cinema brilliance and sheer banality." *Variety*, in its review, called the film a "super spectacle" that nevertheless contained "wooden performances." Still, the film's huge success with audiences certainly raised Bob's stature at the studio in a time when

320 Ivy Mooring to author

321 ibid

all the studios were under siege by television and studios were reviewing the logic of long-term contracts.

Bob continued his recuperation from the hernia operation at his home in Palm Springs while Barbara, emotionally fragile following the announcement of the separation, stayed with Nancy Sinatra, one of her closest friends. Nancy and Barbara would now console each other. Nancy had just recently won a legal separation from Frank Sinatra, who was publically romancing Ava Gardner, one of Bob's former lovers. Barbara and Nancy would spend the rest of their lives pining for the men who got away, and, for a time, hoping that they would see the light and come back to them. Nancy would always have the three children that she and Frank had together. Stanwyck would also have a hold on Bob for the remainder of his life, but one that he grew increasingly bitter about.

Barbara appeared in Los Angeles Superior Court of February 21, 1951. "He said he had enjoyed his freedom during the months he was making a movie in Italy," she told the court. "He wanted to be able to live his life without restriction." Her reaction to his request of divorce? "I was very shocked and grieved. It made me quite ill. For several weeks I was under the care of my physician." The ever-loyal Helen Ferguson was there as a corroborating witness: "I found her in a tragically emotional state." The divorce was granted by the court, which also approved a property settlement that both Barbara and Bob had agreed to. For the rest of her life Barbara would receive fifteen percent of all of Bob's gross earnings until his death or her remarriage.[322] As the years went by, and Bob remarried and had a family, he grew to resent this monetary agreement which Barbara never relented on—it was her way of keeping a piece of him—despite the fact that she had millions. But at the time it seemed the quickest way to get his freedom. Barbara also got the Holmby Hills home, valued at $100,000, as well as all furnishings. Shortly before her death Stanwyck said, "I'm known as someone who takes care of herself, it's true, but I worked hard at the marriage because I wanted it."[323] Bob continued to be publicly gallant toward Barbara. "Let's just say Barbara is a very strong personality," he said.

322 Portland Press Herald & E. Liverpool Review, 2/22/51

323 Stanwyck, pg. 281-282

"I respect her deeply and treasure her friendship . . . I always felt her talent was far greater than my own; it came easier to her, and she made the most of her gifts."[324] In 1953, he would write, "It would be impossible to overestimate what I owe to her [Barbara]. I'm sure I never would have had whatever success has been mine had it not been for her patient help—giving me the benefit of lessons she already had learned and learned the hard way. Her understanding and the happiness she brought me can't ever be forgotten. The one great regret in my life since coming to Hollywood is that our marriage just didn't work out."[325]

A short time later Clark Gable suggested that Bob console himself by seeing an old paramour of his, actress Virginia Grey. Grey didn't initially hear from Bob; instead, a friend called to ask if it would be okay if Bob called her sometime. Fine. Because his divorce wasn't yet final, Bob suggested that they not be seen publicly. They took to having dinner and listening to records at Grey's apartment.

Things must have gone moderately well with Grey for a while because at one point while Grey was in New York doing some television work she sent a note to Bob saying, "What you read ain't true." Bob playfully replied, "That kinda stopped me on accounta all I'd read was that you had knocked them on their asses in New York T.V. and I naturally could only hope that was true! In any case I assume that I was supposed to have read that you and some fella were carryin' on like crazy in N.Y. and that wedding bells were about to ring at any moment! The longer ST 41227 [Grey's LA telephone number] refuses to answer the more I tend to believe that something real good must have entered your life. Right?"[326]

"He would never talk about Barbara," she later recalled, "but his divorce wasn't final yet and I just took it for granted he didn't want to be seen in public with another woman." Grey also recalled that Barbara "was still in love with him—everybody knew it." Years later, Grey would recall that she had a chance meeting with Stanwyck, "what she had to say to me I cannot quote, but I had done the

324 ibid

325 LA Daily News, 5/9/53

326 Robert Taylor to Virginia Grey, 4/8/52 Academy of Motion Pictures Arts & Sciences Library

unpardonable . . . I had gone out with Bob Taylor."[327] Grey wasn't the only ex-flame of Bob's to incur the wrath of Stanwyck. When Lana Turner heard that Barbara was staying at the same Las Vegas hotel as she was, she called Stanwyck to invite her for a drink in her room. "Her response was negative and her tone of voice icy cold. Obviously she held a grudge."[328] Grey recalled Bob as "warm and wonderful," but felt that there was a wall around him. "I don't think Bob liked himself very much and was not a happy man when I knew him. He was a real introvert when it came to a man and woman relationship."[329]

In April, Barbara may have made Bob a bit uncomfortable when she held a four-night auction of some six hundred articles to be sold to the highest bidder. According to contemporary press reports, one of the items which brought the most interest from prospective buyers was Bob's bed. According to the man running the auction, they were swamped with telephone calls. "They all want to know about Taylor's bed," said Max Goldenberg of Goldenberg Galleries. "They want to know what it is like. Most of the callers are women." Among the other items that Barbara put up for sale: pots and pans, a Renoir original and 64 other paintings. The profits were to go only to Barbara.[330]

That same April Bob began a film which he enjoyed making much more than the experience of *Quo Vadis*, in a genre he greatly liked, the Western. The film was *Westward the Women*, a project to be personally produced by Dore Schary and directed by one of Bob's favorites, William Wellman. Bob plays Buck, a tough wagon master whose responsibility it is to transport 140 women from Chicago to California. Along the way the men who accompany Buck are disposed of in a variety of ways, but mostly for trying to take sexual advantage of the women. Eventually, there are only a few men and it's up to them and the women to survive such things as Indian attacks, intemperate weather, disease and wild animals. The film had been originally based on a story by Frank Capra that he hoped

327 Robert Taylor, JE Wayne, pg. 157

328 Lana: The Lady, The Legend, The Truth, pg. 60

329 Robert Taylor, JE Wayne, pg. 157

330 Long Beach Independent, 4/2/51

to make into a motion picture, but he eventually relinquished the rights.

As usual, the Breen censorship office had to give its blessing on the script before shooting could begin. Among the items they found fault with:

> "The mud baths of Buck and the repeated allusions to them make them a symbol not only of drinking bouts, but also of sexual affairs."

> "The illegitimate pregnancy of Rose is treated too lightly. This will be overcome by an indication by the girl that she recognizes that she did wrong."

> Buck kills a man who presumably raped a woman along the way. The production code took exception to the line, "Nothing's happened to her that didn't happen to her before," describing it as "offensively blunt."

> "The use of the word, 'God,' should, of course, be consistently reverent."

> ". . . audiences generally react unfavorably to too much brutality in the treatment of women. While this item has been improved over the first version of the script, we still feel that, in the aggregate, there is a considerable amount of brutality in the treatment of women."

> "Furthermore, care will be needed in the handling of the kiss and dissolve on page 74. So, also, the action, on pages 76 and 77 will need to be handled with care, so as to avoid excessive gruesomeness."

> "In conclusion, we direct your particular attention to the need for the greatest possible care in the selection and photographing of the dresses and costumes of your women. The production code makes it mandatory that the intimate parts of the body specifically, the breasts of women—be fully covered at all

> times. Any compromise with this regulation will compel us to withhold approval of your picture."[331]

The film was shot nearly all on location, in a place called Surprise Valley in the Mojave Desert. Wellman was the kind of old-time rough-and-tumble director who could bring order to such an enterprise. Wellman had just completed similar duty with Clark Gable in another MGM Western, *Across the Wide Missouri*. Wellman's handpicked cameraman, William Mellor, described Surprise Valley as having "every pictorial element we could ask for, from stark desert wastes to deep walled canyons, plus a stream that grew from a rivulet far up the canyon to a good-size river with many pictorial possibilities." Wellman, who had been one of Barbara Stanwyck's favorite directors, was a firm believer in Bob as well. "I was crazy about Bob Taylor," he said years later. "I think Bob Taylor's probably one of the finest men I've known in my whole life. And he was an actor. And he was probably the handsomest one of them all. He did everything I asked him to; he was wonderful."[332]

Wellman made clear to Bob and his predominately female cast that making the picture wouldn't be a cake walk. In fact, just before the film began he brought together all the women in the cast to let them know that "there would be no room for a prima donna" and that the eleven-week schedule would be "long, dirty and tired." He offered them a last chance to back out of the picture. Otherwise, they would be expected to complete it to the end. He then put the women through a three-week period of basic training which included such things as calisthenics, horseback riding, mule team handling, blacksmithing and assembling covered wagons.[333] Meanwhile, Bob was his usual easygoing self. "You know, there's a feller that never growed hisself no ego," an old cowboy who met Bob during the making of *Westward the Women* told Hollywood writer Jane Kesner Ardmore.

But that didn't mean there weren't problems. Much of the cast and crew got sick, including Wellman, within ten days of the film's

331 Dore Schary Papers, WSHSA

332 William A. Wellman by Frank Thompson pages 237-238

333 ibid

production. Schary cabled him, "Please get well soon because we all love you. The stuff I have seen continues to look very very good. But don't think of anything except getting well."[334]

A month later Schary again cabled Wellman: "While this is addressed to you, it is really directed to the cast and the crew, and I do wish that you would read this to them. I know from all that I have heard how much you are going through on the location . . . the sickness, the dust and the extraordinary amount of inconvenience of all kinds. However, with all these things going on, you are getting film that looks exciting and wonderful. All of us at the studio are grateful and proud of the effort being expended to get what I am certain will be a picture you all will be proud of. There is much yet to be done, and I know under circumstances like this all of you have to draw on your patience and strength. Wild Bill Wellman is a hard taskmaster and a good one, but if you know him as well as I do you know that the yells of the morning can be the caress of the evening. I am sorry that I have not been able to come up there and share some of the dust with you, but I do want to take this opportunity to again say thanks and give my heartfelt best wishes and gratitude for the swell job that you are all doing. Fondest to all. Dore Schary."[335]

The wonderful character actress Hope Emerson, who had recently been nominated for an Oscar for her work as a sadistic prison nurse in *Caged*, wrote Schary a couple of weeks later telling him that she "enjoying this part so much," but went on to complain that when she became ill, she was "shocked" that she was docked for the time she missed. "We had worked so hard for MGM, it was a blow. Being docked for getting sick, taking these bad weather conditions. Is that a new rule or what?" Schary placated her temporarily by responding that when she gets back into town "I will discuss the subject of the business you mentioned" and by that time "I will have completed all my investigation about it."[336]

By the end of June principal photography was completed. According to studio records the final cost came to $2,161,660 or about

334 Dore Schary to William Wellman, 4/19/51, Schary papers

335 Dore Schary to William Wellman, 5/14/51, Schary papers

336 Correspondence between Emerson and Schary, Schary Papers

$465,000 over budget. By September the picture was previewed in Pacific Palisades at the Bay Theatre. The preview audience gave it high marks. Out of 262 cards received, 91 rated the picture as "outstanding." 96 rated the film "Excellent." 47 called it "Very Good" while 21 said it was "Good" and only 7 rated the picture as "fair." Taylor rated very well. 174 people rated his performance as Buck as "Excellent" while 64 called him "Good." Only 8 people rated Bob as "Fair" or "Poor." Of the cast only Hope Emerson's portrayal of Patience and Henry Nakamura, who played the Japanese cook Ito, rated somewhat higher. On the pivotal question of "Would you recommend this picture to your friends?" the answer was overwhelming: 215 said "Yes" while only 13 replied "No."

Among the comments of the preview audience:

"A Lot to go through in one evening, but Unforgettable."

"Whole picture very well done."

"Held my interest throughout."

"Outstanding direction."

"A Fine worthwhile picture."

"First picture in which I've ever enjoyed Mr. Taylor."

"Western with a different plan." [337]

That last comment probably summed up what Schary had in mind with *Westward the Women* with its predominately female cast and storyline it was unlike any western ever made up to that time. Film historian Jeanine Basinger has written, it is "one of the few films to present positive, overt sisterhood. It is almost a casebook of traditional attitudes toward women that will be refuted by the visual presentation." Dore Schary would call *Westward the Women*, "A woman's picture for men; a man's picture for women."

The film opened on New Year's Eve, 1951, in New York, and was an immediate hit. Reports to the front office showed that in its first two days at the Capitol Theatre *Westward the Women* grossed a strong $11,232, compared to $4,655 for *Angels in the Outfield*, $3,286 for *Law and the Lady* and $7,491 for *Rich Young & Pretty*, the other MGM releases out over this holiday. The New York reviews were, on the whole, mixed. Frank Quinn, in the *Mirror*, wrote, "MGM has struck oil with *Westward the Women*." Kate Cameron in

337 Preview reports in Schary papers

the *Daily News* lauded Wellman's direction. "He gives every scene a touch of realism and heightens illusions of story." Most of the reviews lauded the female actors, primarily Hope Emerson, overshadowing Bob's contribution, but the critic for the *Brooklyn Eagle* said Taylor was, "rough and tough as his role of an unrelenting train boss requires him to be." Alton Cook, in the *World Telegram & Sun*, pointed out that Bob's more recent roles show him off in a "state of perpetual bad temper that has become his trademark as an actor lately." Otis Guernsey of the *Herald Tribune* was mixed: "Produced by Dore Schary, *Westward the Women*, is not quite persuasive enough to rank as a top-flight example of its type, but it is nevertheless a picturesque novelty." Bosley Crowther, of the *Times*, pretty much was dismissive. "In short, William Wellman, who directed, hasn't got much authority from his cast, but he has got several humorous moments from them, and that's the best to be expected from this film." When the picture opened nationally, it continued on its winning box-office ways. With *Quo Vadis* still bringing audiences in by droves, *Westward the Women* was Bob's second consecutive box-office smash and yet another feather in his MGM hat.[338]

II

MGM was still counting the lucrative box-office receipts of *Quo Vadis* when the decision was made to put Bob in yet another costume picture, based on a bestselling 1819 novel, Sir Walter Scott's *Ivanhoe*. MGM had hoped to make the swashbuckling adventure in the 1930s and, like *Quo Vadis* before it, the young and romantic Robert Taylor had been announced as star. The plan was to shoot it at the MGM London studios. However, these plans were dropped when the Second World War broke out in 1939. Following the war, Dore Schary had plans to make the film when he was head of production at RKO, but that once great studio was in decline thanks to Howard Hughes, the present owner, who was not interested in producing a film which would require such a huge budget.

When Schary left RKO in 1948 for MGM, he brought the Walter Scott property with him. By 1949, the property had been

338 Bob starred in a radio adaptation of the film on The Lux Radio Theatre on 12/29/52

assigned to Pandro Berman as producer, and once *Quo Vadis* proved to be the huge success it became, Schary decided that the time was right to move ahead and produce a big-budgeted, color version of the film to be made on location in England. And, once again, Robert Taylor was to be cast as the heroic Ivanhoe.

Ivanhoe returns to the days of chivalrous knights and damsels in distress set in England during the Middle Ages. There is romance intermingled with politics and court intrigue as Prince John attempts to usurp the throne of his brother King Richard, who is captured and being held in prison. Enter the Saxon Knight Wilfred of Ivanhoe (Bob) who, much to the chagrin of his father, Cedric, becomes a supporter of the Norman King Richard. Furthermore, Cedric had hoped that Ivanhoe would marry the Saxon heiress Rowena. Enter Isaac of York, a Jewish merchant with a beautiful daughter, Rebecca, who enters into an alliance with Ivanhoe to win the freedom of the imprisoned King Richard. Of course, a love triangle soon develops between Rowena, Rebecca and Ivanhoe. In the end, Ivanhoe must fight to save Rebecca from being burned alive as a witch (again, shades of the climax of *Quo Vadis*). The studio wanted to reunite Bob with his *Quo Vadis* co-star Deborah Kerr, as Rebecca, but Kerr became pregnant and had to drop out of the production. The young and beautiful Elizabeth Taylor, in her second and final film with Bob, was cast in the part.[339] Joan Fontaine was cast as Rowena. George Sanders was cast as De Boris-Guilbert, who is in love with Rowena, but willing to sacrifice her. Emlyn Williams, Finlay Currie, Robert Douglas and Norman Wooland are all cast in colorful roles.

Unlike *Quo Vadis* there wasn't a prolonged production schedule. One of the main reasons for this was Pandro Berman's selection of Richard Thorpe to direct. "I picked Mr. Thorpe before I had any cast," Berman told an audience of the AFI in the 1970s. "I picked him for a very specific reason. At that time he was the most efficient, fast-moving, competent, physical director that we had at Metro. I knew that this was going to be a rough picture to make physically." The film was shot from the middle of July to the middle of September of 1951.

339 NY Herald Tribune, 5/9/51

Metro spared no expense. It was felt impractical to use any of the many British castles that peppered the landscape. The existing castles didn't look authentic enough to the MGM researchers and art experts. The solution? The studio built a replica of a 12th-century Norman castle of almost 1,000,000 square feet complete with a ten-foot deep moat dug around it. The moat was filled with some 90,000 gallons of water. In addition to the castle, the studio also authorized the building of an entire medieval village as well as the site for the great Tournament of Ashby sequences when scores of knights in armor perform before Norman and Saxon onlookers.[340] Over 1,000 extras per day were often on call. While the production was expensive, it made sense for the studio to shoot it exclusively in England. The studio had millions of dollars which had accumulated in British banks during the war, but to spend the money there was a provision in British law that they must spend it exclusively in England.

On occasion, Bob would go out on the town with an old friend who was also visiting, Ronald Reagan. Reagan was often seen in the company with Patricia Neal at the time. One night Bob, along with Elizabeth Taylor, met Reagan and Neal for dinner at the Savoy. Neal recalled Reagan as a "delightful and interesting companion. Our conversation more likely than not turned to politics, which meant it was not a conversation but a monologue." She sensed that he was still carrying a torch for Jane Wyman. At the dinner, Neal recalled that Bob "delighted in teasing Elizabeth." Observing that Taylor's legs were in need of a shaving Bob told her, "If you don't shave those legs, Elizabeth. I'm going to shave them for you," causing Taylor to giggle with delight.[341]

Despite dinners with Elizabeth Taylor, Bob wasn't romancing her. She was being courted by the suave and handsome Michael Wilding, more than twenty years older than Elizabeth. This serious romance (they later married) often caused her to be distracted during the shooting. Like Bob, Elizabeth wasn't overly taken with the idea of making a period picture. Joan Fontaine was disgruntled with just about everybody on the film. She thought that Thorpe "cared more about the performances of the horses than the actors. Elizabeth

340 NY Herald Tribune, 9/16/51 & San Francisco Chronicle, 4/20/52

341 Patricia Neal, As I Am, pg. 112

Taylor was being wooed by Michael Wilding. Bob Taylor was nursing his vanity over his divorce from Barbara Stanwyck. George Sanders was his laconic self."[342]

When the film was released in the summer of 1952, *Ivanhoe* proved to be a huge moneymaker. In New York it was the big summer movie at the Radio City Music Hall, the most prestigious movie house in New York, which catered to family audiences and *Ivanhoe* proved to be a family favorite. In 49 days in release at the Music Hall *Ivanhoe* broke box-office records for an MGM film grossing an astronomical (for that day) $1,131,447 breaking the previous record for an MGM film, *Show Boat* ($1,054,673). Furthermore, when the film went into wide release across the country, it did almost as well in some places as *Quo Vadis*. For instance, in Cleveland, *Ivanhoe* grossed $70,378 over three weeks compared to the $72,865 that *Quo Vadis* grossed in a comparable period of time at the same theatre. In Atlanta, *Ivanhoe* actually out-grossed *Quo Vadis*. A memo to Howard Strickling in MGM publicity made the point that, "in relation to comparisons of grosses, please keep in mind fact that *Quo Vadis* admission prices were approximately 25 percent higher than *Ivanhoe*" due to its road show pricing.[343] In the end *Ivanhoe* became Metros highest grossing film of 1952 and the fourth biggest grosser overall for the year with rentals in excess of $6.2 million. It also earned a nomination for Best Picture of the year. Bob, to his surprise, enjoyed making it. "It went very well," he told Hedda Hopper. "It was the most pleasant picture I've ever made over there. Dick Thorpe, who directed, is fast and deficient. We really worked. There was no nonsense. We didn't just sit around."[344] He also denied to Hopper that he had taken out Elizabeth Taylor or Joan Fontaine ("definitely not!") when making the film. When asked if he and Barbara would reconcile, he answered, "I don't know."[345]

Critically, *Ivanhoe* did very well. It placed fifth on *Film Daily's* 30th Annual National Poll of Critics Ten Best List. (The four films

342 Joan Fontaine, No Bed of Roses, pg. 219

343 Pandro Berman Papers, WSHSA

344 Hedda Hopper Papers, Margaret Herrick Library (AMPAS)

345 ibid

which placed above it are: *High Noon, The Quiet Man, The Greatest Show on Earth*, and *The African Queen*.) *TIME* magazine placed it among its ten best of the year. Bosley Crowther, of the *New York Times*, greatly enjoyed the film, calling it a "brilliantly colored tapestry of drama and spectacle." Bob's performance was lauded as "good, sturdy and manly."

III

Since the break-up with Barbara, Bob was staying busy with picture making. He was also re-establishing himself as a potent box-office star at the studio. *Quo Vadis, Westward the Women* and *Ivanhoe* were hugely successful and brought much-needed revenue to the studio which was going through an identity crisis due to a power struggle between Mayer and head of production Dore Schary. Financially, the studios were also struggling due to the soaring popularity of television. Fewer people were going out to the movies when they could get Milton Berle, Ed Sullivan and *I Love Lucy* at home for free. By 1951 the number of television sets in American homes reached 15 million.[346] Also adding to the problem was that the studios were divesting themselves of their theatre chains due to a court ruling that the studio-owned chains were an unfair monopoly.

MGM, like the other studios, was also looking at long-term contracts as being an unnecessary burden. Schary, in particular, was of the opinion that long-term contracts were becoming a thing of the past. He favored keeping fewer stars under contract and instead favored multi-picture deals. Esther Williams, whose poolside epics were still bringing in the dollars, was of the opinion that Schary "didn't like stars, he liked featured players . . . He was a pseudo-snob."[347] Of the stars from MGM's glory days, Judy Garland was gone, fired in 1950 not because her pictures were failing at the box office but because she had become impossible to work with due to emotional and health problems. Mickey Rooney was gone, so too was Myrna Loy. William Powell was still under contract to the studio, but they didn't really know what to do with him anymore and were

346 John Douglas Eames, MGM Story

347 Lion of Hollywood, pg. 458

increasingly loaning him out. Greer Garson's pictures were coming up in the red and her days were numbered. Clark Gable was still the King of the lot but since the war the studio found it difficult to find effective vehicles for him. Spencer Tracy and Katharine Hepburn seemed most successful only when they worked together. So, it was a pleasant surprise for the studio that Bob's fortunes, which had been so uncertain since coming home from the war, were rising.

One of the first contentious moments between Mayer and Schary was dealing with the script of *Quo Vadis* when John Huston was still on the project. Mayer told Huston he wanted more emotion to tug at the heartstrings. Schary liked the script as it was and suggested the best thing to do was to go to Nick Schenck to settle the dispute. Schenck, the head of MGM's parent company Loew's, was a man that Mayer was never fond of and it was mutual. Mayer had never consulted Schenck before about studio disputes and didn't want to begin now. He felt that it showed some spinelessness on Schary's part that he would even suggest such a thing. But the dispute did go to Schenck, who decided in Schary's favor believing that it was now or never to get something done on *Quo Vadis*, which had been in various forms of development at the studio for years.

An even bigger fight between the two came up a few months later over another proposed John Huston film, *The Red Badge of Courage*. Mayer believed that a Civil War picture couldn't make a dime at the box office. Schary countered with *Gone With the Wind*. But Mayer believed that the war was secondary in that picture and the love story and fierceness of the Scarlett O'Hara character dominated. But what he really believed was that *The Red Badge of Courage* was just going to be another one of Schary's message pictures. Again, the dispute went to Schenck, and again the victor was Schary. One of Schary's first pictures as head of production was the much-admired *Battleground*, which became a hit, and he was going to trust Schary's judgment on this. (In the end Schary was wrong and Mayer correct about *The Red Badge of Courage*, which was a box-office flop.)

The breaking point came when Schary renegotiated his contract and got stock options that Mayer didn't. Schenck called Mayer offering to get together and "talk things out," to which Mayer responded that it was best not to, allegedly because he might be tempted to use physical violence. In the end Mayer bluntly told

Schenck he had to decide between him and Schary. Mayer was inflexible and didn't want to discuss his role either with Schenck or Schary. He felt that his record spoke for itself. Schenck, however, believed that the studio needed new blood. He felt that Mayer had spent too much time away from the studio and more time at the race track. He liked that Schary had plans to cut costs. He also believed that it was Schary who was responsible for a rise in Metro profits in 1950. Before he would officially get the word, Mayer decided to render his resignation, effective June 9, 1951.

Richard Anderson (later Oscar Goodman on *The Six Million Dollar Man* and *Bionic Woman*), an MGM contract player, believes that Schary was brought in "because the studio system wasn't working anymore. The personality thing didn't bring in the money. People were finding other things to do with their time. Television was beginning to boom and people were starting to watch it, and that was taking the audience away. That system worked in the thirties, but now what they had to do at MGM was to make a different kind of movie." [348] Still, Anderson recalled MGM as the "Tiffany's of Hollywood. It got the best actors. It got the best stories. It got the best budgets."[349]

Bob's father figure was gone. "Bob loved L.B. Mayer," Ursula Thiess would recall. "Mayer helped guide his career. He was sorry when he left MGM. He didn't really take to Schary. But he did feel that Schary was fair to him."[350] When Mayer died six years later, Bob attended the funeral and later was quoted as saying, "Some writers have implied that Mayer was tyrannical and abusive and a male prima donna who out acted his actors. As I knew him he was fatherly, understanding and protective."

IV

On occasion the press would capture a picture of Bob and Barbara having dinner together and the Hollywood gossip machine would begin to ask if reconciliation was in the making. It wasn't.

348 The Six Million Dollar Boss, Joel Blumberg, Classic Images

349 Richard Anderson to author

350 Ursula Thiess to author

Barbara may have wanted one, but she wasn't the type of woman who would beg to be taken back. She had too much self-respect for that. Bob still respected her opinion and often discussed upcoming film projects with her. They obviously knew that when they did dine together it would cause talk but all they really encouraged was the idea that they were being adult about the break. It wasn't like Barbara was spending all of her nights crying into her pillow. On the set of the Twentieth Century-Fox film *Titanic*, Barbara took a handsome twenty-one-year-old actor just starting out in pictures, Robert Wagner, under her wing. The handsome young actor reminded her of Bob when he was starting out. Like Bob he was often called beautiful rather than handsome and also like Bob, in the early days, he had a lot to learn about acting and life. Barbara gave him an education on how to be a professional in a demanding business and as she had also done with the young William Holden on his first major film, *Golden Boy*, Stanwyck showed him how to act before a motion picture camera. Years later Wagner would reveal that they also began to spend hours away from the set carrying on an affair.

Bob was about to start a film which meant a great deal to him and would team him with one of his favorite leading ladies, Eleanor Parker. The film was *Above and Beyond*, with Bob playing the part of Lt. Col. Paul Tibbets and Parker cast as his wife Lucey. Tibbets was the pilot of the *Enola Gay*, the plane which dropped the Atomic Bomb over Hiroshima in August of 1945. Parker was a beautiful and talented actress who had given a string of outstanding performances in the years prior to this first teaming with Bob. She was nominated for an Oscar for her work in the 1950 prison drama *Caged*, and the following year she was again nominated for her work in the film *Detective Story*.

Col. Beirne Lay, who had written the screenplay for the acclaimed 1949 film *Twelve O'Clock High*, proposed an idea to Dore Schary for a film based on the story of the dropping of the first Atomic Bomb over Hiroshima and the man who led the mission, Col. Tibbets. But he didn't merely want the film to be the story of the military mission. Lay wanted to go beyond that and tell the story of the toll that military service can take on the families of military men. How the days, weeks, and even months away from spouses and children can damage relationships. Lay, in his film proposal, wrote that he wanted the film, tentatively titled "The Story of Colonel Paul Tibbets," to be about "the human caliber of a man who carried out a mission." Schary optioned the story and set Lay to write a treatment, now titled "Heaven High, Hell Deep." As originally written, the film was going to tell Tibbets' story from the time of his small-town boyhood in Quincy, Illinois, up to the time of the dropping of the bomb. This was finally discarded and the story, now titled "Eagle on a Cap," would be told in flashback by Tibbets' wife, Lucey, looking back on the events of the war and the turmoil it took on the Tibbets' marriage. Once the basic story was developed Schary assigned the screenplay to the team of Norman Panama and Melvin Frank, who were best known for writing such comedy films as *My Favorite Blonde* and *Monsieur Beaucaire* for Bob Hope and the Cary Grant comedy *Mr. Blandings Builds His Dream House*, which Schary had produced as head of production at RKO. "Eagle on a Cap" would be there first foray into drama and they would co-direct the picture as well.

While the script was being hashed out, Schary was putting some thought into who to cast in the pivotal role of Tibbets. From very early on Robert Taylor was a leading contender for the part. Other candidates included James Stewart and to a lesser degree Clark Gable. Stewart, however, was reluctant to appear in war films (he felt to do so was cashing in on his war experience) and Gable was beginning to show his age (50 by this time). Among the qualifications that Bob brought to the part was the fact that he was a licensed pilot and a flying instructor during the war. This would give Bob a certain authority during the scenes in the cockpit. Professor and film historian Michael Pressler makes an excellent point in his essay on "The Making of Above and Beyond" (Gettysburg Review, Autumn, 2003), when he wrote of another qualification that Bob brought to the film, which in part dealt with conflict in marriage due to a love of flying. Bob had experienced just such a thing with Stanwyck. "Subsequently Taylor became well acquainted with the strain that frequent flying could put on family life," Pressler wrote. "Less than a month before production began on . . . *Above and Beyond*, Barbara Stanwyck took a cold backward look at the end of their twelve-year marriage: 'It all began when he got that airplane,' she told Louella

Parsons." Schary, who generally disliked stars, seemed to take a liking to Bob, and cast him in the part.

The film of what finally was called *Above and Beyond* would be more than a straightforward account of how Tibbets and his crew came to drop the bomb but would also highlight the personal lives of the Tibbets and the affect that the war and separation had on his personal life. Still, the film is at its best when it focuses on the mission, including the selection and training of a crew and the momentous flight and dropping of the bomb. One memorable scene early on involves how Tibbets is offered to lead the Atomic Bomb mission. Tibbets goes into the office of General Brent and sits down at his desk and is handed a push-button buzzer. The General explains to Tibbets, "Suppose I told you that if you pressed that little buzzer you might stop a war tomorrow. That you'd save half a million American lives and probably as many of the enemy . . . but by pressing that buzzer you have to kill a hundred thousand people in one flash. What would you do?" No wonder Bob looks grim through much of the film. One of the most harrowing scenes in the film is that of the dropping of the bomb itself. For this the filmmakers included actual newsreel footage of the Hiroshima and the mushroom cloud which formed when the bomb made impact. Then the film cut to the interior of the plane when once the bomb has made its impact the entire inside of the plane goes a blinding white.

Bob was justly proud of his performance in this film and it's one of the few times in his career that he actually asked the MGM front office if he could make a personal appearance tour promoting the picture, including television appearances. Up to this time MGM had kept its top talent away from television screens because they wanted to maintain a certain star quality that they believed would be diminished if their stars appeared on TV. Bob was allowed to promote the picture (appearing with Col. Tibbets) on Ed Sullivan's weekly television program. Bob's Tibbets is a man consumed by duty and the weight of carrying out such an awesome responsibility. He is stoic to the point of being utterly humorless, a fact that wasn't lost on several critics, but one which makes complete sense considering what his mission is. It's a very human performance in that Bob is playing a man who truly is carrying the weight of the world on his shoulders. It may be his all-time best motion picture work.

There was talk of an Academy Award nomination for Bob, but when the nominees were announced for Best Actor of 1952 his name was not on the list, despite the film being on many critics' ten best list. Bob's performance was generally applauded. The *New York Herald Tribune* said Taylor, "plays his role with a set jaw and determination—a man with a singleness of purpose." Bosley Crowther in the *New York Times* was lukewarm on the film. "Melvin Frank and Norman Panama, who directed and helped write the scripts with Beirne Lay, Jr., are graduates of musical romances. It is slightly apparent in this film." As for Bob he had a split decision. "Mr. Taylor does not come off in the whole film as fairly and forcefully as he does in the strictly military scenes. He is very good as an airman, but as a husband he overacts." Parker, as the wife, didn't come off much better, "she is utterly theatrical." But some critics liked the love story elements of the film. "It's a love story no woman will ever forget," gushed Louella Parsons in *Cosmopolitan.* The critic for *Today's Woman* called *Above and Beyond*, "a wonderful modern love story, dramatizing sharply the emotional problems of our times." Ironically, the real-life Tibbets and his wife Lucey divorced ten years after the war ended, and only three years after this film premiered. Perhaps it was the subject matter. Did the American people want to support a picture which, regardless of a love story, centered on the dropping of the Atomic Bomb, which came at the height of the Cold War? The film opened well in its first week of release, but by the end of the month dropped out of the ten top grossing pictures in the country. *Above and Beyond* ended the year as the 29th highest grossing film of the year, grossing about 2.5 million. Not bad, but hardly what MGM was hoping for.

The chemistry with Parker was strong off screen as well as on. They began an off-and-on affair that would last almost up to the time of Bob's marriage to actress Ursula Thiess. At the time they began shooting *Above and Beyond*, Parker was in the process of separating from her husband, producer Bert Friedlob. The affair was an open secret among their friends and at the studio, but they worked assiduously to keep it out of the press. Parker went so far as to tell the press that she greatly enjoyed working with Bob, but that their relationship was only friendly and professional. Bob was genuinely fond of Parker, but he never considered marriage. Parker was a take-charge type of woman who wouldn't let any man dominate her. In too many ways she reminded Bob of Barbara.

Shortly after completing *Above and Beyond*, Bob was cast in yet another Western, which reunited him with Ava Gardner, *Ride, Vaquero!* Even though Bob was in process of divorcing Barbara, he and Gardner didn't resume their affair; Ava was very involved with Frank Sinatra. Much of the picture was shot on location in the stifling summer heat of July and August of 1952 near the little town of Kanab, Utah. The temperature during the peak heat of the day could reach as high as 120 degrees. It was not a comfortable production. "It was really the asshole of creation," recalled Howard Keel, also cast in the picture. "Beautiful territory, but we were out there for about, oh, Christ, a month, and there was nothing to do. Nothing!" [351] Much of the cast and crew stayed at the one local hotel, Perry's, unbelievably an establishment with no air conditioning and not even a swimming pool to cool off in. [352]

Ride, Vaquero! offered Bob the opportunity to play a villain, with shades of gray. He plays Rio, the adoptive brother of Esqueda, a vicious murderer (played by Anthony Quinn), and Rio is his brother's right-hand man. When Esqueda, Rio and the rest of their gang attack the ranch of King Cameron (Keel) and his wife Cordelia (Gardner), Cameron and his ranch hands manage to chase them off and capture Rio. While being held captive by Cameron, Rio and Cordelia find themselves attracted to each other. In the end, Rio challenges his adoptive brother.

351 Lee Server, Ava Gardner, pg. 243

352 Charles Higham, Ava, pg. 126

Chapter Ten
A New Love (1953-1955)

Reading the newspaper at his Dorchester Suite, in London, one day in 1952, Bob saw a picture that knocked his socks off. It was of a stunningly attractive woman whom the paper dubbed "The Most Beautiful Woman in the World." Bob couldn't disagree. He thought she was stunning with her full lips, dark hair, expressive eyes and luscious figure. Her name was Ursula Thiess and Bob definitely wanted to get to know her better.

Ursula was born on May 15, 1924, in Hamburg, Germany. She was the daughter of Walter and Wilhelmine Schmidt. Her father was an importer who could have also been a talented carpenter. He built all of the furniture they used at their summer retreat in Lullau, which Ursula would later recall as being a "cobble-stoned village in the heather." They shared a farm house with another family. The upper floors belonged to the Schmidts. Her father made many of the toys she received for birthdays and Christmas as well as "impeccably detailed doll houses."

Ursula was a beautiful little girl. "When Ursula was born, she had large, beautiful eyes. When she was a girl her hair was done up in braids. She was so pretty we used to call her Snow White." [353]

Ursula would recall having a warm relationship with her father while her mother was the disciplinarian. There were times when her mother spanked her so hard she got welts on her bottom. When her maternal grandmother saw the welts and asked who did this to her, young Ursula innocently replied, "Mutti." Ursula recalled that her grandmother gave her mother a hard slap across the face which

353 Parade, 2/27/53

caused the spankings to stop. Still, it was something that always stayed with Ursula. When she became a mother, she was much more inclined to be soothing with her children rather than use a hand or belt.

When Ursula turned eleven, her father disappeared out of her life. For a time she didn't know why. When she would walk into a room, talk about him would suddenly stop. She was only told that he would be gone for "a while." In time, she found out that he had embezzled funds from the firm he worked for and had been sentenced to a year in prison. The financial toll of not having her father's income became evident when Ursula and her mother had to give up their apartment and move in with an elderly couple, sharing their apartment.

To help make ends meet Ursula began taking on work such as cleaning the apartment building she now resided in. Ursula's mother divorced her father when Ursula turned twelve. She soon remarried to a Shakespearean actor with a drinking problem. Ursula got along well with her stepfather. She later recalled that he "helped stimulate my acting ambition."

Every Christmas season he would help her get work in Christmas plays. This gave Ursula a release because she was a shy girl and by playacting she got a chance to explore different sides of her nature which she usually kept hidden. When she was thirteen, she would swoon over a young handsome actor named Robert Taylor who was making movie love to Greta Garbo in *Camille*, one of her favorite movies.

At fifteen, Ursula was forced to leave school due to the Nazi government's compulsory requirement forcing young girls from the cities to work in farm labor. She was given the choice of six months on government owned properties or serving a year as a farmhand. Without any reluctance, she chose the latter because her extreme shyness would make living in a dorm with hundreds of other young girls too much of an endurance test.

When the year's labor was up, she returned to Hamburg and her mother. She was now sixteen years old and wanted to pursue her dream of being an actress. She auditioned at theatres all over the city, but when her turn came up to audition she invariably suffered from stage fright and got the obligatory, "don't call us, we'll call you."

One day she auditioned for a committee of ten directors from various theaters and once again felt she had failed, but when she returned home she found out she had been accepted into a repertoire group within the Ohnsorg Theatre. She was the youngest member of the group, and as such became the pet of the company.

After about a year or two with the repertoire company Ursula met the man who would become her first husband, George Otto Thiess, or G.O. for short. Ursula was seduced by his charm and good looks which she likened to a "cross between Clark Gable and Elvis Presley." Thiess wooed her by sending her long-stemmed red roses before every performance accompanied by a romantic message. Being very young and impressionable she found this irresistible. At the height of their romance, Ursula had the opportunity to audition for a movie contract for Tobis Films, an important studio in Germany at the time. She was among twenty hopefuls selected out of 300 young women who were transported to Berlin for screen tests. Ursula was selected, but Thiess insisted that she put her career on hold and marry him.

Meanwhile, the Second World War was hitting Europe hard. Thiess was sent to make documentary films for the state. Ursula stayed behind with her mother. She was pregnant and while Hamburg was undergoing heavy bombing Ursula gave birth to her first child, a girl, who was named Manuela. Following Manuela's birth, mother and baby were evacuated into the country north of Hamburg, for protection against the constant bombing of the cities. In 1945, when Scottish troops were making their way across the German plains they found Ursula, who was pregnant again and transported her to the Finkenau Clinic just in time to give birth to a son, named Michael. Ursula was very weak after this birth because Thiess had infected Ursula with gonorrhea, and it could only be treated after the birth of the baby.

When the war ended, Ursula decided to leave her husband. It had been a loveless marriage. One day while their children were with their grandmother, Thiess paid Ursula a visit to "talk things over." He wanted her to drop divorce proceedings, but she refused. Her refusal enraged him and he raped her. When it was over he just laughed at her, "There isn't a court in all of Germany that would listen to your complaint. Remember, our divorce has not yet been finalized." The rape caused another pregnancy, which Ursula, reluctantly decided to abort, due to the limited financial resources she had. Finally, the divorce was finalized with the children awarded to Ursula with no visitation rights given to Thiess.

The next several months were hard ones for the family. It was a freezing winter and Ursula, Manuela and Michael spent it in a small room sleeping on one big couch wearing as many layers of clothes to keep warm as possible. She took on as many jobs as she could. Her beauty led to some modeling jobs and eventually she went to Berlin, leaving the children with her mother. She got work dubbing American films. Top modeling jobs followed. A photograph on the cover of *LIFE* magazine announcing Ursula as a "rising German model" led to interest from Howard Hughes and an offer of a seven-year Hollywood contract with RKO pictures, which Hughes owned. Disbelieving at first, she eventually did come to Hollywood. The children stayed behind with their grandmother.

While in Hollywood, Ursula was put up at a hotel by the studio and underwent a strenuous round of being groomed into a starlet. She was given a drama coach whose primary job was to Americanize her accent as much as possible. Ursula was in accord with this, as she later wrote, "I have always felt that struggling to understand someone, on or off the screen can be rather laborious for the listener."[354] One way Ursula increased her English vocabulary was by memorizing a hundred words or so every night. She would wake herself by an alarm clock every few hours to review words.[355] She was getting paid as she was being prepped and sent as much money to her mother as possible. Within four months of her arrival she was on a plane for India to make her first movie, Monsoon, featuring George Nader as her leading man. It was her appearance in this film that resulted in the ensuing publicity that labeled her as the "the most beautiful woman in the world" and attracted the attention of Robert Taylor.

354 Thiess, ...but I have promises to keep, pg. 42

355 Ivy Mooring to author

II

When Bob returned from England he had not forgotten about the beautiful girl who had made such a splash in the papers while he was over there. He was able to locate Ursula thru the help of her agent, Harry Friedman of MCA. Friedman telephoned and told her that Robert Taylor wanted to meet her for dinner and dancing. "Harry's telephone announcement that this world-renowned personality whom I had idolized for so many years would actually like to meet me took me quite off-balance," she later recalled. Bob arrived at her apartment and when Ursula opened up the door there he stood with a smile on his face followed by a simple introduction, "I am Bob Taylor." [356]

Bob took Ursula to the Coconut Grove where they met their companions, Harry Friedman and his wife. The Grove's entertainment that night was provided by the Andrews Sisters. Ursula would recall that when they began to sing "I'll Be with You in Apple Blossom Time" they directed the number toward Bob and Ursula. He asked her to dance and she was in "seventh heaven" until the band changed styles and began to play a rumba. "End of dancing. No Latin rhythms were included in R.T.'s repertoire." [357] At the end of the night he drove her home, took her hand and escorted her to the door of her apartment building and thanked her for a lovely evening, turned and returned to his Cadillac and promptly drove away. Ursula was surprised that he didn't attempt to kiss her or make any other types of advances. He also didn't mention wanting to see her again. This bothered her. She began to wonder if he had not found her attractive or her personality interesting enough. She did recall that he had mentioned that he was leaving with friends on a hunting trip.

It was three weeks later that he called her and told Ursula what a wonderful time he had had. He invited her out to dinner again, this time to the Sportsmen's Lodge. This time it was just the two of them. They spent hours at the Lodge just talking and getting to know about each other a little more. When he took her home this time, he gave her a kiss on the cheek before taking his leave. Again,

356 Thiess, pg. 60

357 Thiess, ...but I have promises to keep, pg. 61

Bob made no mention of any further dates, but "I need not have worried, for we began to see each other now on a rather regular basis, with the signs of a blooming romance at hand." She later recalled that what attracted her most to Bob was his, "down-to-earth, unassuming manner and his beautiful, searching eyes, which were the open windows to his incredible sex appeal." [358]

They began dating quite exclusively and soon enough marriage rumors began to fill the air. Ursula put a stop to them. "We have no marriage plans with each other or anybody else. We are both very serious about these things. Both of us gave it a lot of thought before we were married the first time and we had tragic marriages anyhow. Well, you always learn something from a mistake. Right now we are both too full of ourselves and our own problems to think about marrying anyone." [359]

In the summer of 1953 Bob was scheduled to return to London to make the film *Knights of the Round Table*. Shortly before leaving Bob, Ursula and Ralph Cause flew to Beatrice in Bob's Beech craft. They were met by Ruth, who had arrived a few days earlier and was staying at a local hotel. Bob was sporting the chin beard he would wear in the picture. Also at the airport to meet Bob and his party were a dozen local friends. Bob enjoyed introducing his friends to Ursula and showing her the sights of his hometown.[360] Ursula later recalled that his friends "received us with open arms, making me feel reinstated once more as his woman and his love." [361]

III

Another summer and another film with Ava Gardner. This time instead of a Western shot on location in tiny, hot Kenab, Utah, the two were sent to the MGM studios at Elstree, England, to film *Knights of the Round Table*, yet another reworking of "Camelot" with Bob cast as Lancelot, Gardner as Guinevere and Mel Ferrer as Arthur. Originally, the idea was to reunite Bob with Elizabeth Taylor, his

358 Thiess, pg. 61

359 Photoplay, 4/53

360 Lincoln (NE) Star, 5/20/53

361 Thiess, pg. 63

Ivanhoe co-star, but Miss Taylor was adamant about not doing yet another damsel in distress role. For the studio, Bob was the first and only choice and a must for the role. First, he looked good in costume pictures, and second, his record in such pictures (*Quo Vadis, Ivanhoe*) in terms of box office was overwhelming.

Gardner was more comfortable than on the previous shoot, but no more satisfied with the film or her role. "It was a typical piece of historical foolishness," she later wrote in her memoirs, "with folks in shining armor like my old beau Robert Taylor dashing across the screen and sticking each other in delicate places with horrible-looking pikes." [362] Furthermore, the nightlife in the small English village where the cast and crew were staying was as dull as the nightlife of Kenalb, Utah. Bob was no more enthusiastic about doing yet another costume picture. He reluctantly accepted when he heard that Ava Gardner would be his co-star and besides the studio was adamant. Bob detested the British cooking and before leaving he asked for some steaks sent from New York to the hotel he was staying at in England. When they arrived, he gave the chef of the hotel explicit instructions of how they were to be prepared. When the chef overcooked them, Bob grew into a rage, something he normally never did, usually shaking such things off. One friend said that he never saw Bob so mad. "He got up and stormed out of the room slamming the door—and I mean slammed the door! He wouldn't come back until the table had been cleared off and refused to mention the incident again." [363]

Knights of the Round Table was produced by Pandro Berman, who once again (as he had on *Ivanhoe*) gave the directorial reins to Richard Thorpe. The picture was going to be the first done by MGM in the widescreen process known as CinemaScope, so it was considered a prime project for Metro. The England location selection was made in part because of the castle which had been built on the backlot of the Boreham Wood Studio was still standing. As usual with location shooting there were problems. The weather in England that summer was miserable with rain a good deal of time. Then the many extras that were needed in such a costume picture went on

362 Ava: My Story, pg. 212

363 Robert Taylor, J.E. Wayne, pg. 174

strike, prompting director Thorpe to travel to Ireland to shoot one key battle scene. But the problems didn't end there. The extras in Ireland wanted a bonus for having to endure the heavy armor that the scene required. When the British Association of Motion Picture Producers heard about the Irish extras, they refused to allow it. In the end, Thorpe approached the government which allowed him to use soldiers for the battle scenes. So, no professional extras demanding bonuses were used; instead, professional soldiers who did it for nothing except meals. And those meals were expensive! One day the menu included 975 pork chops, 300 pounds of potatoes, 340 loaves of bread, 150 large cans of peas, 1500 apples and pears, 400 gallons of coffee and tea, and 2,000 cakes and buns.[364]

While Bob got settled into suite 617-8 at London's Dorchester Hotel he wrote his secretary, Ivy Pearson, telling her to "come on over." Bob wanted her to come with him, in part, because it was the Coronation summer of Elizabeth II and he thought it would be a treat for her, an English citizen, to be there and also to visit her family. He also told her that one maid who he recalled from his previous visit "lost several pounds, and I'm sure, thought I'd insist upon her crawling smack into bed with me. However, she's still not quite my type!" He reported that London "seems to be going quite mad with preparations for the Coronation."[365]

Ivy recalls that Bob spent much of his spare time writing letters—primarily to Ursula. He also discussed Ursula with Ivy, who seemed more confidant than secretary. "In your letter you infer that I have found 'another woman who would love me as deeply as my wife did,'" he wrote her. "Do you really think so? I'll be very much interested in your appraisal of Ursula." He went on to write, "Actually I can't quite figure the whole thing out. She has been very good for me, that I know. She's given me fine companionship, apparent devotion, and has been fine for my ego in many ways." Yet, he wondered if Ursula didn't have an ulterior motive, "possibly because I've been such a deceitful old bastard myself at times in my life . . . Maybe I'm wrong—maybe she actually is in love with me."[366]

364 Lee Server, Ava, pg. 138

365 Robert Taylor to Ivy Pearson, 5/2/53

366 ibid

Ivy also recalls that he would occasionally escape the London crowds for "a little spot in Cornwall." Ivy would accompany him and she recalls that he was "horrified" to find that the cottage that they shared with the host couple only had one bathroom! "I assured him I had grown up with only one bathroom and had never felt deprived!" Ivy, being an English girl, got a bit of publicity herself in her role as secretary to the star. She told one newspaper that profiled her that Taylor was "the easiest person to work with" and that because Bob is often on the set from early in the morning to around seven at night she has a good deal of free time on her hands, but that when he gets home, "he will tell me what jobs he wants me to do. He may want a bill paid—he never seems to carry any money around—or some items of personal shopping."

The picture was in production for three months and by October MGM head Dore Schary was crowing to Darryl Zanuck, who had just put out his own CinemaScope picture, *The Robe*, "I thought you would also like to know that I have just screened *Knights of the Round Table* which I believe is one of the all-time big pictures and is certainly helped to be made so by the most beautiful, cinemascope I have yet seen. It is a big, glorious picture that I think is going to help us all keep doing what we like to do."[367]

Overall, Bob got good reviews for his performance. "Robert Taylor handles the Lancelot part with conviction," wrote *Variety*. "Apparently he's right at home with derring-do heroics." *The Hollywood Reporter* called him a "wonderful choice" as Lancelot, "playing him with all the smoldering fire and brooding gallantry described by Malory and Tennyson." Even the *New York Times* was complimentary: "Mr. Taylor is a fine looking specimen of a knight and he acts with bravery and bravura."

The box office was, again, excellent. The picture cost $2.6 million to produce and grossed $8.2 million worldwide and showed a strong $1.7 million dollar profit for the studio. Of the three pictures that Pandro Berman produced for MGM and released in 1954, two starred Robert Taylor and the other, *The Long, Long Trailer*, starred Lucille Ball and Desi Arnaz. All were box-office bonanzas, but *Knights of the Round Table* was the biggest of all. (Bob's other

367 Dore Schary Papers, WSHSA

Pandro-produced film of 1954, *All The Brothers Were Valiant*, grossed $4.7 million worldwide and showed a profit of just over a million dollars.)

While Bob was in London filming, Ursula was keeping busy playing a German countess opposite Robert Stack in *The Iron Glove* for Columbia. She felt Bob's absence keenly. "I thought this was going to be the end of my world, knowing it would be many months before I would see him again."[368] Bob's letters to her were compensation.

After he returned they continued to see a great deal of each other. Because of Bob's moviemaking schedule they would occasionally see one another between scenes on the backlot of MGM eating a picnic lunch that had been packed by Ruth. Meanwhile, Ursula was making plans to bring her daughter, Manuela, to the United States from Germany. Eventually, she wanted Michael to come as well, but he had a deep attachment to his grandmother and it was easier to bring one child over at a time. To prepare for Manuela's arrival she rented a small house in Pacific Palisades.

Ursula was also giving a great deal of thought to her own relationship with Bob. She loved him but felt that there was some kind of barrier between them. They never discussed marriage and she certainly never pressured him. She wanted to provide a stable home for Manuela and didn't know how to explain Bob's presence to her daughter. Besides, if he wasn't interested in marriage what would be the emotional toll on introducing her daughter to him only to have him leave the picture at some future date? "Eighteen months is enough time to give any man to make a decision," she felt.[369] After the failure of his first marriage, Bob was in no hurry to remarry.

They took a week-long trip to the Rouge River. It was Bob's kind of vacation and one he could enjoy with Ursula in a way he never could have with Barbara. For the trip Bob enjoyed the fishing while Ursula was contemplating how to tell him that she felt their relationship had no future. As they drove home, Ursula let him know that the relationship was over. Bob, grim, remained quiet for

368 Thiess, ...but I have promises to keep, pg. 63

369 Thiess, pg. 64

several minutes until he almost defensively asked, "What have I done to make you angry at me?" She assured him he hadn't done anything. It was just her feeling that the relationship had run its course and there was no indication that it was going to go anywhere. The following night, following a farewell dinner, Ursula requested the house key she had given Bob returned. He did so. The following night he showed up on her doorstep and rang the bell. When Ursula came to the door, he requested to come in, obviously wanting to talk things over with her. He must have been surprised when he got a denial and a door shut in his face. Ursula had made up her mind and, though it was killing her on the inside, she was going to stick by her guns. It was useless to prolong a relationship that wasn't going to lead to marriage. The next morning Bob was on his way to Egypt to make a film. He would be gone for at least three months. [370]

IV

The film that Bob made in Egypt, *Valley of the Kings*, tells the story of a team of archaeologists, headed by Bob, who are searching for a tomb which will prove that the biblical account of Joseph in Egypt is based on fact. They must also contend with grave robbers who want to loot the tombs for the treasures they contain. Eleanor Parker was signed to co-star as the daughter of another famous archeologist, who had been engaged in this search years earlier, and now she wants to carry on his work.

Robert Pirosh, who won an Academy Award for his screenplay of *Battleground*, wrote the screenplay for *Valley of the Kings* and though he had only directed two, relatively minor films, previously he was selected by Dore Schary personally to direct *Valley of the Kings*. Pirosh, however, was insecure about his position on the picture. While in Egypt in late October scouting locations for the shoot which would begin in early December, Pirosh's insecurity poured out in a letter to Schary. He was concerned that Andrew Morton, who was brought in to direct second-unit scenes, was actually a stalking horse being prepared to take over the picture from him. He

370 ibid

told Schary he believed that Morton may be "warming the bench while I was in the box." He felt that the flames were being fanned by the unit producer, Stanley Goldsmith, who Pirosh called a "continual thorn in our sides." He believed that Goldsmith may be writing "confidential appraisals of me and my methods of working to the production department." He challenged Schary that if this were the case to contact anybody else in the company and he would be given a completely different estimate.[371]

In reply to this letter, Schary responded that "in no way does anybody lack confidence in your ability," but didn't really relieve his concerns regarding the possibility of Andrew Marton taking over the direction of the picture from him. "The notion about Marton was purely precautionary so that we would not run into any trouble," Schary wrote. "We have made no decision on this, but in any event you must believe what I tell you." Schary then assured him he was confident that "between all of us we are going to get a big, beautiful and very successful movie." Schary also told Pirosh he was sending a special representative, Charles Schnee, to work on restructuring the script. "I am sending him not only as a studio executive," Schary wrote, "but as my voice in the matters he will take up with you. None of the suggestions is serious, but they will all be helpful, particularly the one concerning the ending." Schary also indicated that "I do want Bob Taylor satisfied with some of the things he objects [in the script]; and I want my own point of view accommodated in connection with some of the scenes." It could hardly be a letter to ease the nerves of the director and co-writer of the script.[372] One other problem needed to be determined before the film went before the cameras. According to Executive Meeting Notes of November 4, 1953, one question on the agenda was "Does Taylor wear mustache?" The decision—No.

Schnee, Schary's personal representative, arrived in Cairo on November 12 and reported back that the "company spirit and enthusiasm very high." He also made the suggestion that the cast have two days of rest in Paris and then two days of rest in Cairo before beginning shooting. Five days later reporting again to Schary, Schnee

371 Robert Pirosh to Dore Schary 10/22/53

372 Schary to Pirosh 10/27/53

says he found Pirosh "very difficult but I got what you wanted" in that the director agreed to all of the changes in the script. He also told Schary that Pirosh's nemesis, production manager Goldsmith, was "doing (a) brilliant job." Needless to say, Pirosh agreeing to the script changes and the presence of Schary's personal representative kept him in the director's chair rather than being replaced by Andrew Morton.

Shortly after the film began shooting, on December 2, came the next crisis—this time involving Bob. Executive Meeting notes from 12/7/53 reported that Bob had calcium of the knee and "cannot walk without a limp." X-ray treatments were given to try and relieve the condition. "Taylor will continue as much as possible where walking not necessary. Condition temporarily painful." Apparently, Bob had incurred a very subtle injury when on a hunting trip to Canada which was became more serious once he was in Egypt filming a scene where he had to jump off a camel several times. Bob, in a letter to his secretary Ivy Pearson, wrote that he has been "hobbling like a tired old character actor." Furthermore, he asked her not to mention this injury to his mother, but that if it leaked into the papers she can give her the details to "calm her jangled nerves," but to make sure and assure Ruth that it has "nothing to do with smoke and drink!!!"[373] In another letter to Ivy a few days later he was uncertain if an "accurate diagnosis has really been made." He believed the x-ray treatments did help quite a bit because, "at times, the pain seems to have practically disappeared." Yet it kept recurring at other times. "My personal theory is that there's a slight dislocation of some kind which can only be remedied by manipulation." He told her he would investigate this when he got home.

While in Egypt Bob was writing Ursula nearly every day but, as he reported to Ivy, her lack of warmth indicated that "she's really made up her mind that the whole thing is over and is merely trying to convince me of the fact as quietly and as nicely as possible." He added that he would prefer not to hear any "off the cuff" news of any new boyfriends that Ursula might have because, "strangely enuf, [it] would upset me. And I'm upset enuf by being over here, without seeking additional sources of annoyance." But that didn't

373 Robert Taylor to Ivy Pearson, 12/9/53

mean he was himself lacking in female company. He informed Ivy that while he missed Ursula he has been "taken care of" in the romantic department while he has been in Egypt. "A little location romance has developed which will end the minute I get home and the only result . . . has been that I realize more and more what a nice companion Ursula really was."[374]

Speculation has always been that the nice little on-set romance was with his co-star, Eleanor Parker, something Parker has consistently denied over the years. In July of 1954, more than six months after the picture wrapped, Parker told *Screenland* that "Bob and I both expected there would be romance talk—Egypt is supposed to be a romance background—and we were only surprised that it didn't start sooner. But this old bromide is truly true—I assure you we're just good friends." Since it was almost Christmas he told Ivy that while he didn't know if Ursula was going to be in the United States or Germany for the holiday he was enclosing a card and personal check and instructed her to, "please take it to a very, very good florist and have a beautiful basket or something made up for her at Christmas time."[375]

The picture wrapped filming in Egypt on New Year's Eve, 1953, and Bob flew on to London for a few days before returning to the United States to continue with some interior work at MGM in Culver City. While in London he poured his heart out again to Ivy regarding the situation as he saw it with Ursula. "In only one thing do I disagree with you, Ivy," he wrote, "and that is that she still loves me—I don't think she does." But he took complete blame for the situation, "my own damned fault." He did feel that he might make another try at things when he got home, "However, I'm sure it's all water under the bridge by now. And if guys like [Nicky] Hilton and [Jennings] Lang are hanging around [newspaper publicity items linked Ursula with both men] I know it's all over—I wouldn't compete with characters like that if I never got married again!" He expressed disappointment that a promised letter from Ursula for Christmas never showed up, "but she did send me a brief cable saying that her permission to go to Germany had not been given." He told

374 ibid

375 ibid

Ivy to give Ursula his love, "and when she throws it right back in your face just remember that I warned you."[376]

The picture resumed production on January 11, 1954, and then wrapped for good by the end of the month. By April, the film had been previewed and one Metro executive reported that the preview was "far better than anyone expected." Also in early April, MGM flew in exhibitors to preview several upcoming Metro pictures. A report was prepared for Schary regarding the reaction to several pictures. "Real interest in *Valley of the Kings*," read the report. "The excerpts made the most of background and locale; the screening room actually included audible amazement at some of the scenes, as the camera moved from Pyramid to Sphinx to ancient ruin. Believe this a very good start on *Valley*. (Among the other films screened there was excitement by the exhibitors for both *Seven Brides for Seven Brothers, Beau Brummel,* and *Brigadoon. The Student Prince* had a thumbs down ["they found the story rather tired and old"]; they also had reservations about the latest Gable picture, *Betrayed*, with Gable looking "old and tired.")[377]

When *Valley of the Kings* was released, it produced a modest profit despite mixed reviews. Almost to a review the location scenes were praised rather than the story. *Variety* said that the "backgrounds offer more freshness to the film than does the routine story," but liked the Taylor-Parker pairing, calling them "a good lead team."

V

By the time that Bob returned from Egypt, Manuela was with Ursula. Returning to California, after doing some promotional events for *Valley of the Kings* in New York, Bob called Ursula and requested the opportunity to get together and meet her daughter. Ursula agreed, and when he arrived at Ursula's house to pick them up for dinner he brought along a car full of new toys for Manuela. After dinner and when Manuela was tucked into bed, Bob and Ursula had a long talk, but Ursula was adamant; they could be friends, but that was all.

---

376 Robert Taylor to Ivy Pearson

377 Dan Terrell to Dore Schary, 4/14/54 Schary Papers

At around this time Bob confidentially asked Ivy if he should marry Ursula. "If you don't somebody else will," she told him. Bob had already made up his mind. He brought out a ring he bought and showed it to Ivy. "It was the biggest diamond I ever saw," she recalled. "I asked him if it was real!" [378]

The next night, to Ursula's surprise, Bob called her and asked if they could meet for dinner again. Ursula told him that she had dinner guests already, cinematographer Ernie Haller and his wife. Bob knew the Hallers and was invited to join them. It was an uneasy and plainly nervous Bob Taylor who came to dinner that night. It turned out to be an early evening for the Hallers. They decided to leave early because they could tell that Bob was preoccupied and obviously had something important he wanted to say to Ursula. Once the Hallers left, Bob brought out two packages. He had Ursula open the larger one first, finding some expensive French perfume. He then nervously invited her to open the smaller package. When Ursula opened the smaller box, she found a "beautiful burst of diamonds" sparkling from the engagement ring that Bob had gotten her. "I don't know what took me so long," he told her. "I guess it was my fear of another failure. Darling, would you marry this old goat?" [379] The official announcement of their engagement was made on April 30, 1954.

At the time that the engagement was announced Bob had just begun shooting a crime-drama, *Rogue Cop*, this time giving him a break from the extensive location work of most of his most recent pictures. *Rogue Cop* began its production under the title "Kelvaney"—the last name of the character that Bob plays in the picture. The film was based on a novel by William McGivern (who had also penned the source material for *The Big Heat*, a big hit the previous year, about a cop who is out for revenge), which had been serialized in *Cosmopolitan* in April, 1954, the very month that production on the film began. Bob plays a corrupt police detective who tries to capture his brother's murderer. Janet Leigh, in her last picture of her MGM contract, is cast as a nightclub singer who is also the girlfriend of the murdered brother. Steve Forrest is cast as Taylor's

378 Ivy Mooring to author

379 Thiess, pg. 68-69

brother, an honest cop who is killed by George Raft's gang leader, who has given payoffs to Taylor's corrupt detective in the past. Anne Francis is cast as Raft's mistress. MGM stalwart Roy Rowland directed the proceedings briskly and with style.

Janet Leigh recalled working with Taylor fondly. "My swan song was not too memorable," she wrote in her autobiography, "except that 'Rogue Cop' paired me with Robert Taylor. He was a beautiful man, always modest and self-effacing."[380] Bob was delighted with his part in *Rogue Cop*. "I finally got back into a blue suit," he quipped at the time. "It's much more comfortable than a suit of armor, believe me."[381]

Rogue Cop is a tight, efficient and well-executed *film noir* which gives Bob one of his good-bad guy parts that he always enjoyed. The critics also took noticed and were complimentary to him and the picture in their reviews. In the *New York Times* Bosley Crowther wrote, "It is a well-done melodrama, produced and directed in a hard, crisp style, and it is very well acted by Robert Taylor in the somewhat disagreeable title role." The *New York Post* was equally complimentary. "Taylor handles his tough guy role with ease—never sneering more broadly or hitting harder than necessary."

Within a week of completing *Rogue Cop* Bob had decided the time had come to get married, but he wanted it to be done in complete privacy and without advance notice. Even Ruth would not know. Now that she had her man, Ursula was willing to let him handle all the wedding plans. It was Bob who chose the date, May 24, and the location, Jackson Lake, Wyoming. Only two other people were involved in the wedding party. The two witnesses were, Ivy, who was emerging not only as a close friend of Bob's but Ursula's as well, and Bob's friend and co-pilot, Ralph Crause. It was Crause who flew the wedding party to Wyoming, leaving Los Angeles in the pre-dawn hours of May 24.

Once in the Town of Jackson Lake, Bob and Ursula took care of last-minute preparations, and then left with the wedding party for the lake. Bob decided that the most perfect place to get married would be on a boat in the middle of the lake with the still-snow-capped

380 Janet Leigh, There Really was a Hollywood, pg. 172

381 LA Daily News, 5/4/54

Grand Tetons in the background. Within minutes the ceremony was over. Ursula Thiess was now Mrs. Robert Taylor. The wedding party returned to the hotel where Bob immediately phoned his publicist and the news was released. He then phoned his mother—once more not invited to her son's wedding.

Ruth was furious. Not only because she wasn't invited, but because he never even told her that he was going to marry Ursula. Second, she didn't favor Ursula as a prospective daughter-in-law any more than she had Barbara. According to Ivy, Ruth had many prejudices. She hated Democrats (particularly FDR), Catholics, Jews, homosexuals—and Germans. Earlier in their relationship Ruth tried to dissuade Bob from marrying Ursula because of Ursula's mother. "Ursula's mother was a very large woman," Ivy recalled. "Mrs. Brugh told Bob that later on Ursula, like her mother, would be 'as big as a house.'" Another reason that Ruth didn't want Bob to marry Ursula was because she had two children from a previous marriage. "They will bleed you to death," she told Bob.[382]

The honeymoon was spent in an out-of-the-way cabin in Northern California at a picturesque location along the Russian River near Cloverdale. The only problem was that this romantic setting was actually three miles away from the location shoot of Bob's latest film, *Many Rivers to Cross*. Did Ursula mind? "No, of course not, because I knew before we got married that Bob had to go directly to work on the film. It didn't bother me in the least and I knew at a later time we would have a real honeymoon."[383] Of course there was another little item involved because his leading lady was none other than Eleanor Parker, who had long been linked romantically with Bob, as recently as six months earlier on the set of *Valley of the Kings*. One Taylor biographer would write that Bob told a friend that during the filming of *Many Rivers to Cross* that the presence of Miss Parker came close to breaking up his recent marriage. "No," counters Ursula Thiess. "I'm sure she was surprised just as everybody else on the set was, but there was no tension."[384] Certainly it must have been a considerable surprise for Parker to find out that Taylor

---

382 Ivy Mooring to author

383 Ursula Thiess to author

384 ibid

had married just before showing up on location and that his bride was here with him, despite the fact that there engagement was announced more than two months earlier. If she really did have any inkling of securing Bob it was now a moot point.

The location shooting became a family affair when two days later little Manuela arrived to join her mother and stepfather on their honeymoon. She asked Bob, "What do I call you now? Do I call you Daddy?"

"Of course," he answered, hugging the girl, "unless you can come up with something better."

No tension is found in the performances between Bob and Parker. In fact, they appear as comfortable together in this light-hearted comedy-western as they did in any of their previous films together. The film takes place in 1798 Kentucky and deals with a determined frontier woman (Powell) out to marry a trapper (Taylor) she saved from attack from a group of Shawnee Indians. Of course, Taylor isn't ready to be "bagged" by any female and wants to continue with his wandering life. This is no standard Western fare but in many ways a battle of the sex's comedy set in the late 18th century. While Taylor would rather hunt, fish and trap without any female baggage, Parker is every bit his match as she sets out to get her man. One particularly sparkling scene has Taylor and Parker singing "The Berry Tree," which Sheb Wooley also sings over the opening credits. The proceedings are energetically directed by Roy Rowland and features a top-notch supporting cast, including Victor McLaglen and Josephine Hutchinson as Parker's parents. Two future television stalwarts also appear in the film, James Arness, TV's future Marshal Matt Dillon on *Gunsmoke*, and Alan Hale, Jr., the future Skipper on *Gilligan's Island*.

When the film was released in early February of 1955, it earned good reviews. One critic called it "Slapstick in buckskin." The film also served MGM well at the box office earning nearly $3.7 million and showing a net profit of over $400,000.

Ursula was still working as an actress herself. But her goal was to get out of acting all together and devote herself to her husband and children. It was shortly after making the film *Americano* opposite a leading man she came to despise, Glenn Ford, that Ursula was pregnant with her third child—Bob's first. Bob was ecstatic when he heard the news. Ursula recalled that he "showered me with over-protection and love, of which I became a most willing recipient."[385] In the meanwhile, she was also supervising the building of their own first home together in Pacific Palisades.

Bob was now the top contract star at MGM. With Clark Gable's departure from the studio he was now referred to as "The New King of MGM," a title that Bob would scoff at. Metro made their regard for him clear when they offered him a new six-year extension on a contract which still had a year left. "Well, they wanted me to sign, so I took them up on it," he explained to Hollywood reporter Bob Thomas. "You know, I've made a heck of a lot of money from the studio in 21 years, and I've got doggone little to show for it." (Thomas estimated that in those 21 years Bob had made about $3 million.) He was asked why he didn't pursue freelancing so he could get profit participation and replied, "Oh, Clark [Gable] has got himself all set up. He's in great shape with these new deals. But it would be just my luck to start out my making a couple of bad pictures on the outside and then no one would hire me. No, I'm the kind of guy who likes to stay put. I'm comfortable here and that's where I'll stay."

Just after *Many Rivers to Cross* was released at home in February 1955, Bob was off once again to MGM's Elstree Studio in England to make his fifth film from that location and yet another period piece based on a Sir Walter Scott novel. This time the film was *Quentin Durward*, and his co-star was Kay Kendall. Set in the fifteenth century, the Scottish knight Quentin Durward (Bob) meets his elderly uncle, now impoverished, who wants Durward to carry a marriage proposal to the much younger (and wealthy) Isabelle, the Countess of Marcroy (played by Kendall) in France. As might be expected Durward falls for the lady himself, but doesn't want to reveal himself due to honor and that fact that he is on a mission for another man. Durward agrees to escort the countess on a journey However, French King Louis XI (Robert Morley) plots to have Isabelle captured, for Louis' own amorous pleasures. Naturally it is up to Durward to save the lady. Luckily, by the end of the film the lady is equally in love and the impoverished elderly uncle who sent

385 Thiess, ...but I have promises to keep, pg. 74

Durward on the mission is dead and Durward can openly express his love for Isabelle. Pandro Berman once again produces with Richard Thorpe in the director's chair for the fifth time on a Taylor picture.

Kay Kendall was not the first choice to play Isabella in the film. Originally, the studio wanted the role to go to Grace Kelly, but she ultimately declined the part. Kendall was a beautiful redhead with a winning personality and wit, who was romantically involved with and would eventually marry Rex Harrison before her tragic death from leukemia only three years after this film was released. Kendall was not enchanted by the part. "They shaved my eyebrows and put an orange wig on me," she later wryly observed, "I looked like Danny Kaye having a fit in drag!"[386] In actuality, Kendall looks extremely fetching in the film.

While in London, Bob had dinner with his old flame, Ava Gardner. "Took Ava Gardner out to dinner last night. She seems very happy now—likes her part, enjoys Cukor [she was filming *Bhowani Junction*], isn't all complicated with romance, and all in all, seems much more properly adjusted than I've ever seen her. The date, of course, was with Ursula's knowledge and permission."[387]

The quite pregnant Ursula came over to London to join Bob. Ivy moved into the San Remo house to help look after Manuela. Ivy would recall that Manuela did her best to understand the English language but it was quite a struggle for her. "For her, an assignment would take three times as long as for another person," Ivy later recalled, "and she looked lazy and irresponsible to the casual observer who only looked at how little she had done, not the effort it cost to produce." Ivy also recalls Manuela as a "great kid" who was a bit of a tomboy.[388]

Meanwhile, Bob kept in touch with Ivy by mail. While Bob was working on the picture, Ursula took a side trip to Hamburg to see about bringing Michael home. "Things in Hamburg seem to have worked out satisfactorily," Bob wrote to Ivy. "Michael is rough-and-ready to come back to California with her and, apparently, had only

386 The Brief, Madcap Life of Kay Kendall, pg. 91

387 Robert Taylor to George Nichols,4/14/55, Margaret Herrick Library (AMPAS)

388 Ivy Mooring to author

expressed a contrary desire because Grandma always raised so much Hell at the thought of his leaving." He reported that Ursula would go to Hamburg in March to "get his papers in order and spend a few days pacifying her mother."

Before arriving in London, Bob and Ursula went to France and enjoyed the sights, including a trip to a Parisian club called LIDO to see the show. "It was excellent," Bob told Ivy. "The costuming was beautiful, the acts good, and the nudity refreshing." Bob also reported that the baby, or "little monster" as he called it, inhabiting Ursula's pregnant belly put up a fuss as soon as the nude dancers appeared on stage. "The very minute the first nude appeared on stage 'Junior' starting kicking Ursula around and didn't stop all evening. Unfortunately, his and my tastes don't completely agree—while I'd be ogling the lovely pair of 'lungs' on stage left, he'd be kicking towards stage right! However, I guess it's purely a matter of every man for himself and I can't criticize his choice too much—they were all nice to look at! Wow!"

This time Bob had less to complain about regarding the food. "Food is plentiful, prices have not skyrocked the way they have in France and at home, and there seems to be an air of prosperity I've not seen here since before the war. We've had steaks every night since arriving here—the good old pre-war tounedo type of meat—and the vegetables are wonderful, plenty of fresh fruit, and even the cooking seems to have improved." He closed this letter by telling Ivy to give Manuela his love and also to give a "big kiss to mother . . . If she's run out of anyone to feel sorry for at the moment tell her to come on over here and I can introduce her to an arthritic old scrubwoman on the floor here at the hotel who'll tide her over for a few days. It's pitiful and might fit right into mother's plans."[389]

About a month later Bob was able to report to Ivy that the picture was "going along quite well." He also reported that final arrangements had been made to bring Michael to the United States. In fact, Michael was quite excited about the prospect of reuniting with his mother, "that's all he thinks and talks about." Ursula's mother, of course, was still "mostly tears and sobs" at losing Michael, who had lived with his grandmother for so long.

389 Robert Taylor to Ivy Pearson, 2/27/55

Apparently, Ruth had reported to Bob that the men who had been doing work in the basement of the Taylor home while Bob and Ursula were gone were drinking and stealing from the household. Bob told Ivy that he doubted this was the case. "Maybe they had a few shots of whiskey without asking," he wrote Ivy, "but mostly I found them to be completely reliable." Bob also mentioned that Ruth had written him that his business office was delinquent in paying bills promptly. "Mother, of course, tends to dislike the office and always finds something to criticize them about," he wrote. Nevertheless, Bob instructed Ivy to look into the matter and if she validated what Ruth had said he would write a letter and "really give them a fit if they've let things slide too badly."

Bob wrote that "little one" [Manuela] was "a good little gal but so completely lacking in any sense of responsibility." He hoped that Michael would be the polar opposite. "Of course," he wrote, "when little one arrived in the States she had very good manners and was quiet and well disciplined too. It was only when she learned the language and became acquainted with Ursula and the neighborhood kids that she kinda went haywire." Bob believed that Ursula "must be more strict and try to get a little more punch in the kids than she's doing. Do you agree? Confidentially, of course!" [390]

Ursula and Michael were to arrive back before Bob, who still had to move on to France in either late April or early May for additional location work. He enclosed in the letter some money so that Ivy could buy a "bunch of dark red roses" and have them placed in Ursula's bedroom the day she arrived home, "Perhaps on the desk, in a white vase, would be a good place," along with a personal card from Bob.

Quentin Durward ended production in mid-June and Bob returned home to reunite with Ursula, Manuela and Michael and anticipate the birth of their first child. When the picture was released in October, the box office was weak. The film cost about $2.5 million to produce, but only grossed around $660,000 in the United States. However, it did quite well in foreign markets grossing nearly $1.8 million. Still, when all was said and done, the picture ended up losing about $1.2 million. It proved to Bob that the costume pictures he had done so successfully since *Quo Vadis* had finally had their

390 ibid

run—and he couldn't have been more delighted.

What delighted Bob even more was the prospect of fatherhood. It was while she was out at a movie theater seeing the movie *Seven Brides for Seven Brothers* with Manuela that Ursula began getting labor pains. Though the hospital was only a block from the theater, Ursula made the decision to go home first and let Bob be the one who took her to the hospital. With bags packed and Bob carefully driving himself and his pregnant wife to St. John's Hospital in Santa Monica, Ursula gave birth to a healthy baby boy at 4:28 A.M. on June 18, 1955. They named him Terence, but came to call him Terry. After a suitable amount of time to regain her strength and figure, Ursula went on to make the final film she was contracted to do, *Bandido* (with Robert Mitchum, who she very much liked). She then announced her retirement to devote her time to her children and husband.

Sometime after this Bob and Ursula had a most unpleasant encounter with a drunken Barbara Stanwyck. It occurred at a party that the Robert Mitchums were giving at Romanoff's in Los Angeles. "Bob and I shared a table once more with Lex [Barker], Lana [Turner, his then-wife], and some other friends exchanging gossip and enjoying the evening, when out of the blue there was a disruption," Ursula wrote in her autobiography. "Uninvited and quite drunk, Barbara Stanwyck, accompanied by her publicity agent, marched in and instantly put Bob on edge. When Dorothy Mitchum, confronted her for crashing their party, Barbara arrogantly drawled, 'Do you know who I am?' Apparently Dorothy stood her ground with some strong words to answer to that. But Barbara made no attempt to leave. Lex, who had witnessed this whole exchange, overheard Barbara saying, 'Hell, I don't want your food, lady, I just came in to take a peek at Taylor and his German broad.'"[391]

Ursula later recalled that Bob was excited to be a father, but within days of Terry's birth he was exhibiting signs of jealousy. One day when he walked into their bedroom and caught Ursula looking at her newborn son with the glow of newfound motherhood he stood there and watched and finally said to Ursula, "Are you going to stare

391 Thiess, … promises to keep, pg. 99

at that guy all day?"[392] According to Ivy (who to her great pleasure became Terry's godmother), "He loved the idea [of fatherhood]. He showed Terry off as if to say, 'Look what I was able to accomplish.' He wanted Terry to be somebody who could shoot and hunt with him from the day he was born."[393] He was unsentimental when it came to his son. When Terry was eight months old, he took a tumble from a rubber raft and disappeared in the swimming pool. His stepsister Manuela pulled him to safety. Bob's reaction? "Good—maybe it'll teach him a lesson."[394] It's not that Bob didn't love his son, but he well recalled that he was the child of an overprotective parent and he didn't want his son to be treated the way Ruth treated him.

392 Thiess, pg. 85

393 Ivy Mooring to author

394 Bob Taylor: What Keeps him on Top, Jane Kesner Ardmore, CA. 1957

Chapter Eleven

End of the MGM Line (1956-1958)

In the summer of 1955 Bob began work on one of his most interesting films and one which offered one of his most complex characterizations. The film was *The Last Hunt*, based on a well-received 1954 novel of the same name. That this was going to be one of Metro's most prestigious pictures of the year is the fact that it would be personally produced by studio head Dore Schary. Schary assigned Richard Brooks to write the screenplay as well as direct. Brooks had just directed one of the studio's biggest hits of 1955, *Blackboard Jungle*. For marquee value Schary assigned the film to two of the studio's most stalwart leading men, Bob and Stewart Granger.

Interestingly, Bob didn't believe he was really right for this film. In fact, he initially turned it down. "I didn't think I was good enough, not a good enough actor to play the heavy and play it convincingly. I thought Dick Brooks should have had Douglas or Brando or Lancaster." But Brooks wanted Bob. "He flew all the way to England and convinced me."

Bob plays Charlie Gilson, a buffalo hunter who gets sadistic pleasure out of killing, man or beast. The film takes place in 1883 at a time when buffalo was still king on the prairies of South Dakota. A huge buffalo herd is stampeding grazing land belonging to Sandy McKenzie (Granger) killing all of his cattle. Gilson invites McKenzie to join him in a killing spree to thin out the herd. McKenzie is an ex-buffalo hunter himself but is not eager to join Gilson, a man he has great foreboding about. But as his land continues to be overrun by the stampeding buffalo McKenzie reluctantly joins forces with Gilson. They are joined by Jimmy O'Brien, a half-breed

(Russ Tamblyn) and a former mule skinner with a peg leg named Woodfoot (Lloyd Nolan). Also joining them is a Sioux Indian girl (Debra Paget, on loan out from Twentieth Century-Fox) and her infant son. The Indian girl is adamantly opposed to the hunt, since the buffalo is sacred to the Sioux. Needless to say, the hunt proceeds and, in one of the most brutal sequences ever put before the cameras, we see actual buffalo slaughtered. A turning point comes when McKenzie wants to spare a white buffalo, but Gilson kills the animal without remorse. Later, Gilson attempts to rape the Indian girl—who McKenzie is falling in love with. Eventually, McKenzie and the Indian girl leave Gilson, who then stalks them in the dead of winter, and waits to kill them when they emerge from the cave they are taking refuge in to escape a brutal snowstorm. Gilson, without cover from the storm, kills a lone buffalo and skins it, believing that its hide will protect him from the bitter cold. The next day, when McKenzie emerges from the cave to do battle with Gilson, he finds Gilson frozen stiff under the buffalo skin. This film is not for the squeamish.

The film was shot mostly on location in Custer State Park, which was home to one of the largest buffalo herds still existing in the United States—numbering about 1,500 bison. This would add realism to the project. The big question for the filmmakers was how could they realistically film a buffalo stampede and hunt. Brooks was told that the summer of 1955 would be the start of South Dakota's schedule for trimming its herds, which had grown from less than 400 in 1948 to about 1500 in 1955. Sharpshooters would be brought into the park to thin the herd. Schary and Brooks decided they would coordinate the shooting schedule with this thinning of the herd and would film the slaughter of approximately 75 buffalo and then edit it with shots of Taylor and Granger to give the illusion that they are the ones killing the bison. This would give the picture the "realism" that Schary and Brooks wanted.

South Dakota certainly welcomed the film being shot on location since it would be a boom to the local economy. Rapid City, the largest city in the western part of the state, served as headquarters for the company. It was ideally situated between the Badlands and Black Hills filming sites. MGM brought in a company of about 125 people. In a report prepared by MGM for the Rapid City Chamber of Commerce, "The Company spent directly in Rapid City a sizable amount of money. This money went to many local establishments and individuals such as carpenters, electricians, drivers, laborers, wranglers, also rental for trucks, cars, buses, cattle, horses, lumber and building supplies, medical and hospital costs, laundry, photo service and supplies, hotels, motels, restaurants and cafes. For all of these services MGM spent over a quarter of a million dollars locally." [395]

The filming was not without its hazards. The temperatures in the badlands were often between 100 and 120 degrees for days at a time. The cast and crew had to drink gallons of water to keep from getting dehydrated, but that didn't always do the trick. At least twice during the shooting Granger fainted from the heat. Granger had another close call when one massive bull suddenly charged toward the actor. Granger ran down a 50-yard embankment only to lose his footing; luckily for Granger the bull suddenly turned away from him and ran in an opposite direction, but not before Granger came up with a cut forehead and elbow. On another occasion Russ Tamblyn was driving a runaway mule team that was supposedly stampeded by buffalos. Tamblyn was doing the scene himself without a stuntman (more of that realism that Schary and Brooks wanted) when he was thrown from the wagon and knocked unconscious. After a few moments Tamblyn revived and luckily X-rays proved he had broken nothing more than his pride. There was one casualty in the casting of the picture, very early on. Anne Bancroft, then a young MGM contract player, had been cast as the Indian girl, when she shot a scene with Granger where he had to sweep her into his saddle and ride off with her. Unfortunately for Bancroft she fell from the horse injuring her back. She was out of the picture. That is when Debra Paget was borrowed on little notice from Fox.

Paget has good memories of working on *The Last Hunt*, though at the time it was all a little rushed for the actress. She had just finished *The Ten Commandments* for Paramount when Fox told her she was needed on loan out to MGM for *The Last Hunt*. "I didn't even have a script to read," she recalls. She liked the cast and director, but didn't become close to anybody—including Taylor. "Bob was quiet and very shy and I was quiet and shy so we didn't really get to

---

395 Report found in the Dore Schary papers, WSHSA

know each other very well," Paget recalled over 50 years later. "I was a big fan; I had grown up watching him at the movies, so maybe that was why I was so shy, too. I don't know. But he was extremely nice and so was Stewart Granger. We all got along quite well without really getting to know each other." One thing that Paget does recall is that Taylor was excited about playing the villain in the film. "He played such a different and difficult part and he did it very well," recalls Paget. "He really was quite a fine actor, which some critics seemed to forget because he was so handsome." She remains pleased by how the film turned out despite the difficult subject matter. "I thought the picture was wonderful," says Paget. "Of course it has a tragic story to tell—about the slaughter of the buffalo—but Richard Brooks did a wonderful job on it. It was well made and, of course, I loved making Westerns. I had ridden horses since I was 11 or 12." Despite replacing Anne Bancroft, Paget says that when the picture was completed that Richard Brooks had confided in her that he had wanted Paget all along, "that really pleased me, though, of course, I regretted that I got the part due to Anne's accident." [396]

Bob got on well with director Richard Brooks. That is more than could be said about Granger, who disliked Brooks intensely. He thought that the director "seemed to revel in taking close shots of maggots crawling out of the corpses littering the plains or the skinning and butchering of the stinking animals that had been shot days before." [397] It was a dislike that only grew deeper when only a few years later Brooks married Jean Simmons, who was at the time Stewart Granger's wife.

The only thing about Brooks which Bob didn't like was the fact that he was constantly swearing on the set, and not just a mild expletives but some of the bluest language imaginable. Ordinarily, this wouldn't have bothered a man's man like Bob Taylor, except that on location there were many sightseers who often turned up who could hear Brooks bellowing, "F—this" and "F—that" over a blow horn. Many of these sightseers were women and children and Bob, always the gentleman, wasn't one to use that kind of language

396 Debra Paget to author

397 Stewart Granger, Sparks Fly Upward

in front of them. Bob spoke with MGM publicity director George Nichols about it one night. Bob and Nichols hatched a plan to take Brooks out for a drive with Bob driving and Brooks in the middle. Nichols and Bob would talk back and forth to one another using the dirtiest language imaginable with Brooks not getting a word in edge wise sitting in the middle. The ploy apparently worked because when he returned to the set Brooks stopped using the offensive language.

The climax of the film posed a problem for Schary and Brooks. Basically it was how to kill off the Bob Taylor character. One suggestion was to have the sadistic Charlie get trampled by a buffalo, a sort of poetic beauty, and when Granger and the Indian girl come out of the cave they see Taylor's body in a "grotesque sprawl of death. They turn and walk back together to the fire in peace." Schary vetoed this and went ahead with the idea of Charlie freezing to death during the storm while wrapped in the hide of the buffalo he killed. To produce this effect Brooks sprayed the surrounding hills with a white powder to give the impression of snow and then used airplane engines to create gale-sized winds. It worked very effectively and when Granger discovers the frozen-stiff Taylor, it produces a memorable and disturbing screen moment.

The film was first previewed at the Picwood Theatre in West Los Angeles on December 21, 1955, before an audience which returned some 212 preview cards. Overall the film was deemed outstanding by 25 people, excellent by 70, very good by 45, good by 36, fair by 31 and poor by 3. 134 people said they would recommend the film to their friends while 46 said they wouldn't. 129 thought Taylor was excellent, but he was outpaced by Granger who was found excellent by 156 previewers and Nolan who received 163 excellent votes. Taylor certainly gives a strong performance, but it is probably because he plays such an odious character that it was harder for the audience to praise him.

Among the positive comments that the audience made on their cards included: "The acting was wonderful," "I found the picture unusual and entertaining," "Good photography," "Very different western, which makes it appealing," "An exceptional film," "Very authentic," "Taylor did a job! No swashbuckling at last. A role with meat and dialogue. His best job in my memory," "The three leads gave excellent performances—especially Taylor and Nolan." On the other hand, some of the comments did not bring make Schary stand up and cheer: "Too much buffalo killing," "Most unrealistic," "Robert Taylor should have been killed much sooner," "slow moving—seemed quite silly," "Another western," "A dull bore," "Waste of time for Granger. Taylor should get better material" and numerous complaints about the violence presented by the all-too-realistic slaughter of the buffalos.[398]

Schary wasn't willing to change the picture too much. He felt it was better to let people see what really happened in a graphic manner rather than soft peddle it. In the end he is correct. It's not pretty, but *The Last Hunt* is a compelling film. Many critics agreed. Archer Winsten in the *New York Post* wrote, "The picture-makers have filmed these deaths from the official slaughter of the only big buffalo herd still alive. I can't say it's pleasant, but it does add something authentic to fairly strong-fibered scenes of human conflict. The picture is hard, tough." Bosley Crowther in the *New York Times* put it this way: "It is official and necessary killing, and Metro-Goldwyn-Mayer . . . can be forgiven—indeed it can be acclaimed—for sending its cameras to record this disagreeable incident of modern conservation and integrating it into its fictional film." Taylor garnered some good reviews as well. "Taylor plays the role well," wrote the critic for the *New York Herald Tribune*. "The mean streak is always there, in his thoughts and his smallest actions. He exults in the hunt like a conquering soldier, but the rest of the time he chafes with spite and suspicion. Rages darken his brow like a summer storm, his blue eyes narrow with cruelty, and instinctively his gun is out. He's always ready to shoot."

In the end it's likely that *The Last Hunt* turned off some due to its extreme violence and theme. Schary got several letters from moviegoers offended by what they saw. One letter from a Lyme, Connecticut, man, dated March 26, 1956, summed up the feeling of many of the letter writers. The writer calls the film "depraved" and complains that it's about a "sadist . . . Wherever there was an opportunity to dwell on brutality, the camera took it." Schary replied, "Believe me; I respect your deep concern. I can only tell you that I

398 Dore Schary Papers, WSHSA

am disappointed that THE LAST HUNT upset you as much as it did. There are others who found the picture difficult to watch, but our intent was high and the point we were trying to make we felt was a cogent and valid one."[399] In the two weeks that it played in New York's Loew's State it grossed $36,148, moderately well, but nowhere near as good as the $129,303 that *Blackboard Jungle* made the previous year over a comparable period of time. The film ended up only breaking even at the box office.

II

In 1956 Bob made two films for the director Henry Koster, best known for such whimsical pictures as *The Bishop's Wife* and *Harvey*. The first presented Bob with his first loan out from MGM since *This is My Affair* back in 1937 (which also had been a Fox film). The film is *D-Day the Sixth of June*. Bob reportedly wanted to make this film in part because it reminded him of his own personal favorite, *Waterloo Bridge*.

While the film is titled after the climatic World War II battle, most of the picture doesn't even involve the invasion of Normandy but rather concerns itself with a story of a married American Captain (Bob) and a British officer (played by Richard Todd, who during the war actually participated in D-Day) who, while on board a ship on the eve of D-Day, reminisce about their mutual romantic involvement with a beautiful woman (played by Dana Wynter). It's only in the final twenty minutes or so of the picture that we actually see battle scenes. Six years later Fox would undertake a much more ambitious re-enactment of the events of D-Day with *The Longest Day*.

Koster shot the scenes of the men aboard an actual American cruiser stationed in Wilmington, Delaware. The battle scenes toward the end of the film were shot on the beaches of Point Dume, California. Fox had also gotten the cooperation of the government who provided ships and boats from the Army and Navy. "They were very cooperative to shoot that picture," Koster recalled. "As far as the maneuvers were concerned, I discussed them with the

399 ibid

commanding officer. Then they staged the action and I staged the camera angles."[400]

Like most of Bob's directors, Koster found him very cooperative. "He was really easy to work with, and a wonderful gentleman," Koster recalled. "The only trouble with him was he couldn't give up smoking. He tried and tried, and told me the old joke of Mark Twain, about how giving up smoking was easy; Mark Twain had done it twice a week. Well Robert Taylor tried twice a week, and finally gave up and said he couldn't help it. He hoped that nothing would happen. But it did happen, and he died. Very young, and a truly nice, charming, handsome man." Koster also found Bob insecure with his acting. "Robert Taylor I guess was the handsomest actor there ever was," Koster recalled. "But he always said, 'I'm not an actor. I don't know what I'm doing.' I'd say, "Robert, you did Camille with Greta Garbo.' He said, "Believe me; I didn't know what the hell I was doing. But a beautiful director, George Cukor, told me what to do. He acted it and I just copied him, and out came a good performance. You show me what to do and I'll do it.' He had a complex that he couldn't do the work, that he wasn't born to be an actor. I think Robert Taylor had talent. Maybe he was not a genius like the other great actors, but he grew into a talent. I think you can learn by learning how to relax and not being afraid of the camera."[401]

Bob's co-star, Robert Todd, also commented on Bob's still-romantic good looks. "Robert Taylor [was] still as handsome as he had been before the war with Greta Garbo in *Camille*."[402] Todd maintained that the original ending of the film has Taylor going back to his wife in the United States while Todd's character was, "being left to pick up the pieces with a rather crestfallen ex-fiancée (Wynter)." Todd felt that this was a weak ending and contends that he convinced Koster and the producer, Charles Brackett, to have his character killed off at the end, so that it would be "open to question what the outcome might have been had he lived." According to Todd, both Brackett and Koster adopted his idea and it was filmed

---

400 Directors Guild Oral Interview with Henry Koster by Irene Kahn Atkins

401 Ronald L. Davis, Just Making Movies, pg. 21

402 Richard Todd, In Camera

that way.[403]

The critics were underwhelmed by the film with one calling it a, "soft and sticky story of a wartime love affair in London." Bob wasn't happy with the final result either. "I was impressed with *D-Day the Sixth of June* because it reminded me of *Waterloo Bridge* somehow. Trouble is, reading a script is like reading a book and then seeing the movie—never the same."[404]

Less than two months later Bob was back on the Metro lot making his second Koster-directed film based on a novel, *The Power and the Prize*. Filmed the same year as the similarly themed *The Man in the Gray Flannel Suit*, *The Power and the Prize* is the lesser film. Burl Ives plays a powerful and ruthless business man who wants to groom one of his executives (Bob) as his successor, but first he must demonstrate that he has the same ruthlessness as Ives. Complicating matters is his falling love with a German refugee (played by Elisabeth Mueller) who is wrongly suspected of being a Communist. His love for the Mueller character redeems him. The film has a terrific supporting cast behind the three leads, including Mary Astor, Charles Coburn and Sir Cedric Hardwicke.

This time instead of Bob being loaned out it was director Koster loaned to MGM from Fox. Koster at one time had been an MGM contract director, but his homecoming was hardly sentimental. "Well, frankly, I liked it better at Fox," Koster recalled. "It was more a tightly knit family under the guidance of Darryl Zanuck, who was very good at keeping everything together and was a very active, lively man who always had new ideas."[405]

Bob gives a strong performance in the film; the only thing many critics could find fault with is his age. Clearly the character Bob plays in the film is supposed to be at least a decade or so younger than Bob's actual age (which was 44 at the time). Still he photographs well and his energetic and romantic performance recalls many of his pre-war films. His leading lady, Elisabeth Mueller, a beautiful Swiss actress, made a few German films prior to coming to Hollywood for this picture. Fox had hopes that they had discovered a new star.

403 ibid

404 Robert Taylor, J.E. Wayne, pg. 191

405 Director's Guild Interview with Henry Koster

"They always wanted a new Garbo or Hedy Lamarr," Koster later recalled. But it wasn't to be. Mueller only made one more American film after this one, *The Angry Hills*, opposite Robert Mitchum, before retiring from the screen in 1959.

According to records found in the Dore Schary files, the big executive question regarding this film was whether it should retain the title *The Power and the Prize*. The executives discussed changing the title to "The Business of Love," perhaps in hopes of making the film sound more appealing to female moviegoers. Another agenda on the executive meeting minutes instructs MGM executive Ben Thau, "to discuss Burl Ives with Taylor." (Executive meeting minutes 3/7/56.) What was to be discussed is only speculated, but Ives had been identified by "Red Channels" in 1950 as a Communist and had been blacklisted. However, he had cooperated with HUAC in 1952 where he said he had never been a Communist and had only attended some meetings with a friend and fellow folk singer, Pete Seeger. The blacklist was lifted and Ives' career prospered (by 1959 he had even won an Academy Award), but still it might have been prudent to discuss the casting of Ives first with Bob due to his strong anti-Communist credentials. Needless to say, Ives was okayed for the film. While the reviews were good (one called Bob, "convincingly ardent and courageous as the temporarily diverted tycoon"), the box office was nothing to write home about.

Tip on a Dead Jockey, based on a short story by Irwin Shaw, had appeared in *The New Yorker* in 1954, and was quickly optioned by MGM as a possible film. It's the story of Lloyd Tredman, an emotionally troubled World War II pilot (a bit of a throwback to Bob's character in *The High Wall*). He loses all of the money he had in a horse race where a jockey was killed. Bert Smith (played by Martin Gabel), an international character, wants Tredman to fly a load of smuggled English money between France and Egypt. Needing the money, Tredman agrees to do the job, but then has a change of mind when they learn that the deal includes not only smuggled money but narcotics. Tredman wants nothing to do with such a scheme. This, of course, brings about the usual cinematic complications. Naturally, there is a love interest, his wife (Dorothy Malone), who wants to keep her floundering marriage together.

The film had an interesting pre-production history. This history can be told by notes found in the MGM Executive Meeting Notes:

4/9/56: "Tip on a Dead Jockey title overwhelmingly approved against "32nd Day," (which was what its working title was).

6/19/56: "Protection for a Tough Racket—still no cast—Taylor will play it. 10/25 start date."

7/2/56: "Ten Thousand Bedrooms, Tip on a Dead Jockey, and Protection for a Tough Racket—casting of male lead still up in the air."

7/2/56: "Tip—talk of Lederer (the author of the screenplay, Charles Lederer, also assuming direction of film).

7/17/56: "Tip—script too long. Dore to discuss with Taylor possibility of Lederer directing."

7/24/56: "Tip—Taylor reluctant to accept Lederer as director. We must immediately select another director."

7/30/56: "Tip—Marvin Schenck to find director."

8/6/56: "Tip—possible directors? Norman Krasna, Henry Hathaway, Irving Rapper, Robert Aldrich, Joseph Amboy and Henry Koster."

8/8/56: "Protection for a Tough Racket—choices between Ernest Borgnine, Paul Douglas and Howard Keel, but some consideration to be given to putting Bob Taylor in this role and holding Tip to follow."

9/10/56: "Tip—Dore to see Taylor tomorrow regarding his decision to make film Tip on a Dead Jockey."

Meanwhile, Orson Welles had somehow entered the picture.

9/17/56: "Tip—Taylor definitely wants to do this with Orson Welles directing. Check on Welles' price."

9/24/56: "Tip—Marvin Schenck to give Orson Welles a 1/2/57 starting date—script should come in under 1.5 million."

10/1/56: "Tip—Discussion of Orson Welles going over time in our commitment to him if we start him 12/3."

10/29/56: "Tip—Lederer to start on screenplay as soon as Scherck and Cohn meet with Orson Welles to arrange his starting date."

11/5/56: "Tip—Still follow up on Welles deal."[406]

But Welles ultimately didn't do the picture, though he was clearly interested. According to Welles biographer Frank Brady, "MGM was another studio that also had no luck in enticing Orson to the United States, for reasons perhaps even obscure to him, even though he was immensely interested in directing Robert Taylor in Irwin Shaw's crime story, *Tip on a Dead Jockey.*"[407]

With Welles out of the picture the film ultimately went to MGM stalwart and frequent Taylor director, Richard Thorpe. The film *Tip on a Dead Jockey* involved more character study than it did action and as a result the film under Thorpe's direction seems stilted and muddled, not helped by the disjointed script by Charles Lederer. Taylor was disappointed by the end result and by missing out on the opportunity of having Welles direct him. As it turned out at the very time that *Tip on a Dead Jockey* went into production at MGM in February, 1957, Welles was over at Universal shooting his later day masterpiece, *Touch of Evil. Tip on a Dead Jockey* ended up with a net loss of $510,000 at the box office.

406 Executive Meeting Notes found in Dore Schary Papers (WSHSA)

407 Frank Brady, Citizen Welles, pg. 490

Bob's penultimate Metro film was *The Law and Jake Wade*, a Western shot over a seven-week period from early November to late December of 1957. Bob is Jake Wade, a reformed outlaw who is now a marshal of a New Mexico town. Richard Widmark is cast as Clint Hollister, the leader of Wade's old outlaw gang, who is awaiting execution for murder. In the complex code of the old west Wade decides to come to Hollister's rescue, since he owes him a favor. If Wade expects gratitude he is wrong. After saving Hollister's neck, Hollister ends up kidnapping Wade and his fiancée (played by Patricia Owens, fresh off of *Sayonara*). Hollister expects Wade to lead him to missing money from an old bank robbery from years before.

The film is a solid action-packed effort directed by John Sturges just a year after his big-budget *Gunfight at the OK Corral*, a major moneymaker for Twentieth Century-Fox. The film was shot on location in the California High Sierra mountain range, Lone Pine and Death Valley. In addition to the star power of Taylor and Widmark, the cast includes such solid players as Robert Middleton, Henry Silva and DeForest Kelley, about a decade before his iconic portrayal of Dr. "Bones" McCoy on *Star Trek*.

Kelley was excited to be working with Robert Taylor, who he idolized as a kid. As a matter of fact, he first encountered Bob years before when he and a buddy had snuck onto the Metro lot. "We walked for what seemed like miles and finally saw the lights and all the action going on outside," Kelley later recalled. "And we walked up there and we're standing around, and all the grips [were working], and I looked over, and there was Robert Taylor sitting there in a chair. I nudged Mike and said, 'There's Robert Taylor' . . . and Taylor looked up, and he said, 'You two guys slip in here?'" And Kelley and his friend admitted it. They probably thought that the gig was up and that Taylor would have guards remove them from the studio property, but that wasn't the case. "Well, when these guys [the grips] start to move around something, get over there and start pushing it with them so that they'll think you work here, and they'll let you stay in." [408]

408 From Sawdust to Stardust by Terry Lee Rioux pg. 19

III

In April 1958, Bob celebrated twenty-four years under contract to Metro-Goldwyn-Mayer. Only character actor Lewis Stone had served the studio longer in such a capacity. Bob was the last of the major stars of the thirties still under contract to the studio. Little by little as the television revolution took over, and the studios liquidated their movie houses, the star system was being phased-out. It made more sense now that the studios weren't producing the massive amounts of product they were at the height of the studio system. The studios had begun letting their long-term contract players go and offered multi-picture deals instead. Also, the stars wanted a piece of the box-office action. In return for signing on for two or three pictures they wanted a percentage of the gross.

One of the reasons why Bob outlasted such stars as Clark Gable, Spencer Tracy, Katharine Hepburn, Van Johnson and so many others was because he was so easy to work with. Metro producer Joe Pasternak called Bob, "the nicest guy in the picture business." He went on to say, "he stays out of trouble, he does his job and does it well, and the crew loves him." When Hollywood writer Bob Thomas interviewed Bob on this anniversary, he did so in the MGM commissary, where Bob was still sitting at his usual seat in the middle of the room. "Been sitting here for over twenty-years," Bob told him. "The ranks are thinning out now, but it used to be fun when we had such guys at this table as Clark Gable, Spencer Tracy, Vic Fleming, Scott Fitzgerald. I'm about the only one left. I guess that makes me the grand old man."

But on this auspicious occasion he, too, had come to the realization that his time was about up. "This MGM bunch is great to work for, always has been. I'd never want to sever my connections completely," he said. "But when you have no contract you have a wider range of scripts to choose from."[409]

It was a mutual decision and no bitterness on either part. MGM gave him his pension and offered him an option for three more films as a freelance star, an agreement he accepted. Bob hoped that he would have more choices as a freelancer and set a price of $200,000

---

409 Reading Eagle, 4/23/58

up front with a piece of the box office. He also hoped he could make some big money in just a few years so he could retire. He told Hollywood columnist Sheilah Graham that he wanted to retire by the time he was fifty in 1962, "unless I'm in fabulous demand. Otherwise, I'm going to quit."[410]

He still had one more picture to make for MGM under his existing contract. *Party Girl* is a terrific *film noir* which casts Bob as lawyer Tommy Farrell, defender of mobsters in 1930s Chicago. He is a good lawyer, and also one not above using tricks to gain sympathy from the jury by exploiting his crippled leg. He is a rich and successful lawyer and also one stuck in an unhappy marriage to a wife who finds him physically unattractive due to his disability. The mob mouthpiece, Tommy, finds himself coming under the spell of a nightclub dancer, Vicki Gaye (Cyd Charisse), who performs in one of the clubs owned by Chicago gangster Rico Angelo (Lee J. Cobb). The feeling is mutual as Vicki gives him the love that his wife never has. Tommy, who has been scared by his disability, plans to go to Sweden to get an operation which will straighten out a deformed hip, and he plans to send for Vicki. When he sends for her and she comes, it is a Tommy standing on his own two legs and walks forward to take her into his arms. They plan to stay in Sweden and try to make a new life when gang leader Angelo sends for his top mouthpiece to handle some delicate court proceedings. Vicki urges him not to go, and Tommy tries to break off with Angelo, who then threatens to kill Vicki. With no other way out Tommy takes the case. Eventually, the prosecutor (Kent Smith) convinces Tommy to turns state evidence against Angelo. He agrees to do so, which makes Tommy a man with a contract on his head.

As director, the studio selected Nicholas Ray, who had made a name for himself by directing such ambitious films as *In a Lonely Place*, *Rebel without a Cause* and *The True Story of Jesse James*. According to Ray biographer Bernard Eisenschitz, Ray chose to do this film at a studio where directorial freedom was tempered, due primarily to its setting, 1930s Chicago during Prohibition, an era and place that Ray had lived in. The original producer was Charles Schnee, but when Schnee dropped out the film went to old reliable MGM

410 Deseret News, 11/12/58

stalwart, Joe Pasternak, who made his name by helping save Universal from bankruptcy by producing a series of successful films starring Deanna Durbin. One of Pasternak's most acclaimed films, however, came in 1955, with the musical-drama bio-pic *Love Me or Leave Me*, which had starred James Cagney and Doris Day. It was an excellent combination of a dramatic story with musical numbers. This was one reason why Pasternak was eventually selected to produce *Party Girl*.

Bob had been offered a Pasternak-produced picture months earlier, *Ten Thousand Bedrooms*, but had turned down the flimsy script. The part went to Dean Martin, and proved disastrous for him at the box office, in his first solo film without former partner Jerry Lewis. When Pasternak offered Bob *Party Girl*, he enthusiastically accepted the part. For the "party girl" of the film Pasternak considered Doris Day, which would have put more emphasis on singing in the musical sequences, but in the end the studio decided to cast one its own—Cyd Charisse—which changed the musical numbers from song to dance.

Ray came to admire Bob's dedication to his part and growth as an actor. He would recall that when he went to the movies in his youth he, "first saw the favorite actor of the day, Paul Muni. My impression was that he was always playing in front of a mirror. Then came *Camille* and Robert Taylor, pale, handsome, remote. Two decades later, I saw Taylor working for me like a true Method actor." As an example of this Ray recalled how Bob prepared for the part of playing a crippled man, both physically and emotionally. "I wanted Taylor to feel the injury, so that he could be aware of what part of his body the pain was in at all times when he moved." So Ray took Bob to see an osteologist and was impressed by the way he asked the doctor questions and prepared himself to play a handicapped man. "After that, he needed no kind of aid to create his limping. It is only very rarely that you find this kind of ambition, sensitivity and humbleness which Taylor stood for."[411] One of Ray's strongest contributions to the picture was the use of color and atmosphere. In the words of Richard Brody, "Ray's direction, with its garish, searing streaks of color (red has rarely slashed the screen so violently),

411 Bernard Eisenschitz, Nicholas Ray, pg. 343

sharp diagonals, and quickly jerking wide-screen views, reflects its characters' raging energies and inner conflicts."[412]

As was typical of the day, Ray would direct the dramatic scenes while the musical numbers featuring Cyd Charisse were directed by the choreographer Robert Sidney. Sidney was more of a studio man than the maverick Ray, and that led to some conflict between them. According to Ray's biographer, "A natural alliance formed between producer, female lead, and what Ray described as this 'very efficient' but 'very dull' choreographer. Sidney felt that Ray's ideas, shaped by jazz and black music, were aberrant."[413] Charisse found Ray a strange man to work with and one who was often absent from the set. But she relished working with Bob. "From Rock Hudson to Robert Taylor, I worked with two of the handsomest—and nicest—of men in successive pictures. *Party Girl*, which I did with Bob, was a good role for me and a good picture . . . I had known Bob Taylor before because he was a good friend of Tony's [her husband, singer Tony Martin]. He was a very pleasant man, but kept himself aloof on the set, just paling around with his own cronies. He drank coffee all day long and chain smoked. I have a hunch that, around four or five, there was something in the cup besides coffee. It didn't affect him; he was always a gentleman on the set and a thoroughly professional artist."[414]

One Ray biographer later wrote that *Party Girl*, "moves effortlessly from action-packed scenes of violence to more meditative and touching sequences that helps the film to surpass its generic origins. Marked throughout both by his [Ray's] great professionalism and by his feelings of sympathy for his ill-starred lovers, the movie transcends the conventions of the nostalgic gangster picture to become a passionate, involving tale of moral and emotional rebirth."[415]

Filming of *Party Girl* took forty-two days, six over schedule, at a cost of $1.7 million, $50,000 over budget. The reviews were overall on the positive side, including this one from *Variety* which said, "Taylor carries considerable conviction as the attorney, suave

412 The New Yorker, 7/20/09

413 Bernard Eisenschitz, Nicholas Ray, pg. 343

414 Charisse & Martin, The Two of Us

415 Geoff Andrew, The Films of Nicholas Ray, pg. 135

and virile." The *New York Post* said Bob is a "grim but stalwart operator who is as convincing as might be expected in a well-worn role." The film made a modest profit and provided Bob with a fitting end to his long-term MGM contract.

PORTRAIT GALLERY #4

Bob as Marcus Viniqius in *Quo Vadis*, at the time the second biggest grossing film of all-time, after *Gone with the Wind*.

Bob and Deborah Kerr in costume in the lavish epic, *Quo Vadis* (1951)

Bob surrounded by some of the women he leads across the west, *Westward the Women* (1952)

Publicity photo of Ursula Thiess, prior to becoming Mrs. Robert Taylor, 1952 (Photo courtesy of Terry Taylor).

Bob had another big hit with *Ivanhoe*, here with Joan Fontaine.

Bob in his second film with Elizabeth Taylor, *Ivanhoe* (1952)

Bob gave some of his best acting in *Above and Beyond* (1952)

Bob was romantically linked to Eleanor Parker, here in *Above and Beyond*

Howard Keel, Ava Gardner, Bob and Anthony Quinn, *Ride Vaquero!* (1953)

Bob and Ann Blyth in *All the Brothers Were Valiant*, (1953)

***Knights of the Round Table* (1954)**

Valley of the Kings **(1954)**

Studio publicity photo, mid-fifties.

A good-natured romp, Eleanor Parker and Bob in *Many Rivers to Cross* (1955)

Victor McLaglen holding a gun on Bob in *Many Rivers to Cross*

A favorite photo of Ursula and Bob (COURTESY OF TERRY TAYLOR)

Bob was happy that *Quentin Durwood* (1955) with Kay Kendall was his last medevel costume picture.

M-G-M presents
in
CINEMASCOPE
"THE LAST HUNT"
Starring
ROBERT TAYLOR
STEWART GRANGER
LLOYD NOLAN
DEBRA PAGET
RUSS TAMBLYN
Screen Play by RICHARD BROOKS
Based on the Novel by Milton Lott
Directed by RICHARD BROOKS
Produced by DORE SCHARY

***The Last Hunt* (1956) offered Bob a fascinating role.**

D-Day: The Sixth of June **(1956) with Dana Wynter was Bob's first picture on loan-out from MGM in nearly twenty-years.**

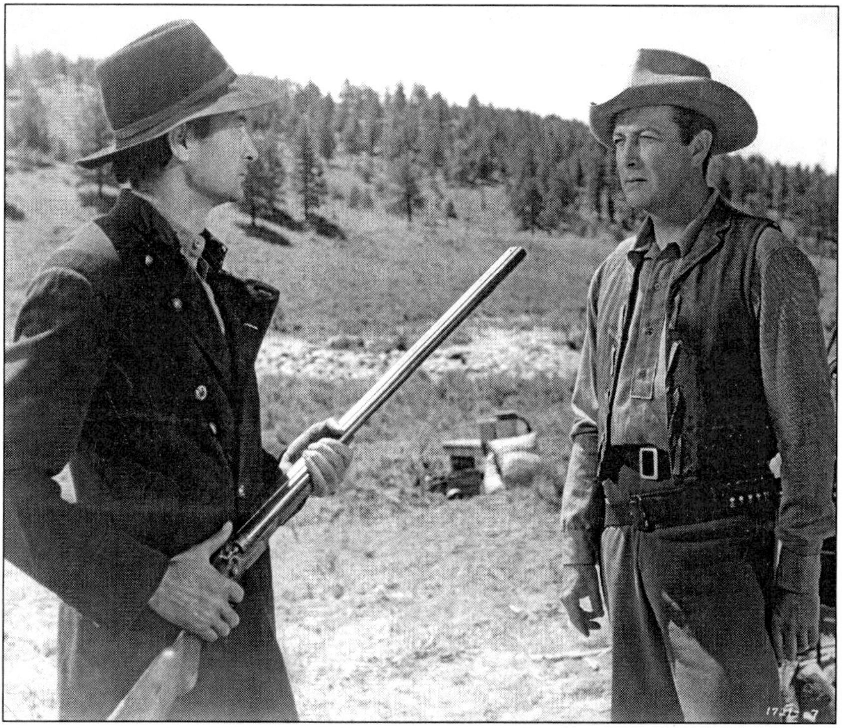

Another western—*Saddle the Wind*, Royal Dano holding a rifle on Bob.

Chapter Twelve

A Freelancer at Last (1959-1962)

Bob's first post-MGM film was made at Paramount, a studio he had never previously worked for during his long career. As a freelance actor Bob was looking forward to making some real money. He asked for and received $200,000 upfront along with a percentage of the gross. It wouldn't be any surprise if Bob's price was the largest amount budgeted for *The Hangman*, a cheaply made, yet effective little Western, based on a short story by Luke Short.

Initially, Edward Dmytryk was penciled in to direct the film, but was instead side-tracked into directing the Henry Fonda-Anthony Quinn Western *Warlock* instead. Paramount contacted Michael Curtiz to direct as well as produce the picture. While the film is clearly shot on the backlot on a shoestring budget, the cast is excellent. Fess Parker, fresh out of his Disney contract, is cast as the sheriff and Tina Louise, who had scored well in the film version of *God's Little Acre*, is the female lead. Jack Lord, a decade before enforcing law and order in Honolulu on *Hawaii Five-O*, is cast as the chief villain of the picture.

The premise of *The Hangman* is quite good. Bob plays a marshal who has a reputation for getting his man and seeing him hanged (thus the title). He tracks an outlaw (Lord) to a small town and is confronted with a town which is protective of the outlaw and will fight to keep him safe. Parker is the town sheriff whose allegiance to Taylor is shaky.

Fess Parker recalls *The Hangman* as "early obscure." He further recalls that "Paramount didn't spend a dime on it. Unlike other Westerns, which were shot on location, we had to make do with the backlot." Despite this Parker was excited to be working with Taylor.

"I enjoyed it greatly," he recalled. "He was a legend and I grew up watching his films." As usual on the set Bob was pleasant but not overly effusive. "He sort of did his own thing and I did mine," Parker recalls. "That's not to say he was standoffish or anything like that. He was just reserved. But we would sit side by side on the western street between scenes, and he was pleasant but not forthcoming. We would shoot the breeze about his ranch and horses." Unfortunately, one thing in particular does stick out in Parker's memory about Bob. "He smoked an awful lot of cigarettes—just a very heavy smoker."[416]

Another thing which stands out about the film in Parker's mind is Jack Lord. Lord was a Method actor who "prepared for a scene by running around the stage two or three times so that he could approach the scene in a heightened physical state." As for being directed by Michael Curtiz, who helmed such classics as *The Adventures of Robin Hood, Yankee Doodle Dandy, Casablanca* and *Mildred Pierce*, Parker remembers him as being "surprisingly calm given his reputation. This was late in his career so maybe he had mellowed because he just basically put us in the scene and called 'Action!'"[417]

The reviews were, on the most part, lackluster. Paramount decided to release it on double bill with the Danny Kaye musical-drama, *The Five Pennies*. The *New York Post* critic reviewed the film and wrote, "One of Robert Taylor's chief assets has always been his quality of conviction. He contributes a great deal of this to his role, but it is a hollow figure despite cursory attempts at providing reasons for his being a hangman." The film performed as lackluster at the box office as it did with the critics. Bob, himself, was reportedly unhappy with the film and particularly its box-office performance, an inauspicious beginning for his post-MGM career.

The same year as *The Hangman*, Bob had been offered the starring role in *Operation Petticoat* for Universal. It would have been a welcome change of pace for him to do a comedy. But two factors came against him. The first was his own lack of confidence in his comedic ability and the second was Tony Curtis, who had emerged as one of Universal's top stars in recent years. He was going to co-star, but he

416 Fess Parker to author

417 Fess Parker to author

felt the part called out for Cary Grant and not Bob Taylor. Grant ended up doing the picture which became a huge box-office success. Bob didn't give it much thought; however, he was philosophical regarding the films he turned down. "I can point with pride to some I've sent back. I can point without pride to some I didn't. I sent back *Battleground*, an excellent script, but I knew I wouldn't help the picture and it wouldn't help me. And I still think I was right even though Hodiak did a great job. I turned down *Wings of Eagles* because I didn't see that part either. I couldn't believe myself in it."

II

June Allyson invited Ursula to attend the baby shower of their mutual friend Nancy Reagan at her home high above Mandeville Canyon. At some point during the shower Ursula looked down at the breathtaking scenery in the canyon below: "I looked down on a ranch, reminding me of a small village. The main building, far removed from the road and sitting at the foot of the mountains, sprawled into a rambling ranch house, surrounded by acres of lawn. Closer to the road were two more structures, one being the barn, the other apartments for the help as well as guests. I was looking at about twenty-five flat acres of pastures for the horses to roam on, plus all the buildings and lawns. The total property, including the hills, spread into 113 acres. As luck would have it, the place was up for sale and it didn't take me all that long to arouse Bob's curiosity to take a look."[418]

Bob liked the idea of a ranch, especially with an expanding family. He thought it would be a great way for his children to grow up with plenty of time for the out of doors on 113 acres. It also reminded him of his upbringing in rural Nebraska. But the property needed a great deal of repairs which would be on top of the asking price. Ursula, however, was very excited about the challenge of decorating the new home. "I'm the assertive dreamer when it comes to houses and I easily visualized our new quarters into completion."[419] Bob was impressed by his wife's passion and decided to buy the ranch.

418 Thiess, pg. 112

419 Thiess, pg. 112

They put their Pacific Palisades home on the market and to their surprise it was sold within two days to the first couple who looked at it. "I think it was a sign that we were meant to move," recalled Ursula.[420] Bob paid tribute to his wife by naming the ranch Ursulor Rancho.

Bob also set about hiring a foreman for the ranch. Ultimately, he came to select a man who would become a great friend, somebody he could always depend on, Art Reeves. Art came to work for Bob sometime in 1959. "I remember because I was there when Tessa was born." The first man who had the position of ranch manager was leaving because he got a job as a stuntman in the John Wayne film *The Horse Soldiers*, which would require him to be on location for several months. Art, who also, on occasion, worked as a stunt actor in films, was acquainted with the man who offered to get him an interview with Bob for the position of ranch manager. When Art arrived for the interview, Bob was with another candidate, "while I sat there drinking coffee—waiting my turn." As it turned out the other candidate did get the job, but he didn't last long. "He and Bob had a falling out about something or other," and Bob remembered Art and hired him. "I was staying at the bunk house of a cowboy actor named Wild Bill Elliot when Bob called and offered me the job and I jumped at it." Art was very much impressed with Bob's interest in the ranch and unlike some actors, "he was a real good horseman—who could ride unlike some others in pictures."[421]

Shortly after becoming foreman of Ursulor Rancho, Art married his sweetheart, Barbara, in Bob and Ursula's house where a reception held afterwards. They lived in a little house on the property, not far from the main house. Eventually, Art and Barbara became part of the family. "We were treated like one of the family. Bob used to call me 'Uncle Art' even though I was younger than he was. He would say to me, 'Uncle Art, I can't tell you how glad we are that you are here.' Bob was really a cowboy at heart. On the ranch we raised chickens, Bob used to go to Nebraska to visit he would always come back with baby chickens he would buy out there. He really took an active interest in the ranch. We even raised a few rabbits. We thought

420 Ursula Thiess to author

421 Art Reeves to author

about cattle and we looked at Black Angus but it never filled the bill. I'm sure we must have gotten on each other's nerves from time to time but we never had a cross word in all the time we worked together."[422] They were always included at festive occasions such as Thanksgiving and Christmas.

Ursula was put in charge of organizing their new home right away. She began, with typical enthusiasm, decorating the main family house. Also under construction would be a swimming pool and pool house, as well as a garage to store the farm equipment. Ursula was on her own at this point because Bob, soon after moving in, was off to Europe to make back-to-back films, *The House of the Seven Hawks* and *The Killers of Kilimanjaro.*

The Killers of Kilimanjaro, for Columbia, was filmed from mid-April to late May of 1959 and shot on location in Tanganyika and at Sherperton Studios in London. Bob plays an engineer put in charge of building the first African railroad running from Mombasa to Lake Victoria in East Africa. The singer/songwriter Anthony Newley was cast as Taylor's sidekick. Anne Aubrey plays an English girl searching for her missing father and fiancé who joins up with Taylor to explore the interiors of Africa. Naturally, they engage in a romance along the way. Chosen to direct was the stalwart Richard Thorpe. The location filming is truly breathtaking, but the film itself is mediocre, which the studio seemed to realize since it held back its official release for nearly a year. Bob himself later considered *Killers of Kilimanjaro* to be one of the films he should never[423] have made, a list which also included *The Hangman.*

Bob shaved the mustache he wore for *Killers of Kilimanjaro* and went straight into production on *The House of the Seven Hawks. The House of the Seven Hawks* is the first of three films that Bob committed to do for MGM when he officially severed his long-term contract. Bob plays a skipper who operates a small boat in the waters off the coast of eastern England. He is hired (for a large sum) by a man of mystery to take him across the North Sea to Holland. Along the way the man dies and the skipper finds in his procession a map. When he arrives in Holland, his boat is met by a woman (played by

422 ibid

423 Ocala Star Banner, 3/15/67

Linda Christian) who claims to be the dead man's daughter, but she is actually an imposter. Ultimately, he meets the real daughter and they wind up looking for missing treasure on an island called The House of the Seven Hawks. It turns out that the treasure was stolen by Nazis during the war and hidden on the island. Naturally, there is adventure because other, dangerous, people are also in pursuit of the treasure (which turns out to be diamonds). As in *Killers of Kilimanjaro*, Richard Thorpe is Bob's director. It was to be their eighth and final film together in a collaboration that began in 1938 with *The Crowd Roars*. Thorpe once paid tribute to Bob to writer Joe Hyman: "He's a rarity. A lot of big stars are really heels off screen and the public doesn't know it at first. It takes them awhile to discover it. But Bob is really a nice guy and it comes through on screen."

Luckily for the tight shooting schedule the cast enjoyed each other's company. Beautiful Linda Christian once called Bob the actor she worked with who most impressed her. "He was so natural whenever he spoke his lines, he never seemed to be acting. He impressed me so much with his talent. He also made all the other actors feel comfortable, which is also important." [424] The film was shot at M-G-M's Borehamwood Studios near London, and on location in Holland at The Hague, Massaluis and the Hook of Holland. They began shooting in late May of 1959 and thanks to six-day weeks and fourteen-hour days it was completed by mid-June. When it was released, the *Los Angeles Times* review was full of praise: "acted and directed in the tradition of some well-remembered American Film melodramas (*The Maltese Falcon* comes to mind)." Taylor's, "grim, tight-lipped portrayal comes across well."

Ursula and Terry flew to London to be with Bob for the final couple of weeks of shooting on *Killers of Kilimanjaro*. However, before arriving in London, Ursula left Michael in the care of his grandmother in Germany. Michael had been suspended from two schools for poor study habits and lack of attention. It wasn't easy for either Michael or Manuela adapting to a new country and culture. "Their classmates didn't speak the same language," Ivy Mooring later related. "Even their teachers couldn't understand them. Their

424 Screen Sirens Scream! Pg. 44

school work, such as social studies, was Greek to them. They couldn't read their textbooks or understand the schoolyard games."[425] As a result, according to Ivy, they began to act out in school and at home.

In an attempt to help Michael, Ursula consented to having the boy stay with the brother-in-law of Ivy's second husband, Wyn, and his family which included his wife and their five children. It was hoped that Michael might flourish in a family-orientated situation, but it didn't happen and thus the decision to place Michael with the German grandmother. Ursula thought that maybe he could find his footing in the school system where he spent his early elementary years and by being reunited with the German grandmother who he loved so much. One area where Ivy condemns Bob is in his understanding of raising children, more his stepchildren than his own children. "Bob knew nothing about raising children," she says. "He thought they came out of the womb as miniature grownups and needed only a firm hand and all would be OK. He didn't understand the confusion of either Ursula's son or daughter when they arrived here to a totally different world than they had experienced with their grandmother in war-ravaged Germany."[426] The decision to send Michael to Germany was made independently of Bob who was "more than surprised" when he heard the news. Bob never thought that overprotective mother Ursula would ever allow her children to be separated from her again. According to Ursula, Michael accepted this fate stoically by trying to "cheer me up and spent endless flying hours entertaining his three-year-old brother Terry."[427]

While with Bob in London, Ursula developed a cold ("Whenever traveling out of California, I invariably get a cold"). She was harboring a rasping cough when she and Bob were invited to dinner at the London apartment of Audrey Hepburn and her husband, Mel Ferrer. Over Audrey's homecooked Kidney Pie, Ursula's cough got progressively worse. Without saying a word, Audrey quietly departed the room and called a pharmacist to prescribe some medication to ease Ursula's suffering. "Whatever it was, it certainly

425 Ivy Mooring to author

426 ibid

427 Thiess,...but I have promises to keep

helped," recalled a grateful Ursula.[428]

Soon the picture was completed and the family returned to California and Bob's first look at the renovated ranch. "I shall never forget my husband's expression of total acceptance and appreciation when he entered the house," recalled Ursula. "He simply loved what I had done, in terms of color, fabric, and furnishings, each carefully selected for total male comfort." Especially pleasing to Bob's eye was a cabinet built into the den which held Bob's gun collection.[429] Eventually, it was a working ranch with 80 chickens and 26 horses. Of his 113 acres of land, Bob said, "I like plenty of room to breathe."[430]

III

Even though Bob had two films in release in 1959, and one in the can for release in 1960, he made a decision which raised some eyebrows in Hollywood. He consented to star in a television series. Film stars of Bob's stature had, on the whole, kept their distance from the medium. At the time it was believed that if a star began appearing on television it would mean the end of his career in motion pictures. That was the snobbery of the time. Why would anybody want to pay to see you on the big screen if they could see you for nothing in the comfort of their homes? Even Bob, who made his television series debut in a cameo appearance on the MGM produced *Thin Man* television series in 1957, dismissed the idea. "This is my first and last TV appearance. I don't like the medium. Can't say that I enjoy watching it either."[431]

So what changed? In part it was the opportunity to make some big money. Four Star Television made an offer to Bob which meant partial ownership of the show. If the show was successful and sold into syndication it could mean millions. Another reason for Bob's decision to tackle television had to do with his family. In late 1958 thru the spring of 1959, Bob had made two films on location outside

428 ibid

429 Ibid

430 LA Times, 7/30/61

431 Hollywood Citizen News, 6/13/60

of the United States. This took him away from Ursula and Terry for months at a time. And, now, Ursula was pregnant with another baby, and more than ever, Bob began to believe that he should settle down closer to home so that he could spend more time with his growing family. Television, whatever its shortcomings, offered him this opportunity. Ultimately, he went to his friend Clark Gable to ask his opinion. Gable didn't exactly dismiss the idea. "A weekly show's gotta be tough to do," Gable told him, "but you've got ten years on me."[432]

On August 15, 1959, Bob and Ursula were dining with their good friends Rory and Lita Calhoun, at the Beverly Hills Hotel. Ursula was well along with her pregnancy and could give birth at any moment. Bob, sat nervously with his wife at dinner, and was anxious that they not make it a late night. He wanted the mother-to-be to get enough rest. Ursula was enjoying the evening out and wasn't in a rush. Finally, she consented and the Taylors were off for the ranch. As they drove up the long driveway to their house, they noticed that the horses seemed spooked. Bob guessed it might be a mountain lion and went for his shotgun to scare it off. After several shots, Bob and Ursula went to investigate the pasture and Ursula couldn't help suppress a laugh when they saw that it was only a trouble-making skunk that had driven the horses to distraction, with good reason, as the skunk immediately went into defensive mode and sprayed the pregnant Ursula with its pungent scent. Luckily for Bob, the skunk hit only one target, Ursula. As he led her back to the ranch house, Ursula discovered that she was going into labor. But they couldn't possibly expect to go to the hospital with Ursula smelling like skunk. Bob had heard that tomato catsup would take away the sting of the smell and doused Ursula with it and gave her a bath. Unfortunately, the smell still lingered, but they had no choice but to get back in the car and drive off to St. John's Hospital in Santa Monica. "The two ladies at the admissions desk looked at each other in utter disbelief," Ursula recalled, "but let me register just the same, while cautiously baking away from the odor. Finally I found my room and bed and started labor without restraint."[433]

432 Clark Gable, J.E. Wayne, pg. 277-278

433 Thiess, ...but I have promises to keep

Out of this farce came a very special gift, a baby girl. She was born in the early morning hours of August 16. There was an early scare when it appeared the baby's heart stopped beating, but it was short-lived and the baby was soon breathing on her own. She was named Tessa, after the character from the book *Tess of the Storm* Country, which Bob had read as a child. As often happens with a father and his daughter, the little baby girl brought out a side of Bob that the birth of his son didn't. "Bob's attitude had taken a complete turn," recalled Ursula. "While he was reticent to even touch his son as a small baby, this new little female was overindulged with attention." [434] He affectionately nicknamed her puss-puss.

For godparents Bob and Ursula asked their good friends Ron and Nancy Reagan. In return the Reagans asked the Taylors to be the godparents of their daughter Patti. As the years went on Bob's relationship with Ronald Reagan only strengthened. When they initially met in late thirties and through the war years they were friends but not as strong as they would become. For one reason while both Bob and Ron enjoyed discussing politics they were polar opposites on this subject when they first met. Bob had always been a rock-ribbed Republican while Ron was a New Deal Democrat. In fact, he really didn't begin to change his political ideology until the late forties. In 1948, while Bob strongly supported Republican nominee for President Tom Dewey, Ron was a strong Truman supporter and even made speeches for the president when he visited California. But by the late 1950s, Bob and Ron were political comrades. Ron hadn't yet changed his voter registration from Democrat to Republican, but he had supported Eisenhower for president in 1952 and 1956 as a "Democrat for Ike." On the issues, too, Ron had moved increasingly to the right.

Politics was by no means the only subject that Reagan and Taylor had in common. They were also men who grew up in the Midwest and had an appreciation for the out of doors, and horse flesh. Nancy Reagan would recall that it was their "shared values and upbringing" which helped to bond them. They both loved to ride horses and could spend hours riding and discuss horses and their ranches. Patti Reagan would later write that Bob Taylor "was the

434 Thiess, ...but I have promises to keep

only time I observed my father being close friends with another man."[435]

Ursula and Nancy became equally good friends. "The first time I met her," Nancy later recalled, "I thought to myself, she is the most beautiful woman I've ever seen. She looks like the type that has breakfast in bed, dozens of servants to wait on her and who must spend hours grooming herself. Was I wrong! Ursula is a very deceiving girl in many ways. When I got to know her, I found her to possess unbelievable strength. She is exactly the opposite from the type of woman she appears to be on the surface. She is a wonderful housekeeper, a fabulous cook. And she truly loves all the things that a lot of women consider the drudgery of housework."

Shortly before the birth of Tessa, Bob had begun production on his new ABC-TV series, *The Detectives*. It was a good deal which would bring Bob some big money immediately and hopefully pay off in the years ahead. He would draw $150,000 for 32 shows, but he would only star in six or seven episodes, and take on a smaller part in the other 25 or so. At most it was only going to be about three days per week of work. This would allow him plenty of time for ranch work and being a daddy. Bob was cast as Captain Matt Holbrook, a tough cop, and leader of a dedicated band of special case detectives. Bob was perfect for the part. Bob had no illusions about television and often was exasperated by the rapid shooting schedules. "He didn't like doing the show," Ursula later recalled, "but he had nothing better to do, and he felt it was the best thing for his family because of the hours and he wouldn't have to be off to far-away locations."[436] Publicly, he never made any bones about why he took on a weekly series. "It's as simple as ABC—a five letter word pronounced money," he told his friend columnist Hy Gardner.[437]

Though Bob certainly didn't love television he threw himself into it with his usual professionalism. Twenty-four-year-old Mark Goddard had just come off of the television series *Johnny Ringo* when he joined the cast of *The Detectives* during its second season:

---

435 The Way I See It, Patti Davis, pg. 25

436 Ursula Thiess to author

437 NY Herald Tribune, 10/13/59

"I chose doing 'The Detectives' because I really wanted to work with Robert Taylor, who I admired very much—I grew up watching movies like 'Johnny Eager' and 'Quo Vadis,' etcetera. I knew that he was the ultimate professional and that I would learn a lot from him. I was very happy and very fortunate to work with him for three years. When I went into that show, it was like I was the star of the show and Robert Taylor was like the sidekick as far as the publicity was concerned. They threw a lot toward me during that first year. They wanted another 'Kookie' Byrnes, they wanted that look. It wouldn't work today, but in those days it did . . ."

Goddard recalls that on the set, however, there was never any question as to who the star was. "Let's say there was going to be a medium two-shot, Robert Taylor and myself. They'd spend about thirty-five, forty minutes lighting Robert Taylor. I'd be just in the back of him, my head over his shoulder. Then they'd say, 'Okay let's go, let's shoot.' And they'd been lighting only Taylor all that time. I'd say to the cameraman Howard Schwartz, 'What about me? Do I get any light or what?' And Howard said, 'Mark, you just get all the leak light. All the light that's left over, that Robert Taylor doesn't use, you get."

Veteran actor Ed Nelson, who would make a name of himself in the primetime soap opera *Peyton Place*, as well as a ton of TV movies during the 1970s, made several guest appearances on *The Detectives*. "Robert Taylor was one of the few people who was a regular guy who had been under contract to the studios," he later recalled. "Most of them were pampered and acted like it on the set, but not Bob Taylor. When he came to television, he didn't act like he was too big for the small screen. Many of those film stars were babysat and pampered for years by the studios and would look their noses down on those in television when they were working in television, but Taylor was an exception." [438]

On the set Bob was considered a no-nonsense pro that, while not humorless, was very focused on getting done with the job and getting home to his family. The cast sometimes looked for ways to get his attention and throw him a bit off balance. Veteran television actor Tige Andrews (who would go on a few years later to be the

438 Ed Nelson to author

commanding officer of *The Mod Squad*) decided to play a prank on Bob one afternoon when he found an old pair of work shoes, with inch-thick soles. They looked to be big enough to fit Boris Karloff's Frankenstein monster. Andrews put the huge pair of shoes in Bob's dressing room along with a note: "Bob, A friend of yours stopped in while you were at lunch, left these shoes and said he'd be back this afternoon." Andrews obviously expected that Bob would return and get a big laugh out of it, but after returning and finding the shoes he came out of his dressing room with the note and said, "Tige, I don't think I know this man. What did he look like, and when did he say he'd be back?" Andrews replied that Bob's visitor was "a big fellow, about 7 feet 6, with a bolt in his neck." Finally, Bob got the joke and allowed a huge guffaw.[439]

While working on the first season of the series, Bob looked back on his earlier screen persona. "In a way, I'm happy to be rid of that 'great lover' tag. It was more commercial than fact. Take Greta Garbo, for instance. All during *Camille* I called her Miss Garbo—even when we were all tangled up in each other's arms, ready to go into a romantic close-up." This particular week Marsha Hunt was guest-starring on an episode titled "The Prowler." "With all the plot line to go through in a half-hour, we don't have much chance for romance," Taylor said. "But I do get to take a couple of admiring glances at Marsha. Just enough to show there's life in the old boy yet!"[440]

Arthur Hiller, who directed three segments of *The Detectives*, also recalls Taylor's professionalism. "He had it in his contract for television that he would not film after six p.m. and he stuck to that. Well, on one of the shows I did with him I needed another fifteen minutes to get the scene just right. I told the producer that I was going to ask Taylor if he could give us about fifteen more minutes. I was told he would never agree to this, that he was out at six no matter what. So I go to him and I explain to him that if we got another fifteen minutes the scene would be right and we wouldn't have to reshoot it the next day. He said, 'fine' and gave it to me. He was a total professional."[441]

439 TV Guide, 12/16/61

440 LA Times 4/17/60

441 Arthur Hiller to author

It was during the second season that Bob began appearing in more of the segments and Ursula was brought in as a love interest on the show, playing a girl reporter who hangs around the station looking for a story. "I did it for only one season," Ursula recalled. "But it took me away from the children for too many hours and I decided, and Bob agreed, that after that one year that I would retire from the show and become a full-time wife and mother again. I never regretted that."

It was while working on the second season of the show that Bob's good friend and the "King of Hollywood," Clark Gable, died at age 59 of a heart attack on November 17, 1960. It was the end of an era. It was a star-studded crowd that turned out for Gable's funeral on November 19. Bob joined such former MGM colleagues as Spencer Tracy, James Stewart, Howard Strickling and Eddie Mannix as a pallbearer (less than three years later Bob and Stewart served the same function at the funeral of Eddie Mannix). Hundreds of people turned out to catch a glimpse of the stars as they arrived and left. They weren't disappointed. Bob drove his station wagon and shot a short wave at the crowd.[442]

During the third season the show moved to NBC and expanded to an hour. Bob put as positive a spin as possible on his working in television versus films. "Actually," he explained, "TV is much like the picture business was when I started. By that I mean that in those days we were making lots of B, C and D pictures. We made them fast, and we had to make them at a price to realize any profit. And they would use anyone, whether they'd ever heard of him or not, including me. The difference is that even in those B, C and D pictures, there wasn't the rush there is in television." It was clear that despite his current situation in television that he didn't think that the talent the medium produced equaled that of motion pictures. "I honestly don't believe there ever will be a star in television that will last as long as, say, Gable did in motion pictures. The reason is simply that people get tired of seeing the same face every week." He also didn't think, by and large, that television stars could make the transition to the big screen. "It's easier to become a working actor today because there are more jobs, thanks to television. But I strongly

442 LA Times, 11/20/60

doubt that it's easier to become a so-called star. There are lots of good people in TV. We're constantly finding new ones—new to me anyway—who are really fine. But TV simply hasn't developed many stars of the sort who can go into motion pictures and pull customers by themselves. Dick Boone can, and James Garner has made the transition beautifully, but who else is there?"[443]

Adam West was still several years away from playing *Batman* in the campy ABC series when he accepted a co-starring role on the show during its third season, when the show expanded to an hour and was broadcast in color on a new network (NBC) under the title *The Detectives Starring Robert Taylor*. "Taylor . . . was a fine if formal gentleman who didn't socialize much with his fellow actors," West later recalled. "Though he was utterly professional, I got the feeling that he didn't enjoy the show much. His own MGM movie contract had not been renewed, and with nothing else to do he turned to TV to pay the bills. There's nothing wrong with that, of course, though he seemed to resent having gone from co-starring with Jean Harlow and Joan Crawford and Katharine Hepburn to uttering weekly variations of 'Hold it right there!' and 'Put your hands up!'" Still, West says he gained valuable insight from working with Taylor. "I learned a lot about acting from Robert Taylor, and about acting for the close-up camera in particular. I also learned more about the silences. He taught me how not saying or showing things gives the viewer's imagination a chance to fill in the emotional painting."[444]

Bob was busy filming *The Detectives* on November 5, 1961, when he got a call at the studio from Ursula. She had spent some time that morning riding with a friend in the hillside above the ranch. From a certain point she could see smoke rising from Bel Air, an exclusive area a few miles from the canyon. This naturally alarmed her. She called Terry's school and was told that as far they knew everything was fine and not to worry. But within minutes the school was evacuated and the children were sent home in a school bus. By two that afternoon the fire department had issued an order urging residents to evacuate as the fire was making its way toward

443 LA Examiner, 1/28/62

444 Adam West, Back to the Bat Cave

the canyon. It was at this point that she called Bob at the studio to alert him of the situation. Bob told Ursula to gather up the kids and evacuate to Nancy and Ronald Reagan's Pacific Palisades home. He would meet up with the family there. Ursula quickly gathered up Terry, Tessa and their housekeeper, and loaded all in her car along with such treasures as family photo albums and left for the Reagan home.

They were all watching news reports of the fire when one reporter erroneously reported that the fire had hit the property of actor Robert Taylor. Bob and Ursula realized that the report couldn't possibly be correct since the fence on the property that the reporter was at didn't look like theirs. At this point, Bob and Ursula decided to drive to the mouth of the canyon and survey the situation themselves. At Paul Revere Junior High School, located on Sunset Blvd., at the foot of Mandeville Canyon they found there horses residing (as well as Bob's hunting dogs), safe and sound, in the school's playground. They later found out that the Taylors' ranch foreman, Art Reeves, along with other neighbors, including Steve McQueen, herded the horses to a safe haven away from the danger and put into makeshift corrals. After persuading the authorities to allow them to return to their home, Bob and Ursula arrived back at the ranch to find it in perfect condition, relieved that the television report was wrong; they also found that their phone worked as well as their electricity. They would spend the rest of the night standing guard over the property and, with Art and his wife Barbara, keeping the roof of the house well watered. Throughout the night they could see the damage the fire was creating on the other side of the canyon. Ursula would recall a "beautiful large, eucalyptus tree went up like a Roman candle on our neighbor's property. It was a horrifically beautiful sight. When it exploded, it ignited buildings surrounding their property." It was the property which had once belonged to their friends Dick Powell and June Allyson; luckily, the fire fighters were able to save the buildings. It was a long night and a challenging next day, but with luck the fire had skipped their property. "They're calling this the miracle of Mandeville Canyon," Bob later told a reporter.[445]

445 LA Times, 11/8/61

At the end of the third season, with 97 episodes filmed, *The Detectives* called it a day. It did go on to syndication but never became the huge hit Bob hoped for. Today, it's rarely seen. A year later, plans were made for Bob to return to television in a new series tentatively titled *The Robert Taylor Show.* The show was to be based on the files of the Department of Health, Education and Welfare. Bob was enthusiastic when he spoke with Louella Parsons about the new series. "The show was sold before we shot a foot of film. There's an unlimited amount of fascinating material in the department files. You know the HEW, besides its obvious functions, covers such things as veterinary medicine, dope traffic and immigration." Unfortunately, the plug was pulled before the show saw the light of day, reportedly because HEW expressed dissatisfaction with the scripts.

IV

Luckily, Bob had a movie waiting for him when *The Detectives* ended its run. *Miracle of the White Stallions* is based on the true story of Colonel Alois Podhajsky, who was the director of the Spanish Riding School in Vienna, which since 1572, the school had focused on the training of Lipizzaner horses in the art of Classical dressage. Colonel Podhajsky also was an Olympic gold medalist in the sport of dressage. The focus of the film deals with Podhajsky's concern for the safety of stallions due to bombings during World War II. He, along with General George Patton (also an expert equestrian, who competed against each other in Olympic Games), and American troops, helped evacuate the stallions to the city of St. Martin in Upper Austria. There were many obstacles along the way. It was a colorful role for Taylor, and one he greatly enjoyed doing given his love of horses.

The film was produced by Walt Disney, one of the most respected producers in the business and one of the cheapest in compensating his actors. "The money ain't the best—least wise it ain't what I used ta get—but that figgers and I AIN'T PROUD NO MORE!" he wrote his buddy Tom Purvis. [446] But a Disney picture had a built-in

446 Robert Taylor, J.E. Wayne, pg. 217

audience and it was a good bet to be a successful return to the big screen after a three-year hiatus.

Ursula and the children would occasionally join Bob on location for one of his films or television programs. It meant a lot to Bob to have his family with him when possible, such as when the children's school schedules allowed. One of the most memorable experiences for the family was joining Bob when he was filming the Walt Disney film *Miracle of the White Stallions* on location in Vienna.

Arthur Hiller, a prominent television director with a resume a mile long, including three episodes of *The Detectives Starring Robert Taylor*, was selected by Disney to make his motion picture debut with this film. "A.J. Carothers [who wrote the screenplay, based on Podhajsky's autobiography] was a friend of mine and I had directed a TV show of his and he really liked my work and suggested me to Walt Disney," Hiller later recalled. "Disney wasn't so sure because I was so young. He looked over another couple of directors and still wasn't satisfied, so he asked Carothers, 'Who was that kid you wanted me to look at?' and arranged an interview. So I had my meeting with Disney, and I should say, very nervously, on my part. But all went well and within twenty minutes I felt that I would be the one doing this film. He said, 'You know the frame work of a Disney film—keep within that framework, but within that framework you can do different things' and when I had problems with the associate producer, who was with us in Vienna, about different things I wanted to do, I would telegraph Disney, who would back me up."

According to Hiller, Bob had already been signed to star in the film by the time he was selected to direct. "I think Bob was the first person Disney hired for the picture," Hiller said. "But I cast most of the other roles, including Curt Jergens (who plays a sympathetic Nazi), Lili Palmer (cast as Podhajsky's wife) and Eddie Albert (cast as Otto, Podhajsky's chief rider)." Hiller says he couldn't have asked for a better leading man than Bob for his film debut. "It was a tremendous relationship," recalled Hiller. "I liked him a lot personally, too. He always wanted more direction than he really needed. He would say, 'Should I do this or that?' and I would assure him that what he was doing was fine. He was aware that he wasn't a great actor, but within his range he was quite an effective actor.

He always gave me everything I wanted. He was a very intuitive actor and went a great deal by feel. It was such a pleasure to work with him and that entire cast." [447]

According to Hiller, the film itself was nearly problem-free, "the only problem that I can recall was that we had some odd problems bringing some horses into the country but eventually that was resolved—probably because of Disney and his reputation which could cut thru red tape. We had a terrific production head who if something came up and we had to cut here and there to keep within the budget would not cut key scenes which would hurt the story but look for little things here and there."

Prior to the start of shooting, Bob came to Hiller with a potential problem. "'Arthur,'" he said, "I would prefer it if I could be filmed on my left side—if at all possible.' I told him that Lili Palmer also wanted to be shot on her left side. He just kind of smiled at me and said, 'That's okay, Arthur—just go with her.' He was always a great gentleman." [448]

Bob arrived in Vienna and was soon followed by Ursula, Terry and Tessa. In her autobiography Ursula recalled the trip over, "The threesome of Terry, Tessa, and me was to follow, expecting to spend two months on location with him. Those were the days in the early sixties, when the airlines (in this case, Scandinavian Airlines) would send limousines for their most preferred customers. The compliment of a neatly-packaged orchid was usually waiting on the seat of the plane for the female passenger. Since this was still before jet transportation, I was anticipating a long, twenty-four-hour flight. Terry had just turned seven and Tessa was not yet three years old. However, they adjusted very well and after many hours of flying, I was told that my two offspring were just about the best behaved they had ever had the pleasure of flying with." A stopover in Iceland presented the children with their first experience with snow, "they rolled in it, tasted it, pounced on it, and most likely envisioned old man Santa on his sleigh in the far distance," recalled Ursula. [449]

---

447 Arthur Hiller to author

448 Arthur Hiller to author

449 Ursula Thiess, ...but I have promises to keep

The children had a good time as well. Terry later recalled that he had been cast in a small walk-on role in the film but that in the end, "it must have been left on the cutting room floor." But he did have a companion in Eddie Albert's young son, Edward, who was then eleven years old. According to Ursula, Terry developed a case of "hero worship" with Edward, "It's not often that an older boy shows interest in a mere seven year old."[450] Tessa would recall that being on location with her father in Vienna was "the first time I realized what Daddy did. I didn't realize or understand that he was a movie star. I was so proud of seeing him riding these horses."[451]

After a month with Bob on location, Ursula managed to persuade Manuela to join Michael, who was at that time living with his father in Hamburg, and herself and the younger children for a vacation to the Baltic Sea. Ursula hoped that in the calmer atmosphere of a family vacation that she could reach out to both Manuela and Michael and better understand their problems and hopefully bring about some closure. "I remember only too well Bob taking me and our two little ones to the train station," Ursula later recalled. "He was greatly concerned and hugged me tightly, for he knew this would be a very emotional trip for me." Despite her best efforts Ursula would recall that she "didn't even come close to the core" of resolving their problems. (Though Manuela did accept a job in Berlin working in an orphanage for a few months, "which put her right in her element as she has an incredible ability to relate to children of all ages." Michael was not so lucky, it was shortly after this vacation that he was arrested and charged with attempting to poison his father.)[452]

Back in Vienna, Ursula and Bob were invited to join Arthur Hiller, Eddie Albert and his wife, Margot, at the circus. "A circus came to town while we were filming," Hiller recalled. "And the circus people wanted to watch the filming and they were so thrilled that they extended their thanks by inviting us all to watch them perform." This gave Eddie Albert an excuse to pay a light-hearted prank on his pal, Bob Taylor. "It was a Saturday night and we all went, except

450 ibid

451 Tessa Taylor to author

452 Thiess, ...but I have promises to keep

for Eddie. He had to beg off, but his wife attended with us. The circus opened with a Volkswagen entering and about twelve clowns falling out of it. How they all fit in there I don't know! The clowns came out and did their routine. Then they came over to the boxes and began playing with people in the audience. Then one clown came over to Bob Taylor and was having fun with him and Taylor and the audience was just eating it up. After about four minutes Bob finally took a good look in the eyes of the clown and he realized that the clown was none other than Eddie Albert! Eddie always wanted to be a clown and talked the circus into letting him do this so he could have his dream come true and have a bit of fun with Bob in the meanwhile."[453]

After two months abroad it was time for Ursula and the children to leave and return to the United States, Bob stayed on a bit longer to finish the picture. It had been an, overall, idyllic time for Bob, Ursula and the two youngest children. Bob was very high on the film. "I've admired Disney for a long time," Bob told Hollywood columnist Vernon Scott. "If I had to dump my career in someone's lap I'd just as soon have it Disney's." Bob went on to explain to Scott that he was entering a new phase in his career. "I won't be playing the romantic lover roles any more. Those are for younger men. I'll play more mature parts in what I like to think of as commercial pictures. That's why I accepted this Disney movie. I want to be in entertainment films, not trying to settle people's problems, or creating new ones for them on screen."[454]

Arthur Hiller was also pleased by how his first motion picture turned out. "I thought it turned out very well, and I was very pleased that Walt was very happy about it."[455] When it was released in May 1963, the critics were not as kind, but overall the box office was solid, if not spectacular. The *New York Times* dismissed the film and called Bob, "weatherworn and weary" as well as a "rather dull sort," but conceded that "the youngsters should like it." On the other hand the *New York Post* raved calling it a "beautiful film" and complimented Bob. "Robert Taylor, weathering prettily with the

453 Arthur Hiller to author

454 Daily Review, 9/10/62

455 Arthur Hiller to author

years, seems more and more able to portray hard-bitten men. This, for an actor who used to be too beautiful for words, is high praise." But for the family the important thing is that they got to spend quality time with Bob, and for the children got to enjoy the wonders of Vienna.

Shortly after completing *Miracle of the White Stallions*, Bob began work on the second of the two-picture deal he had signed with MGM in 1959 when he was released from his long-term contract. The film was a Western called *Cattle King*. It had a simple story, written by Thomas Thompson, which cast Bob as a Wyoming rancher who wants to protect the land against a rival cattle man (Robert Middleton), who wants to open up the lands to his benefit. The film was inexpensively filmed, much of it on location in Kernville, California, with a shooting schedule of just under two weeks. To maintain the pace the studio put the picture in the capable hands of stalwart Tay Garnett, who had last directed Bob some twenty years before in *Bataan*. The studio also surrounded Bob with a topnotch supporting cast, in addition to Middleton, there were Joan Caulfield, Robert Loggia, Larry Gates (playing President Chester A. Arthur) and William Windom. Despite its low budget, the picture was photographed in pleasing Metroscope-Eastman Color.

Robert Loggia[456] was a thirty-two-year-old actor of mainly television dramas at the time. Television would be his bread-and-butter for the next twenty-odd years, but after playing a toy company president who dances to "Chopsticks" with Tom Hanks in *Big* he increasingly worked in major motion pictures as a character actor. Loggia was impressed to be working with a star of Bob's caliber. "Bob was an extremely talented artist," Loggia later recalled. "He was also the ultimate gentleman and a true professional who followed the rules of the day—arrive on time, know your lines and be willing to do what had to be done to make the picture successful. Here was a guy who could convincingly play the romantic lead opposite Greta Garbo in a picture like *Camille* and be just as convincing playing a cowboy. Now that's range, but the critics really never gave him his due." Loggia has fond memories of the film and its director, Tay

456 Bob described Loggia as a "nice person and a good actor—one of the best," to Hedda Hopper in 1963.

Garnett. "It was terrific," he recalled. "It was old-time moviemaking. It really was a 'B' picture, but we didn't treat it as such. We worked as hard on it as we would have on any big, expensive picture—harder because we had such a tight schedule. And Tay was personable, but knew he was on a tough deadline and pushed us all to get as much done as we could in a day."[457]

Bob and Loggia got close enough that Bob wanted Loggia to work with him in a television series that NBC was planning for him based on the case files of the Department of Health, Education and Welfare. "The network wanted to call it *The Robert Taylor Show* to cash in on his name," Loggia recalled.[458] Ultimately, Loggia passed on the offer, and a pilot was made, but the show never came to air. Apparently, the Department of Health, Education and Welfare, which provided the case files (much the same way the LAPD would for *Dragnet* and the FBI for *The FBI*), was not happy with the scripts and pulled a plug on their participation with the series. With that NBC also lost interest.

457 Robert Loggia to author

458 ibid

Chapter Thirteen

THE FAMILY MAN (1963-1967)

To Robert Taylor acting was a job—it wasn't his life. He and Ursula were not into the Hollywood party scene. Bob still found his happiness when he was able to enjoy the outdoors by hunting, fishing or flying into some primitive location and roughing it. He enjoyed the income a star salary could command and the benefits it brought not only for himself but for his family, especially the ranch, but he always lamented that it came with a price: the high taxes that had to be paid on such a salary, for instance. The ranch was Bob's refuge and the place he loved the most. "When I think of Daddy, I think of the ranch," his daughter Tessa says. "It was a great place to be. A great way to grow up."[459]

Bob liked the fact that Terry and Tessa were growing up on a ranch and finding an appreciation for the outdoors and learning respect for the land and the animals that inhabited it. It reminded him of his upbringing in Nebraska. "I think it had a lot to do with the upbringing he had," Tessa says. "That is what he tried to do with us. Give us the kind of upbringing on the ranch that he had."[460] Above all he liked that his children were not really part of the Beverly Hills/Hollywood scene. He had seen too many bad seeds emerge from overindulgence by many Hollywood celebrities toward their offspring. He wanted Terry and Tessa to grow up as normal as possible. Terry Taylor would recall his dad as, "generous, stern when I deserved it, as hands-on as he could be considering he was still making movies until I was 10-11 years old. He taught me how to

459 Tessa Taylor to author

460 ibid

ride a bike, ride a horse, ride a motorcycle, fish, shoot, walk properly (I was pigeon-toed, and he would call me 'Pidge' so often that I straightened it out on my own), throw and hit a baseball, train dogs, Bar-B-Q, and countless other things that a kid might take for granted were it not for a father paying attention."[461]

Tessa recalls that she was a "little doll for him"[462] and he doted on her the way a loving father could dote on his daughter. "They had a wonderful relationship," Ursula would recall of Bob and Tessa. "She had him wrapped around her little finger. One thing I remember is that we had stools on the patio with little holes in the seats and she put her finger in there and it got stuck and Terry came and told us about it, and I said we better take her and the stool to a doctor. Bob said, 'No, I'll take care of it.' He went into the work room and got a pair of scissors and took about a half hour to get her finger out—without a scratch. 'You got to trust your father,' he would say soothingly to her, 'I won't hurt you.' She was only three and it's a memory which still lingers with me because it was such a wonderful example of his gentleness with his little girl." Ivy Shelton-Mooring would recall that Bob was "seduced by his baby daughter. From the moment she was born, a beautiful blonde, with his blue eyes, and Ursula's porcelain skin. She could do no wrong and grew up feeling she had to live up to those expectations."[463]

Ursula completed Bob. "I've never known such complete happiness as I have since I've been married to Ursula," he told Hedda Hopper. "She's a really attractive woman . . . She's so self-sufficient. Nothing seems to upset or worry her. She's well-adjusted. She can be alone or with people. I've never seen her in a situation she was unable to handle in a quiet sort of way." She did her best to learn and enjoy Bob's hobbies with him. "To this day I don't know how sincerely she enjoyed hunting, fishing and riding with him," Terry Taylor later said.[464]

Bob and Ursula rarely quarreled, and if they did have a disagreement it was largely over child-raising. "He was a disciplinarian," Ursula

461 Terry Taylor to author

462 Tessa Taylor to author

463 Ivy Mooring to author

464 Terry Taylor to author

would write in her autobiography. "While I was more the negotiator. I would rather compliment and reward the children on even the smallest effort to please, while Bob was tempted to criticize for better performance. "Ursula later conceded that all of this was true, but it "had much to do with how he was raised and in the end he was always hardest on himself." Bob conceded that he liked being a father, "but I'm a stern one." Despite their differences on discipline Bob was full of respect for Ursula's gifts as a mother, "Not only is she a most perfect wife," he wrote privately to Hedda Hopper in 1956, "she's also one of the best damned mothers I've ever seen. For fear of seeming prejudiced I can't comment too strongly on your opinion of Terry; however if, as you say, he's cute and healthy and well behaved it's largely to her credit. Naturally I've got a big old 'piss elm club' which I use occasionally but that's only when Ursula ain't around to talk me out of it." [465] Terry recalled that on occasion Bob would give him, "the belt on the backside a few times." One time in particular, he recalled, was for walking in wet grass in his dry slippers, but Terry also concedes that Bob had "warned me many times against (this)." But Terry also recalls Bob's "generosity with whatever spare time he had and with material things like Christmas, Easter, birthdays and so on." [466]

Ursula was an exceedingly patient and resourceful wife and mother. Few things seemed to rile her. Bob loved to tell the story about how, shortly after they married, he had planned a fishing trip with his friend and pilot, Ralph Couser. "We were going to take our camping outfits and sleeping bags and I told him I'd meet him at the corner of Sunset and Sepulveda at 5:00 A.M. Saturday morning," he told Hedda Hopper. "Ursula and I got up at 4:00 and she took me to the corner . . . and we took off. We arrived in Provost, Utah that night about 8:00 . . . I needed some money so I reached in my pocket—and there were the keys to Ursula's Ford. I'd left her sitting on Sunset and Sepulveda at 5 o'clock in the morning with no car keys. I called her, and she said, 'Did you forget something this morning?' She'd walked up to the shopping center and telephoned the automobile club; they came out and put the wires together so she could drive

---

465 Hedda Hopper Papers, Margaret Herrick Library, AMPAS

466 Terry Taylor to author

home. Then she called the Oldsmobile people . . . and he sent somebody out to make her a new key . . . I apologized for causing her all the trouble. She said, 'I didn't mind. It was a beautiful morning and I loved the walk.'"[467]

Of course, Bob was also stepfather to Ursula's children from her first marriage, Manuela and Michael, and with them he seemed to struggle, not that he didn't have provocation. 1962–1963 was a particularly tough time for Manuela and Michael, not to mention Bob and Ursula. In April 1962, Manuela, then 18, pleaded guilty to a misdemeanor charge of being under the influence of drugs in public. A year later, she pleaded guilty to a public drunkenness charge. While these can easily be attributed to youthful indiscretions, Michael's transgressions were much more serious. Just before Christmas, 1963, Michael, 18, who was now living in Germany with his father, was arrested for trying to poison him. George Thiess refused to drink the tea that Michael had brought to him because, "It smelled funny." When questioned about the incident, Bob simply stated, "It's a tragic thing when this thing happens to any young boy or girl." (Eventually Michael would be sentenced to a year in a reformatory.) Ivy Pearson-Mooring, a keen observer of the family, and godmother to Terry, believes that Bob was inadequate in understanding both Manuela and especially Michael. "Bob didn't understand mental illness," Ivy explained. "Michael was a very disturbed young man. He may have been a sociopath. He could be unkind to people and say rude things. This of course upset Bob, but he didn't understand mental illness and in many respects Bob didn't understand kids. He thought with children it should be like in the army, 'yes, sir,' 'Right away, sir.'"[468]

Ursula was a very giving and generous mother who always made time for her children. When asked what she most recalls about her childhood, Tessa replied, "The ranch and Daddy and Mother are all part of it. She made the Halloween costumes and would take us around. She cooked, she was a housewife, and we ate dinner together every night. We were allowed only an hour of TV every night; shows like Disney's *Wonderful World of Color*. It was a great environment

---

467 Hedda Hopper Papers, Margaret Herrick Library, AMPAS

468 Ivy Mooring to author

to grow up in. I even remember a mountain lion came down out of the hills to drink out of our pool." [469]

Tessa also fondly recalled the presence of two other special people in her life, Art and Barbara Reeves. Art was the foreman of the ranch. "Art took care of the land and the property," recalls Tessa. "He was probably Daddy's best friend, particularly later on when he was sick. Art was so much fun to be around. He knew so much about nature and animals. I always wanted to be where Art was. He was the stability of the ranch and Barbara, being a teacher, helped me with my homework." [470]

One early morning Art informed Ursula and Bob that one of the mares was in labor. Bob and Ursula believed it was time that both Terry and Tessa had the opportunity to see the miracle of a mare giving birth since so many of the animals on the ranch had done so. It was frankly a part of a working ranch. "The beautiful mare, lying on the ground, struggling for the delivery, was the first one bred to our stud horse Showbar, a rather spectacular animal," Ursula would later recall of the incident. "Terry and Tessa showed great concern for the visibly uncomfortable mare, now in the last thrashes of foaling, and breathed a sigh of relief with the rest of us when the stalky, wobbly, wet body of a miniature horse emerged. With Art's announcement that we had a boy, it became a family effort contemplating what to call him. Our smart son, knowing that the stud's identity must be reflected in the off-springs name, came up with the ultimate statement. Trying to impress his dad with his lately-acquired musical knowledge and skills exhibited on his piano, he said, 'Let's call him Chopin. He'll be the only violin-playing horse west of the Mississippi.'" [471]

Art Reeves recalls Bob as a man who always made the maximum effort in any job he attempted. "Bob was a perfectionist in a way I'm not. He was very sure of what he was trying to do and very methodical. He would get frustrated a little bit as perfectionists do. One day he found that there was a board on a fence that needed to be fixed and he said, 'I'd fix it myself if I could find the hammer

469 Tessa Taylor to author

470 ibid

471 Thiess

and nails.' You see Bob would have put the hammer and nails in a very specific place, but not me, so I got him the hammer and nails and he went on and fixed the fence. As the ranch manager I worked 12-14 hour days but he still worked more hours than I did because when he was working in television or movies he would put in hours at the studio and then would come home and work around the ranch."[472]

Art and Barbara became part of the family. "We were treated like one of the family. Bob used to call me 'Uncle Art' even though I was younger than he was. He would say to me, 'Uncle Art, I can't tell you how glad we are that you are here.' Bob was really a cowboy at heart. On the ranch we raised chickens—when Bob used to go to Nebraska to visit he would always come back with baby chickens he would buy out there. He really took an active interest in the ranch. We even raised a few rabbits. We thought about cattle and we looked at Black Angus but it never filled the bill. I'm sure we must have gotten on each other's nerves from time to time but we never had a cross word in all the time we worked together." They were always included at festive occasions such as Thanksgiving and Christmas. Art and Barbara lived in a separate house about 300 yards from the ranch house that the Taylors lived in. In addition to Bob, Art came to appreciate Ursula and the children. "She was very, very close to the kids—just a super mother," he would say about Ursula.[473]

As for Terry and Tessa, Art came to like both of them very much. "Terry was a typical kid, one of the most normal kids of any motion picture star. He was always into something, and I mean that in a good way. When he was younger, we had a driveway which was as long as a city block. One day he was digging a hole in it and I ran him off with a broom! As he got older he wanted to earn money and so he and his friends latched on the idea of selling firewood to our neighbors by chopping down some of the dead trees on the property. So he came to me and I got him a chainsaw and he paid me back for it, too. I pointed out the trees he could cut down and they sold the firewood around the neighborhood. I was very proud

472 Art Reeves to author

473 Art Reeves to author

of him and so was Bob." Art recalls Tessa as "a very beautiful girl, just a sweetheart. I've always liked her." Years later, Art and Barbara attended one of Ursula's Christmas open houses and Tessa, now an adult and an actress in her own right, came up to him and suggested that he get an agent. "She told me to send her a picture and she got me an agent for commercials and I did quite a few of them, too, thanks to Tessa." [474]

Occasionally, Bob and Art would travel together on ranch business and Art would get a revealing glimpse in how Bob handled his celebrity, or, perhaps tried to hide it. "One time we drove down to Paris, California, to Audie Murphy's place where Bob was going to look over some of his stallions. As a rule he usually wouldn't stop along the way because he didn't want to be recognized. He would take a thermos of coffee and a sandwich and eat it as we drove. Well, this time we stopped at this little café and we took a seat at the counter. After a few minutes the cook in back came out and said, 'Don't I know you?' And Bob said, 'I don't think so.' So the cook went back and then a few minutes later he came out and asked Bob, 'You look so familiar—did you ever work in pictures?' And Bob would say, 'Oh, off and on.' But he never told that cook who he was, and the cook never figured it out." [475]

Bob took an active interest in horses and liked the people who shared his passion. One such person was Don Burt, horseman, trainer and seller. According to Burt, Bob offered to help him make a sale when he had somebody who was taking a little too much time to decide if they wanted to buy. They cooked up a scheme where Bob would suddenly call while this prospective client was talking business in his office. Burt would take the call and after a few seconds, would cuff his hand over the phone and tell the prospective buyer that he had "Robert Taylor, you know, the movie actor" on the line and would he mind if he spoke with Mr. Taylor for a few minutes. Naturally, the prospective buyer was impressed and was fine with it. After the call, Burt would tell his prospective buyer that the business with Taylor was a little more complicated and would he mind accompanying him to Taylor's nearby ranch for dinner? And they

474 ibid

475 Art Reeves to author

could discuss their own business matters on the way over and way back. Naturally, the prospective buyer was thrilled and delighted to have this opportunity not only to meet Robert Taylor but also dine with him.

Once at the ranch, Bob and Ursula would warmly greet their guests. Bob would say just the right things, such as "Don found every one (horses) for me" and generally build Don and his horses up to the prospective buyer. After dinner Bob and Don would excuse themselves for Bob's den where they were going to discuss "business" leaving Ursula to charm the prospective buyer. After a few minutes they would come out and announce a deal had been made with Bob very excited and again touting Don's product. Of course this was a bit overwhelming for the prospective buyer and convincing since Don usually had no trouble following up with a sale.[476] On occasion there would be a surprise for Taylor as well, such as the time he answered the door and the prospective buyer, who happened to be a woman, fell into a dead faint at meeting Robert Taylor.

When not at the Mandeville Canyon ranch, the Taylors enjoyed a cabin at Big Horn Mountain, Wyoming. One of the pleasures of the environment was the fishing. Bob later pointed out that Terry, "catches all the fish in the stream when we go out." He also pointed out that he and Terry enjoyed skeet shooting. "I like that kind of physical fitness for children rather than walk marathons." Bob hoped that the outdoor activities, which also included horseback riding, would keep the children so occupied they wouldn't become as obsessed as some kids with television. He pointed out that the children earn their TV hour each day by doing chores, homework and eating their dinner, in addition, to spending a half-hour reading. "It's reading that suffers when kids get the television bug."

One of the most cherished times of the year in the Taylor household was Christmas. "It was a wonderful time of the year!" Terry recalled. "During our Christmas dinner Dad would at some point have our housekeeper ring a small bell from the kitchen that would 'allegedly' be Santa's sleigh arriving. At that point he would excuse himself and sneak away to an intercom in another room with nuts

476 Don Burt, Horses and Other Heroes, pg. 109-110

stuffed in his cheeks to ho-ho-ho more effectively as Santa. Tessa and I would run to the front door where a gunny sack full of gifts had already been dropped off for each of us (by Art)." After a few minutes the excited children would return to the dinner table and Bob would rejoin them saying, "Its cold here. Do you think it's snowing outside? Maybe Santa is due for a visit." [477] The children, wide-eyed with excitement, would tell him, "You missed him again, Daddy. He was already here!" And they would point out the sack of toys that the jolly old elf had already left them. Bob got a great deal of joy in his young children's reaction to this stunt and performed it for years.

But Christmas was more than just Santa and toys for the children; it was also the homey atmosphere that Ursula provided. She, more than anybody, made the holiday special. The house would be lovingly decorated with lights and candles throughout. The smells of goodies baking in the kitchen. A large tree was bought every year and put up the day before, but hidden behind locked doors until after the Christmas Eve meal so that the children could imagine that it was Santa himself who had magically made the huge, lighted, tree appear. "My German heritage of celebrating Christmas rather dominated my family, and my husband was beginning to see it through my eyes," Ursula later wrote. "Until the introduction of what this season really meant to me, he (Bob) had looked at it as commercialism rather than a holiday to be enjoyed. But once he appointed himself Santa Claus to his children, his whole attitude changed." [478]

Christmas dinner was a feast to be enjoyed, often enhanced by Ursula's German desserts. Bob always helped out by cooking a special roast beef recipe (he was no turkey lover, per Ivy Mooring). Close friends like Art, Barbara and Ivy were perennial guests. Also Ruth and Ursula's mother would be occasional guests. "Even though our two mothers spoke different languages, there was definite communication between them, as we observed them laughing quite a lot." When Ursula's mother first visited the ranch and entered the front door and saw the height of the ceiling, she was so impressed that

477 Terry Taylor to author

478 Thiess

she assured Ursula, "Now this is a house." Over the years Ursula had managed to do something that Barbara never did, nor had the inclination to do, she won over Ruth. "Ursula won Bob's mother over by her kindness, devotion to Bob and wonderful homemaking skills," accords to Ivy Shelton-Mooring.[479] The atmosphere was further enhanced by neighbors who came caroling and the warmth of a fire crackling inside the huge fieldstone fireplace. The look and atmosphere of Christmas at the Robert Taylors' couldn't be surpassed by even Currier and Ives.

II

Bob joined a strong ensemble cast which included Shelley Winters, Cesar Romero and Broderick Crawford in a film called *A House Is Not a Home*, based on Polly Adler's autobiography. Adler (played by Winters, of course) was a notorious New York City madam during the 1920s. Bob was cast as racketeer Frank Costigan. One of the reasons that Bob undertook this role was because he felt it would provide him with some of the grit that *Johnny Eager* and *Party Girl* provided. Like in *Eager* and *Party Girl*, Bob grew a mustache to play Costigan. The film, however, had little grit. Lawrence Quirk in his *The Films of Robert Taylor* wrote, "The critics were frankly derisive, noting that there was little sex in a movie that was supposed to be about just that, and that Shelley-Polly came across as a sort of dormitory housemother rather than as a tough, money minded Polly." Despite the watered-down script, producer Joseph E. Levine produced a lush production for his Embassy Productions. Levine alternated between producing films such as *The Carpetbaggers, Where Has Love Gone? The Oscar* and *Harlow*, films with star names and top productions values, but decidedly trashy, with more prestigious films like *Long Day's Journey Into Night* and *Lion in Winter*. Unfortunately, *A House Is Not a Home* belongs in the former category.

Bob did his usual professional job and won praise from members of the cast in the process. "Like Ronald Colman, he was the sweetest man to work with," recalled Shelley Winters. "By that I mean he was cooperative and understanding in contrast to most leading men

479 Ivy Mooring to author

today, who try either to elbow you out of camera range or are off in a corner somewhere practicing 'method acting.'"[480] He could also make a movie newcomer like Kaye Ballard feel at ease. Ballard, a cabaret comedian, was cast in a small role in the picture. "On the first day of shooting I was surprised that Robert Taylor's hands were shaking," recalled Ballard. "I said, 'Mr. Taylor, you're not nervous, are you?' 'Oh yes, Kaye,' he answered, 'I'm always a nervous wreck on the first day of shooting.' Can you imagine? Robert Taylor! He held Garbo in *Camille*, for God's sake—and he's nervous."[481]

The Taylor film that drew the most attention in 1965 was a low-budgeted horror/suspense picture produced by William Castle. It wasn't the script or the production values that drew the attention but the fact that Taylor's leading lady was none other than his ex-wife, Barbara Stanwyck. Obviously, this could be used by that master showman Castle as a marketing tool for the film. It wasn't exactly new that a divorced couple was cast in the same film, but it was rare. Henry Fonda and Margaret Sullavan were divorced when they starred together in the 1936 film *The Moon's Our Home* and the same year divorced, but still pals, and William Powell and Carole Lombard worked together effortlessly in *My Man Godfrey* made a few years after they were Mr. and Mrs.

In 1962 when Bette Davis and Joan Crawford had starred together the low-budgeted *What Ever Happened to Baby Jane?* They surprised the industry when the film went on to be one of the most successful of the year and rejuvenated the careers of both Davis and Crawford. Since then many aging actresses let go of their typical glamour and consented to appear in such films as *Shock Treatment, Strait-Jacket, The Caretakers, Hush . . . Hush, Sweet Charlotte, Lady in a Cage,* and *The Nanny.* Barbara Stanwyck tried to resist as long as she could. But her sixties film roles had thus far consisted of portraying a madam in *Wild in the Streets* and playing second fiddle to Elvis Presley in *Roustabout.* Stanwyck, if nothing else, was a working actress and to be a working actress she had to work and when William Castle offered her *The Night Walker* she wasn't in a position to turn it down since she had nothing better on her plate.

480 Reluctant Witness, Linda Alexander, pg. 347

481 Kaye Ballard, How I Lost 10-pounds in 53 Years

But reporters learned not to call *The Night Walker* a horror film to Miss Stanwyck's face. "It is not a horror film," she would reply. "It's a shocker. A suspense movie. There's a difference! Horror is with heads rolling and the blood and gore and all that sort of thing. This is a shocker-suspense film." So how did Bob get involved in this shocker-suspense film? According to Stanwyck, "It was Mr. Castle's idea." Castle had sent the script to Stanwyck and when she went to discuss the picture with him he asked her, "I have an idea, and I don't know how you will feel about it, but how would you feel about Robert Taylor playing the other (role)?" Stanwyck professed that she thought it would be a "wonderful" idea, but that "you'd better ask him. And Mrs. Taylor."

Well, Mrs. Taylor was no problem. Ursula knew that Bob had no lingering feelings for Stanwyck beyond the fact that she was a very good and professional actress. To the press Bob put it this way: "Any actor who failed to appreciate the chance, and privilege, of playing opposite Barbara Stanwyck under any circumstances would be out of his head. She's one of the all-time greats in the picture business. Not only that, but we're still fine friends." It didn't hurt that Stanwyck and Taylor both shared the same business manager who urged them both to work together, since each had a piece of the pictures box office. The more interest in the picture, the bigger the potential pay-off.

On the set they were congenial with one another. Hollywood columnist Bob Thomas was on the set and later recorded Bob, Barbara and Castle seated next to each other enjoying a quiet few minutes between scenes. Castle asked Bob how old he was when he made *Camille*—30?

"No, I was 25," Bob replied.

"I was the one who was 30," Barbara happily piped up.[482]

While Bob spoke of he and Barbara still being "fine friends," and it is true that on the rare occasions when they met that they were perfectly cordial to one another, but Bob still carried a lingering bitterness toward his one-time spouse for the way she would embarrass him during their marriage. One night after Ursula had tucked Terry and Tessa into bed she heard Bob talking in their den. She wondered

---

482 Reading (PA) Eagle, 6/4/64

if somebody had dropped by and entered the den to find Bob talking back to the TV set. According to Ursula, on the set was an image of Stanwyck appearing on the TV series Rawhide about to horsewhip a young Clint Eastwood. Bob was saying to the screen, "Okay, lady, do what you do best. Whip him, humiliate him, squash his ego. I know you enjoy doing that." [483] Bob was embarrassed to find Ursula had walked in on him and tried to laugh it off, but told her that he thought that she had accepted the TV show just for the opportunity to perform that scene. Bob also came to the sad conclusion that even though he got a piece of the picture that, too, would be to Barbara's advantage since she still got fifteen percent of his income. "Do you realize that every penny I just made on that movie ends up in Barbara's pocket?" he complained to Ursula.[484]

Still, the filming of *The Night Walker* went well. Bob later stated, "It felt like we had never been married." Stanwyck played a wealthy woman, married to a blind man (*I Dream of Jeannie* co-star Hayden Rourke) who suspects that she is having an affair with his attorney (Taylor). Furthermore, Stanwyck is experiencing terrifying and amorous dreams. Eventually, her husband is killed in an explosion—or was he? In her still recurrent dreams he is still alive and out for vengeance. Stanwyck confides in Taylor, who she trusts, but should she? Given that the stars of the film were once married to each other the press clamored to visit the set. "Bring 'em on. All they'll see are a couple of actors at work," was Stanwyck's reply.[485]

The film turned out to be a box-office dud. The result was a setback for producer William Castle, who up till this point had made a series of profitable low-budget films. More than a decade later, in his autobiography, after devoting nearly a chapter on a Joan Crawford shocker called *Strait Jacket*, Castle dismissed *The Night Walker* in a short paragraph. "I felt the declining box office on my next picture, *The Night Walker*, co-starring Robert Taylor and Barbara Stanwyck, both big stars that I felt would be strong enough to pull customers in," he wrote. "The picture played to almost empty theatres." The *Los Angeles Times* critic liked the film. "Robert Bloch's

483 Ursula Thiess, …but I have promises to keep

484 Thiess, pg. 166

485 LA Times, 7/9/64

screenplay provides more punch and plausibility than regularly offered in these amusements . . . builds up some suspense and moves on to a surprising ending." Ironically, this would be Barbara Stanwyck's final feature film. She would spend the rest of her career appearing on television.

Shortly after completing *The Night Walker* Bob was offered a part he was really enthusiastic about in a film tentatively titled *The Cry of the Laughing Owls*. Bob felt it would be an important film which would finally allow him to graduate to character roles. Bob was cast as a widowed school teacher (he even gets to wear glasses in the film) who teaches underprivileged Seminole children on an Indian reservation in the Everglades. Eventually, the picture was retitled *Johnny Tiger* after a character in the film, the grandson of a Seminole chief who finds himself pulled in two directions: the traditions of his ancestors and the modern world. The widowed professor played by Taylor has three children, one of whom (played by Brenda Scott) falls in love with Johnny. Filming got underway in October of 1964 on location in the Florida Everglades near Wekiwa State Park. "This is the first semi-character part I've played," Bob recalled. "It was an interesting experience, but those spectacles (the glasses he wore for most of the picture) were an awful nuisance. I was always either taking them off at the wrong time or forgetting I had them on." [486] Just prior to the start of shooting Bob and Ursula spent a couple of days visiting Tom Purvis and his wife at their home in Bradenton, Florida. While there he let it be known that he no longer had a plane. "I have a license but I haven't kept it up. I had a plane for several years but it got to be too much of an expense and I gave it up. It takes a lot of time to keep up a license." [487]

Cast in the pivotal role of Johnny Tiger was a young actor named Chad Everett, who, like Bob had been, was under contract to MGM (though loaned out to Universal for this picture) and, also like Bob, reviewed more on his looks than his abilities as an actor. This led to a bond between the two of them. Everett would later recall that he was always "shadowing" Bob on the set, studying him, realizing that here was a man with more than thirty years' experience

486 LA Times, 4/28/66

487 Sarasota Herald-Tribune, 10/10/64

behind him and understanding that he could obviously learn a great deal from him. The film, like *Cattle King* and *The Night Walker*, was shot on a shoestring budget with a fast-paced production schedule. On those long hours of shooting Bob came to realize that he had become kind of an idol to Everett and decided to take the young actor under his wing. Everett told author Linda Alexander that Bob, "would get up very early when he was fresh, and he would do the majority of his studying for his day's work at that time . . . He was always prepared." Everett was impressed that Bob not only knew his own lines but everybody else's too. ". . . he knew everybody's stuff," he told Alexander. "And he never flaunted it or showed it off." According to Everett, Bob "taught me, both verbally and by example." To this day Taylor remains a "giant" to Everett, and one who "never got the credit he deserved to from the critics . . . though the public was always with him." Their friendship lasted for the remainder of Taylor's life and Everett would occasionally be a guest at the ranch where he observed the obvious love that Bob and Ursula felt for one another, "they were hand holders." [488]

Bob was proud of his performance in *Johnny Tiger*. "I felt that part—it was me," he said in an interview at the Florida premiere of the picture. [489] When the film came out, reviews were generally positive. The *New York Post* complimented Bob, calling his performance, "a worthy piece of acting." Even the *New York Times* favorably reviewed his performance. "Mr. Taylor may be slightly obtuse as an educator, but he handles his role naturally and with ease." Universal, however, didn't do much to promote the picture and it eventually hit neighborhood theaters on the bottom half of a double-bill with *Munsters Go Home.*

After *Johnny Tiger* Bob was to make only four more feature films—one of which, *Where Angels Go Trouble Follows* (1968), allowed him only a cameo appearance (as a rich cattleman who helps a group of nuns and their teenage charges on a road trip to California). His more substantive films took him outside the United States. He went to Spain for the Western *Savage Pampas* (1967), to play the commanding officer of an Argentinean outpost during the 1870s. In between

488 http://www.dvdclassicscorner.net/taylor.htm

489 Robert Taylor, JE Wayne, pg. 241

filming he was able to enjoy one of his favorite recreations, hunting. Originally, it seemed that Ursula would not be able to join Bob in Spain due to being unable to find a decent sitter for the children, but in the end she did find someone and was able to join Bob for several days. To Bob's great relief she also brought along some of his favorite instant coffee as he disliked the Spanish coffee.

Then it was off to Egypt for *The Glass Sphinx* (1968), a semi-remake of his own *Valley of the Kings*. Bob's leading lady was the buxom Swedish actress Anita Ekberg. At the time he felt he wasn't in the best of shape and was carrying around an extra twenty pounds or so. "The big problem is purely a technical one," he wrote his tailor, a man he affectionately nicknamed Nudie. "Anita Ekberg has an enormous pair of 'lungs'—and to find a camera lens which can hold HER LUNGS and MY ASS in the same scene is a difficult thing to solve!"[490] Miss Ekberg also had a mischievous sense of humor. Ursula had been able to get away and join Bob on location for about ten days during the filming. One day after Bob and Ursula had arrived back to their hotel room from an afternoon of sight-seeing they walked in to find what appeared to be a blonde woman in Bob's bed. On closer examination what they found was one of Ekberg's blonde wigs draped over a pillow giving the illusion of a woman in the bed. Bob laughingly told Ursula that it was another of a series of practical jokes perpetrated by his leading lady and her husband.[491] It wasn't a picture that Bob particularly wanted to do. "It was a job—and I needed the money," he told Ivy.[492] When a reporter asked Bob if the film would ever be seen in the United States, Bob replied, "I hope not, although I haven't seen it."[493]

The final picture filmed outside the United States was a Cold War spy romp, *The Day the Hot Line Got Hot* (1968), filmed in Paris and Barcelona. The advantage of this film, for Bob, was the presence of his co-star, Charles Boyer, a man he greatly admired and enjoyed the company of. Of these last three films it's the most entertaining and enjoyed a modest success upon release in the United States, but

490 Robert Taylor, J.E. Wayne, pg. 254

491 Thiess, pg. 168-169

492 Linda Alexander, Reluctant Witness, pg. 330

493 Ocala Star Banner, 3/15/67

is hardly considered one of his best.

By this time Bob had come to the conclusion that his motion picture career was waning. "You can't have too many mediocre pictures and maintain an extremely high status," he told Hollywood columnist Bob Thomas.[494] He also had no time for so-called "message pictures." "I don't want any part of them," he said. "I think we've had enough messages on film to last several generations. I belong to the old, old school that says films belong to entertainment. Of course, with some of the kooks we've got running around today, you've got to have a message."[495]

Television had once again come to the rescue. When his pal Ronald Reagan announced that he was going to run for Governor of California, TV stations in the Golden State couldn't use Reagan's introductions as host of the syndicated Western series *Death Valley Days* under the fairness doctrine, so a series of co-hosts, including Bob, were used to introduce the series. Naturally, Bob supported his old friend. "Actually he's too nice a guy for politics," he wrote a friend, "and I wouldn't envy him the job—but maybe it's time some good people got into that racket!"[496] When Reagan was elected Governor in November of 1966, *Death Valley Days* had to come up with a replacement. Reagan enthusiastically recommended Bob Taylor, and the choice made sense to the producers. After all, Bob had been an even bigger star than Reagan had ever been in films and like Reagan, he made a convincing cowboy.

It was an easy and lucrative gig. *Death Valley Days* produced 26 half-hour episodes (sponsored by Borax Bleach) and Bob's hosting duties introducing those 26 stories took about four weeks to film with an additional 2-3 days each to film the roughly four episodes that Taylor would actually star in. For 4-5 weeks of work Bob was paid a cool $75,000.[497] The producer of the series, Bob Stapler, kept sending scripts to Bob of the stories he thought would be good for Bob to star in and was amazed when Bob would continually reject them. "Bob kept refusing scripts but not telling me why,"

494 Elyria (Oh) Chronicle-Telegram, 3/17/67

495 LA Times, 6/26/66

496 Linda Alexander, Reluctant Witness, pg. 328

497 LA Times, July, 1967

Stapler recalled. "I knew he was anxious to star in several episodes—it was written in his contract—but he was sending the best ones back to me without comment. One day I approached him about it. Taylor said he was not going to play the part of a young man and that was that."[498] It seems that the scripts that Stapler sent to Bob seemed to indicate a lead actor considerably younger than Bob himself, now in his mid-fifties. "I got the message but outsmarted him," recalled Stapler. "I told my secretary when I found a good story for Taylor to simply change the age of the leading man to forty-five and from that time on he accepted every one!"[499]

Naturally, the press began to wonder if Bob, like Reagan, would become a corporate spokesman on the chicken-and-peas circuit and perhaps use it as a stepping stone to a political career. Another MGM leading man, George Murphy, was elected to the U.S. Senate in 1964, so why not Bob, whose conservative credentials were as strong as anybody's. Bob let the press know in no uncertain terms, "Not on your life. I'd rather go huntin' and fishin'." And he meant it.[500]

In the spring of 1967 Bob was invited to co-host the popular syndicated afternoon talk show *The Mike Douglas Show* from Philadelphia. The producers had done their research on Bob carefully and planned a little surprise for him on the show. Douglas engaged Bob in conversation of his early pre-Hollywood days and discussed the fact that he had been a singer and musician with a trio called "The Harmony Boys." At this point Douglas asked Bob to sing a little something. Well, it had been years since Bob had sung publically and was reluctant to do so now in front of a studio audience and audience of millions of people who would be watching. Douglas continued to egg him on, finally using his trump card, "Well, we have a couple of guys back here to help you out." Out from behind the curtain came the other members of "The Harmony Boys": Gerry Wiebe, now Dean of the College of Communications at Boston University, and Russ Gibson, an office manager of a Lincoln, Nebraska laundry and cleaning firm. A visibly surprised Bob was excited to

498 Robert Taylor, J.E. Wayne, pg. 251

499 ibid

500 Appleton (Wi) Post-Crescent, 8/6/67

see his two old friends and they did a brief song together. "It was great fun for all of us, although too brief," Gibson recalled of the incident. "We did a number together, but it wasn't very professional, I'm afraid." [501] Not that the audience seemed to mind.

501 Lincoln (NE) Sunday Journal, 4/30/67

Chapter Fourteen

"How to Say Farewell to a Friend Named Bob" (1968-1969)

In February 1968, Bob was selected to serve as honorary director of the Winchester Claybird Tournament. He accompanied the winning American team on a worldwide trip that took him (and Ursula, who accompanied him) to Hawaii, Australia, Thailand, Italy, Germany and England. It was a publicity coup for Winchester, and Bob had the right image for the job. In announcing the worldwide tour Winchester described Bob this way: "All his life Mr. Taylor has been deeply involved in outdoor sports—particularly shooting. He is a fine actor, an excellent shot and a gentleman. We feel his association with this Clay bird Tournament will greatly add to the luster of the shooting sport."

Bob knew full well what was expected of him on this trip. "I hope, honey, you realize, that we are only window dressing this affair," he told Ursula, "but I sure would like to meet some of those sharpshooters abroad. Besides, how often do we get a free ride halfway around the world, without any obligation other than being on the spot with a smile and the know-how to carry a gun?"[502]

Bob began the trip looking exceptionally well. He sported a suntan and had recently lost twenty extra pounds he had been carrying around for a few years. He gave the illusion of being an extremely fit man for his then fifty-five years. Ursula, however, knew that for months Bob had been battling fatigue. No matter how much rest he got he just couldn't shake it and it made him irritable and occasionally he would take that irritability out on Ursula. Ursula knew that this was unlike him and urged him to slow down and try

502 Thiess, pg. 170

and to rest more. But Bob was, as always, concerned with providing for his family, and so he continued a back-breaking schedule, which included filming *Death Valley Days* and two films in 1967.

One of these films was a Western called *Return of the Gunfighter*, which reunited him with his friend and protégé Chad Everett. One of the featured players in this made-for-television movie was Johnny Crawford, who had found fame as Chuck Connors' son Mark on the successful television series *The Rifleman*. Crawford was excited to be working on a film with one of the idols of his youth, Robert Taylor. "I looked around and he wasn't on the set, so I thought he was probably back in his trailer. This was in Old Tucson, Arizona. There was one old guy there that had a long face, but good features. He looked like the kind that hung around Hollywood and if the breaks had been better he could have been somebody. He was talking to people, and as time went by the assistant director said, 'Mr. Taylor, come on in.' that old guy was Robert Taylor." Later on, Crawford understood that Bob probably was already suffering from the cancer which would ultimately kill him. "He would have been excused to lie in the trailer and rest until his next shot, but he wouldn't do that. And when they called him he went on a dead run just like a new kid. He did not hold you up." [503]

Veteran character actor Harry Lauter also worked with Bob on this film and noted his decline. "Robert Taylor was a very dear friend of mine, one of the nicest men in the business," Harry stated. "I did one of his last pictures (*Return of the Gunfighter*). He was very ill, and I knew it. They came in for a close-up on me, and they say, 'We'll get Mr. Taylor.' He was lying down in his bungalow, and I said, 'No, don't bother him. Let the script girl read the lines.' I usually liked the actors there—but in this case, and gosh, I looked up and there he was. I said, 'Bob, you don't have to.' He said, 'No, you deserve the courtesy as an actor for me to be here and read the lines, just as well off camera as on.' That's one of the things you don't get anymore from people. I'll never forget that." [504]

Ursula hoped that this free around-the-world trip watching a sport he greatly enjoyed and meeting the type of people he liked

503 Goldrup, Tom & Jim, Feature Players: The Stories Behind Their Faces
504 ibid

being around would relax him by giving him a break from the rigors of acting.

The trip began with meeting the U.S. winning team in the Bahamas. Also in attendance was Prince Rainier of Monaco who, at dinner that night, exchanged stories on raising children with Ursula. From this meet and greet in the Bahamas the actual tournament began in Hawaii. Bob seemed to be greatly enjoying himself and the mild weather of the Bahamas and Hawaii agreed with him. However, when the tournament made its way to Thailand, and encountered hot, sticky weather, Bob's fatigue returned with a vengeance. He was able to make the rounds of tournaments, dinners and even meet the king of Thailand, but his weariness kept him from making sightseeing tours with Ursula. Instead, he would stay in his room and rest up.

The final year of Bob's life was not only difficult for Bob, but also for Ursula as she had to deal with concerns not only for her husband but for her eldest son. Shortly after the New Year, Michael was back in the news when he slashed his left wrist at a Santa Monica hotel. It was certainly a cry for help because right after Michael cut his wrist he sought help at the hotel's front office where an ambulance was immediately called. Michael was taken to Santa Monica Receiving Hospital where his wounds were addressed.[505] Ursula, who was with Bob in Australia, received a call from Manuela to alert her before she heard it from the press. She assured Ursula that Michael was getting psychiatric care and that it wasn't a serious suicide attempt. Then, a week later, Michael was arrested in West Hollywood on suspicion of being drunk and disorderly after he was found wandering in somebody's yard and "yelling like a banshee," the description given by a deputy sheriff. Ursula decided to try tough love with her eldest son, and refused him bail. After this latest arrest he spent several weeks at Camarillo State Hospital where Ursula, who came back early from her trip, would drive weekly to spend a day with her son. At the end of the day Ursula would recall that Michael would hug her with "such intensity and tell me over and over again how much he regretted causing me pain, and that one day he would make good, would make me proud

505 Hollywood Citizen News, 2/8/64

of him."[506]

While Michael's life was still in turmoil, Manuela was getting hers together and following her dreams. She had matured, at age 21, into a strikingly beautiful brunette, every bit as attractive as Ursula. She was cast in a film by producer A.C. Lyles, and made such an impression that Paramount picked up her option. She was one of a group of children of celebrities who were profiled in a February 1968, *Los Angeles Herald-Examiner* article titled "The Cruelty of Fame" about the highs and lows of offspring who attempt to follow their parents in show business. Manuela, like Ursula, also worked as a model. But she didn't start at the top. Her first assignment was as a mannequin at a specialty shop. Later, designer Helen Rose saw some pictures of her and put her under personal contract.[507] Manuela later summed up her feelings for her stepfather this way:

"As for me, I can only tell you that while I was the kind of teenager that rebelled fiercely against any kind of authority, including parents, I can tell you that in retrospect, I see my stepfather as a man of conviction, a man of principles, and a man who was honest to the best of his ability. He spoke his own truth, and once, when he was asked to run for Governor, he refused because he felt he didn't have the type of qualifications, such as a law degree, that people should have to run for governor. In other words, he was not easily flattered, nor given to hubris. Did he have faults? Certainly, but probably no more than the average man, and it would be unseemly to speak of those for a man who is not here to defend himself."[508]

Upon returning home from the Westchester trip, Bob plunged back into work on *Death Valley Days*. The producer, Bob Stapler, had also noticed that Bob had a persistent cough and was not quite himself. They took a trip together by plane shoot location scenes and then flew back to Los Angeles. For the entire return trip Stapler could hear him hacking away. When they arrived back in L.A., Stapler found an empty box of tissues under Bob's seat on the plane,

506 Thiess, pg. 172-173

507 Hollywood Citizen-News, 4/11/69

508 Manuela Thiess to author

"It was full when he started home."[509]

Occasionally, Ursula and the children would join him on location in Kenab, Utah, when filming *Death Valley Days*. "I always enjoyed spending time with him in the actor's trailers and while he had his make-up applied," recalled Terry.[510] Terry recollects that his father was "uncomfortable" watching himself on screen either in dailies or on a TV or movie screen. "Never once did he share with me a favorite film that he made." One of the most memorable moments of watching television with Bob was when Terry watched the Beatles appearing on *The Ed Sullivan Show*. "All he kept muttering was 'those long-haired hippies!'" By September, Bob had completed his work for the season on *Death Valley Days*.

Bob had had a lingering cough for years, but by 1968 it was occurring with increasing regularity. It was particularly cruel at night when he and Ursula tried to sleep. The hacking kept both of them awake at regular intervals throughout the night. Ursula realized something was radically wrong when one night upon returning from a dinner party and enjoying a nightcap Bob suddenly turned white and bent over in pain so acute it caused him to groan in agony. He confessed to Ursula that the attack wasn't the first time it had occurred, but that it was the worst of its kind. "When I had them before," he told her, "it felt like indigestion, but this one is different—like being cut in two pieces."[511]

Ursula urged Bob to get a complete check-up. That Bob was hesitant to do so, while enduring such extreme pain, makes one think he may have guessed the truth. In 1962 doctors had found a spot on his lung and had diagnosed Rocky Mountain Spotted Fever, a bacterial infection that's transmitted to people by tick bites. But Bob also had confided to his friend Tom Purvis that an X-ray taken in 1966 had clearly shown a growth on his lung. It appears that he kept this information from Ursula and in the meanwhile the growth was not only eating away at Bob physically, but mentally, with a change in temperament caused not only by lack of sleep but, probably, living with the knowledge that he had something far worse

509 Robert Taylor, J.E. Wayne, pg. 257

510 Terry Taylor to author

511 ...promises to keep, pg. 175

than Rocky Mountain Spotted Fever. Ursula kept the pressure up and finally a reluctant Bob decided to have a complete check-up. The result of the check-up was that his doctors recommended immediate surgery. On October 8, 1968, Bob entered St. John Hospital in Santa Monica and underwent surgery for the removal of his right lung. The operation was successful in removing the lung and the press and public were told that Bob was "doing very well" recuperating in the intensive care unit. They also disclosed that the lung had been removed due to "a fungus infection commonly referred to as valley fever." But more ominously they had discovered small tumors on the removed lung, but they had not yet determined if they were cancerous.

The doctors assured Bob and Ursula that all was well and that the malignancy was cut out, but told Bob that to ensure total recovery he would need to submit to radiation therapy. Bob's surgery made headlines in newspapers from across the country and the response was immediate from his fans with thousands of letters flooding the hospital and later the ranch. Among those sending messages of encouragement were former President Dwight D. Eisenhower and his former MGM colleagues, Rosalind Russell and Greer Garson. But, probably, the message which meant the most to Bob was from John Wayne, who had survived the removal of a lung back in 1964. If Duke could survive, so could he. Of course, at this point, Bob was confident he would survive given what his doctors were telling him that the malignancy was gone. All he needed was to gain some weight and he would be back on his feet. When Bob was released from the hospital and he returned home, one of the first things he did was have twelve-year-old Terry see his surgical scar, a scar which began at the center of his chest and reached all around to his back. Bob told him, "Terry, here you see the results of a very bad habit. Don't ever even think of picking up a cigarette."[512]

The next several grueling weeks involved almost daily radiation treatments at the hospital which further depleted Bob's strength. An elevated temperature caused his doctors alarm, believing that he had developed an infection within his surgical scar. In November he was back in the hospital having his chest reopened to insert a

512 ibid

drainage tube. Bob didn't want to stay in the hospital and the doctors released him suggesting he have a daily morphine shot to ease his pain and around the clock nursing care. Bob didn't want any of that. He was tired of hospitals, tired of doctors and tired of nurses. He told them to explain what needed to be done to Ursula and she would handle it. The day before his discharge Bob's doctors demonstrated what she needed to do. Bob's bandages were unwrapped from his chest and the small incision to insert the tube that Ursula expected to find was instead a gaping hole, "the size of a golf ball." Taken totally by surprise, she fainted. When she regained consciousness only seconds later, she heard Bob reading the riot act to the doctors regarding their insensitivity in not preparing Ursula for what she would see. The demonstration continued without further incidence. Ursula never totally got over the revulsion she felt over the gaping hole, "but I had to do it and I did."[513]

By this time Bob's weight was down to around 150 pounds. His old clothes were hanging loose on him and he needed to have some lounge suits made for him. Just before Thanksgiving he sent a tape-recorded message to Tom Purvis. "I'm as breathless as a bride," he told him, "and I'm so God damn weak I can hardly get my pants on and I'm not kiddin.' Every time I breathe this damn hose talks back to me." He also paid tribute to Ursula, "God Damn—this gal has been takin' care of the ol' man and the whole damn family, too." The next day was Thanksgiving Day, but Bob had no appetite and he was forcing himself to eat. "Ursula makes up a batch of milk shakes," he told Purvis, "with lots of eggs and milk and malt and I siphon off a small one of those every morning and in the afternoon, but I'm not eatin' cause I'm not hungry."[514] Art would recall that Bob "lost a lot of weight . . . He didn't feel well enough to see lots of people and with the exception of some people he stopped seeing people all together because he didn't want them to see him the way he looked."[515]

Meanwhile, Bob was trying to evade the press in his daily excursions to the hospital for cobalt treatments. Bob didn't want

513 Ursula Thiess to author

514 Robert Taylor, J.E. Wayne, pg. 260

515 Art Reeves to author

them to snap any pictures of him in his weakened condition and reduced weight. To throw them off he would often lay on the backseat of the station wagon while Ursula drove him to the hospital. But press speculation was intense and finally on December 3 it was revealed to the public that Bob's surgery in October wasn't due to a fungus condition as initially revealed but was as many privately speculated, lung cancer. By Christmas Bob was back in the hospital after developing a high fever. The cause was staph infection. One doctor outraged Bob by asking Ursula if she had been careful in how she had been disinfecting the surgical wound properly when inserting the drainage tube. He made it clear to them that nobody on their staff could do a better job of taking care of him than Ursula had been.

It was a sad and dispirited Christmas. Bob would spend this, his last Christmas, in the hospital. On Christmas Eve, Ursula spent the morning preparing her annual Christmas Eve meal and then spent the afternoon at the hospital with Bob. That night during dinner, Bob called and tried to sound a merry tone even giving one of his "Ho-Ho-Ho" Santa impressions for the kids.

For the children it was a difficult time. Terry at 13 was at an age where Ursula did let him know certain facts about his father's condition, but by no means all. "I think my mother did a remarkable job of hiding it from the kids," Terry later said. "At least in my case the idea that he was away somewhere was nothing new. The fact that it was the hospital was something my mother chose not to share . . . or at least I chose not to accept if she did. It really didn't sink in for me that he was sick until he was home from the surgery in his TV chair with a white towel draped across his chest to cover the exposed hole. I could literally hear his breathe through it, especially when he coughed to bring up some of the infection inside of him."[516] Yet Terry felt that his father would almost certainly beat the cancer. "As young and naïve as I was, of course I thought he would beat it and be back out front one day soon playing catch and riding a horse or his motorcycle. I don't think that it ever dawned on me that he would leave . . . until he did." Bob did his best to shield his children from whatever discouragement he might have

516 Terry Taylor to author

felt. "He seemed to have a sense of hope throughout most of his battle because he never led me to believe that it was that serious . . . and neither did my mother. In hindsight, I don't know if telling me the whole truth along the way would have been good or bad for me."[517]

At nine years old it was a confusing time for Tessa. She especially remembers the constant coughing, "a very nasty cough" and the fact that he always needed a hanky due to it. She also recalls how upset Bob got when she walked in study while his nurse was changing his bandages and seeing the gaping hole in his chest, certainly something Bob would have wanted to shield her from.[518]

The doctors were never really open with Ursula (or for that matter with Bob). They told her that he would be sent home once his infection was cleared up but they never really discussed with her his long term prognosis. On Christmas morning, Ursula found out the truth. On her way to visit Bob at the hospital she stopped off at the home of Ron and Nancy Reagan to extend holiday greetings to them. Nancy's parents were present, as usual at the holidays, and Ursula knew them well. Nancy's father, Dr. Loyal Davis, was a well-respected neurosurgeon. Obviously, the Reagans had discussed Bob's case with Dr. Davis, who in turn had consulted with Bob's family physician. It was clear to Dr. Davis that Ursula had no real understanding of her husband's prognosis. He laid it out on the line to her this Christmas morning. "For heaven's sake, Ursula," he told her not mincing his words, "Bob is not dying of infections. He is dying of the disease." It was as if she were struck by lightning because up to this moment the possibility of Bob dying had never been discussed with them by the doctors treating him. Ursula became defensive and began to argue with Dr. Davis that Bob's doctors had been telling them that "there is still a good chance of winning the battle." Dr. Davis told her he understood what they were doing but thought it was wrong. "You have to face the inevitable."[519]

Nancy Reagan later recalled that Bob "smoked too much and had a wracking cough that worried us all. We tried to get him to see a

517 Terry Taylor to author

518 Tessa Taylor to author

519 ...but I have promises to keep, pg. 179

doctor but he wouldn't." Mrs. Reagan also believes that Bob may have suspected what was wrong with him which was one reason why he delayed the inevitable. [520] There is a hint that Bob did know how hopeless his situation was. In February he had written to Purvis, "The doc's tryin' to make me think everything's O.K., but I know different. I'm losin' this one, Curly." [521]

Ursula's eyes were now open to the fact that Bob was likely to die and the only question was when. But she also agreed with his doctors that telling him might depress him so much he would lose any ability to fight and the end would come sooner rather than later. Ursula decided to keep Bob in the dark about his actual diagnosis to keep his spirits up. When he was released from the hospital, Bob's physicians suggested that perhaps now it was the time for him to have a professional nurse on duty, but Bob and Ursula always declined the necessity of doing this. Bob felt that he could get as fine of care from his loving wife as he could from any professional. Bob's family doctor could only see so well Ursula's fatigue and appealed to her. No, she understood that Bob had a need for privacy which would be shattered if there were strangers in the house providing him nursing care. She would manage, she assured the doctor.

By March, Bob and Ursula consulted with two more surgeons at St. John's. Bob was still in great pain and obviously had continued infections due to his elevated temperature. The doctors examined the opening in his chest and told them that the opening was about three inches too high to give him proper drainage and suggested that another opening be made below it. So once more another surgery was performed and Bob managed to come thru it fairly well. However, after this third surgery, Bob's pain was still quite acute and he finally gave in to morphine injections which were performed each day in the late afternoon by a sympathetic and attractive younger nurse. The morphine did the trick of allowing Bob to sleep better at night.

In late March Bob and Ursula were at the hospital where a new set of x-rays were read. The doctor doing the reading seemed almost giddy with delight when he told Bob, "I'm really pleased with these,

520 Nancy pg. 138

521 Robert Taylor, J.E. Wayne, pg. 267

Mr. Taylor. When I saw your first batch, last October, I wouldn't have given you more than two or three months to live." Bob was shocked. This was the first time he had been given any inclination by any doctor that he was on borrowed time. With a drained face, but a controlled voice he asked the doctor how much time he would give him now. "You could possibly enjoy another year," was the reply. From that day forward, according to Ursula, Bob gave up any attempt to fight on. He refused any further radiation treatments.

Bob realized he would never return to *Death Valley Days* and called producer Robert Stapler to ask for a cancellation of his contract. Stapler told him, "No way, Bob." He wanted to give Bob hope that he would indeed return in August when filming for the new season began. Stapler went so far as to ask Bob if he could come over with a sound man to record a couple of his introductions for the upcoming season. "Don't worry," he told Bob. "We'll wait for you. We don't have to start filming until August."[522]

Stapler's sympathetic gesture meant the world to Bob and gave him a temporary boost, but it was short-lived. By this time Ursula was helping Bob with such physical needs as showering, dressing, and, most humiliatingly, to and from the toilet. By May, Bob was back in the hospital. Bob saw only selected friends in the hospital. People he felt comfortable with such as Ron and Nancy Reagan, Dale Robertson and old MGM stalwarts like George Nichols and Howard Strickling. Naturally, Ivy and the Reeves were among those admitted. When in late May, the doctors had proposed doing a spinal tap for "research" purposes as well as to provide more relief, Bob and Ursula had given their consent. However, when the long needle was planted in his back, Bob cried out in excruciating pain. Ursula was livid. From that moment forward no more experimenting would be conducted on her husband. She told the doctors, "Can't you see that your patient has nothing else to fight for but his dignity? At least grant him that. Just leave him alone."[523]

In March Michael had been released from Camarillo and seemed to be an entirely new man. He had gotten himself a job doing office work for a construction firm in Westwood. Because he suffered

522 Thiess, pg. 185

523 ...but I have promises to keep, pg. 188

from a seizure disorder he was unable to drive a car, so he found temporary lodgings at a motel which was within walking distance of his job. He spent his weekends at the ranch. Ursula would recall that Michael was especially attentive and sensitive to her needs during this difficult time. On Mother's Day he had given an expensive gift of Chinese figurines. He then surprised her with the news that he had been approached by a modeling agency and signed a contract. He proudly presented the contract to Ursula and appeared to be happier than he had been in quite some time. The next weekend he had asked Ursula for some family pictures, as he wanted to make a collage. She supplied the requested photos and drove him to his motel where he showed her some photos of himself that the modeling agency he had just signed with had taken. "Viewing the pictures of my handsome, tall, blonde son, I had no doubt that jobs would soon be available to him," she recalled.[524]

The next morning Ursula awoke to find that she had forgotten to give him his weekly supply of Thorazine, the medicine he was taking to control his moods. She quickly changed her clothes and drove over to the motel that Michael was staying at. When she arrived, she knocked at his door, there was no answer. She tried again and still no answer. Finally, she decided to try opening the door and found that it was unlocked, and entered. When she saw Michael in bed, it appeared that he was still fast asleep. Ursula decided to look around the room. It was neat and the laundry that she always picked up was neatly folded in a cardboard box awaiting her. She then turned her attentions to her son and looked down at his face, he seemed so still, yet with a small, faint smile. She bent down to give him a kiss and then a crushing realization hit her—Michael was dead. She took his face into her hands and stroked him as tears began to flow. Her husband was dying and now her oldest son, only twenty-three, was dead. What more could she endure? She composed herself and walked over to the motel's front office to report a death on the premises. She called the family doctor who soon arrived to verify that her son was, indeed, dead. She also called Manuela, who arrived hysterical that her final words to her brother the day before had been said in anger. A few weeks later the results

524 Ibid, pg. 189

of an autopsy indicated that Michael had died of an overdose of morphine.

Ursula was in no condition to see Bob. She needed to be by herself and her thoughts before she could go and see her dying husband. Bob was informed of Michael's death by their doctor and immediately his thoughts turned to Ursula. "My poor baby, how is she going to deal with all this?" he repeated over and over. When, later in the day, Ursula arrived, Bob was sitting up in a chair and offered his sympathy. He told her, "Darling, I don't really know what to tell you, but if it was his own choice, I'm sure he is better off now. Possibly even happier." [525]

Ursula didn't have a lot of time to prepare for Michael's funeral because the following day Bob took a sudden turn for the worse. Friends, like Nancy Reagan, were supportive as always. Michael's funeral was an impersonal affair. Among the fifty or so mourners were friends of Michael's and people who attended in part to lend their support and love to Ursula such as Nancy Reagan and Rhonda Fleming. A wake was held at the ranch following the funeral. Ursula recalled that his friends saw Michael as one of the "beautiful people" while all she could remember was a tormented soul who never found the peace he was continually seeking.

The day after Michael's funeral Bob was insisting to his doctors that he wanted to go home because his place was with his wife. Ursula was told pointblank by the doctors that he was losing muscle control and that soon the cancer would begin to affect his brain and that she was not strong enough to deal with it. They told her that in their opinion it was best that Bob not be released. This was one wish that Ursula could not deny Bob: the chance to go home to the ranch he loved so much. She arranged to have an ambulance take him home. When he arrived home, he saw his children and the ranch as if it were for the first time. Heavily leaning on Ursula as he walked into the house he was soon helped to bed with the aid of a male nurse. The nurse was dismissed soon afterward and Bob was to spend the next four days at home, in his bed or in the den reclining in his chair and watching television. "All the things which bothered him before became nothing," Ursula recalled. "I remember he used

525 ...but I have promises to keep, pg. 192

to hate the cry of the coyotes in the hills and now that didn't bother him anymore." [526] But much of the time he would be sleeping. The nurse who assisted in his care in the afternoons sympathetically assured Ursula that Bob wasn't in pain because the cancer had now metastasized throughout his body, including his brain, which numbed the pain.

On the fourth day Bob lost all body control. Ursula called for his doctor who told her, as sympathetically as possible, that he had been expecting the call, and that there was no way that she could deal, alone, with Bob in the condition he now was in and recommended that Bob return to the hospital. An ambulance was summoned. Ursula rode along next to him. As they were driving Bob suddenly began looking nervously around for something. "Damn it, darling," he said, "I don't know what I did with my script. Can't find my script." [527] It was now apparent that the cancer had affected his mind. Ursula assured him that it was fine; the script would show up on location. Over the next few days Ursula moved into the hospital room to be with Bob. The only time she left was for a few hours when Terry graduated from junior high school on June 5. In these last few days some of Bob's closest friends were invited to come and say goodbye. Ivy came by and told him that she was soon to be married to a professor of Economics at UCLA. Bob had long held academia in suspicion as a bunch of loony liberals. He had previously warned Ivy not to marry him because he was a "commie." But now he simply took Ivy's hand and told her, "I'm sorry, I don't think I can make it, honey, but be happy and tell Ursula to be happy too." Ivy recalled that his once handsome face was now so gaunt and his eyes had sunk into hollow cheeks. [528]

On June 7 it was made public that Robert Taylor was dying. Nancy Reagan immediately flew down from Sacramento to keep Ursula company for a few hours. "Ursula was amazing during that time dealing not only with Bob's terrible illness but the devastating loss of her son at almost the same time," Nancy later recalled. "She

---

526 Ursula Thiess to author

527 ibid

528 Ivy Mooring to author

was tireless in her devotion to Bob."[529] When she left to return to Sacramento, Nancy stepped outside the room and was in the hospital corridor when she suddenly felt an urge to turn around and see Bob one last time. "I returned to his room and kissed him on the cheek."[530] Ursula stayed by her dying husband's side. In the early morning hours of the 8th Art Reeves woke up in the middle of the night with an intense feeling that he needed to see Bob. "I just had to go and I got to the hospital just before he went into a coma."[531] Bob opened his eyes once more and told Ursula, "Mutti, I love you," before slipping quietly and painlessly into his final coma. Bob died at ten A.M. on June 8 with Ursula still holding him in her arms.

Nancy Reagan, back in Sacramento, turned right around knowing that Ursula needed her. Nancy "took over for me," Ursula later recalled. "I was in shock. She made all the phone calls, all the arrangements, picked out my wardrobe—everything. Nancy could never separate herself from Ronnie for more than a day if she could help it, and she stayed with me several days and took care of me." Reagan offered to do the eulogy for his good friend. "Ronnie wrote it himself," recalled Nancy. "The only thing he was afraid he wouldn't get through it without breaking down." Nobody could recall Reagan looking so devastated. In the months ahead even his sixteen-year-old daughter Patti would recall her father's despondency over his friend's death. "He would come home from work at five every day," she recalled, "but he didn't seem part of those months."[532] According to Ivy Mooring, Bob's death which came so soon after the passing of her oldest son left her "emotionally drained" and "the most devastated I have ever seen her. She sobbed on her bed as I tried to comfort her."[533]

Bob's funeral was held in the Church of the Recessional at Forest Lawn Memorial Park in Glendale. Over 700 friends and fans attended and heard the Governor of California, Ronald Reagan,

529 Nancy Reagan to author

530 ibid

531 Art Reeves to author

532 Ronnie & Nancy pg. 404

533 Ivy Mooring to author

eulogize his departed friend. It began, "How to say farewell to a friend named Bob. He'd probably say, 'Don't make any fuss. I wouldn't want any trouble.'" It was a eulogy which would be remembered long by all because it truly came from the heart. Reagan reviewed Bob's life from the time he was born Spangler Arlington Brugh in Nebraska to achieving the heights of fame in Hollywood. He even spoke of the his discomfort with the "pretty boy" tag, "Now there were those in our midst who worked very hard to bring him down with a label, 'pretty boy,' . . . It's only in the recent years of our friendship that I've been able to understand how painful all of this must have been to him—to a truly modest man . . ." He spoke of Bob's love for his family. "He loved his home and everything that it meant. Above all, he loved his family and his beautiful Ursula—lovely Manuela, all grown up!—little Tessa; Terry, his son, a young man in whom he had such great pride." He revealed to Ursula what Bob's last wishes for her were, "Ursula, there is just one last thing that only you can do for him—be happy. This was his last thought to me." Reagan managed to make it through without breaking down, which is more than could be said for those listening to the beautiful words and reflecting on the man they were directed toward.

Portrait Gallery #5

Bob and Tina Louise in his first post-MGM film, *The Hangman* (1959)

Killers of Kilimanjaro, 1959

Bob and Nicole Maurey in *The House of the Seven Hawks* (1960)

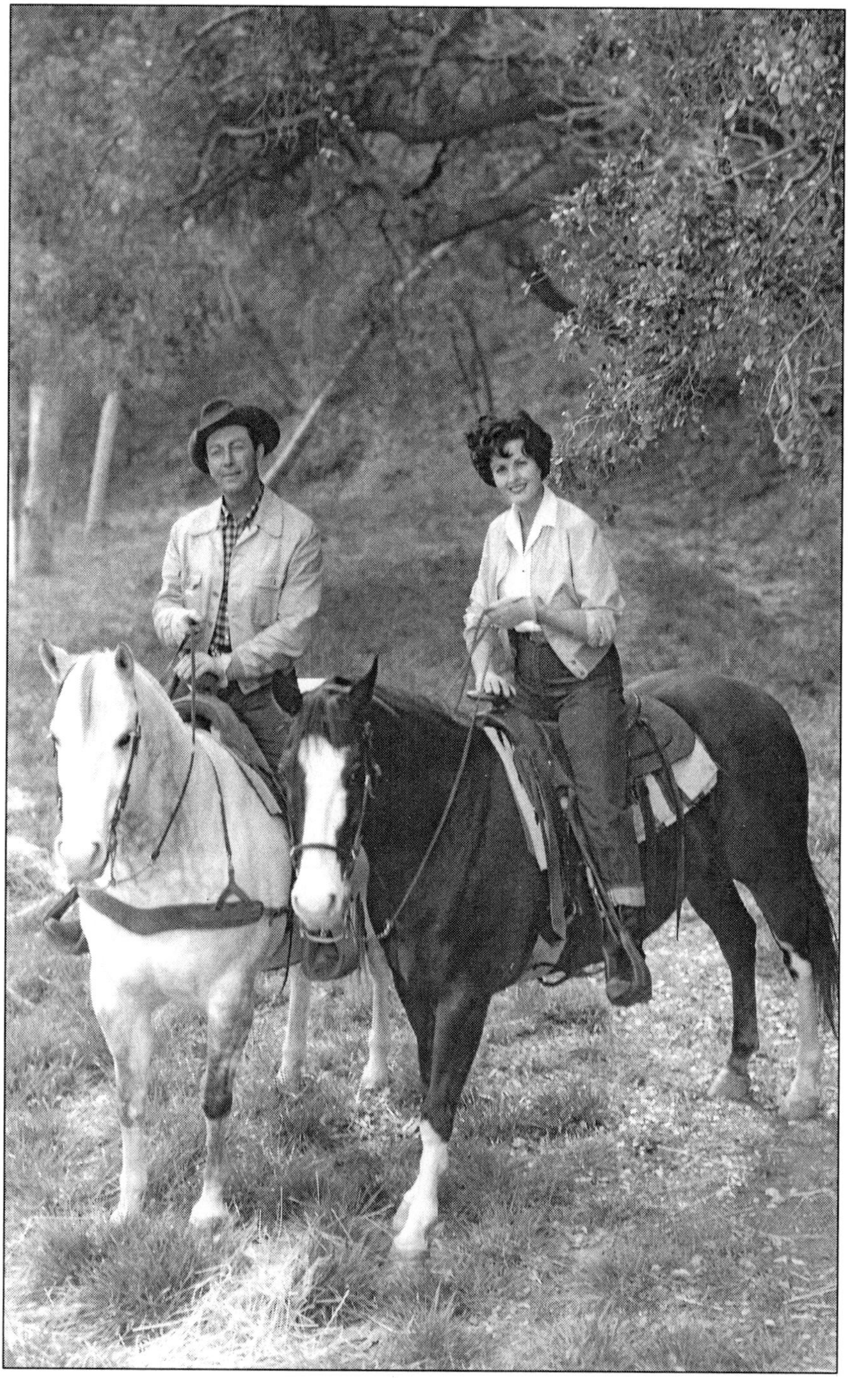

Bob and Ursula on horseback (circa, 1960)

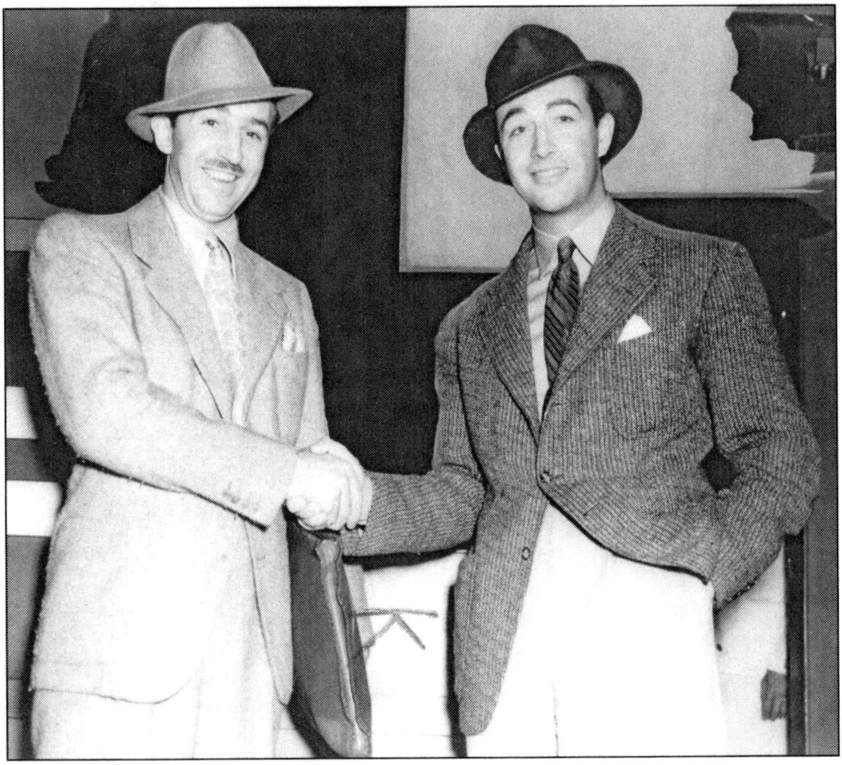

Bob shaking hands with Walt Disney in late thirties, years before Bob made *The Miracle of the White Stallion* (1962) for Disney.

***Cattle King* (1963)**

Bob and Maggie Pierce, *Cattle King*.

Bob and Barbara reunited for ***The Night Walker*** **(1965), 13-years after their divorce.**

Bob and a grotesquely made up Hayden Rourke in *The Night Walker*.

Bob (center) with an ensemble which includes Jesse White, Broderick Crawford, Cesar Romero and Shelly Winters, *A House is Not a Home* (1964)

Bob and Geraldine Brooks in the underrated *Johnny Tiger* (1966)

Mid-sixties studio photo of Bob

A mid 70's shot of Bob's family: Manuela, Tessa, Ursula and Terry
(COURTESY OF TERRY TAYLOR)

Bob's children, Terry and Tessa (courtesy of Terry Taylor)

Afterword

Barbara Stanwyck was among the mourners at Bob's funeral on June 11, 1969. She was invited by Ursula to attend and at first she declined, but on the morning of the funeral she changed her mind and then wearing a bright yellow dress and dark glasses she arrived. During Governor Reagan's eulogy, no longer able to contain herself, she "broke down in loud sighs and tears."[534] Ivy Mooring would recall Barbara's sobs as an "Academy Award performance,"[535] but heavily sedated and supported by two aides, it is probable that Barbara's grief was real. After the funeral ceremony Ursula invited her to the ranch where several of the mourners were gathering to "have one in Bob's memory." This gracious offer was accepted and Stanwyck was driven out to Mandeville Canyon. Equally gracious of Ursula was returning to Barbara some of the jewelry that she had given Bob during their years together, many of which had been inscribed—including St. Christopher pins. Another item had been a gold cigarette lighter inscribed, "To Lt. Robert Taylor with my admiration and love from Mrs. Robert Taylor."[536] At one point the two ladies excused themselves for a private conversation outside on the Taylors' driveway.[537] Ursula would later say that "repeatedly" Barbara had told her, "If there is anything I can do for you, Ursula, anything, just let me know."[538]

534 Axel Madsen, Stanwyck, pg. 342

535 Ivy Mooring to author

536 Al DiOrio, Barbara Stanwyck, pg. 212

537 ibid, pg. 343

538 Ursula Thiess,...but I have promises to keep, pg. 204

But then only a few days after the funeral Ursula was shocked to receive a letter from Barbara's lawyers asking for back payments of alimony that Bob owed her. It seems that in Bob's last months Barbara released him from the obligation to pay her alimony while he was undergoing treatments and hospitalizations, but now she wanted to collect. Ursula later recalled that it "couldn't have come at a worse time, as so many financial obligations had to be met all at once."[539] It seemed that even in death, Barbara wanted a piece of Bob.

Barbara Stanwyck would live another twenty-one years after the death of her second husband. She never remarried. Her feature film career ended with *The Night Walker*, but she continued to be active on television. As she grew older the industry that she devoted her life began paying tributes to her. The Film Society of Lincoln Center surprised her with a tribute in 1981. After four Best Actress Oscar nominations, the Academy selected Barbara for a special award for lifetime achievement in 1982. She still proved to be one of the most formidable of actresses when she portrayed Mary Carson in the highly successful ABC-TV miniseries, *The Thorn Birds*, in 1983, and was awarded an Emmy for her performance. Then a few years later she was honored with the American Film Institute's Life Achievement Award. Her reception at this ceremony by her peers was so overwhelming that she held back tears and said, "Honest to God, I can't walk on water."

In her final years she suffered from Emphysema; she and Bob had cigarettes in common. In 1985 there was a fire at her house and she reportedly lost many mementos, including letters from Bob that she treasured. After this was a long, slow decline as she continued to battle Emphysema and bouts of pneumonia. She was on oxygen and got around by wheelchair. The end for Barbara Stanwyck came on January 9, 1990; she was 83. There was to be no funeral.

Ruth had not attended the funeral. She was in an assisted living facility when her son died suffering from dementia. Ruth had watched television reports of the funeral without grasping that the man that had died and whose funeral was being reported was her own son. "As I looked at the sad lady, who had raised that exceptional human

539 ibid

being I called my husband, I wished for an instant to trade places with her. But only for an instant."[540] Bob's estate would continue to pay for Ruth's care. She would outlive her son by four years in the haze of Alzheimer's disease.

It was a period of adjustment for Terry and Tessa. Tessa found emotional support by sleeping for a time with her mother and was haunted by nightmares, "what her mind had not yet fully comprehended, her body acted out in no uncertain terms."[541] Terry was now the man of the house and, according to Ursula, she began noticing, "Too much bravado when in the company of his friends."[542] Even today Terry says he still blocks out the time of his father's death, "as being something much greater than anything else I had experienced before." Yet, the older he gets he wishes, "I had paid more attention or had been more inquisitive during that period."[543] Tessa grew into a tall and strikingly beautiful woman. She eventually became an actress herself. Her mother would later write that Tessa has a "persistence of study, unquestionable talent, and a determination I can only admire."[544] She lives in the Los Angeles area. Terry grew into a tall, handsome young man and, in 1985, he married and remains married to this day to the same woman. He works in the cable industry on the East coast. Ursula is proud of both of her children, as well as her firstborn, Manuela. They, in turn are devoted to her.

For Ursula the first years after Bob's death were a painful and difficult time. Not only did she have to cope with the grief of losing her husband and bringing up two children she had to bear the burden of financial problems. Terry recalls that his mother "remained very private about her feeling about his loss, at least with me." Ursula would go off by herself, sometimes for hours at a time, horseback riding—alone with her thoughts. She immersed herself into hobbies such as painting as a way of dealing with the loss. Terry recalls that she converted the galley of a dry-locked riverboat into a studio and

540 Ursula Thiess, ...but I have promises to keep, pg. 204-205

541 ibid

542 ibid

543 Terry Taylor to author

544 ibid, pg. 222

gallery. Eventually, due to increasing debts, she needed to sell the land around their ranch and eventually the ranch house itself and move into a smaller residence. Perhaps it was because of mounting debts or more personal reasons, Ursula held a garage sale shortly after Bob's death and ended up selling such things as horse tackle and saddles. "I still wish I had stepped in to discourage her," says Terry, "as so many things are gone that I remembered as a child."[545] Friends continued to be supportive of Ursula, and a few tried to set her up, but she wasn't ready. It would take time and more healing before she could do so. Eventually, she met a businessman named Marshall Schacker, a Gregory Peck look-a-like. He turned out to be exactly what she needed and was sensitive to her needs and understanding of the place Bob still held in her heart. In short, he was a good man. After they married he moved into Ursula's home and she felt it was best to remove photos and other mementos of her years with Bob. He put a stop to this, telling her, "They represent the most important part of your life, don't deprive yourself or your children of those memories." He also took an active interest in her children and they came to care for him very much. "Marshall often looked for opportunities to focus my children's attention to their father's accomplishment and fame and how he should be remembered," Ursula later wrote.[546] They were married for thirteen happy years, but then Ursula became a widow for a second time when Marshall died of cancer.

Over the years Ursula has devoted her time to her children, friends and volunteer work at the Pediatrics Unit of UCLA. Today she is 86 years old and lives in an assistant-living facility near her daughter Tessa. According to her son Terry, they were able to move many of her personal belongings in with her and "she has since warmed up to the place."

Sadly Ursula passed away on June 19, 2010.

What is Bob's legacy since his death? In 1970, his western legacy was saluted by his being inducted into the Hall of the Great Western Performers by the Cowboy Hall of Fame in Oklahoma City; he was the sixth western actor to be so-honored. In 1986 the Lion's Building

---

545 Terry Taylor to author

546 Ursula Thiess, ...but I have promises to keep pg. 214

on the Lorimar Telepictures Lot (formerly the MGM Studio Lot) was renamed in March 1988 as the Robert Taylor Building, "honoring what many consider to be one of the most professional, consummate actors of our time." It was also a tribute to Bob's extraordinary quarter of a century at the studio.

The honor, however, was short-lived. In 1990 fifty Lorimar writers petitioned to have the building they worked in stripped of the name "The Robert Taylor Building." According to director Judy Chaikin, the reason was the days of the blacklist and the belief that, "Taylor was the only one on film actually naming names."[547] (Of course many named names in private.) The petition passed and the building was renamed "The George Cukor Building" after the man who directed Bob in two films. Ironically, in 1983, Cukor was quoted as saying, "Robert Taylor was my favorite actor. He was a gentleman—that is rare in Hollywood." The building, *sans* Bob's name, has since been demolished.

Bob's home state of Nebraska has always embraced its favorite son. On October 2, 1994, a twelve-mile section of U.S. Highway 136 between Beatrice and Filley was dedicated as the Robert Taylor Memorial Highway. It was a proud day for Ursula and his children. Turner Classic Movies (Turner owns the MGM library), saluted Bob as its "Star of the Month" twice, most recently in April of 2010. More and more of Bob's films are coming out on DVD and Blue-Ray, including deluxe editions of *Magnificent Obsession, Camille, Waterloo Bridge* and *Quo Vadis.*

547 Axel Madsen, Stanwyck, pg. 363

BIBLIOGRAPHY

Alexander, Linda, *Reluctant Witness: Robert Taylor, Hollywood & Communism*, Tease, 2009

Andrew, Geoff, *The Films of Nicholas Ray*, London: Charles Letts & Co., 1991

Arnaz, Desi, *A Book*, William Morrow & Company, 1976

Atkins, Irene Kaho, *Henry Koster*, Director's Guild of America Oral History, 1987

Ballard, Kaye, *How I Lost 10 Pounds in 53 Years: A Memoir*, Watson-Guptill, 2006

Basinger, Jeanine, *Anthony Mann*, Wesleyan, 2007

Benny, Jack (with Joan Benny) *Sunday Nights At Seven: The Jack Benny Story*, Warner Books, 1990

Buhle, Paul (and Dave Wagner), *Blacklisted: The Film Lover's Guide to the Hollywood Blacklist*, Palgrave, 2003

Burt, Don, *Horses and Other Heroes: Recollections and Reflections on a Life with Horses*, The Lyon's Press, 2004

Colacello, Bob, *Ronnie & Nancy: Their Path to the White House*, Warner Books, 2004

Cole, Lester, *Hollywood Red: Autobiography of Lester Cole*, Ramparts Press, 1981

Davis, Ronald L, *Just Making Movies: Company Directors on the Studio System*, University Press of Mississippi, 2005

DiOrio, Al, *Barbara Stanwyck: A Biography*, Coward-McCann, Inc., 1983

Deutsch, Armand, *Me and Bogie*, G.P. Putnam's Sons, 1991

Dumont, Herve & Kaplansky, Jonathan, *Frank Borzage: The Life and Films of a American Romantic*, McFarland, 2006

Eames, John Douglas, *The MGM Story*, Crown Publishers Inc., 1979
Eliot, Marc, *Jimmy Stewart: A Biography*, Harmony Books, 2006
Eisenschitz Bernard, *Nicholas Ray*, Faber & Faber, 1993
Eyman, Scott, *Lion of Hollywood: The Life & Legacy of Louis B. Mayer*, Simon & Schuster, 2005
Fishgall, Gary, *Pieces of Time: The Life of James Stewart*, Scribner, 1997
Flamini, Roland, *Thalberg: The Last Tycoon and the World of MGM*, Crown, 1994
Fontaine, Joan, *No Bed of Roses*, William Morrow & Co., 1978
Friedrich, Otto, City of Nets, *A Portrait of Hollywood in the 1940's*, Harper & Row, 1986
Gaonowicz, Antoni, *Garbo: Her Story*, Simon & Schuster, 1990
Gardner, Ava, *My Story*, Bantam Books, 1990
Garnett, Tay, *Light Your Torches and Pull Up Your Tights*, Arlington House, 1973
Geist, Kenneth, *Pictures Will Talk: the life and films of Joseph L. Mankiewicz*, Da Capo Press, 1983
Gordon, Bernard, *Hollywood Exile: Or How I Learned to Love the Blacklist*, University of Texas Press, 1999
Goldrup, Tom & Jim, *Growing Up On the Set*, McFarland, 2005
Goldrup, Tom & Jim, *Feature Players: The Stories Behind Their Faces*, self-published, 1986
Graham, Sheila, *Hollywood Revisited*, St. Martin's Press, 1984
Granger, Stewart, *Sparks Fly Upward*, Granada, 1981
Hadleigh, Boze, *Conversations with my Elders*, St. Martin's Press, 1986
Harmetz, Aljean, *The Making of the Wizard of Oz*, Hyperion, 1998
Harris, Warren, *Gable & Lombard*, Simon & Schuster, 1974
Higham, Charles, *Ava*, Delacorte, 1974
Hirsch, Foster, *Acting Hollywood Style*, AFI Press, 1991
Hirschhorn, Clive, *Gene Kelly: A Biography*, Henry Regency Company, 1975
Hopper, Hedda (and James Brough) *The Whole Truth and Nothing But*, Doubleday, 1962
Kael, Pauline, *Kiss Kiss Bang Bang*, Bantam Books, 1968
Kobal, John, *People Will Talk*, Alfred A. Knopf, 1985

Lambert, Gavin, *Norma Shearer: A Life*, Knopf, 2004
Leigh, Janet, *There Always Was a Hollywood*, Doubleday, 1984
LeRoy, Mervyn (with Dick Kleiner), *Take One*, Hawthorn, 1974
Loy, Myrna (and James Kotsilibas Davis), *Being and Becoming*, Knopf, 1987
Maltin, Leonard, *Movie Crazy*, M Press, 2008
Mann, William, *Kate: The Woman Who Was Hepburn*, Henry Holt & Co., 2006
Martin, Mary, *My Heart Belongs*, William Morrow & Company, 1976
Martin, Tony & Charisse, Cyd, *The Two of Us*, Mason/Charter, 1976
McGilligan, Patrick, *George Cukor: A Double Life*, St. Martin's Press, 1991
Minnelli, Vincente (with Hector Arce), *I Remember It Well*, Samuel French, 1974
Mordden, Ethan, *The Hollywood Studios: House Style in the Golden Age of Hollywood*, Alfred A. Kropf, 1988
Navasky, Victor, *Naming Names*, The Viking Press, 1980
Norman, Barry, *Talking Pictures: The Story of Hollywood*, BBC Books, 1987
Parla, Paul (and Charles Mitchell) *Screen Sirens Scream!*, McFarland, 2006
Quirk, Lawrence, *The Films of Robert Taylor*, Citadel Press, 1975
Quirk, Lawrence, *Margaret Sullavan*, St. Martin's Press, 1986
Reagan, Ronald, *Where's the Rest of Me?* Duell, Swan & Pearce, 1965
Rioux, Terry Lee, *Sawdust to Stardust: The Biography of Deforest Kelley*, Simon & Schuster, 2005
Schatz, Thomas, *The Genius of the System*, Henry Holt & Co., 1988
Server, Lee, *Ava Gardner: Love is Nothing*, St. Martin's Press, 2006
Sheppard, Dick, *Elizabeth: The Life and Career of Elizabeth Taylor*, Doubleday, 1974
Shipman, David, *The Story of Cinema*, St. Martin's Press, 1986
Stevens, George, Jr., *The Great Moviemakers of Hollywood's Golden Age*, Alfred A. Knopf, 2006
Swindell, Larry, *The Last Hero: A Biography of Gary Cooper*, Doubleday & Co., 1980
Taraborrelli, J. Randy, *Elizabeth*, Warner Books, 2006

Thiess, Ursula, . . . *but I have promises to keep*, Creative Arts Book Company, 2003

Thomas, Bob, *Joan Crawford: A Biography*, Simon & Schuster, 1978

Thompson, Frank, *William A. Wellman*, Scarecrow Press, 1983

Todd, Richard, *In Camera*, Hutchinson, 1989

Tornabene, Lyn, *Long Live the King: A Biography of Clark Gable*, Putnam, 1976

Troyan, Michael, *A Rose for Mrs. Miniver*, University of Kentucky, 1999

Turner, Lana, *Lana: The Lady, the Legend, The Truth*, E.P. Dutton, Inc., 1982

Vickers, Hugo, *Vivien Leigh*, Hamish Hamilton, 1988

Walker, Alexander, *Vivien: The Life of Vivien Leigh*, Weidenfeld & Nicolson, 1987

Wayne, Jane Ellen, *Robert Taylor*, Manor Books, Inc., 1973

Wayne, Jane Ellen, *Clark Gable: Portrait of a Misfit*, St. Martin's Press, 1993

Wayne, Jane Ellen, *Leading Men of MGM*, Carroll & Graf, 2004

Weaver, Tom, *Double Feature Creature Attack*, McFarland, 2003

West, Adam (& Ravin, Jeff) *Back to the Batcave*, Berkley Trade, 1994

Yudkoff, Alvin, *Gene Kelly: A Life of Dance & Dreams*, Watson-Guptill, 1999

Zierold, Norman, *Garbo*, Stein & Day, 1969

INDEX

LaVergne, TN USA
23 March 2011
221267LV00003B/89/P

9 781593 936150